S0-AZO-786

Encino-Tarzana Branch Library
18231 Ventura Boulevard
Tarzana, CA 91356

BACCANO!

Original Story *Ryohgo Narita*

Art
Shinta Fujimoto

Character Design
Katsumi Enami

YA

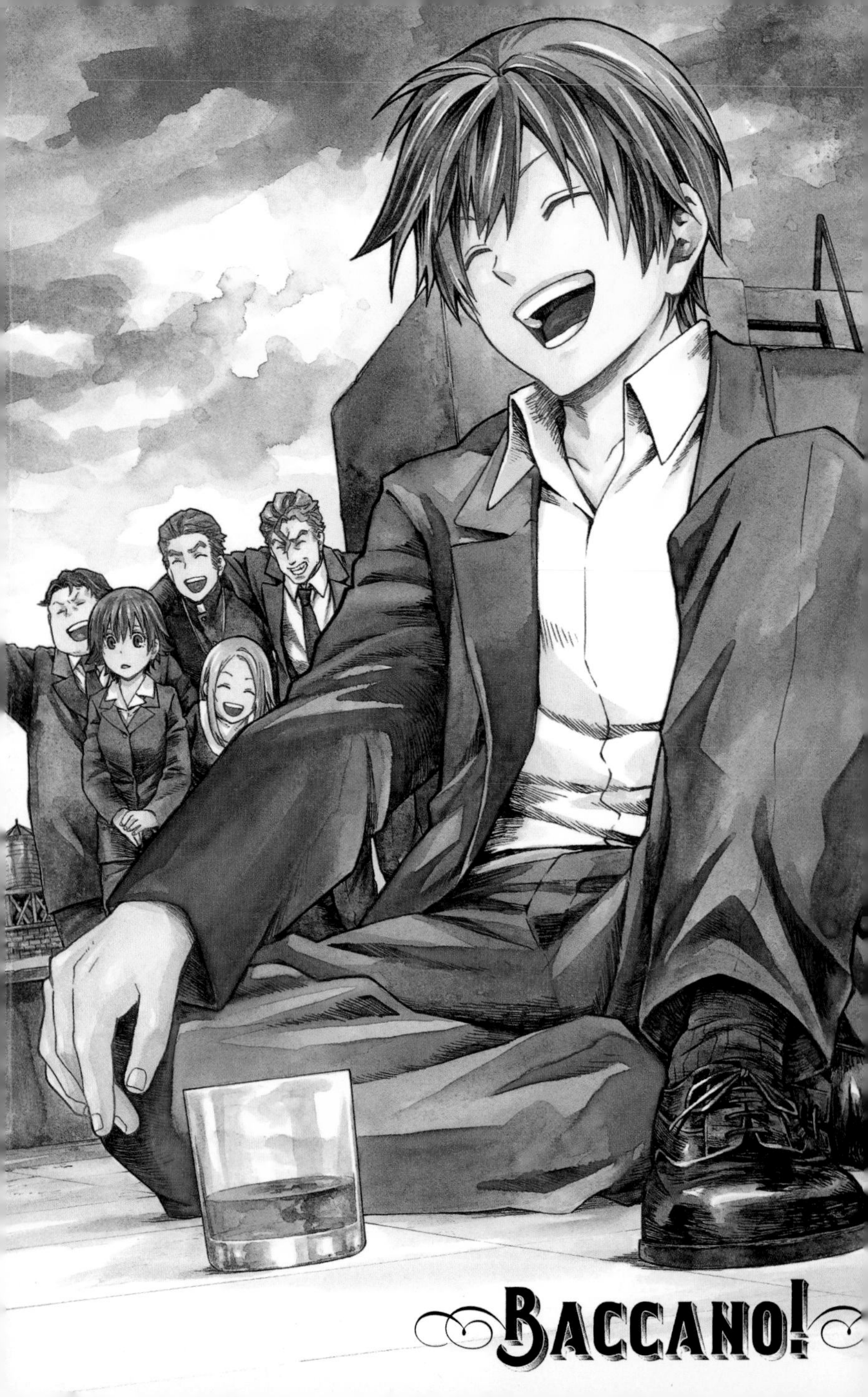
BACCANO!

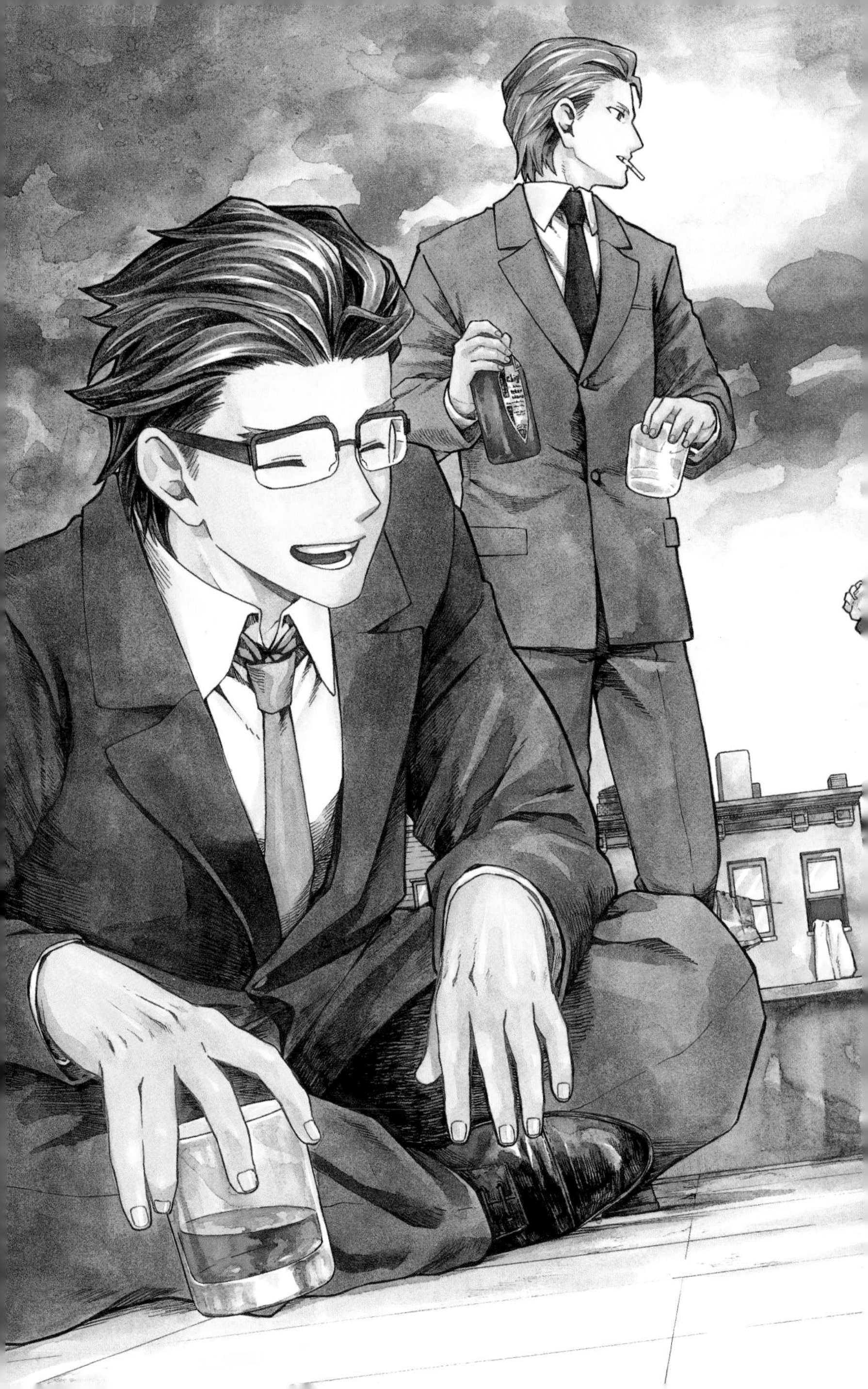

Alveare

Baccano! 3

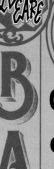

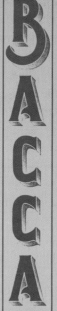

Contents

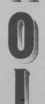

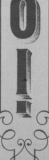

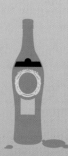

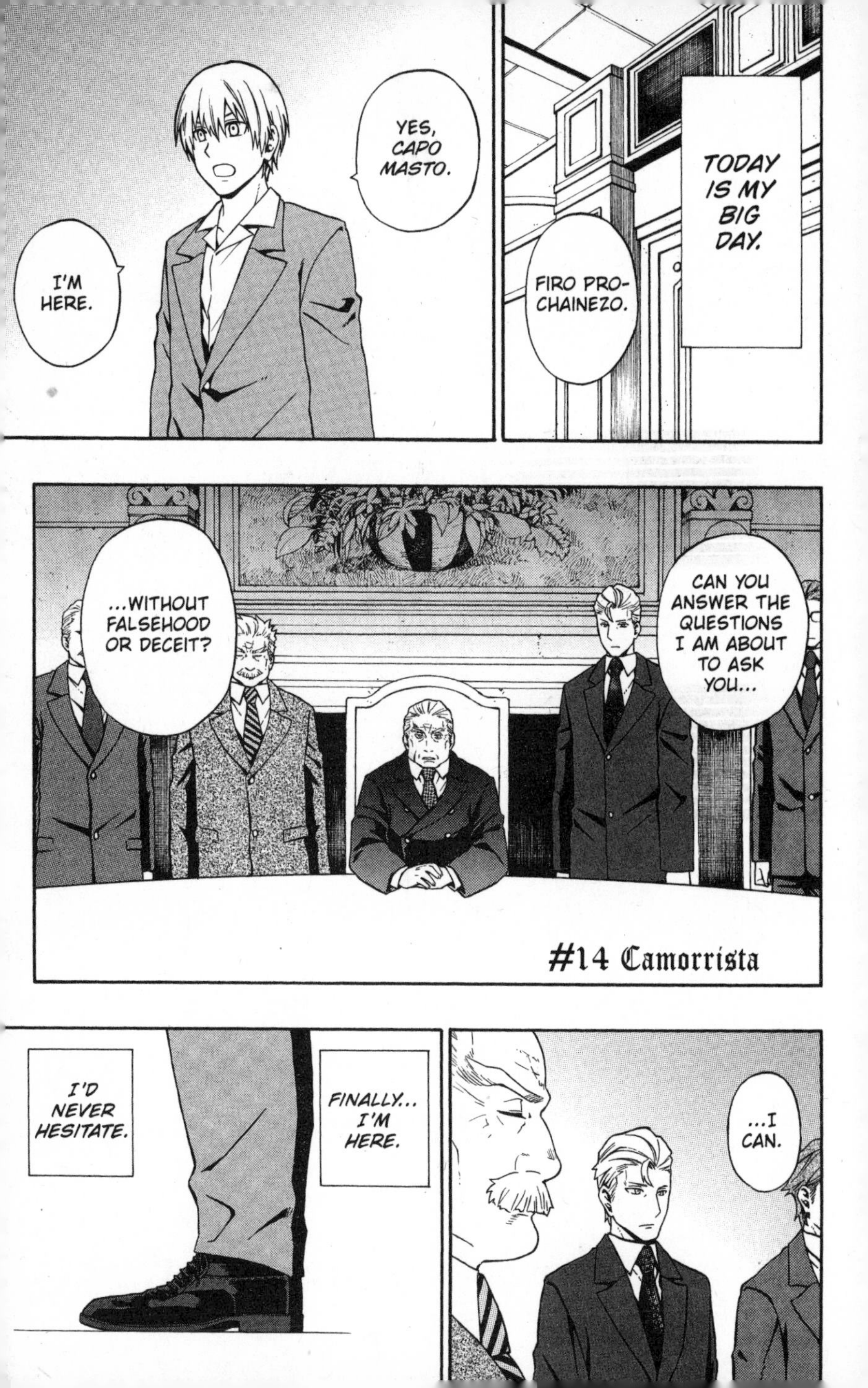
TODAY IS MY BIG DAY.
FIRO PRO-CHAINEZO.
YES, CAPO MASTO.
I'M HERE.
CAN YOU ANSWER THE QUESTIONS I AM ABOUT TO ASK YOU...
...WITHOUT FALSEHOOD OR DECEIT?
#14 Camorrista
...I CAN.
FINALLY... I'M HERE.
I'D NEVER HESITATE.

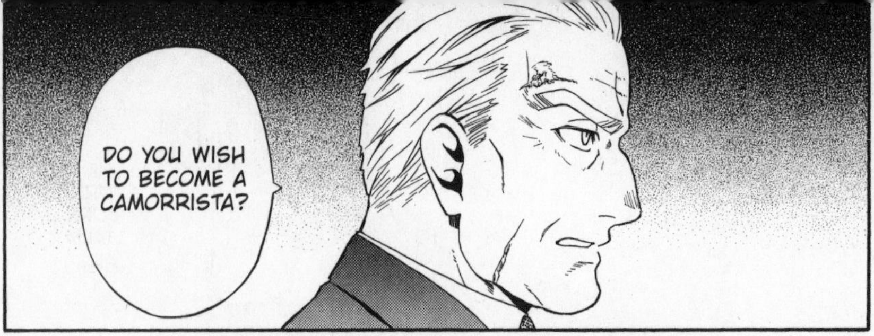
DO YOU WISH TO BECOME A CAMORRISTA?

AFTER ALL, THIS IS THE PATH I'VE WALKED ALL THIS TIME......

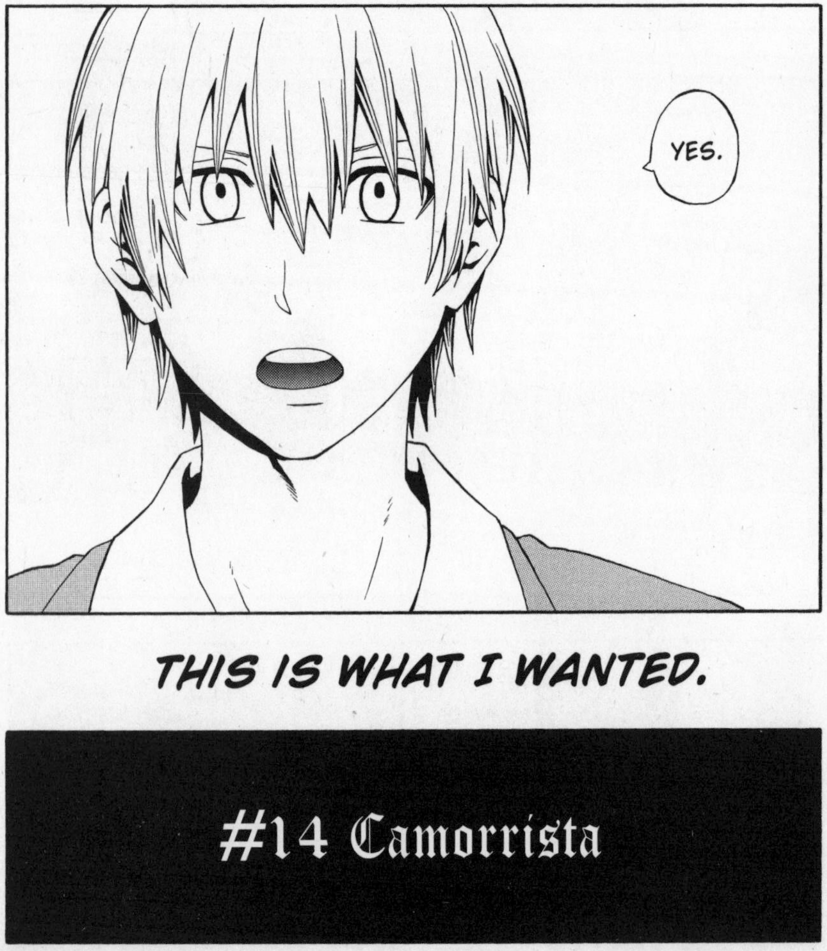
YES.

THIS IS WHAT I WANTED.

#14 Camorrista

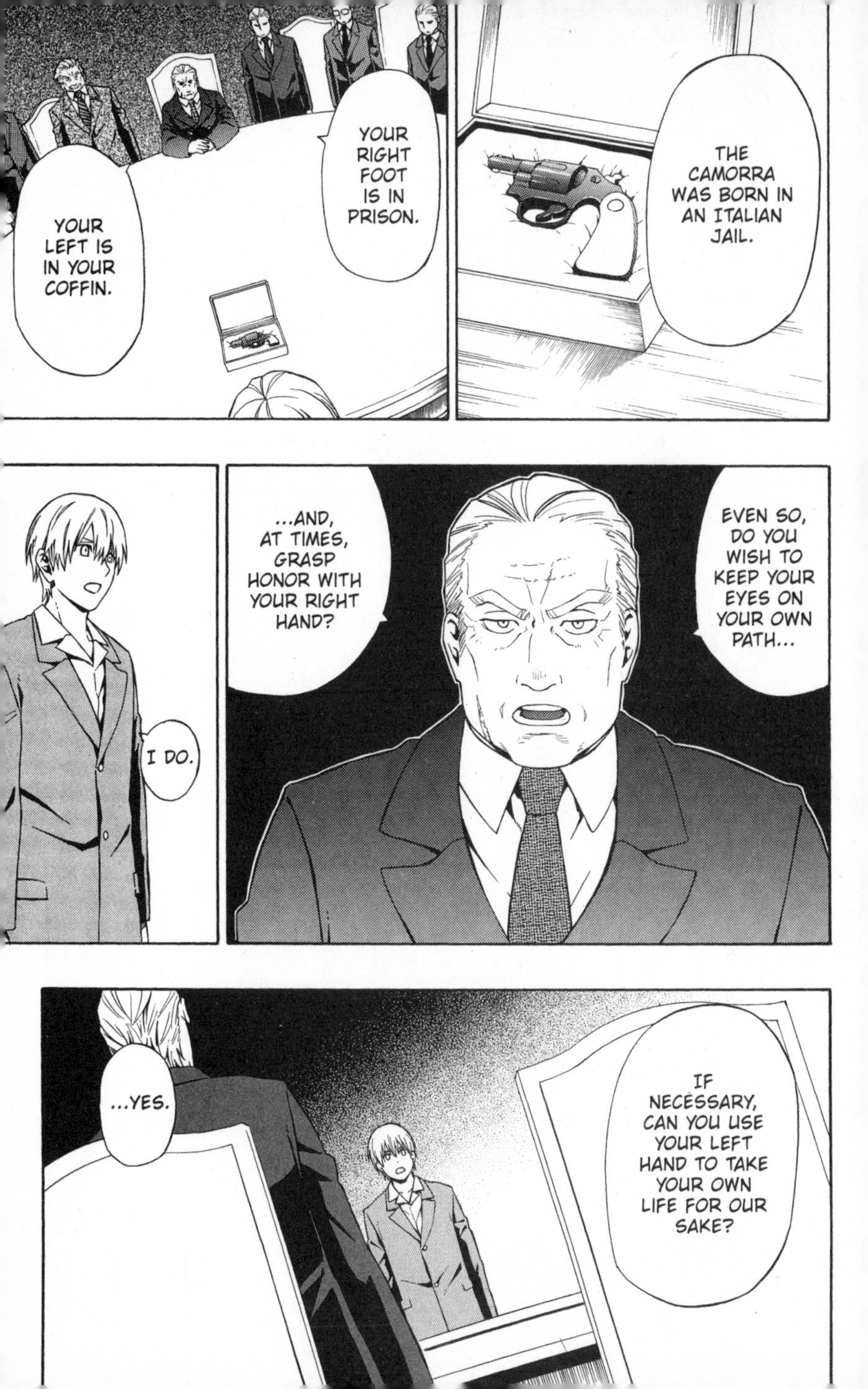
THE CAMORRA WAS BORN IN AN ITALIAN JAIL.
YOUR RIGHT FOOT IS IN PRISON.
YOUR LEFT IS IN YOUR COFFIN.
EVEN SO, DO YOU WISH TO KEEP YOUR EYES ON YOUR OWN PATH...
...AND, AT TIMES, GRASP HONOR WITH YOUR RIGHT HAND?
I DO.
IF NECESSARY, CAN YOU USE YOUR LEFT HAND TO TAKE YOUR OWN LIFE FOR OUR SAKE?
...YES.

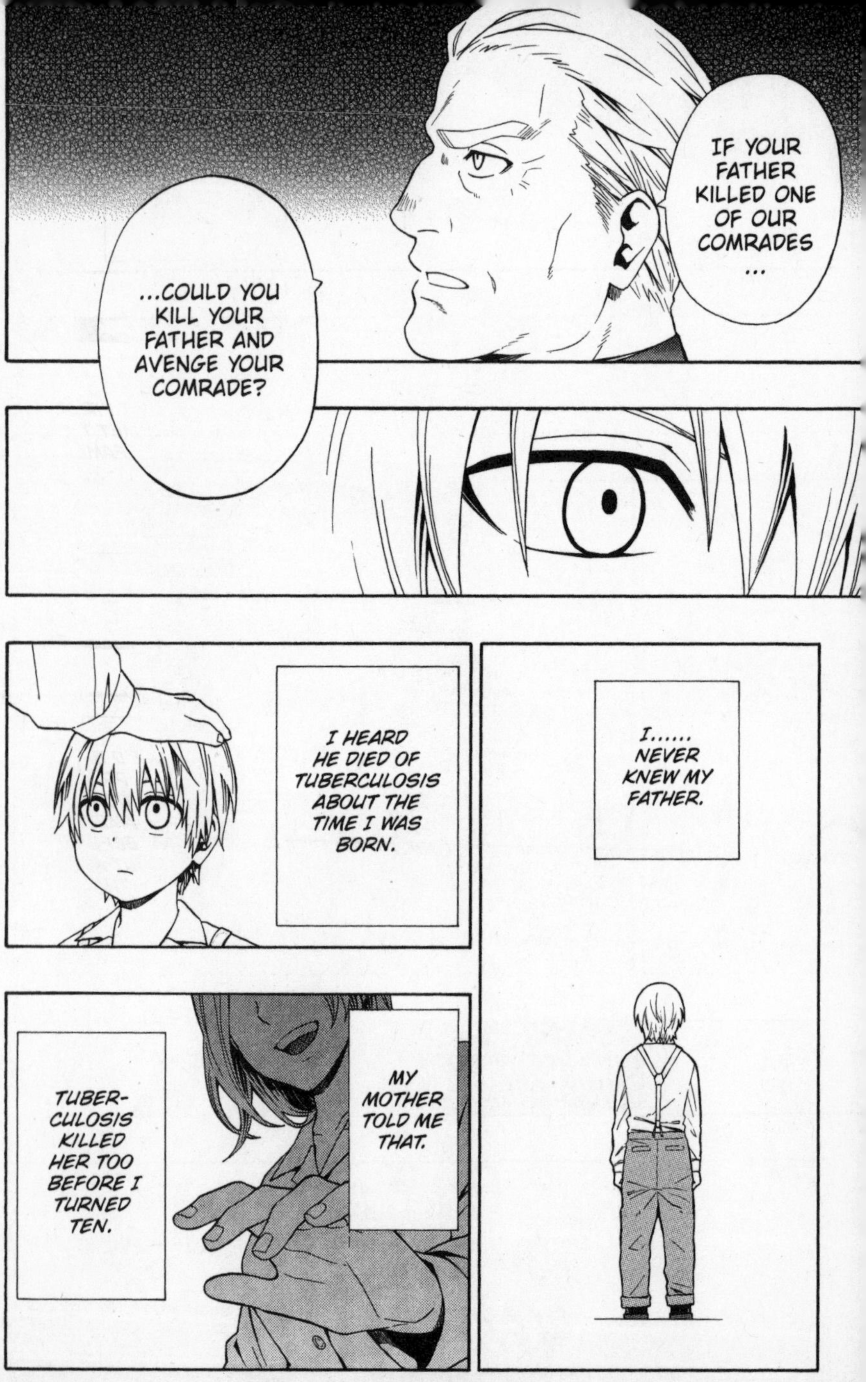
IF YOUR FATHER KILLED ONE OF OUR COMRADES ...
...COULD YOU KILL YOUR FATHER AND AVENGE YOUR COMRADE?
I...... NEVER KNEW MY FATHER.
I HEARD HE DIED OF TUBERCULOSIS ABOUT THE TIME I WAS BORN.
MY MOTHER TOLD ME THAT.
TUBER-CULOSIS KILLED HER TOO BEFORE I TURNED TEN.

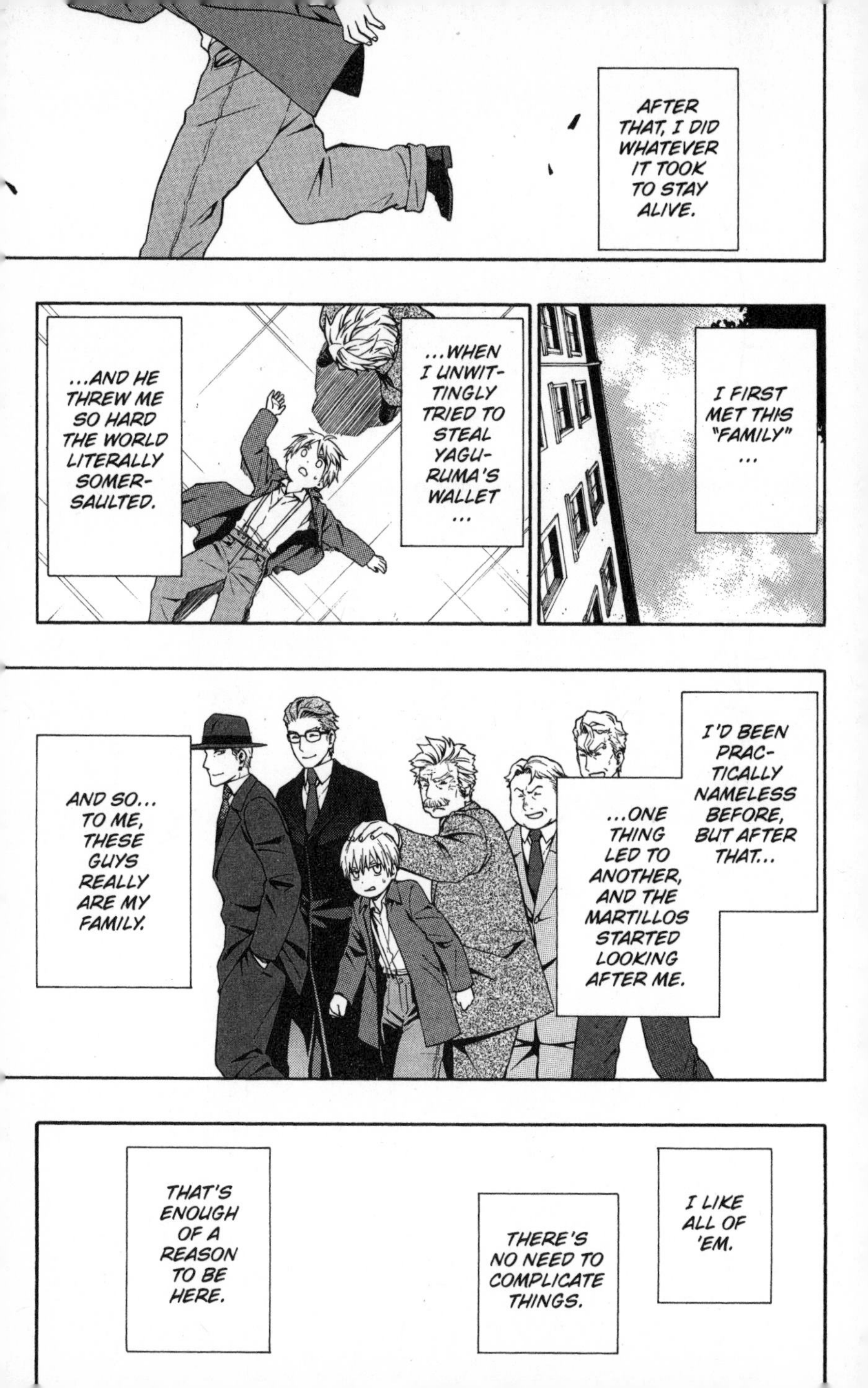
AFTER THAT, I DID WHATEVER IT TOOK TO STAY ALIVE.
I FIRST MET THIS "FAMILY" ...
...WHEN I UNWITTINGLY TRIED TO STEAL YAGURUMA'S WALLET ...
...AND HE THREW ME SO HARD THE WORLD LITERALLY SOMERSAULTED.
I'D BEEN PRACTICALLY NAMELESS BEFORE, BUT AFTER THAT...
...ONE THING LED TO ANOTHER, AND THE MARTILLOS STARTED LOOKING AFTER ME.
AND SO... TO ME, THESE GUYS REALLY ARE MY FAMILY.
I LIKE ALL OF 'EM.
THERE'S NO NEED TO COMPLICATE THINGS.
THAT'S ENOUGH OF A REASON TO BE HERE.

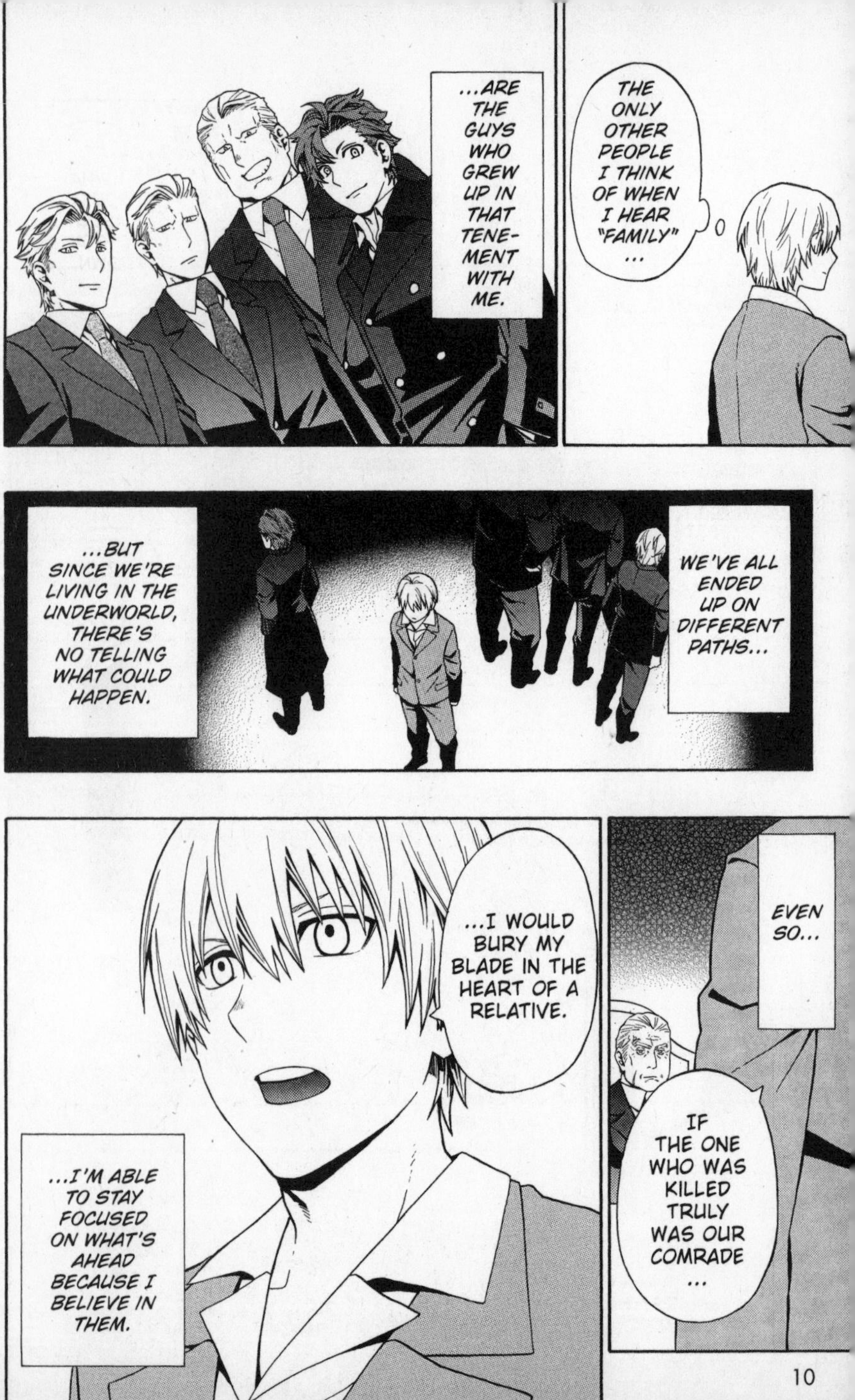
THE ONLY OTHER PEOPLE I THINK OF WHEN I HEAR "FAMILY"...
...ARE THE GUYS WHO GREW UP IN THAT TENEMENT WITH ME.
WE'VE ALL ENDED UP ON DIFFERENT PATHS...
...BUT SINCE WE'RE LIVING IN THE UNDERWORLD, THERE'S NO TELLING WHAT COULD HAPPEN.
EVEN SO...
IF THE ONE WHO WAS KILLED TRULY WAS OUR COMRADE...
...I WOULD BURY MY BLADE IN THE HEART OF A RELATIVE.
...I'M ABLE TO STAY FOCUSED ON WHAT'S AHEAD BECAUSE I BELIEVE IN THEM.

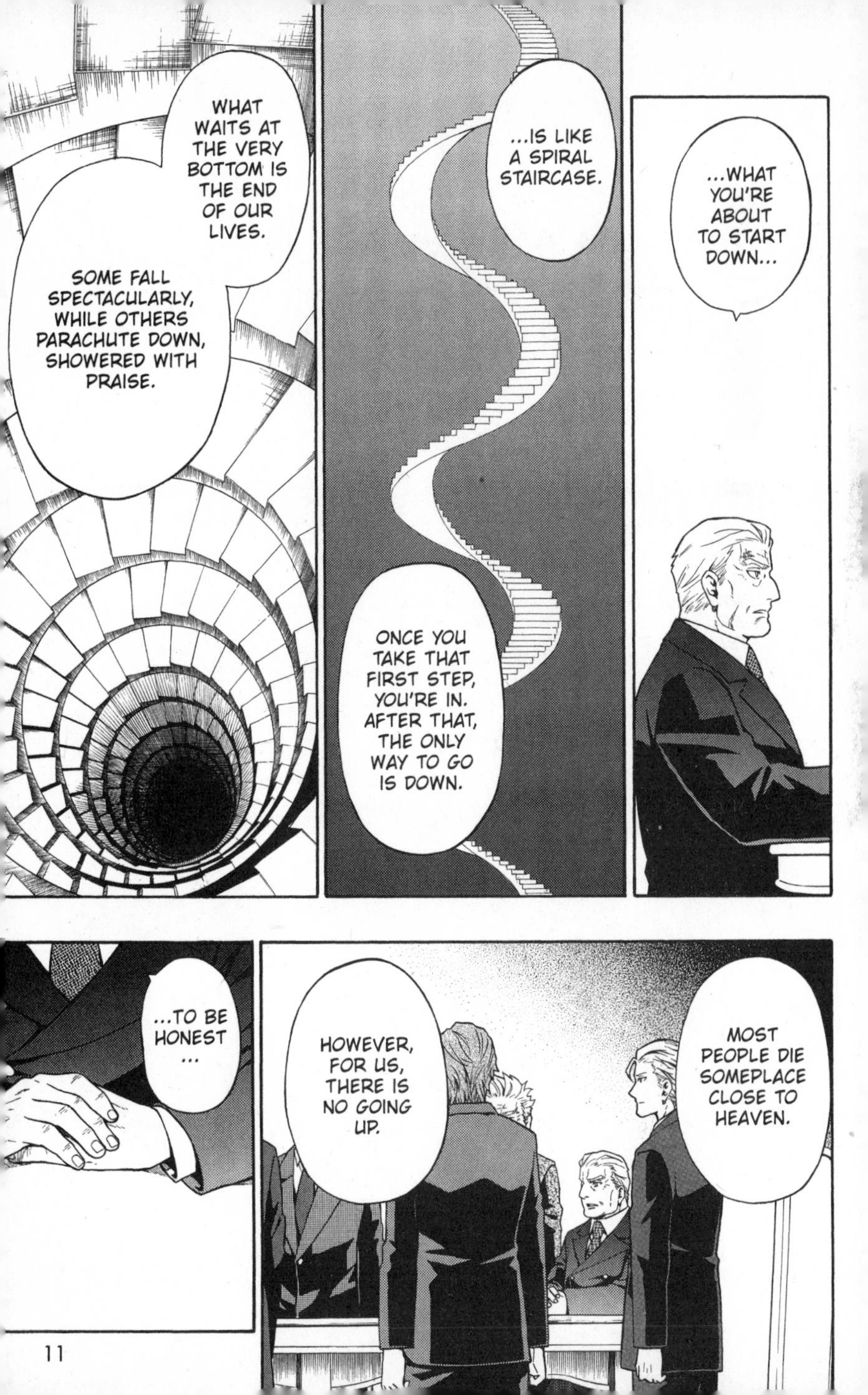
...WHAT YOU'RE ABOUT TO START DOWN...
...IS LIKE A SPIRAL STAIRCASE.
ONCE YOU TAKE THAT FIRST STEP, YOU'RE IN. AFTER THAT, THE ONLY WAY TO GO IS DOWN.
WHAT WAITS AT THE VERY BOTTOM IS THE END OF OUR LIVES.
SOME FALL SPECTACULARLY, WHILE OTHERS PARACHUTE DOWN, SHOWERED WITH PRAISE.
MOST PEOPLE DIE SOMEPLACE CLOSE TO HEAVEN.
HOWEVER, FOR US, THERE IS NO GOING UP.
...TO BE HONEST ...

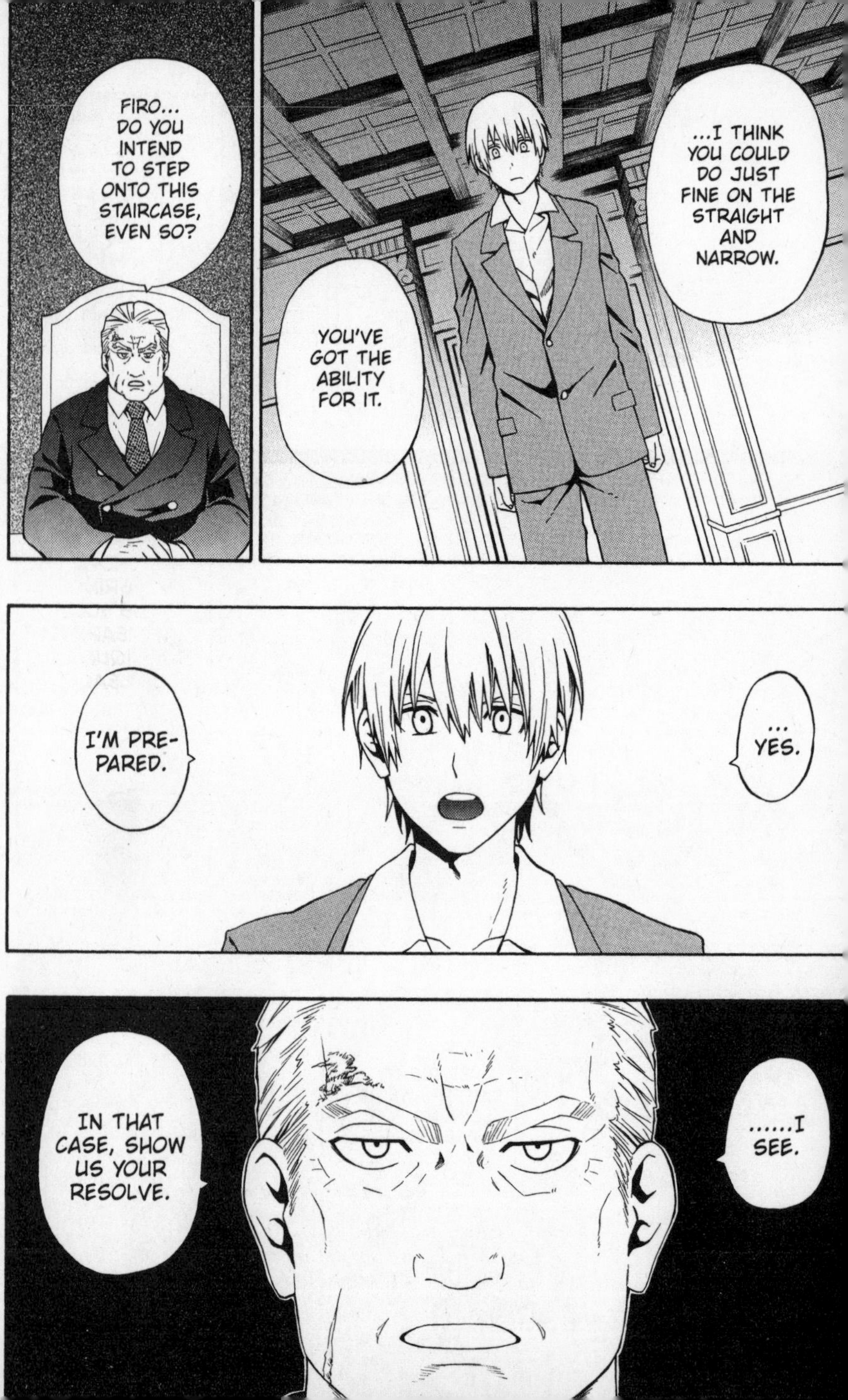
...I THINK YOU COULD DO JUST FINE ON THE STRAIGHT AND NARROW.
YOU'VE GOT THE ABILITY FOR IT.
FIRO... DO YOU INTEND TO STEP ONTO THIS STAIRCASE, EVEN SO?
... YES.
I'M PRE-PARED.
......I SEE.
IN THAT CASE, SHOW US YOUR RESOLVE.

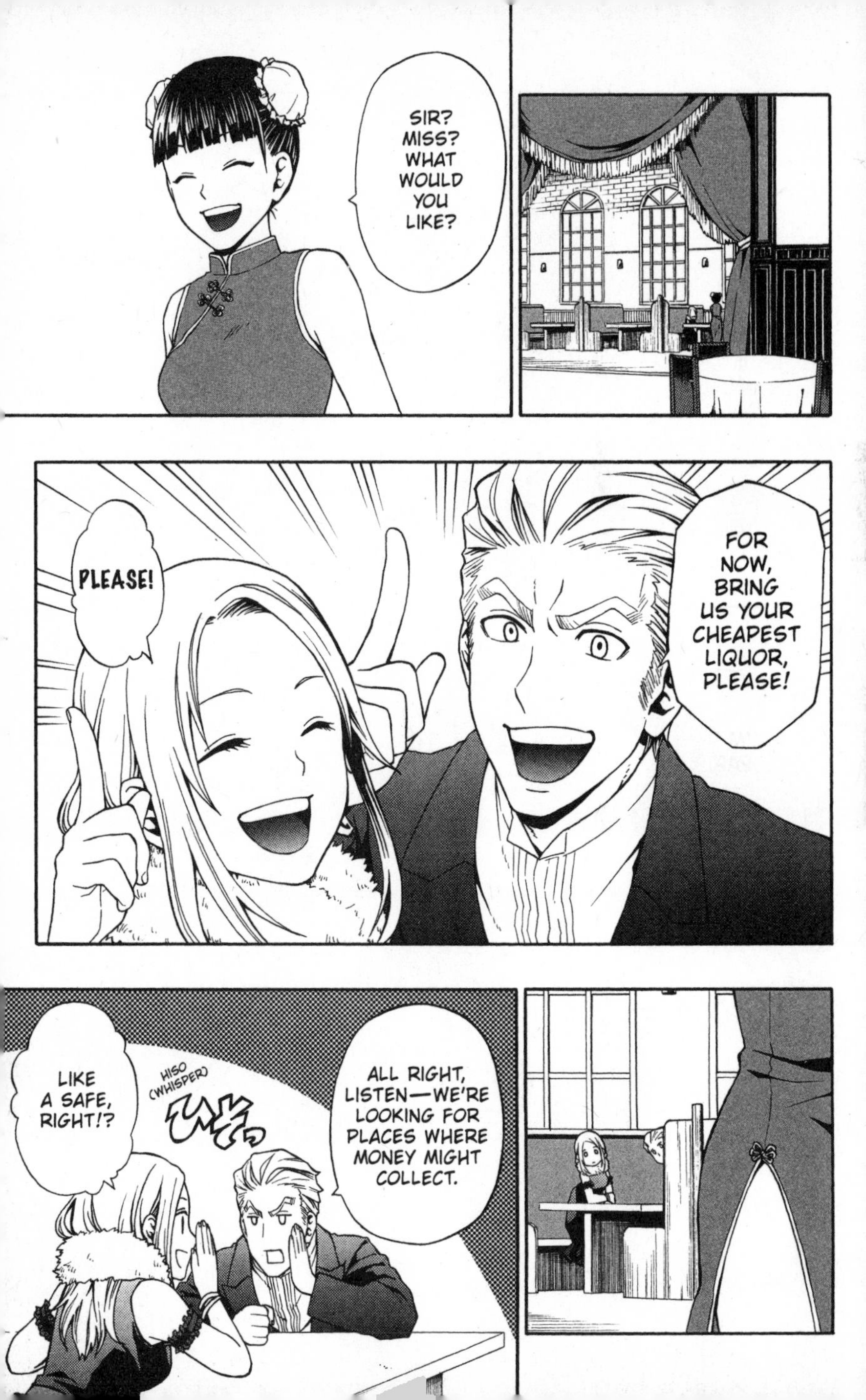
SIR? MISS? WHAT WOULD YOU LIKE?
FOR NOW, BRING US YOUR CHEAPEST LIQUOR, PLEASE!
PLEASE!
ALL RIGHT, LISTEN—WE'RE LOOKING FOR PLACES WHERE MONEY MIGHT COLLECT.
HISO (WHISPER)
LIKE A SAFE, RIGHT!?

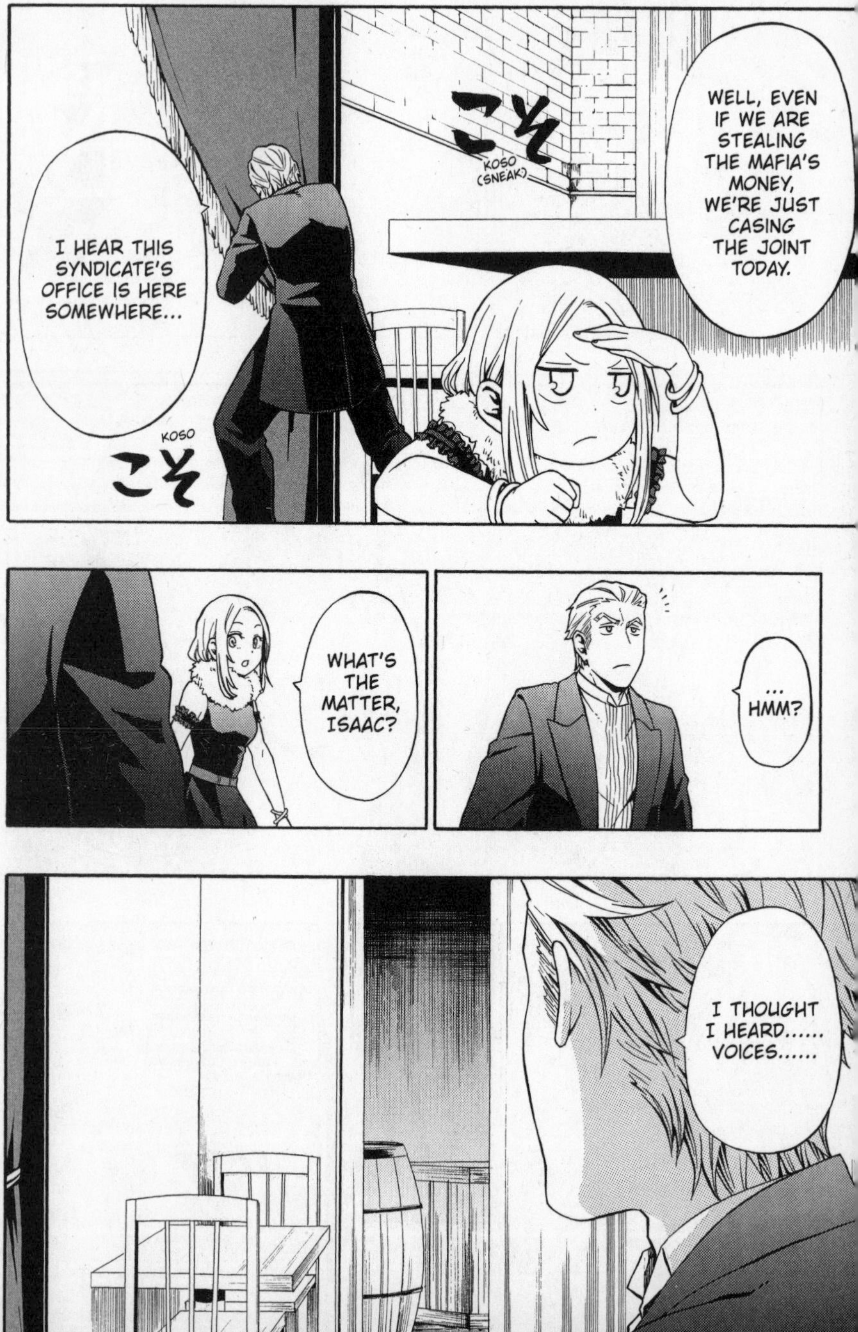
WELL, EVEN IF WE ARE STEALING THE MAFIA'S MONEY, WE'RE JUST CASING THE JOINT TODAY.
こそ
KOSO (SNEAK)
I HEAR THIS SYNDICATE'S OFFICE IS HERE SOMEWHERE...
こそ
KOSO
... HMM?
WHAT'S THE MATTER, ISAAC?
I THOUGHT I HEARD...... VOICES......

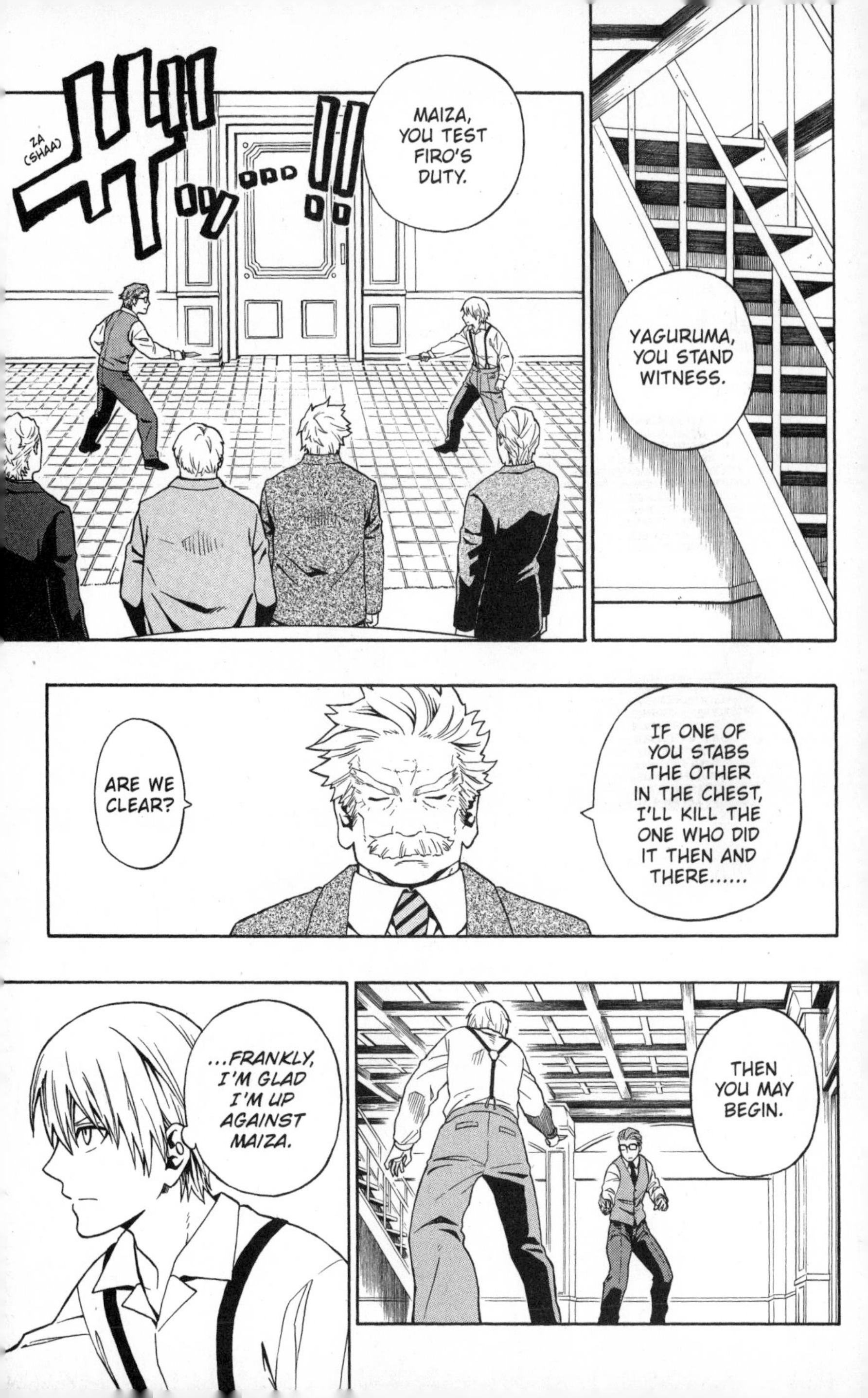
YAGURUMA, YOU STAND WITNESS.
MAIZA, YOU TEST FIRO'S DUTY.
ZA (SHAA)
IF ONE OF YOU STABS THE OTHER IN THE CHEST, I'LL KILL THE ONE WHO DID IT THEN AND THERE......
ARE WE CLEAR?
THEN YOU MAY BEGIN.
...FRANKLY, I'M GLAD I'M UP AGAINST MAIZA.

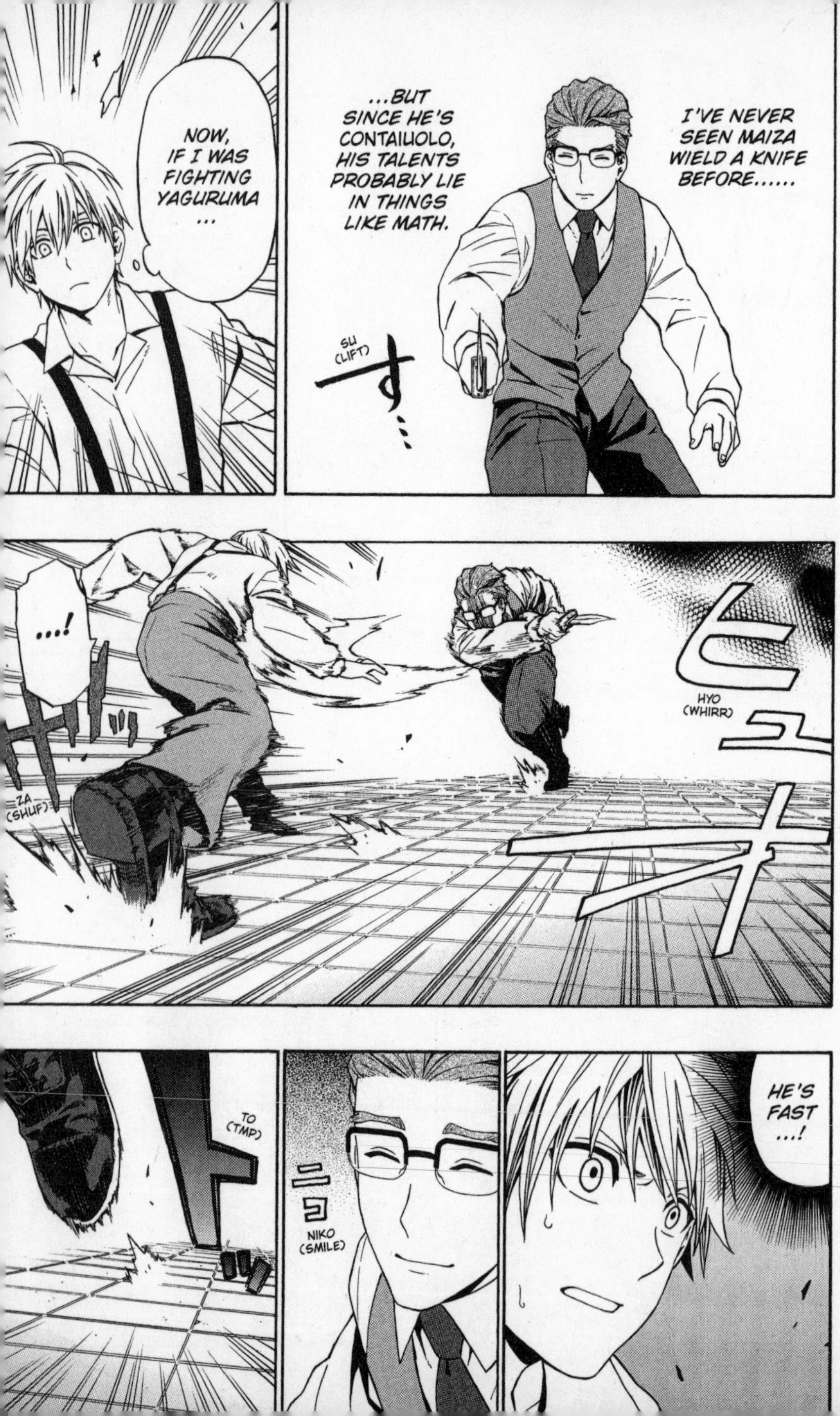
I'VE NEVER SEEN MAIZA WIELD A KNIFE BEFORE......
...BUT SINCE HE'S CONTAIUOLO, HIS TALENTS PROBABLY LIE IN THINGS LIKE MATH.
SU (LIFT)
す
NOW, IF I WAS FIGHTING YAGURUMA ...
HYO (WHIRR)
...!
ZA (SHUF)
HE'S FAST ...!
NIKO (SMILE)
TO (TMP)

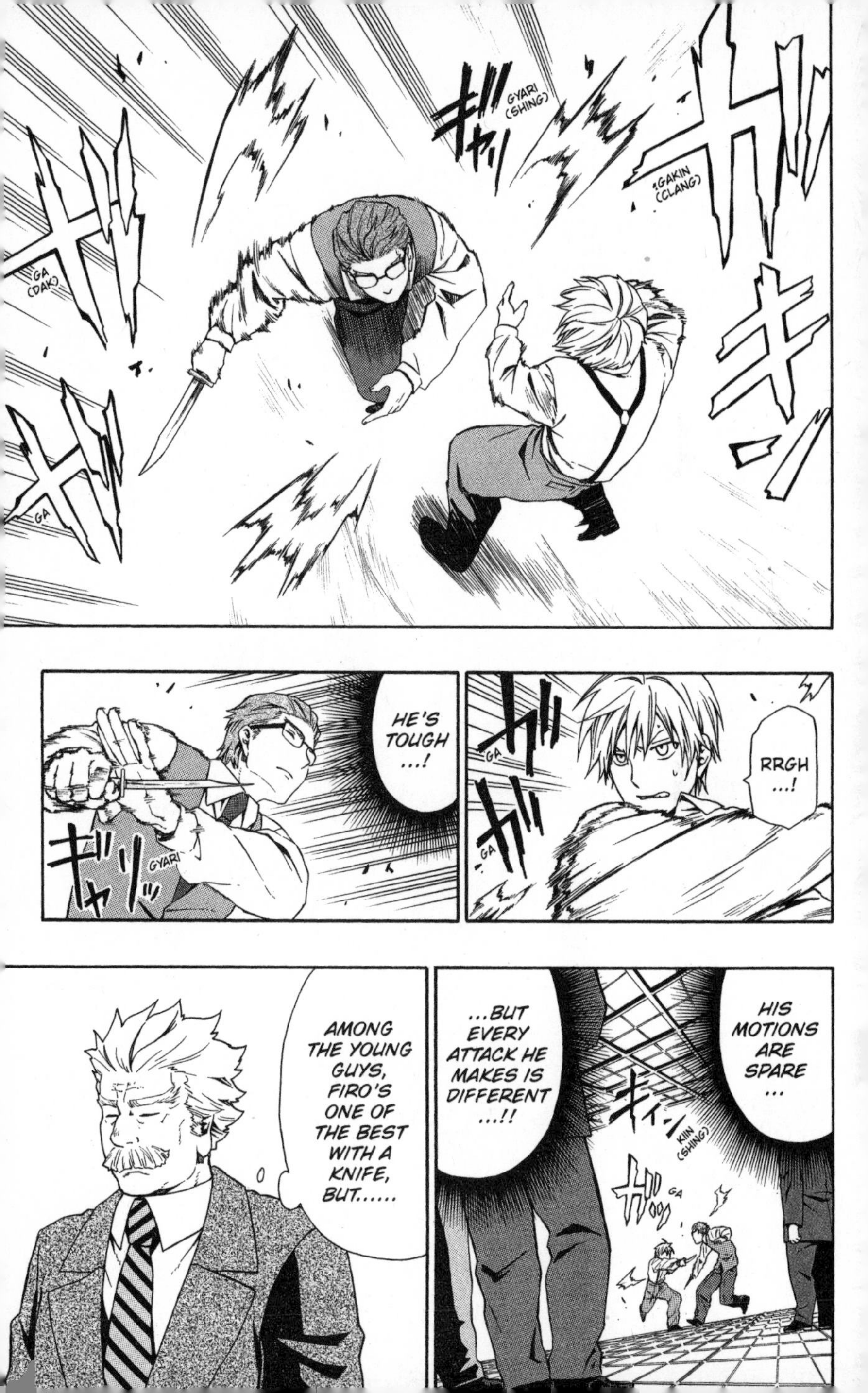
GAKIN (CLANG)
GYARI (SHING)
GA (DAK)
GA
GA
GA
RRGH ...!
HE'S TOUGH ...!
GYARI
HIS MOTIONS ARE SPARE ...
...BUT EVERY ATTACK HE MAKES IS DIFFERENT ...!!
KIIN (SHING)
GA
AMONG THE YOUNG GUYS, FIRO'S ONE OF THE BEST WITH A KNIFE, BUT......

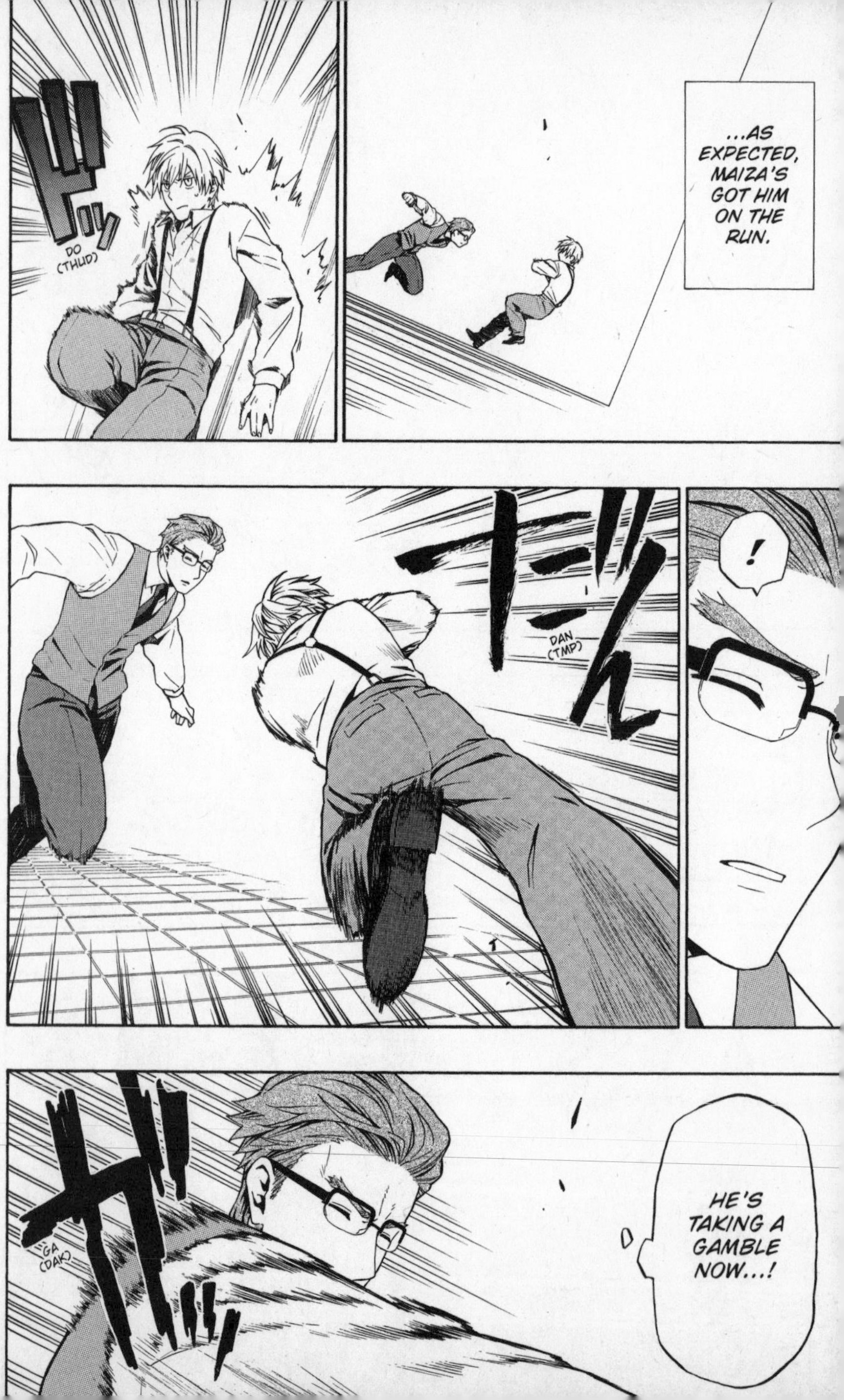
...AS EXPECTED, MAIZA'S GOT HIM ON THE RUN.
DO (THUD)
!
DAN (TMP)
HE'S TAKING A GAMBLE NOW...!
GA (DAK)

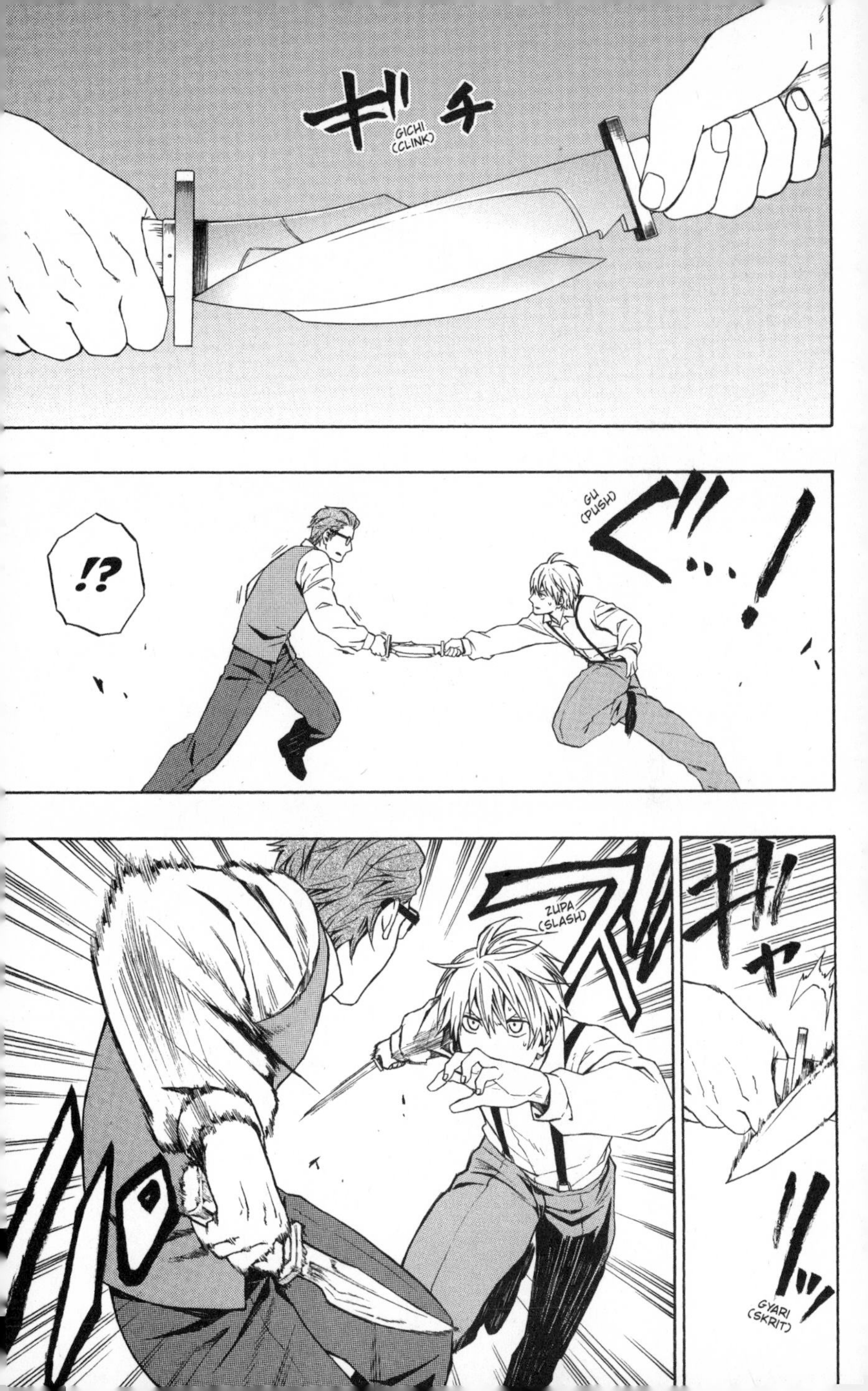
ギチ
GICHI (CLINK)
ぐ…!
GU (PUSH)
!?
ギャリッ!!
GYARI (SKRIT)
ZUPA (SLASH)

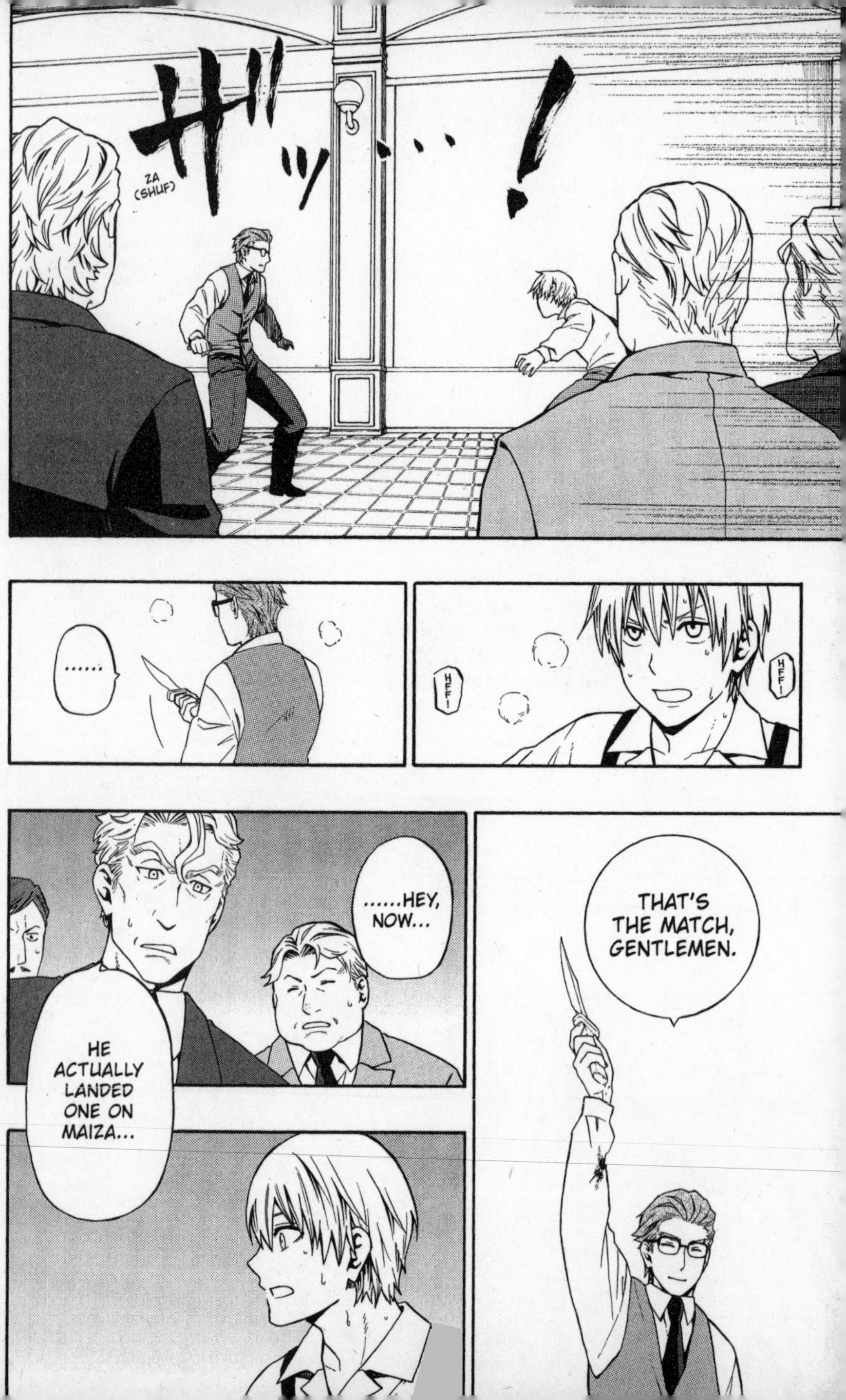
ザッ…!
ZA (SHUF)
HFF!
HFF!
......
THAT'S THE MATCH, GENTLEMEN.
......HEY, NOW...
HE ACTUALLY LANDED ONE ON MAIZA...

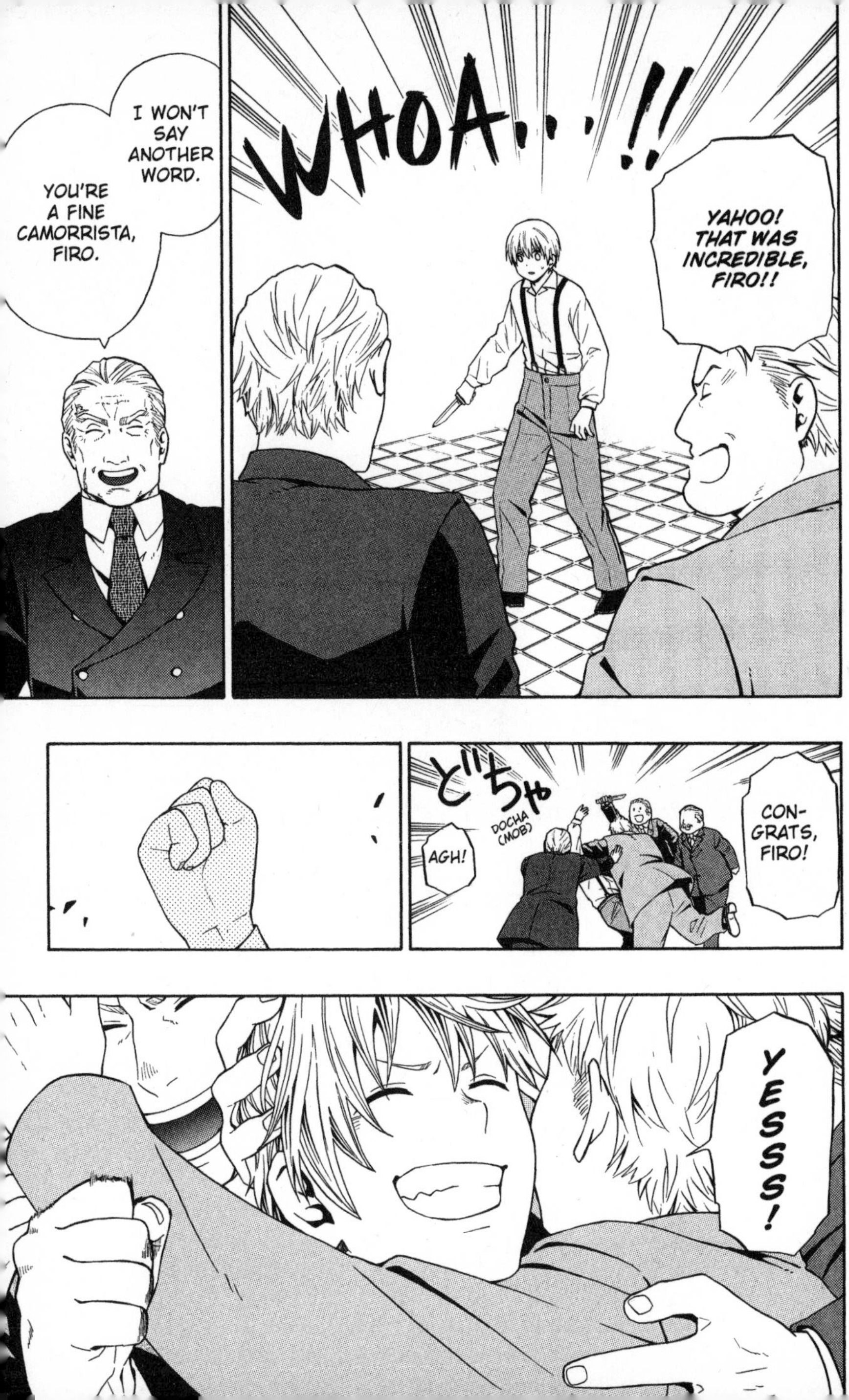
WHOA...!!
YAHOO! THAT WAS INCREDIBLE, FIRO!!
I WON'T SAY ANOTHER WORD.
YOU'RE A FINE CAMORRISTA, FIRO.
CON-GRATS, FIRO!
どちゃ
DOCHA (MOB)
AGH!
YESSS!

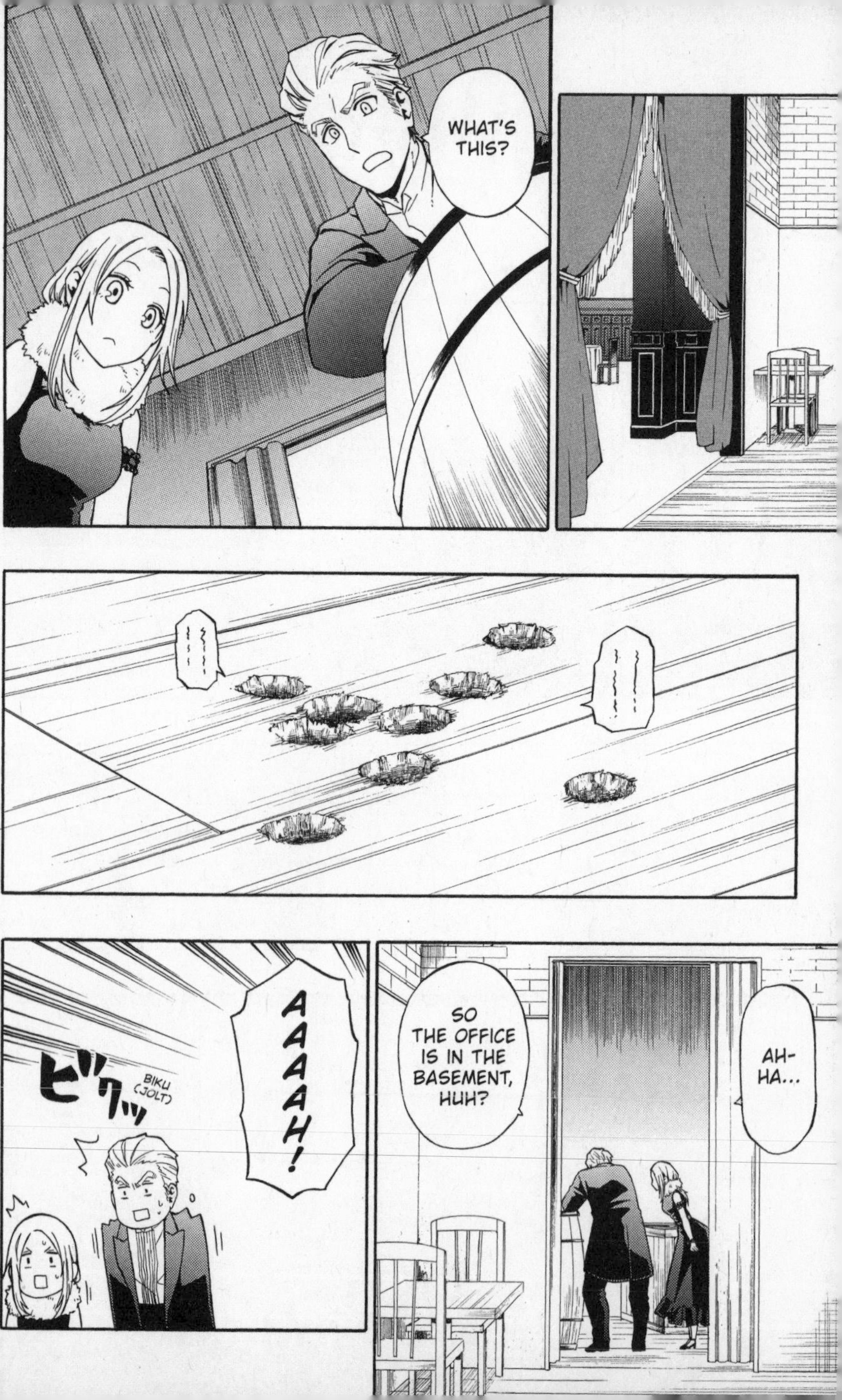
WHAT'S THIS?
AH-HA...
SO THE OFFICE IS IN THE BASEMENT, HUH?
AAAAAH!
BIKU (JOLT)

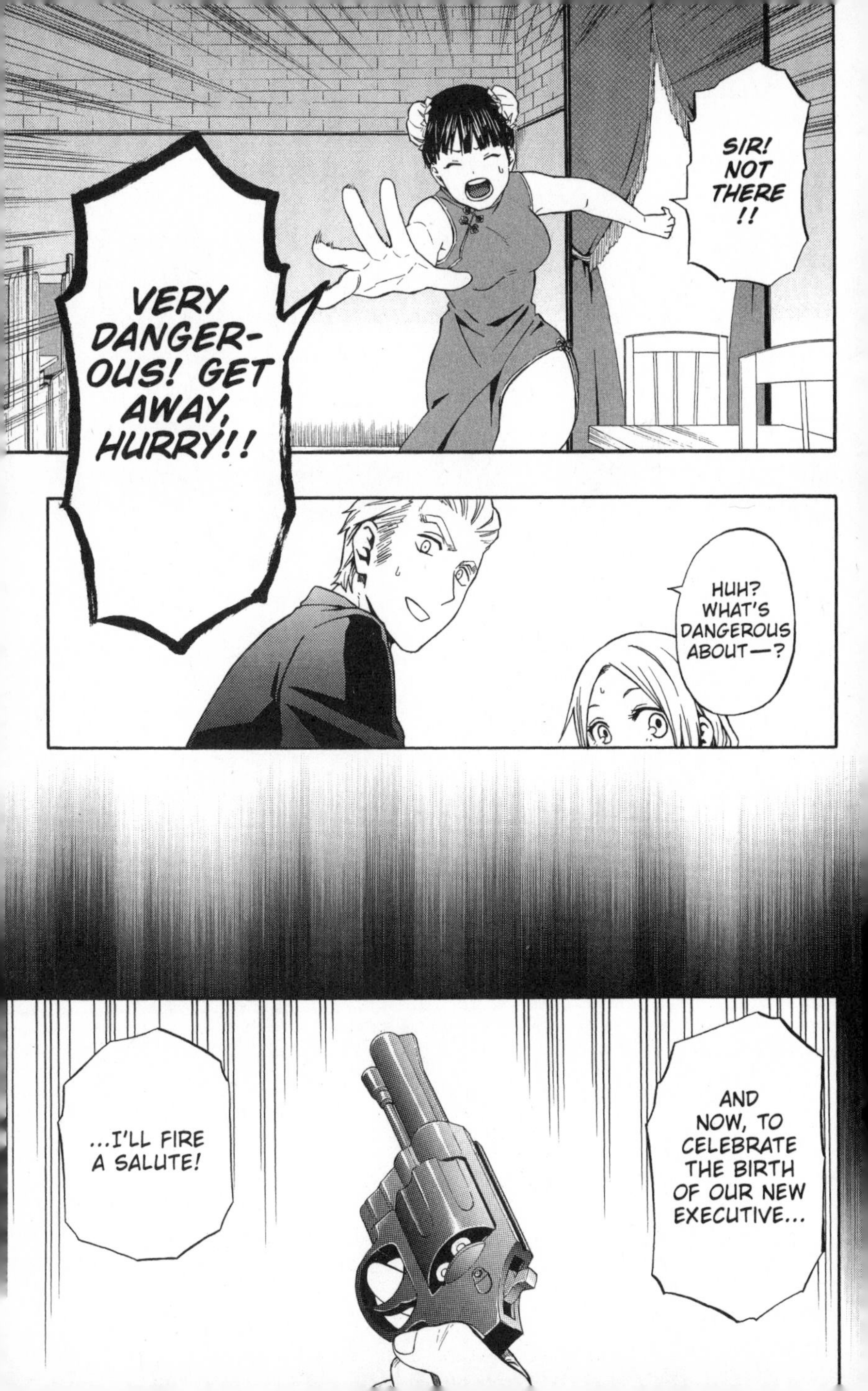
SIR! NOT THERE!!
VERY DANGER-OUS! GET AWAY, HURRY!!
HUH? WHAT'S DANGEROUS ABOUT—?
AND NOW, TO CELEBRATE THE BIRTH OF OUR NEW EXECUTIVE...
...I'LL FIRE A SALUTE!

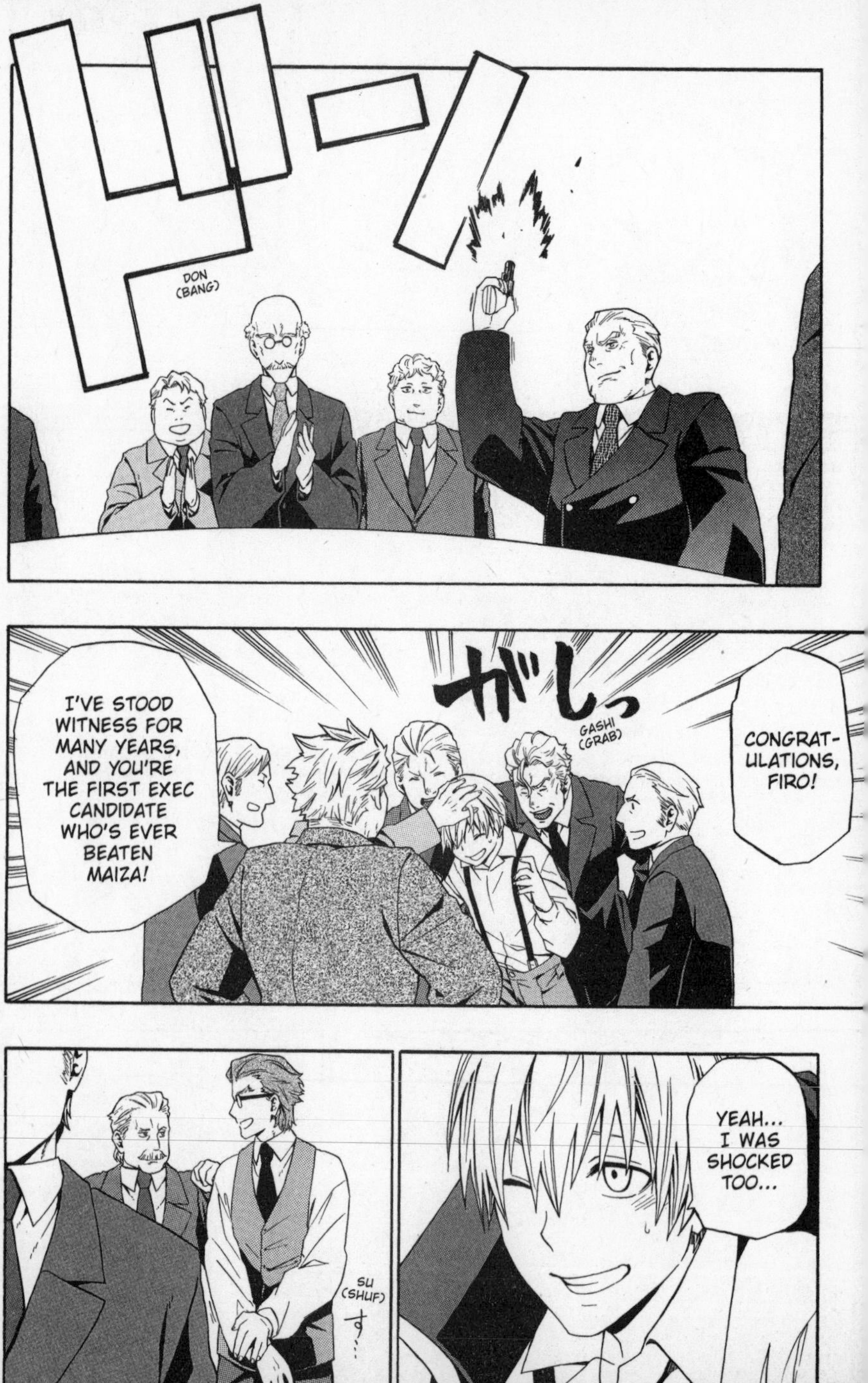
ドーン
DON (BANG)
CONGRAT-ULATIONS, FIRO!
がしっ
GASHI (GRAB)
I'VE STOOD WITNESS FOR MANY YEARS, AND YOU'RE THE FIRST EXEC CANDIDATE WHO'S EVER BEATEN MAIZA!
YEAH... I WAS SHOCKED TOO...
SU (SHUF)
す…

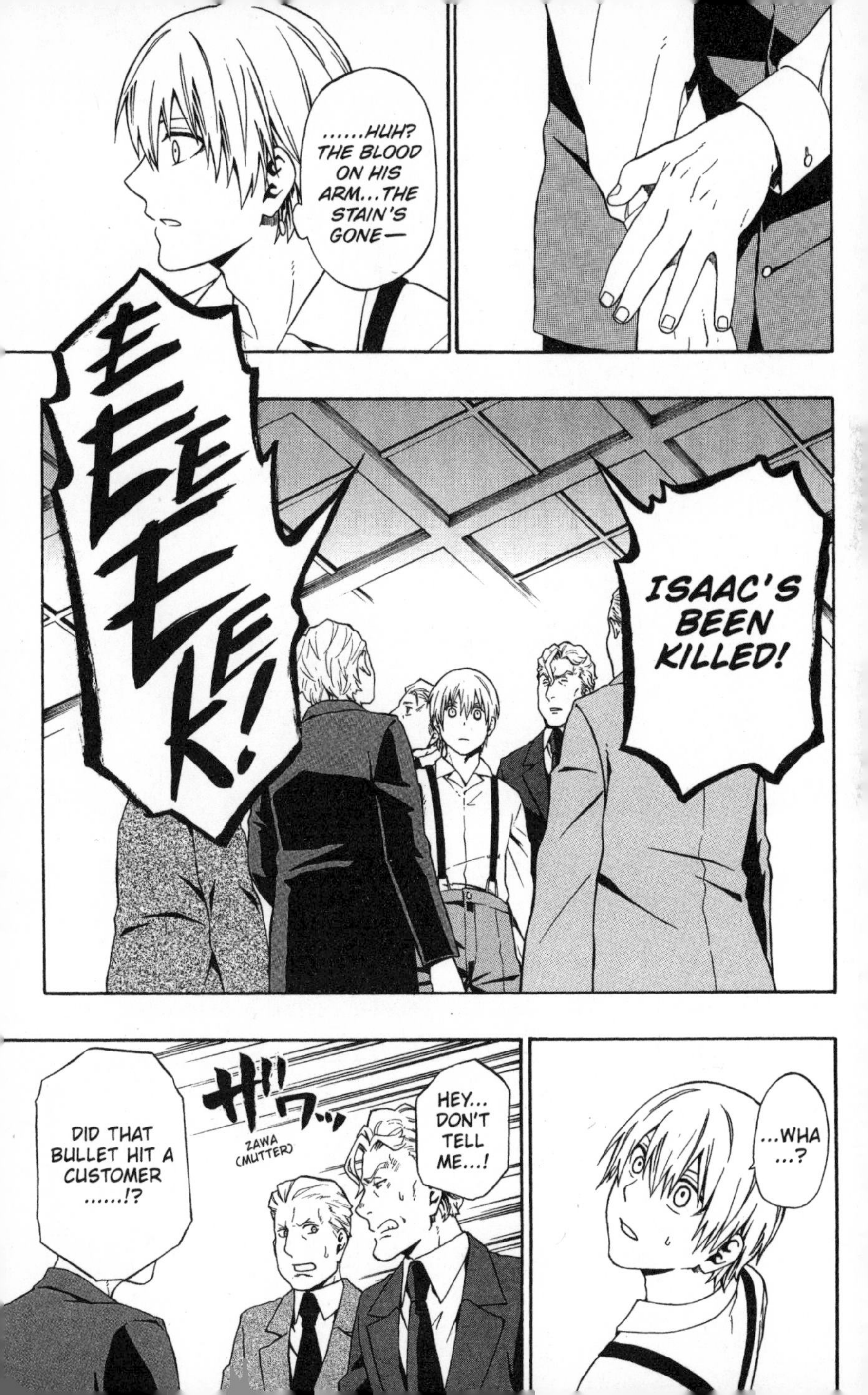
......HUH? THE BLOOD ON HIS ARM...THE STAIN'S GONE—
EEEEK!
ISAAC'S BEEN KILLED!
...WHA ...?
HEY... DON'T TELL ME...!
ザワッ
ZAWA (MUTTER)
DID THAT BULLET HIT A CUSTOMER ......!?

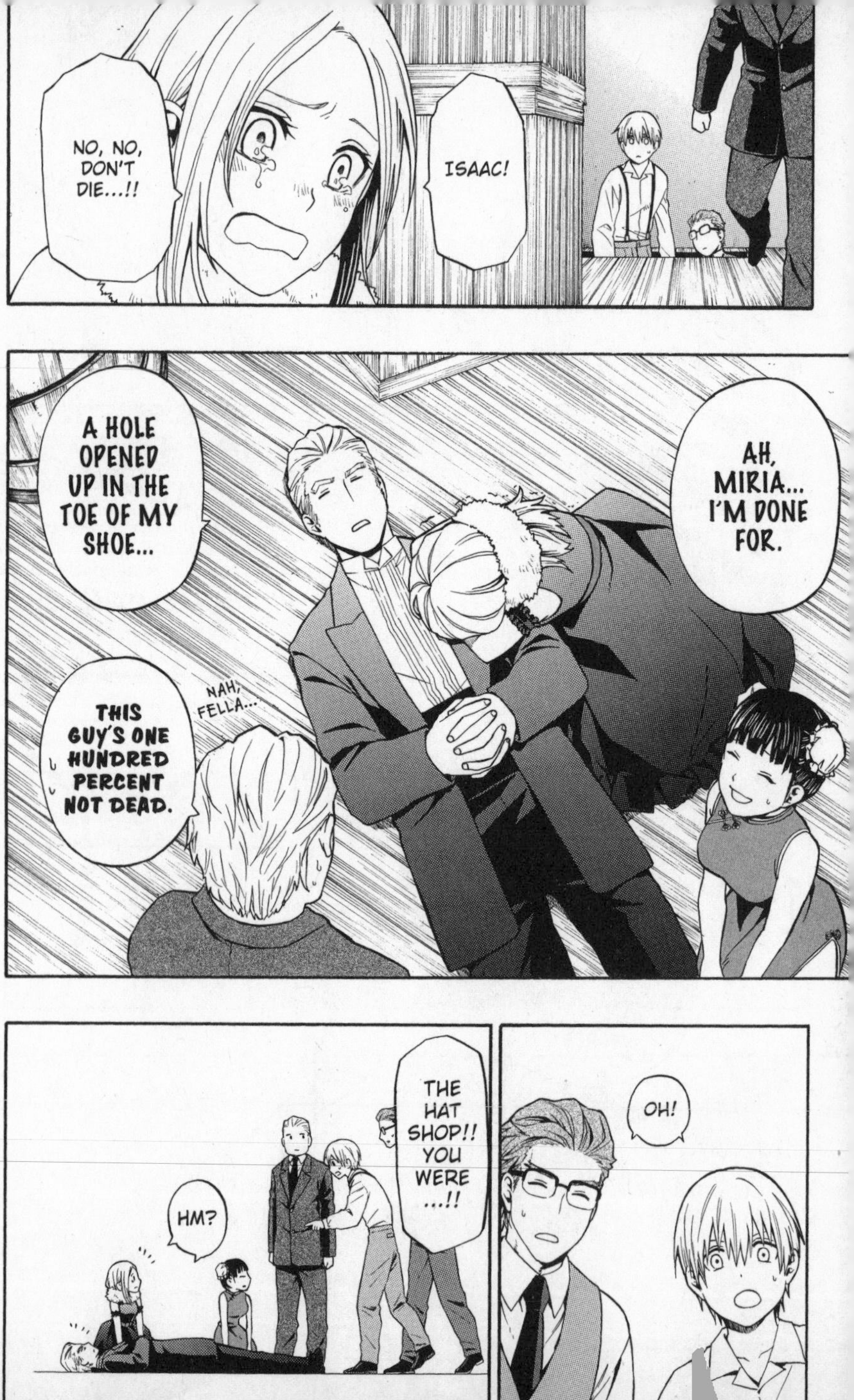
ISAAC!
NO, NO, DON'T DIE...!!
AH, MIRIA... I'M DONE FOR.
A HOLE OPENED UP IN THE TOE OF MY SHOE...
NAH, FELLA...
THIS GUY'S ONE HUNDRED PERCENT NOT DEAD.
OH!
THE HAT SHOP!! YOU WERE...!!
HM?

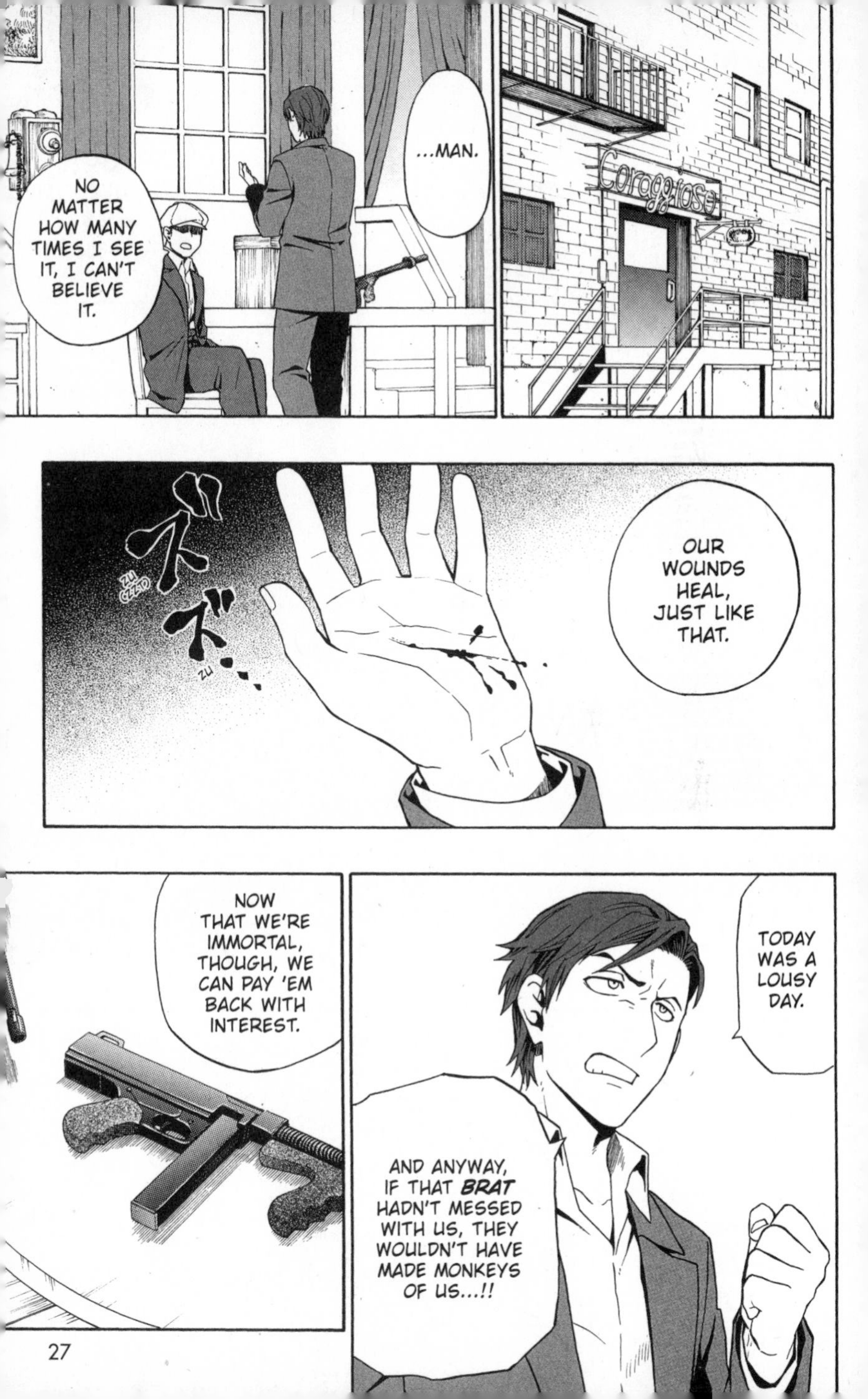
Coraggioso
...MAN.
NO MATTER HOW MANY TIMES I SEE IT, I CAN'T BELIEVE IT.
OUR WOUNDS HEAL, JUST LIKE THAT.
ズズ...
ZU (Z-Z-T)
ZU
TODAY WAS A LOUSY DAY.
AND ANYWAY, IF THAT *BRAT* HADN'T MESSED WITH US, THEY WOULDN'T HAVE MADE MONKEYS OF US...!!
NOW THAT WE'RE IMMORTAL, THOUGH, WE CAN PAY 'EM BACK WITH INTEREST.

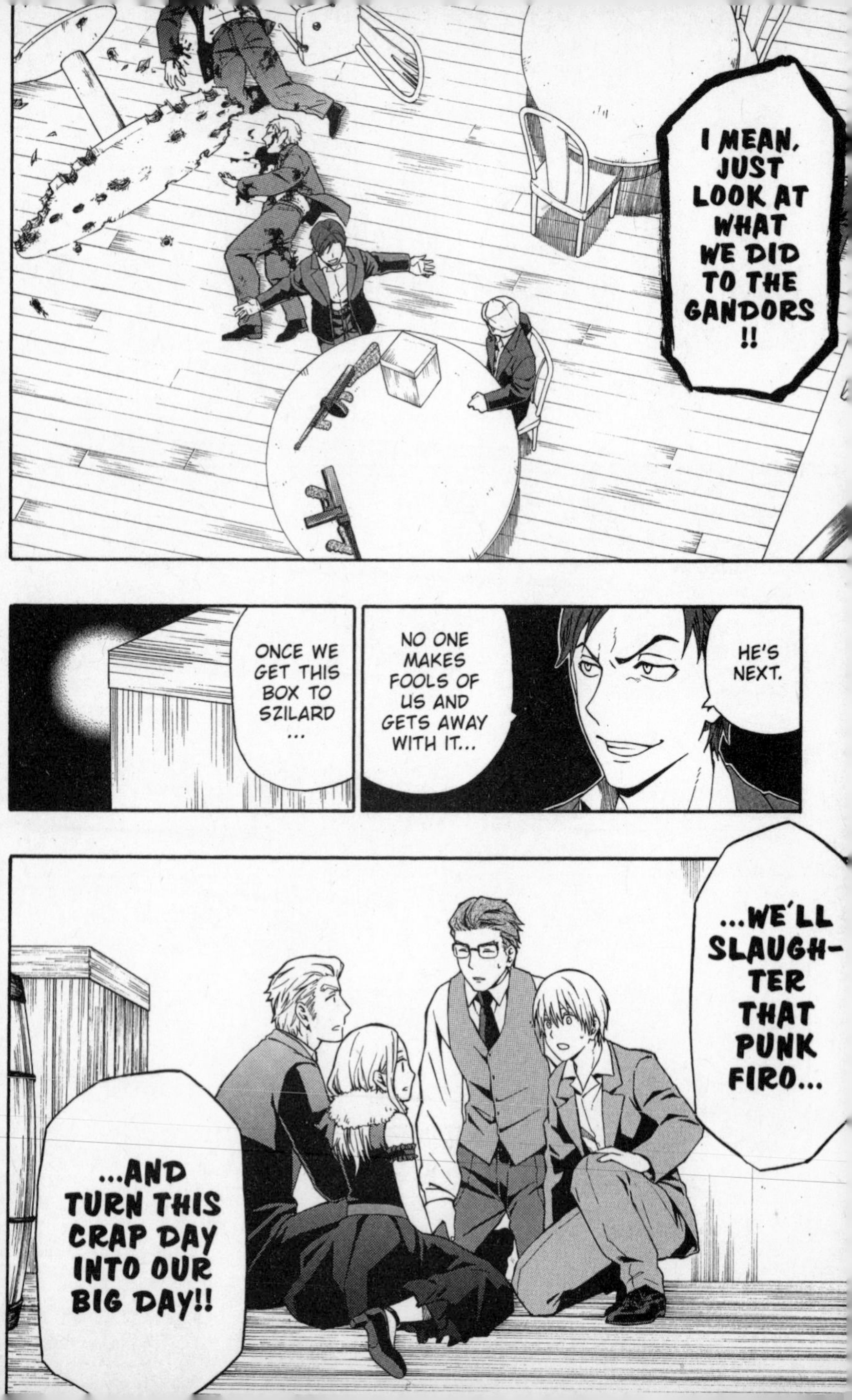
I MEAN, JUST LOOK AT WHAT WE DID TO THE GANDORS !!
HE'S NEXT.
NO ONE MAKES FOOLS OF US AND GETS AWAY WITH IT...
ONCE WE GET THIS BOX TO SZILARD ...
...WE'LL SLAUGH-TER THAT PUNK FIRO...
...AND TURN THIS CRAP DAY INTO OUR BIG DAY!!

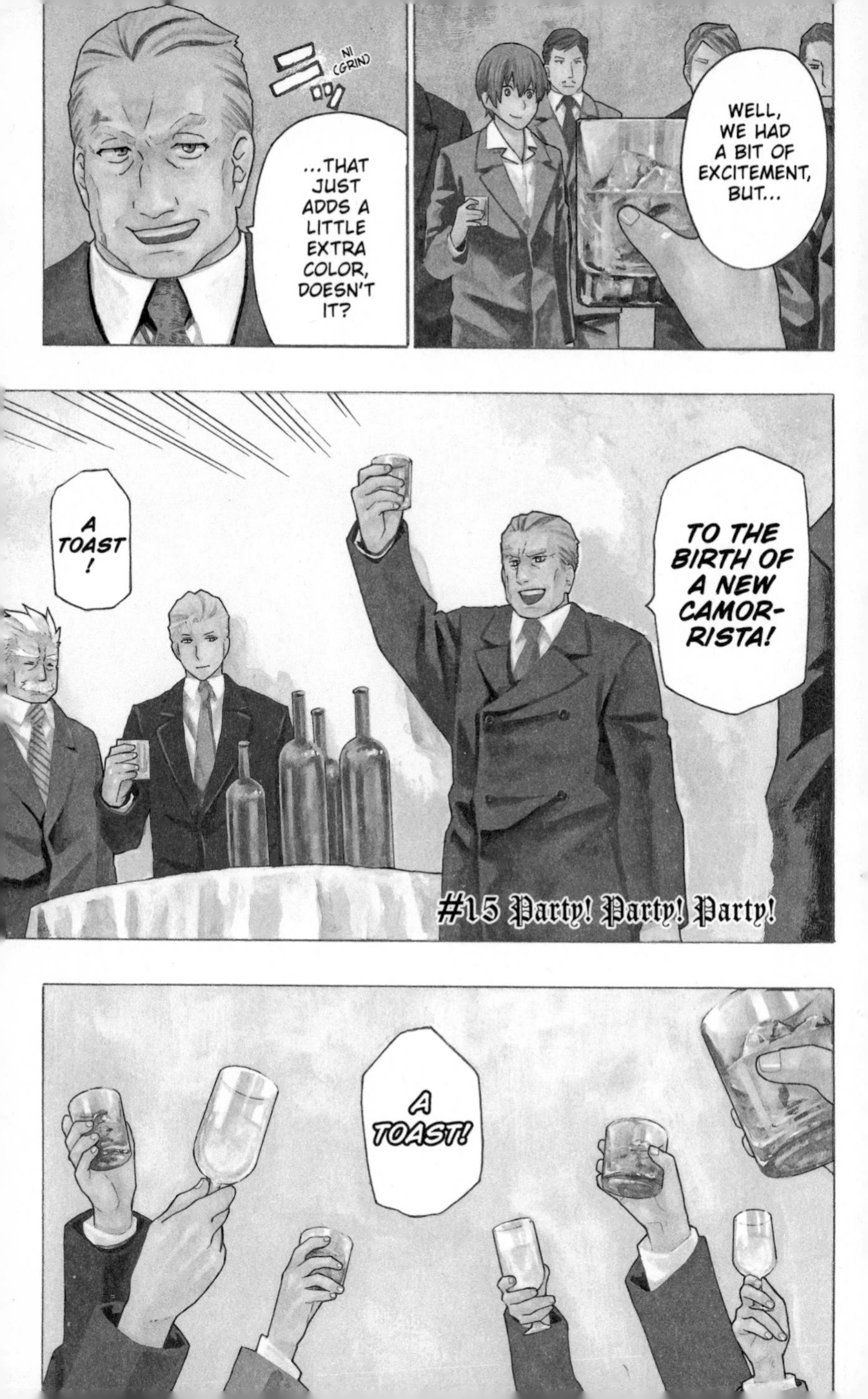
WELL, WE HAD A BIT OF EXCITEMENT, BUT...
NI (GRIN)
...THAT JUST ADDS A LITTLE EXTRA COLOR, DOESN'T IT?
TO THE BIRTH OF A NEW CAMOR-RISTA!
A TOAST!
A TOAST!

#15 Party! Party! Party!

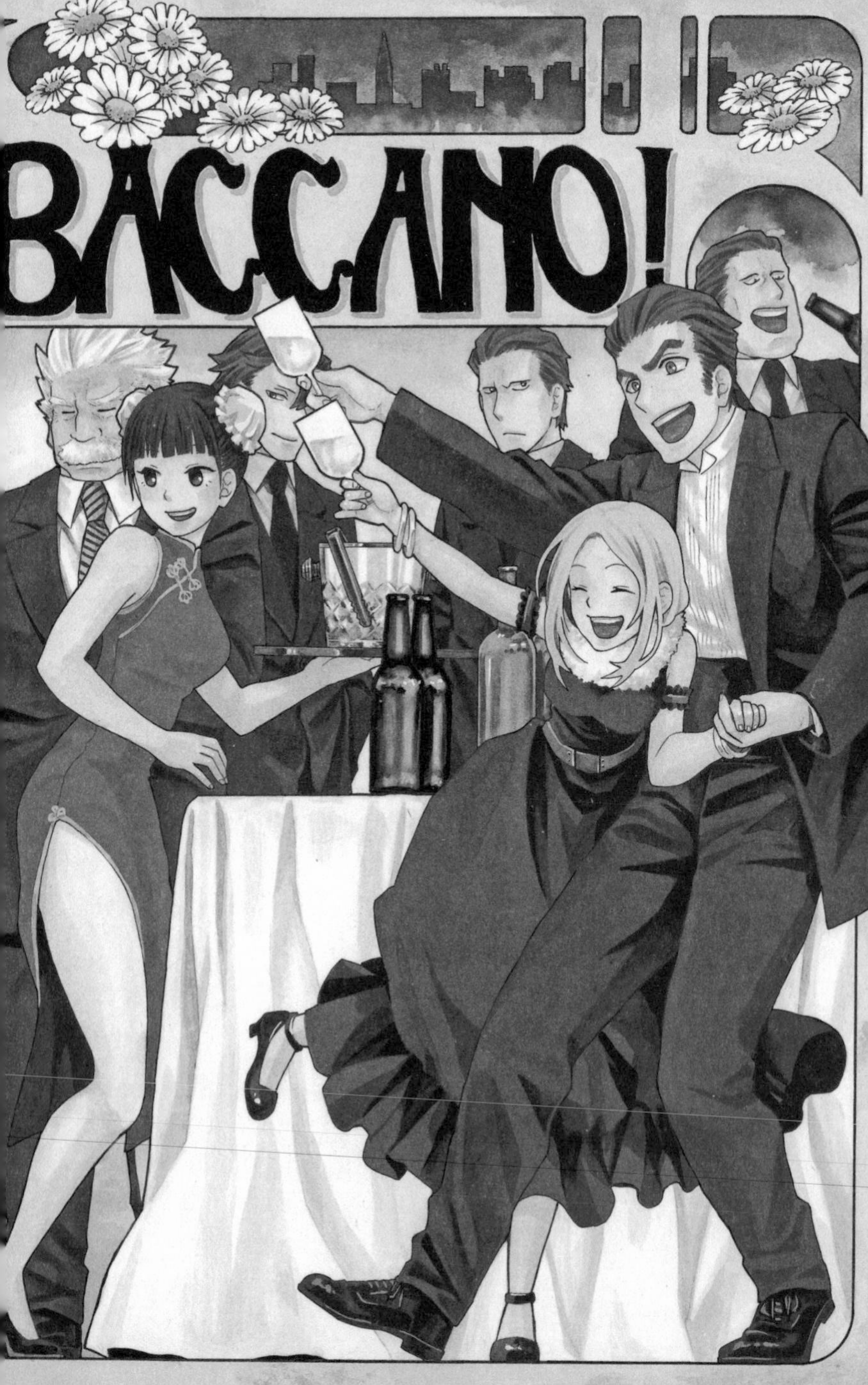
BACCANO!

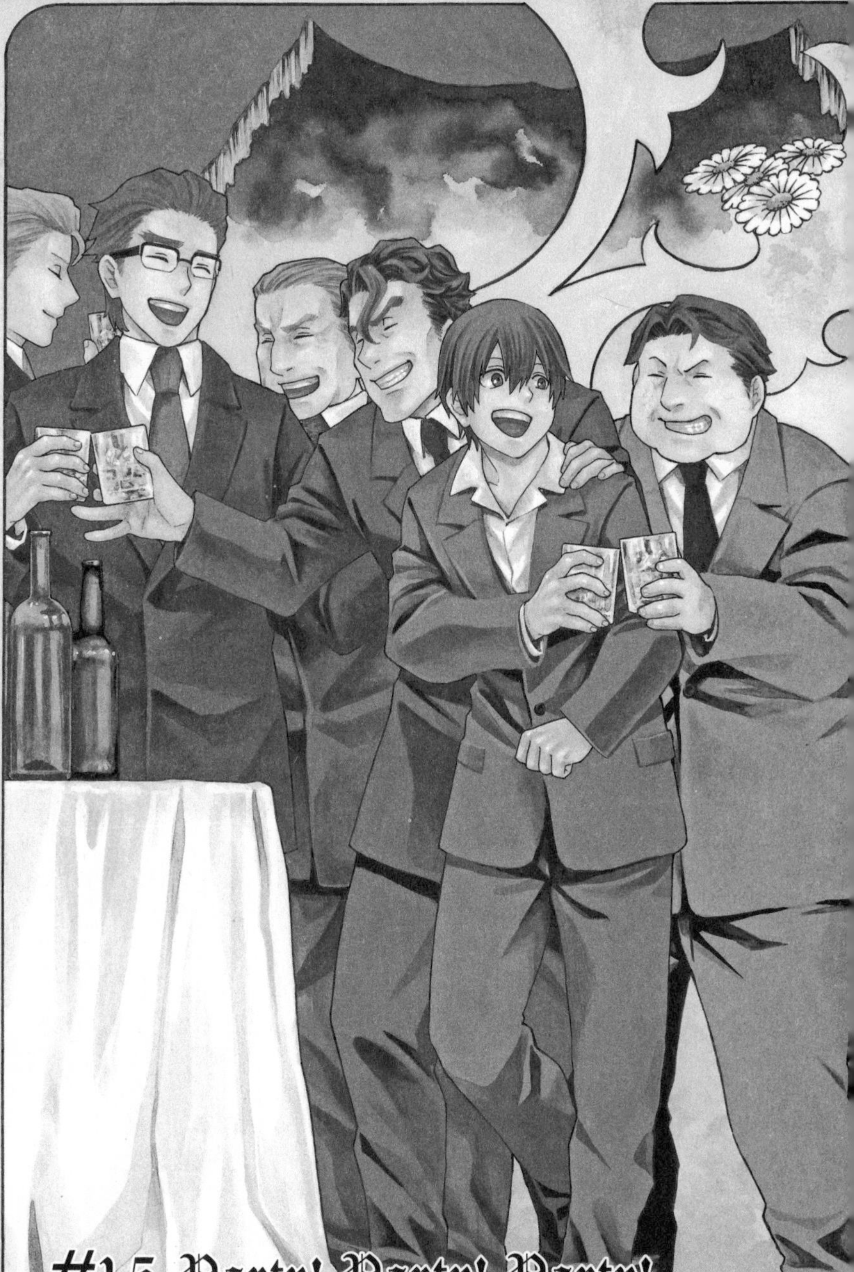
#15 Party! Party! Party!

BACCANO!

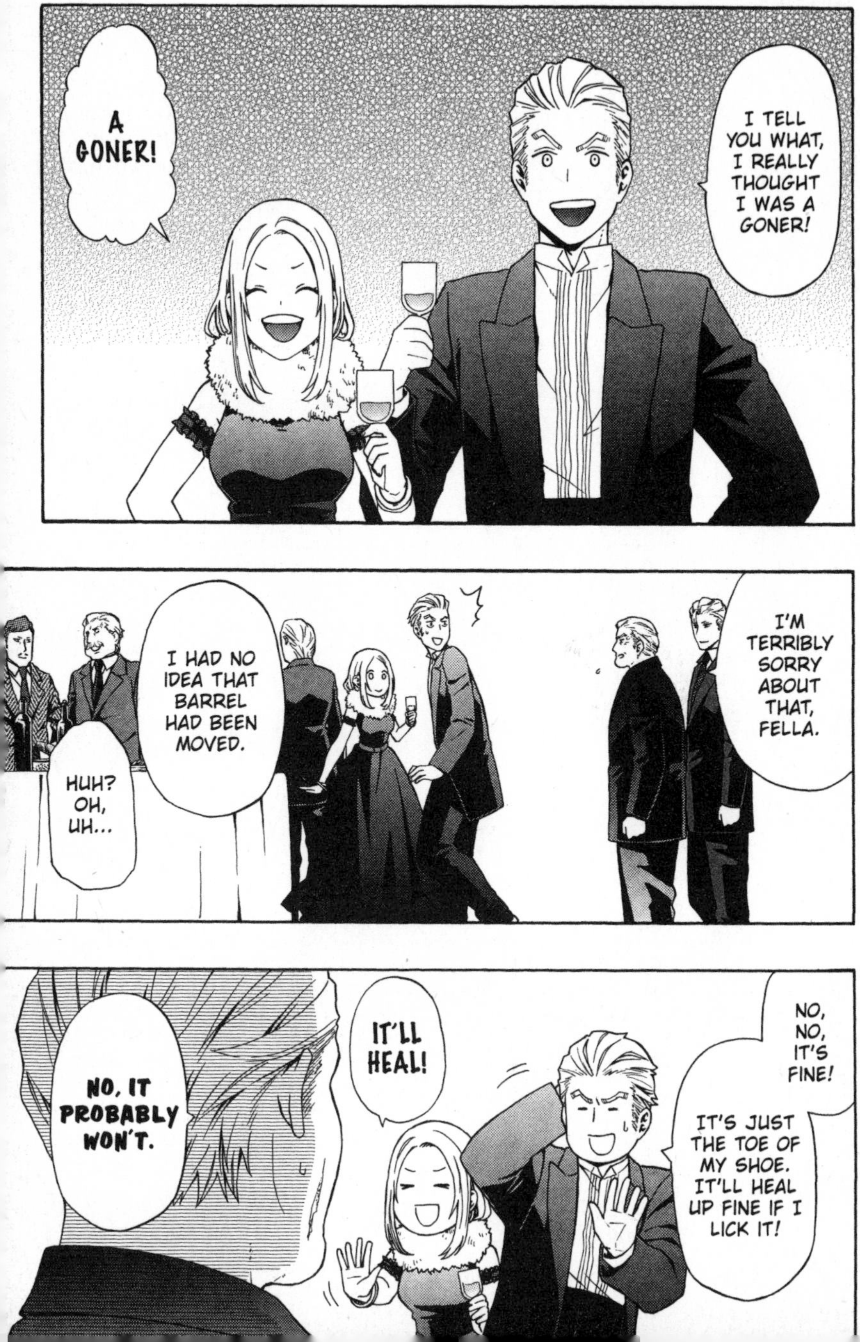
I TELL YOU WHAT, I REALLY THOUGHT I WAS A GONER!
A GONER!
I'M TERRIBLY SORRY ABOUT THAT, FELLA.
I HAD NO IDEA THAT BARREL HAD BEEN MOVED.
HUH? OH, UH...
NO, NO, IT'S FINE!
IT'S JUST THE TOE OF MY SHOE. IT'LL HEAL UP FINE IF I LICK IT!
IT'LL HEAL!
NO, IT PROBABLY WON'T.

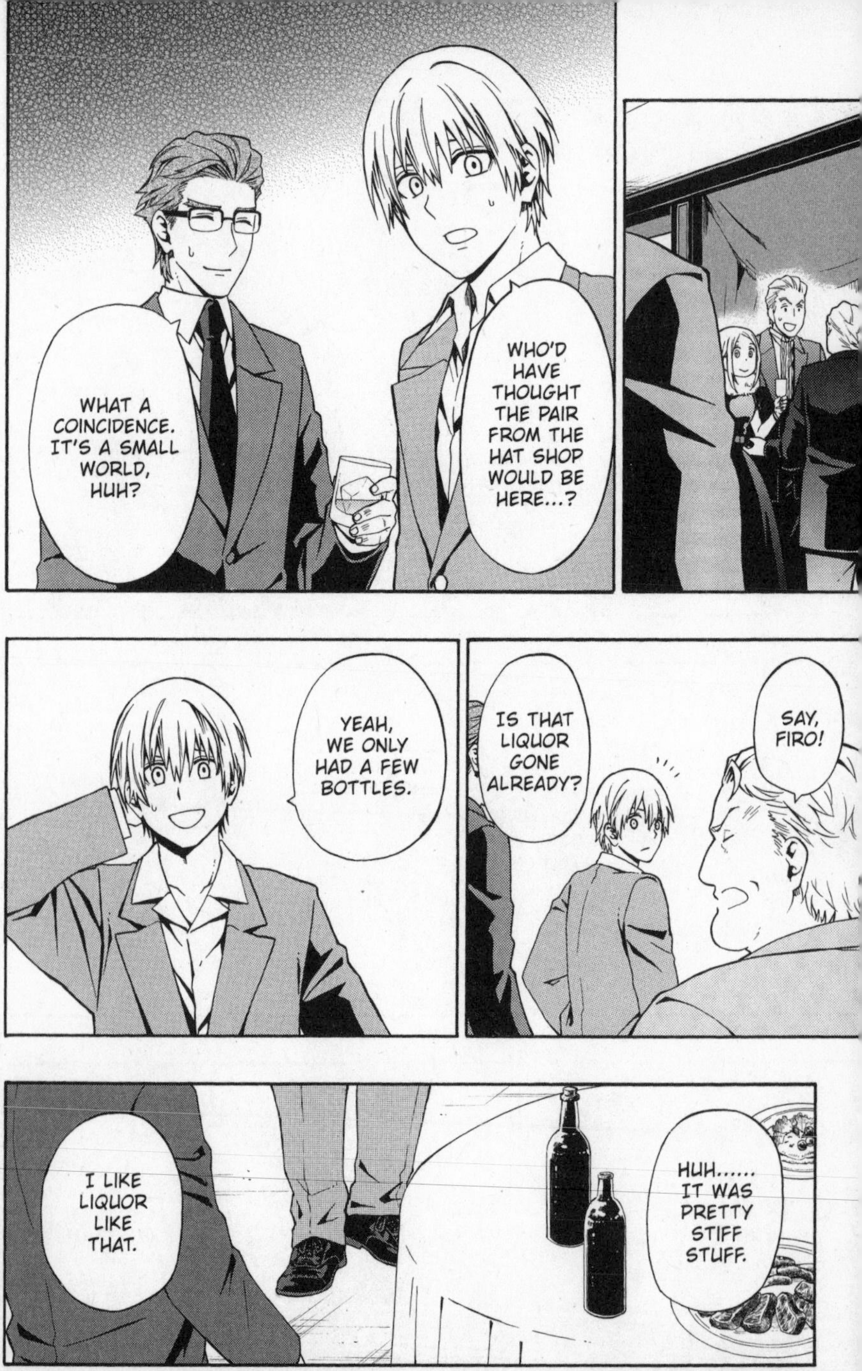
WHO'D HAVE THOUGHT THE PAIR FROM THE HAT SHOP WOULD BE HERE...?
WHAT A COINCIDENCE. IT'S A SMALL WORLD, HUH?
SAY, FIRO!
IS THAT LIQUOR GONE ALREADY?
YEAH, WE ONLY HAD A FEW BOTTLES.
HUH...... IT WAS PRETTY STIFF STUFF.
I LIKE LIQUOR LIKE THAT.

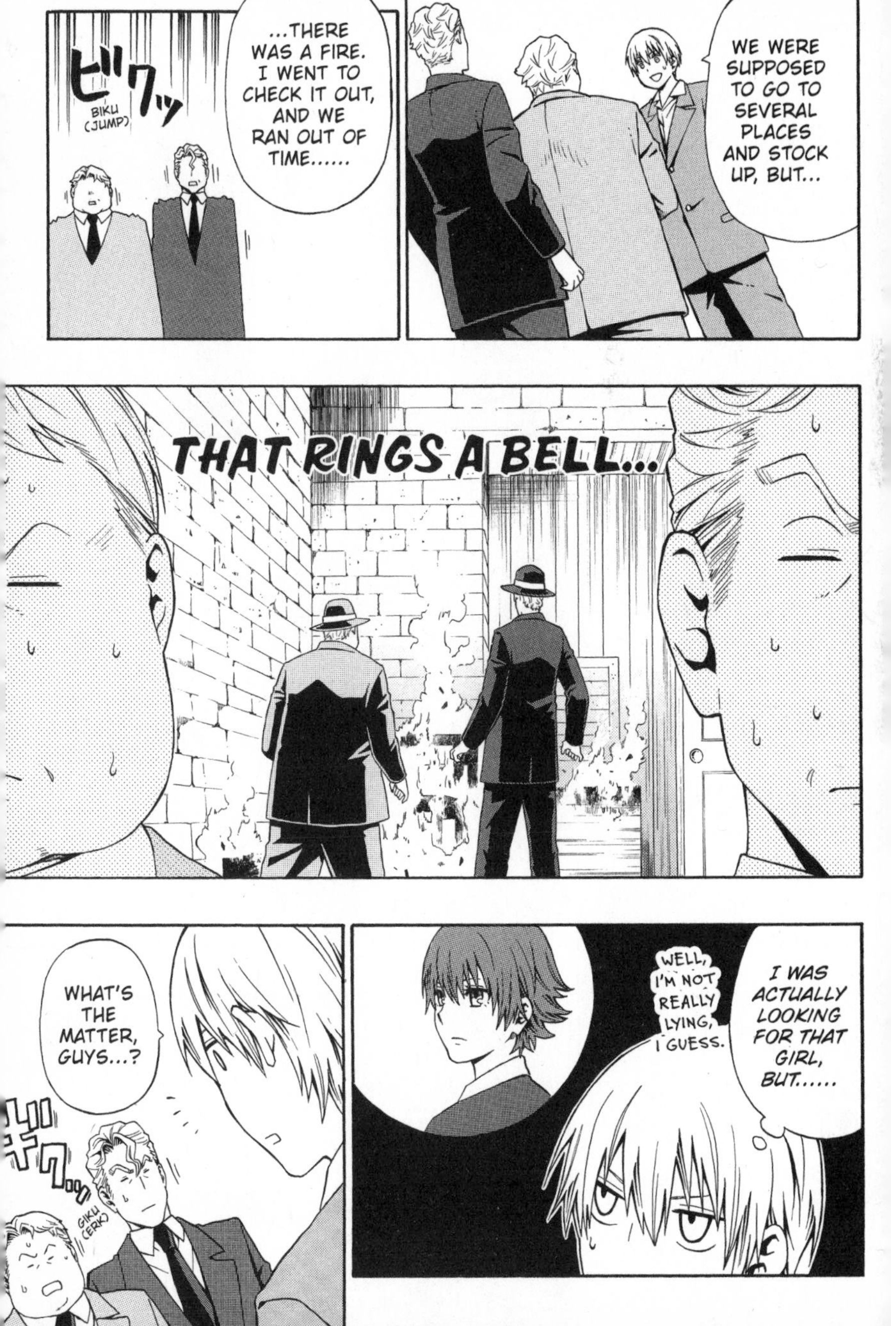
WE WERE SUPPOSED TO GO TO SEVERAL PLACES AND STOCK UP, BUT...
...THERE WAS A FIRE. I WENT TO CHECK IT OUT, AND WE RAN OUT OF TIME......
ビクッ
BIKU (JUMP)
THAT RINGS A BELL...
I WAS ACTUALLY LOOKING FOR THAT GIRL, BUT......
WELL, I'M NOT REALLY LYING, I GUESS.
WHAT'S THE MATTER, GUYS...?
ギクッ
GIKU (ERK)

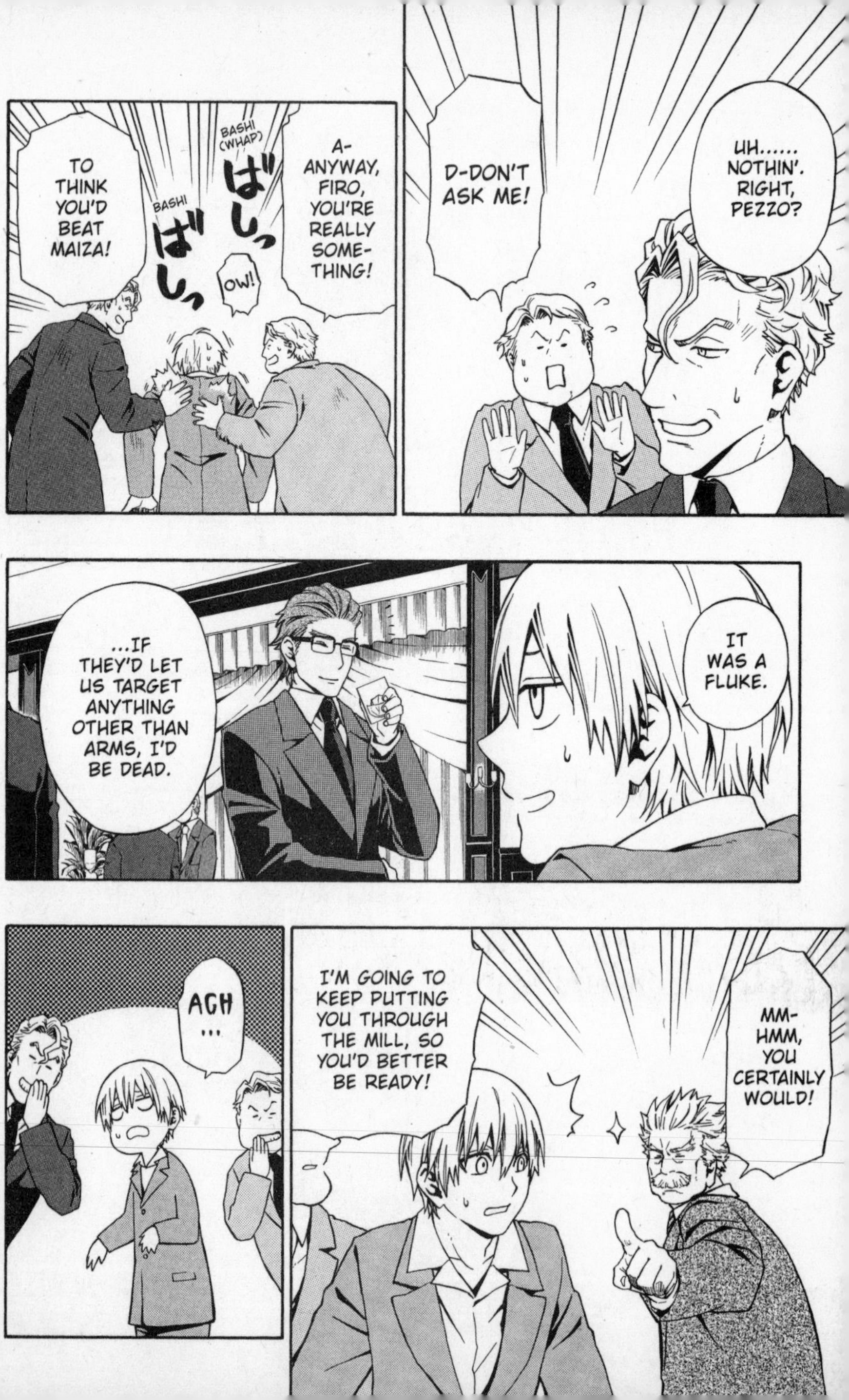
UH...... NOTHIN'. RIGHT, PEZZO?
D-DON'T ASK ME!
A- ANYWAY, FIRO, YOU'RE REALLY SOME-THING!
ばしっ
BASHI (WHAP)
OW!
ばしっ
BASHI
TO THINK YOU'D BEAT MAIZA!
IT WAS A FLUKE.
...IF THEY'D LET US TARGET ANYTHING OTHER THAN ARMS, I'D BE DEAD.
MM-HMM, YOU CERTAINLY WOULD!
I'M GOING TO KEEP PUTTING YOU THROUGH THE MILL, SO YOU'D BETTER BE READY!
AGH ...

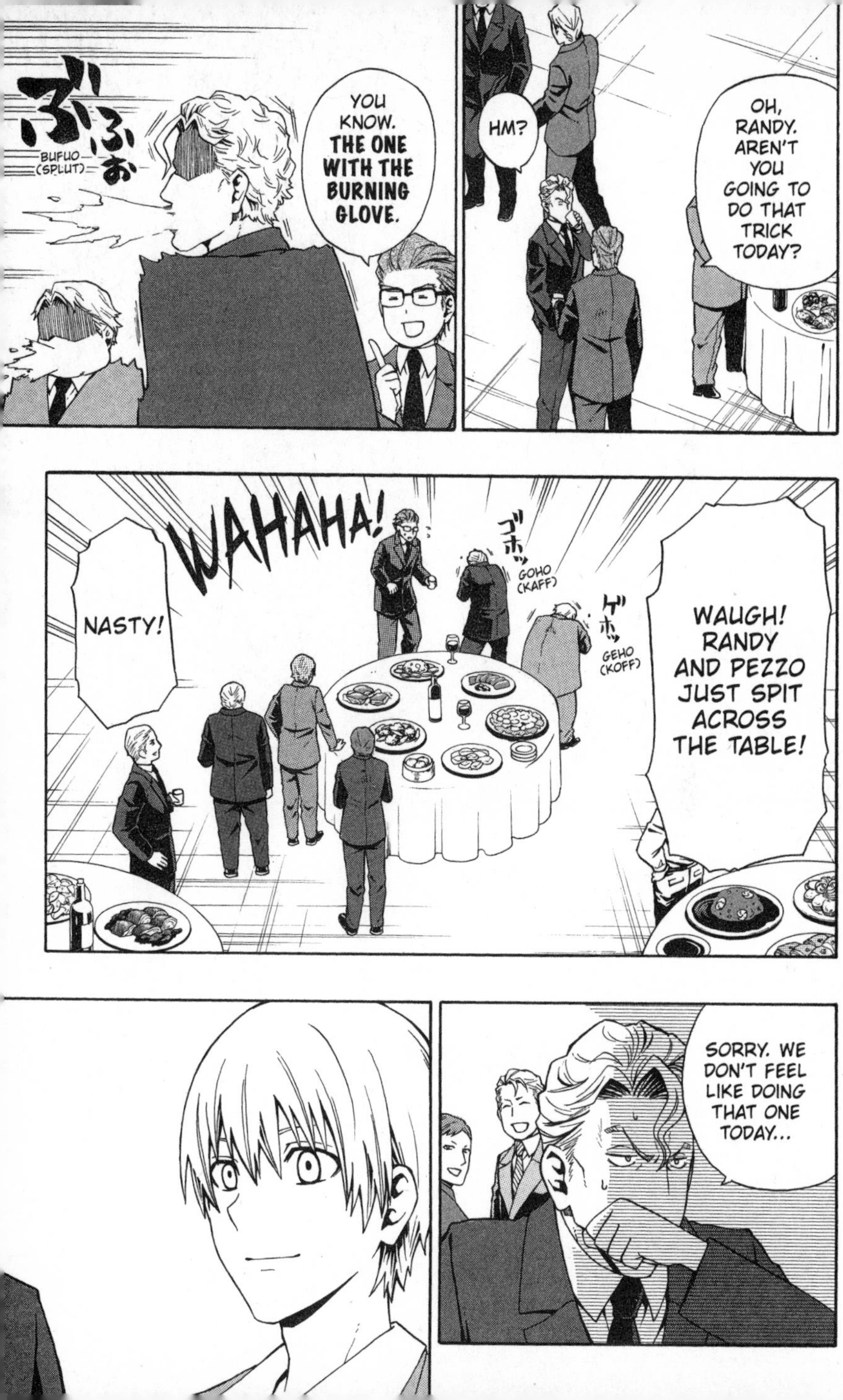
OH, RANDY. AREN'T YOU GOING TO DO THAT TRICK TODAY?
HM?
YOU KNOW. **THE ONE WITH THE BURNING GLOVE.**
ぶふぉ
BUFUO (SPLUT)
WAUGH! RANDY AND PEZZO JUST SPIT ACROSS THE TABLE!
ゲホッ
GEHO (KOFF)
ゴホッ
GOHO (KAFF)
WAHAHA!
NASTY!
SORRY. WE DON'T FEEL LIKE DOING THAT ONE TODAY...

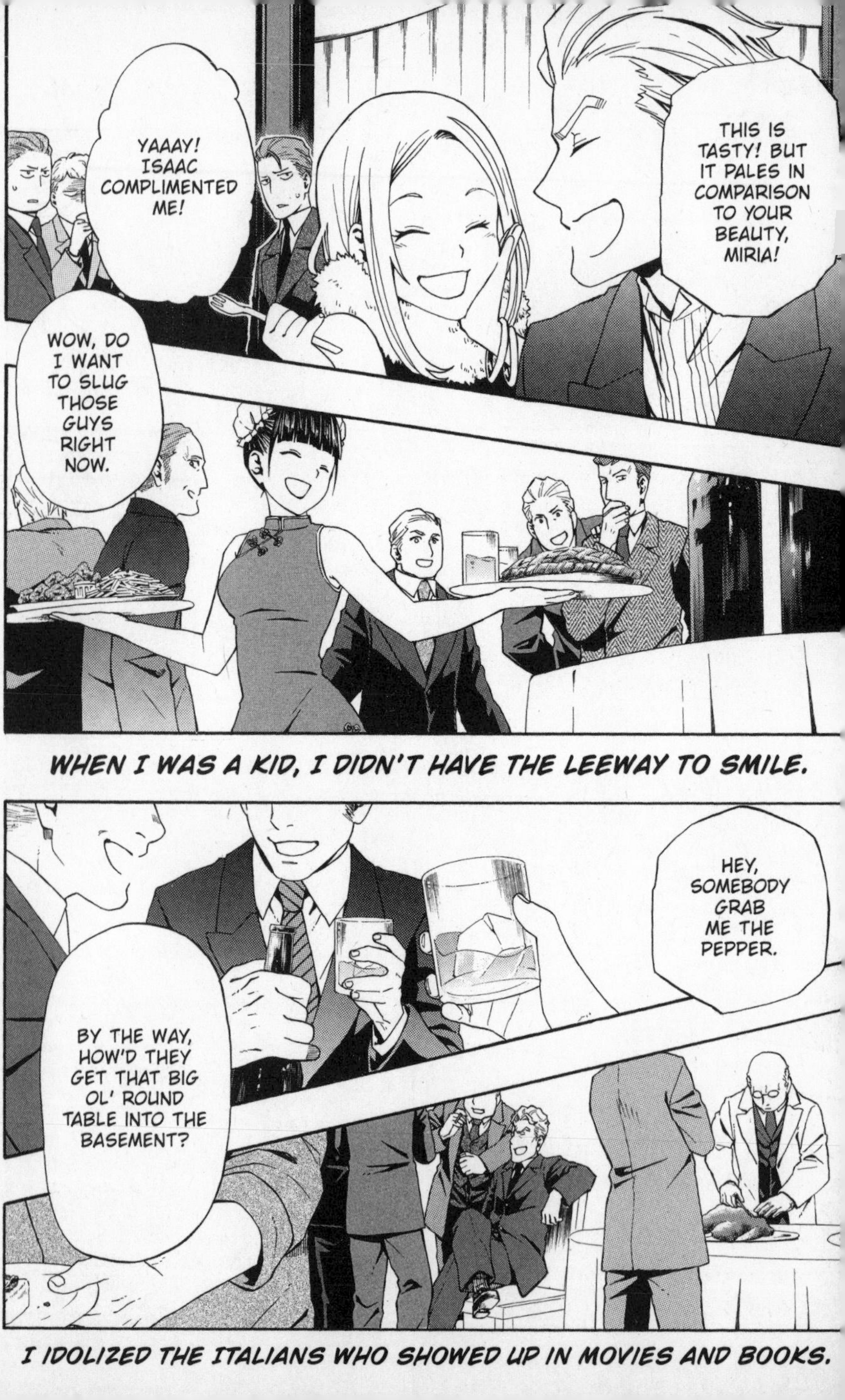
THIS IS TASTY! BUT IT PALES IN COMPARISON TO YOUR BEAUTY, MIRIA!
YAAAY! ISAAC COMPLIMENTED ME!
WOW, DO I WANT TO SLUG THOSE GUYS RIGHT NOW.
WHEN I WAS A KID, I DIDN'T HAVE THE LEEWAY TO SMILE.
HEY, SOMEBODY GRAB ME THE PEPPER.
BY THE WAY, HOW'D THEY GET THAT BIG OL' ROUND TABLE INTO THE BASEMENT?
I IDOLIZED THE ITALIANS WHO SHOWED UP IN MOVIES AND BOOKS.

I DREAMED ABOUT SMILING CHEERFULLY, LIKE THEM.

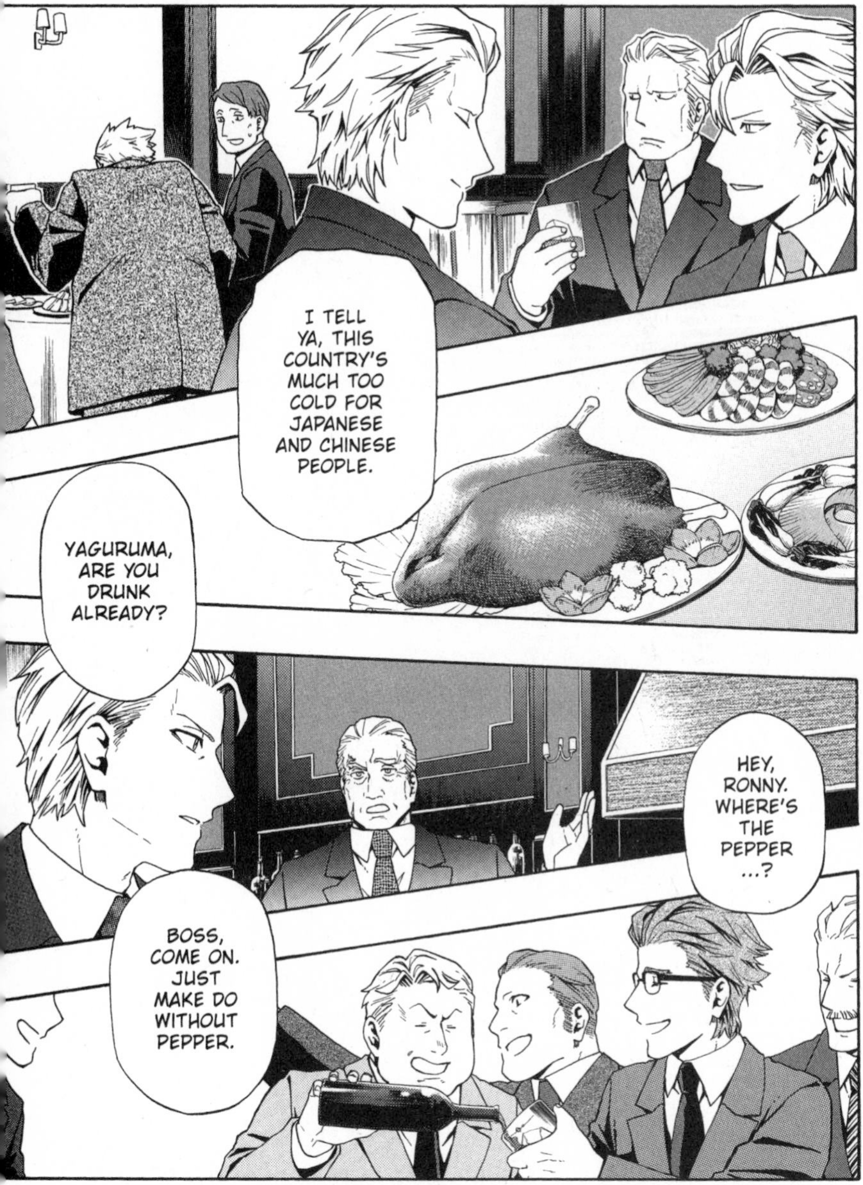
I TELL YA, THIS COUNTRY'S MUCH TOO COLD FOR JAPANESE AND CHINESE PEOPLE.
YAGURUMA, ARE YOU DRUNK ALREADY?
HEY, RONNY. WHERE'S THE PEPPER ...?
BOSS, COME ON. JUST MAKE DO WITHOUT PEPPER.

AND NOW—THAT DREAM'S COME TRUE.

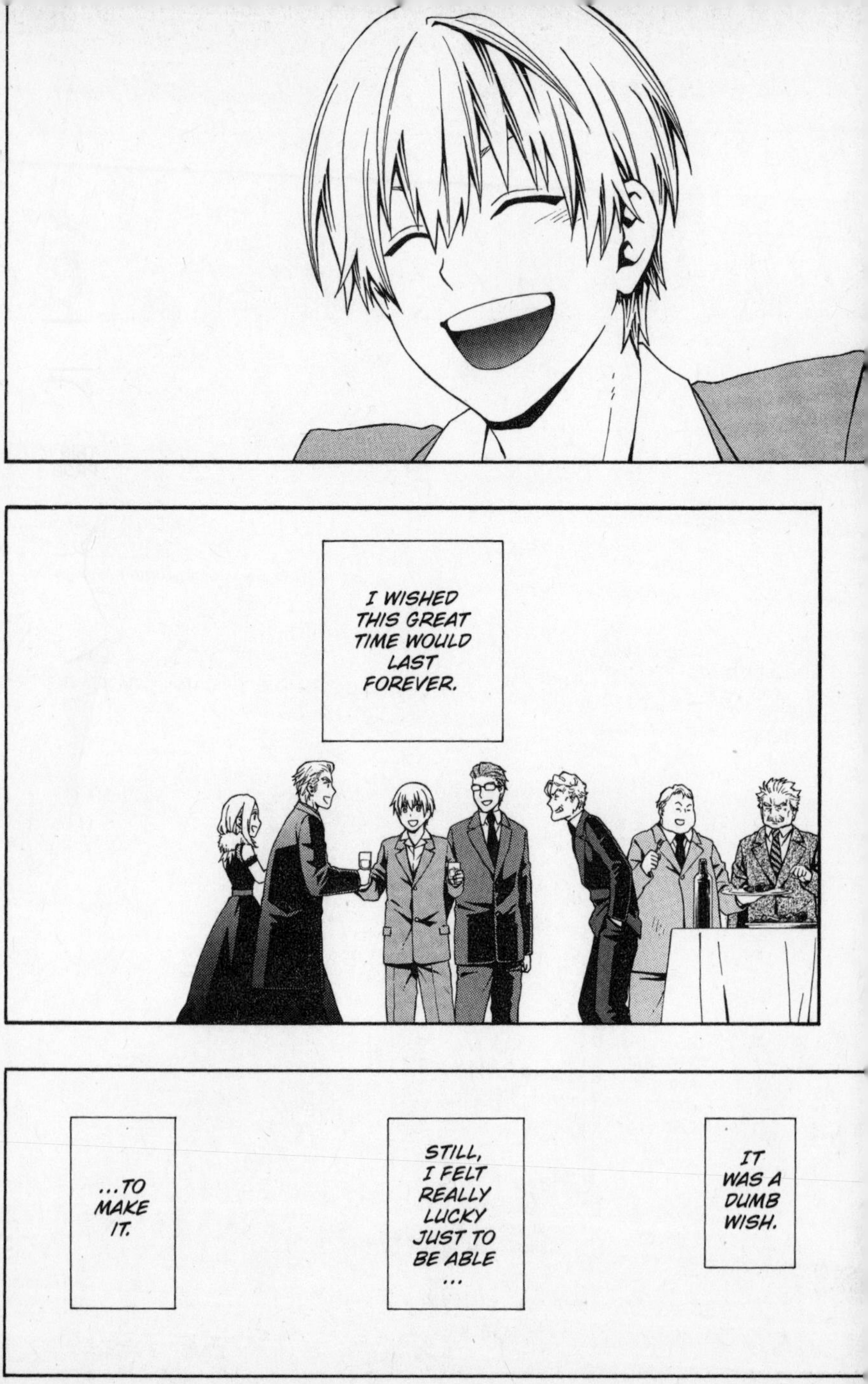
I WISHED THIS GREAT TIME WOULD LAST FOREVER.
IT WAS A DUMB WISH.
STILL, I FELT REALLY LUCKY JUST TO BE ABLE...
...TO MAKE IT.

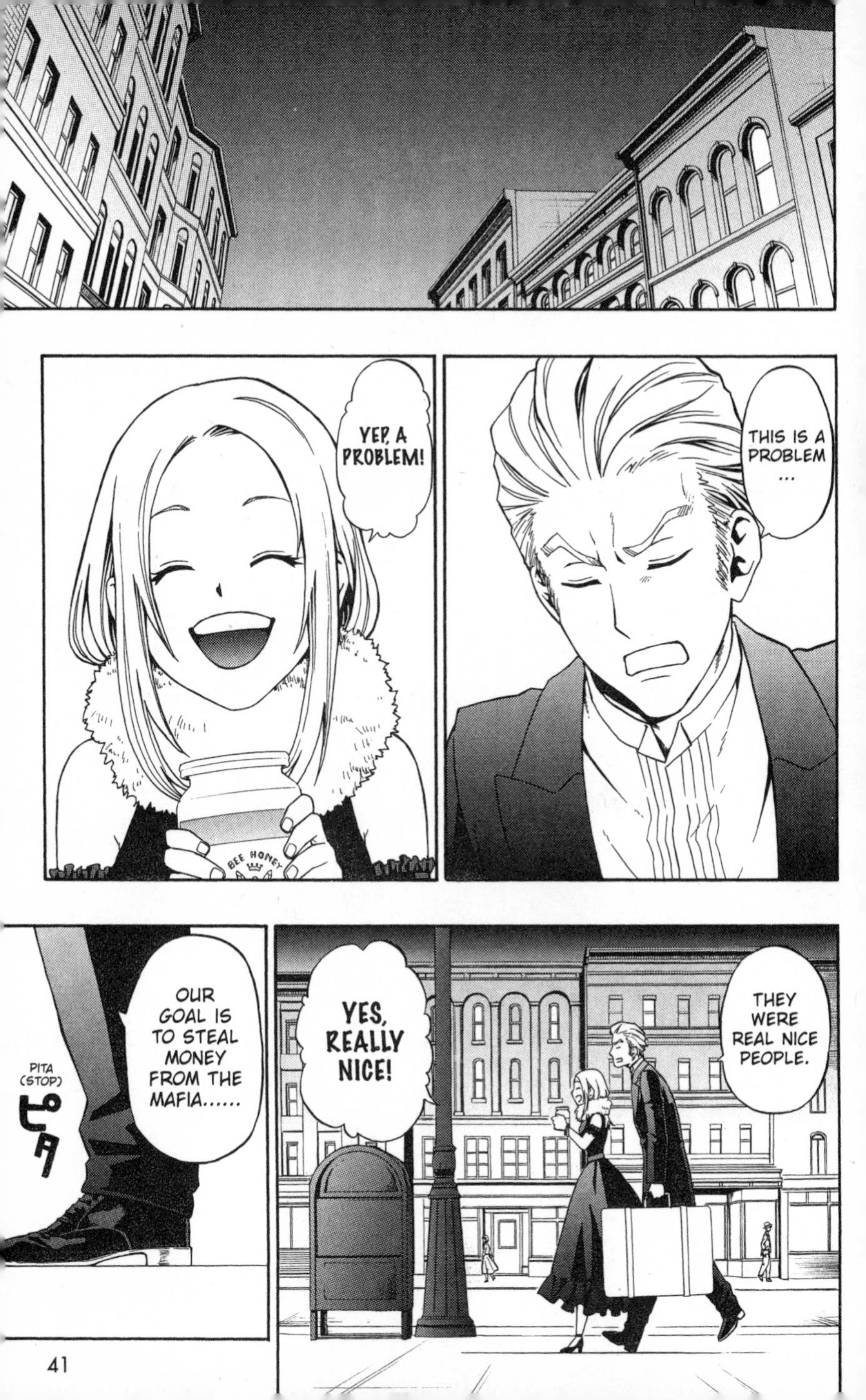
THIS IS A PROBLEM ...
YEP, A PROBLEM!
BEE HONEY
THEY WERE REAL NICE PEOPLE.
YES, REALLY NICE!
OUR GOAL IS TO STEAL MONEY FROM THE MAFIA......
PITA (STOP)
ピタ

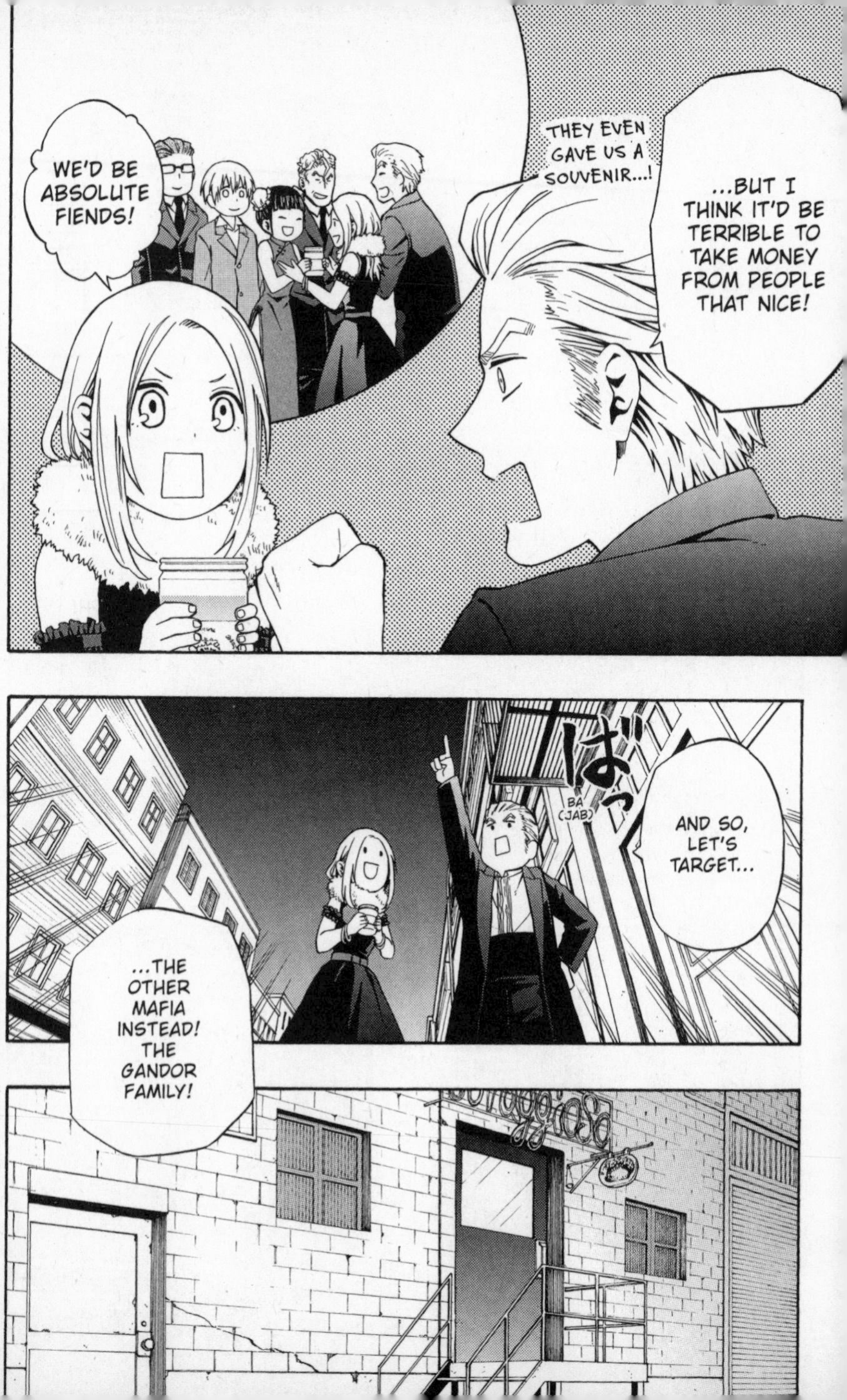
THEY EVEN GAVE US A SOUVENIR...!
...BUT I THINK IT'D BE TERRIBLE TO TAKE MONEY FROM PEOPLE THAT NICE!
WE'D BE ABSOLUTE FIENDS!
ばっ
BA (JAB)
AND SO, LET'S TARGET...
...THE OTHER MAFIA INSTEAD! THE GANDOR FAMILY!

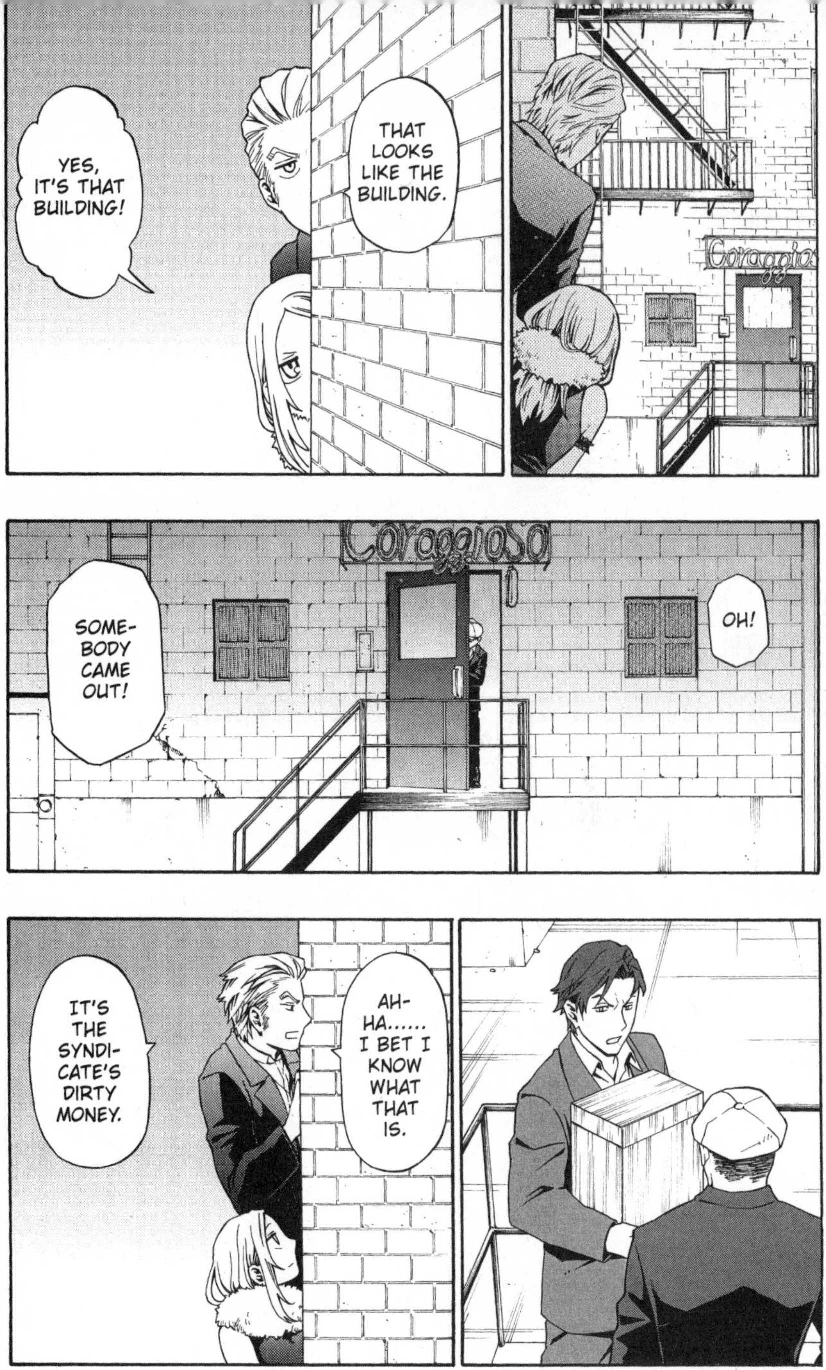
THAT LOOKS LIKE THE BUILDING.
YES, IT'S THAT BUILDING!
Coraggioso
OH!
SOME-BODY CAME OUT!
AH-HA...... I BET I KNOW WHAT THAT IS.
IT'S THE SYNDI-CATE'S DIRTY MONEY.

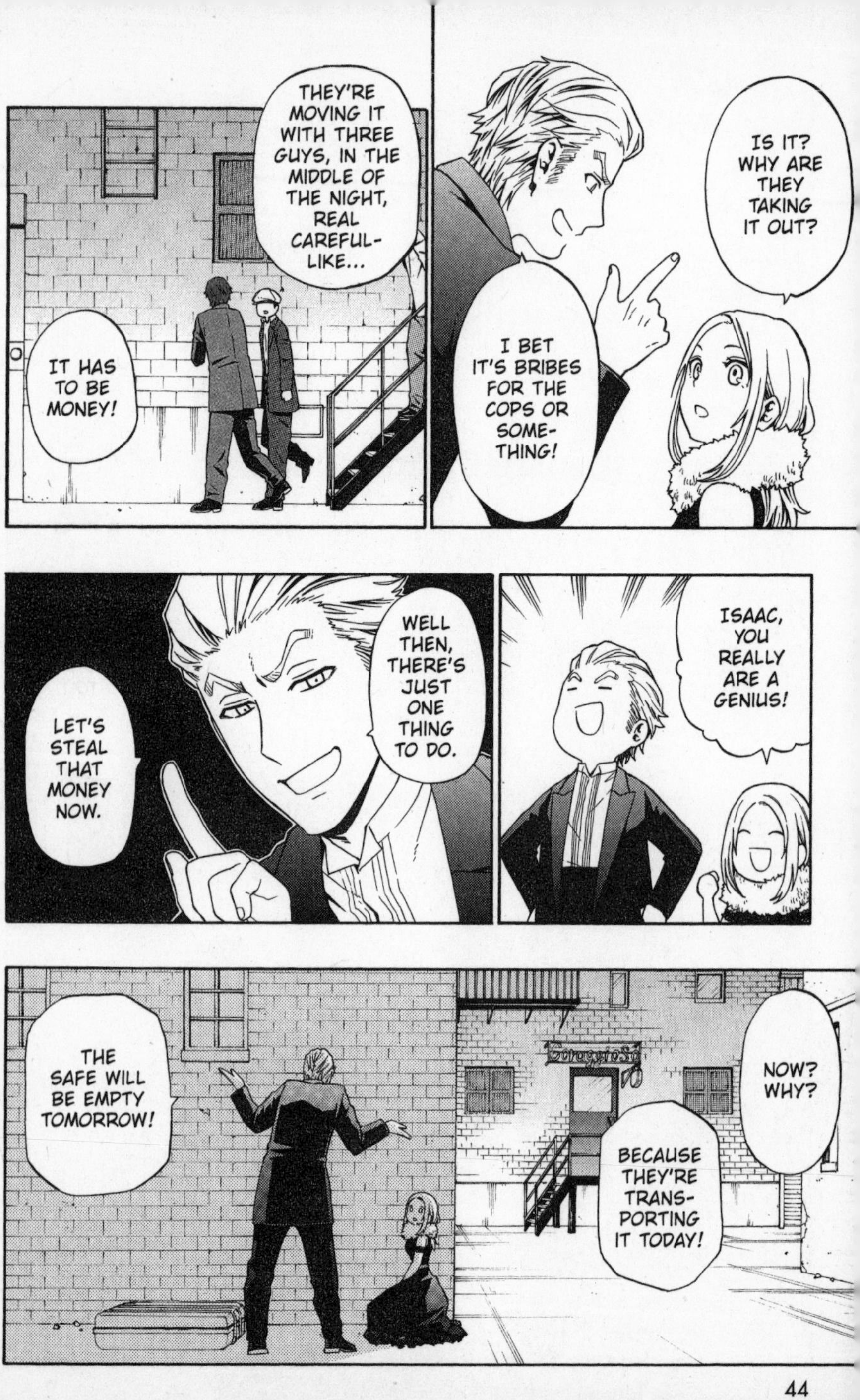
IS IT? WHY ARE THEY TAKING IT OUT?
I BET IT'S BRIBES FOR THE COPS OR SOME-THING!
THEY'RE MOVING IT WITH THREE GUYS, IN THE MIDDLE OF THE NIGHT, REAL CAREFUL-LIKE...
IT HAS TO BE MONEY!
ISAAC, YOU REALLY ARE A GENIUS!
WELL THEN, THERE'S JUST ONE THING TO DO.
LET'S STEAL THAT MONEY NOW.
NOW? WHY?
BECAUSE THEY'RE TRANS-PORTING IT TODAY!
THE SAFE WILL BE EMPTY TOMORROW!

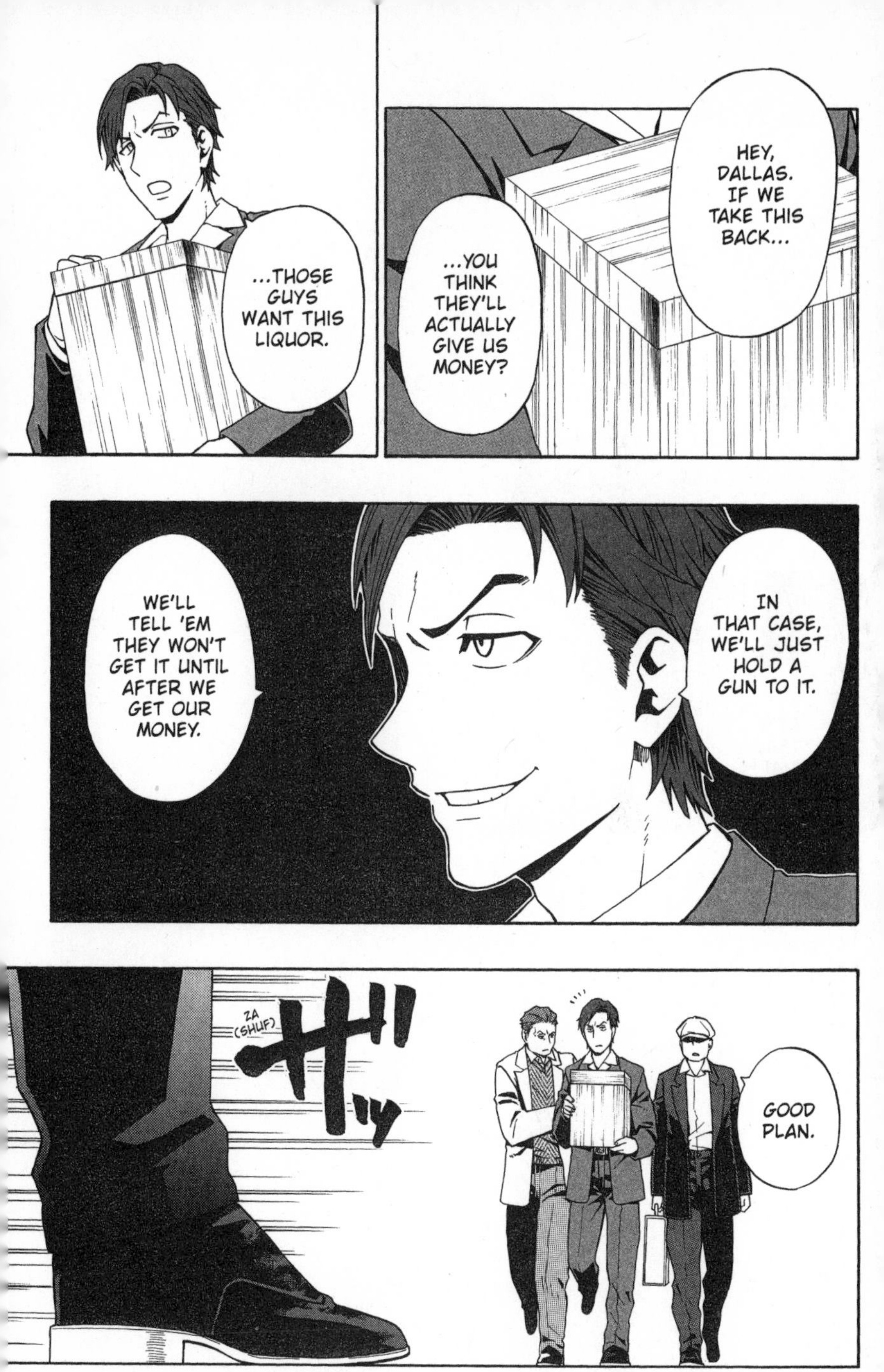
HEY, DALLAS. IF WE TAKE THIS BACK...
...YOU THINK THEY'LL ACTUALLY GIVE US MONEY?
...THOSE GUYS WANT THIS LIQUOR.
IN THAT CASE, WE'LL JUST HOLD A GUN TO IT.
WE'LL TELL 'EM THEY WON'T GET IT UNTIL AFTER WE GET OUR MONEY.
GOOD PLAN.
ZA (SHUF)

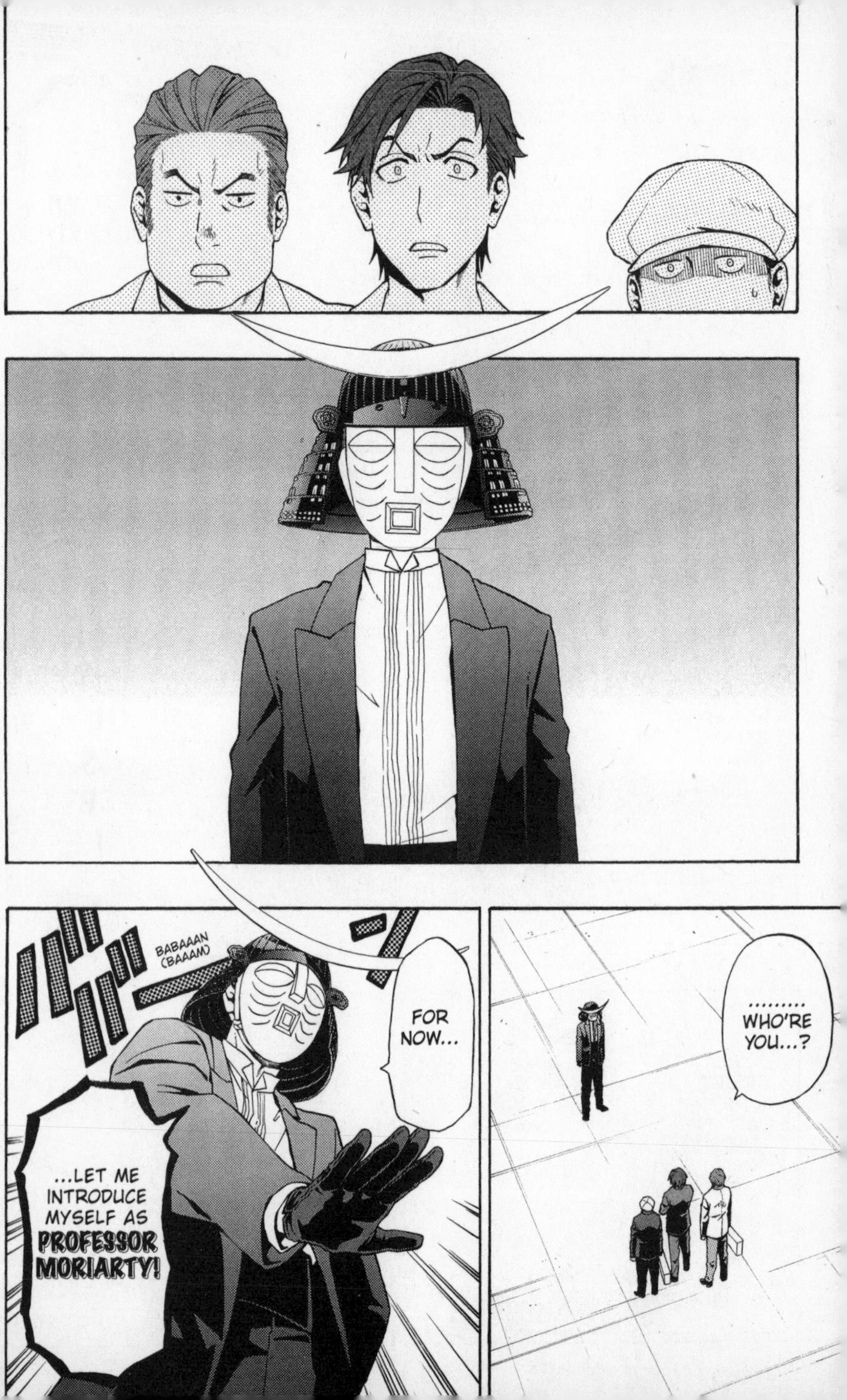
....
WHO'RE YOU...?
FOR NOW...
BABAAAN (BAAAM)
...LET ME INTRODUCE MYSELF AS PROFESSOR MORIARTY!

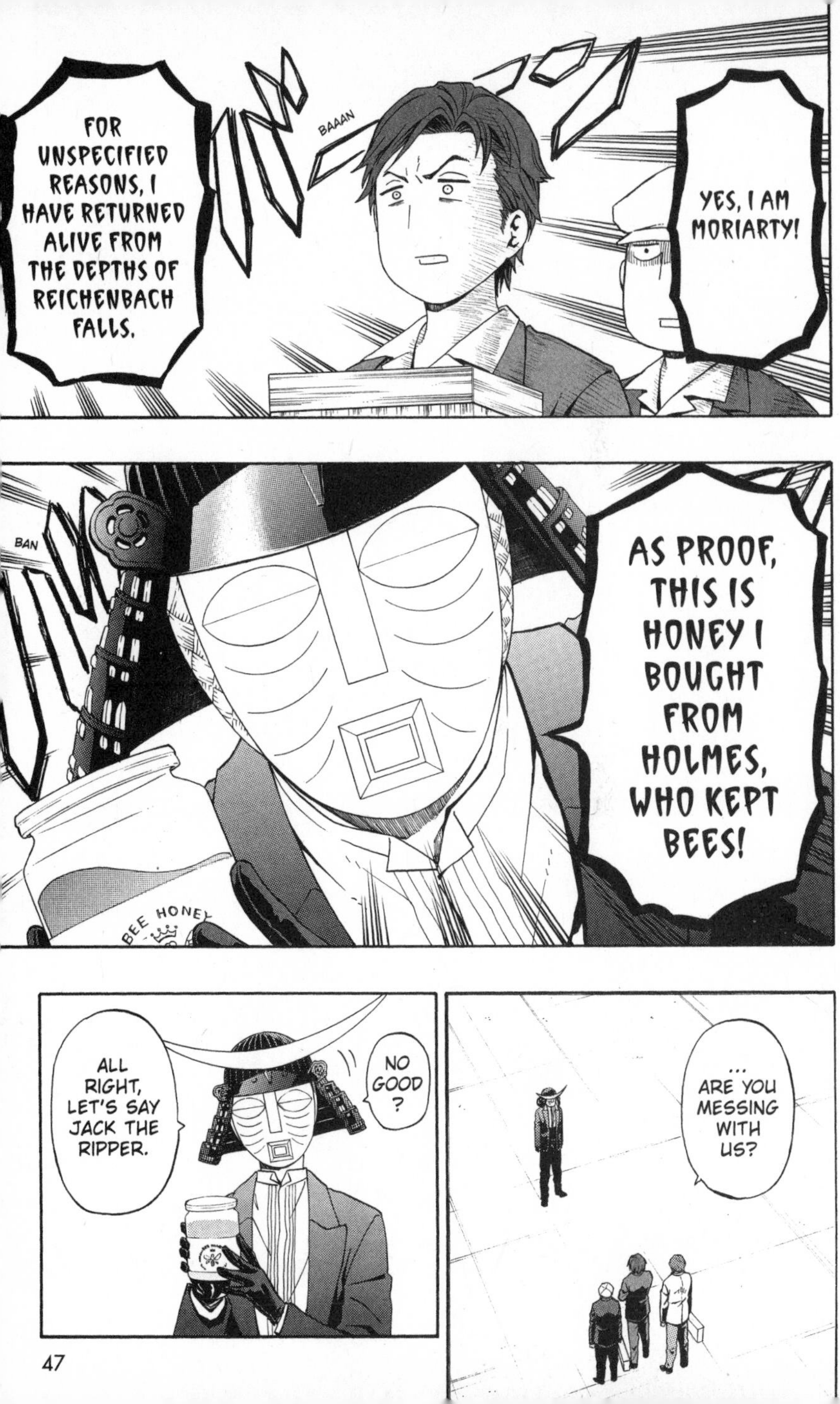
YES, I AM MORIARTY!
BAAAN
FOR UNSPECIFIED REASONS, I HAVE RETURNED ALIVE FROM THE DEPTHS OF REICHENBACH FALLS.
AS PROOF, THIS IS HONEY I BOUGHT FROM HOLMES, WHO KEPT BEES!
BAN
BEE HONEY
... ARE YOU MESSING WITH US?
NO GOOD?
ALL RIGHT, LET'S SAY JACK THE RIPPER.

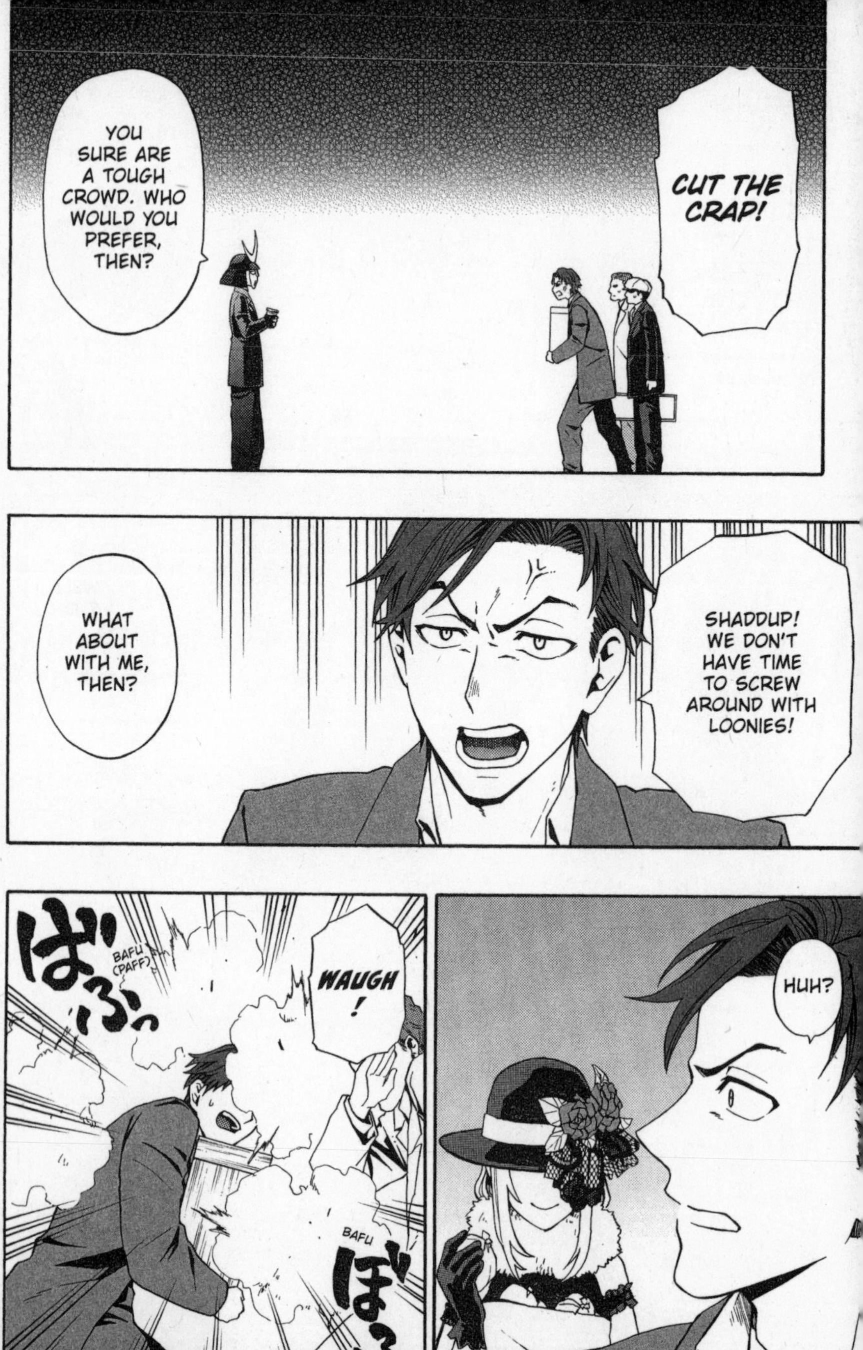
CUT THE CRAP!
YOU SURE ARE A TOUGH CROWD. WHO WOULD YOU PREFER, THEN?
SHADDUP! WE DON'T HAVE TIME TO SCREW AROUND WITH LOONIES!
WHAT ABOUT WITH ME, THEN?
HUH?
ぱふっ
BAFU (PAFF)
WAUGH!
ぼふっ
BAFU

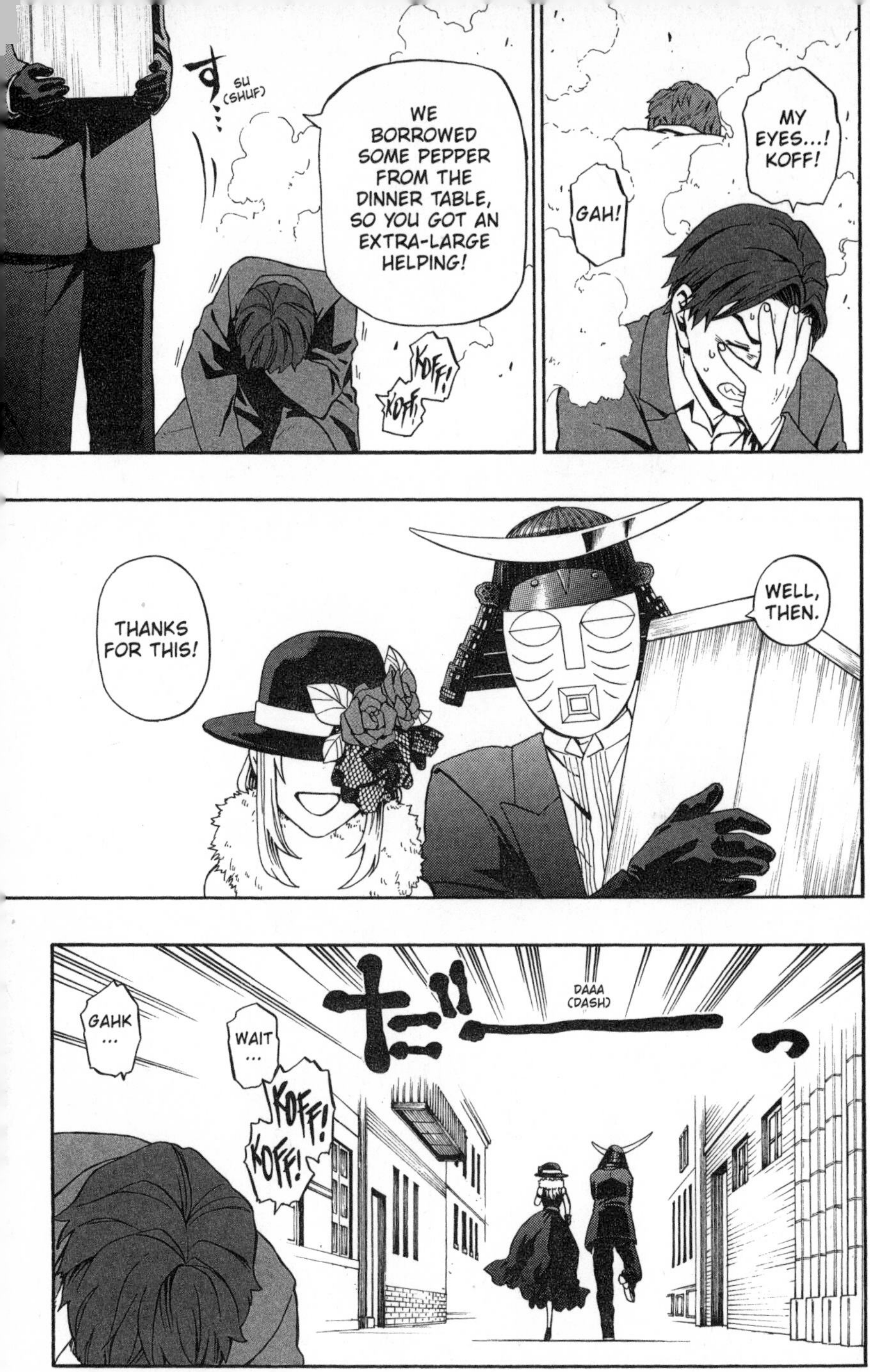
MY EYES...! KOFF!
GAH!
す
SU (SHUF)
WE BORROWED SOME PEPPER FROM THE DINNER TABLE, SO YOU GOT AN EXTRA-LARGE HELPING!
KOFF!
KOFF!
WELL, THEN.
THANKS FOR THIS!
だーっ
DAAA (DASH)
WAIT...
KOFF!
KOFF!
GAHK...

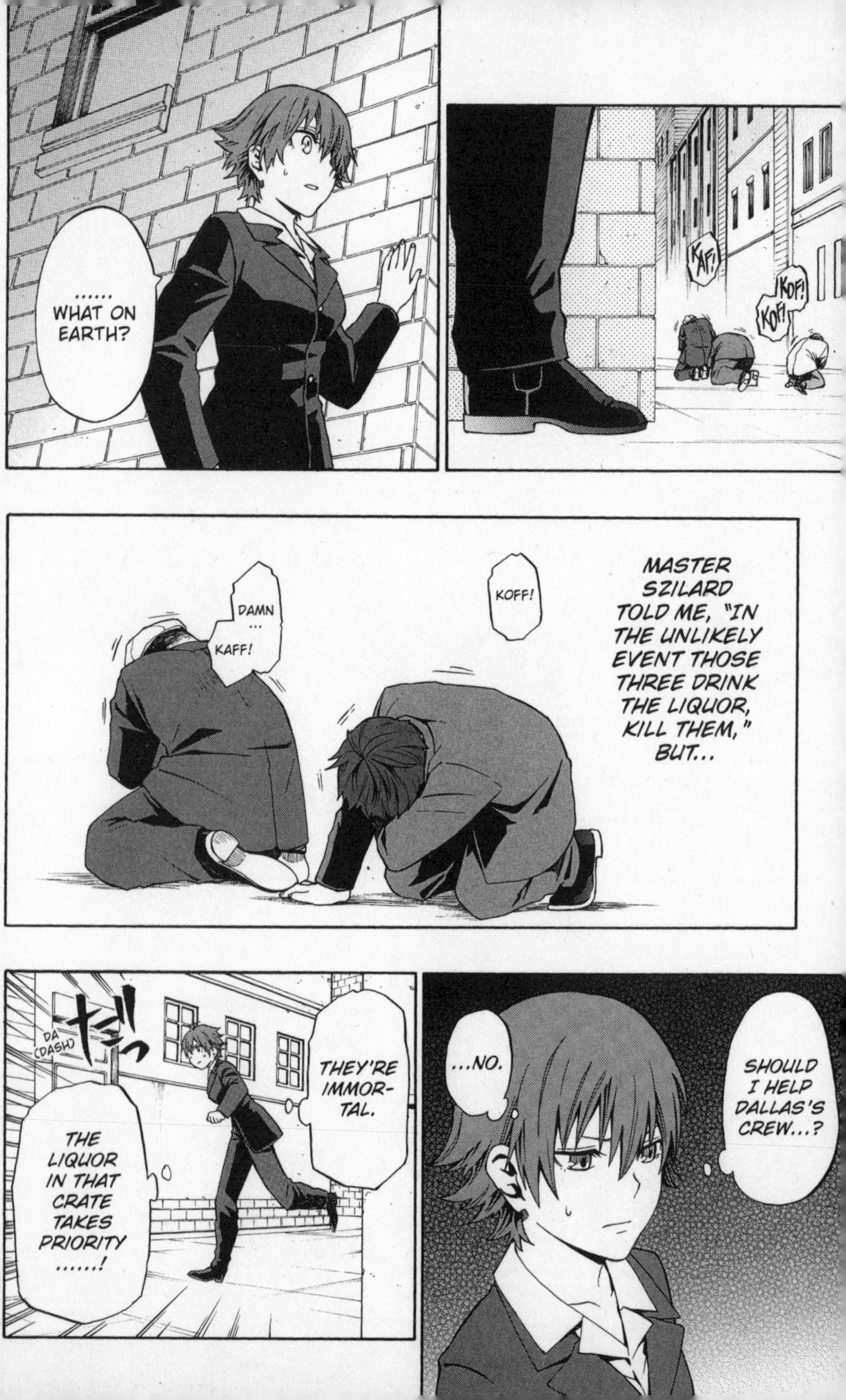
KOF!
KAF!
KOF!
...... WHAT ON EARTH?
MASTER SZILARD TOLD ME, "IN THE UNLIKELY EVENT THOSE THREE DRINK THE LIQUOR, KILL THEM," BUT...
KOFF!
DAMN... KAFF!
SHOULD I HELP DALLAS'S CREW...?
...NO.
THEY'RE IMMOR-TAL.
DA (DASH)
THE LIQUOR IN THAT CRATE TAKES PRIORITY......!

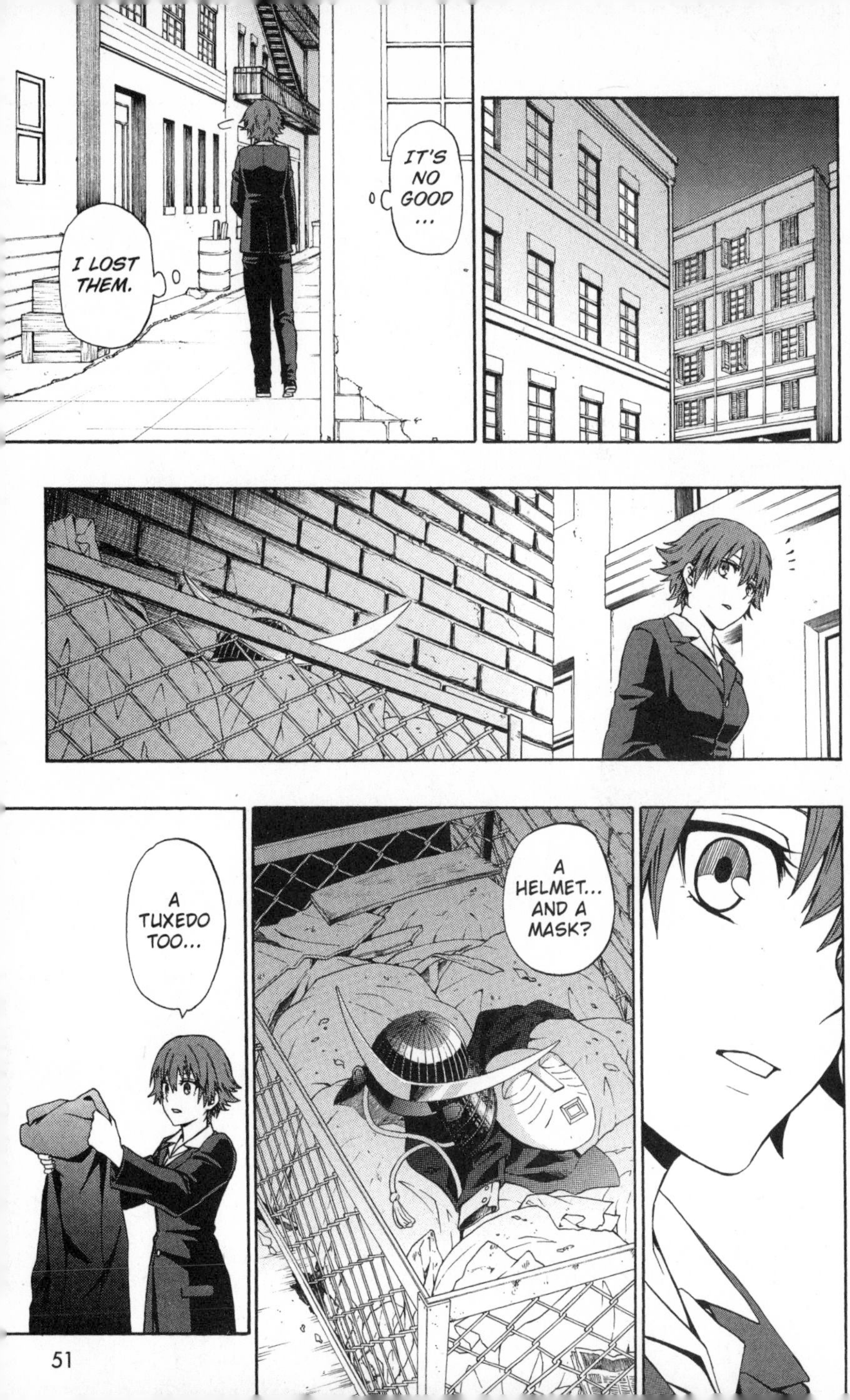
IT'S NO GOOD...
I LOST THEM.
A HELMET... AND A MASK?
A TUXEDO TOO...

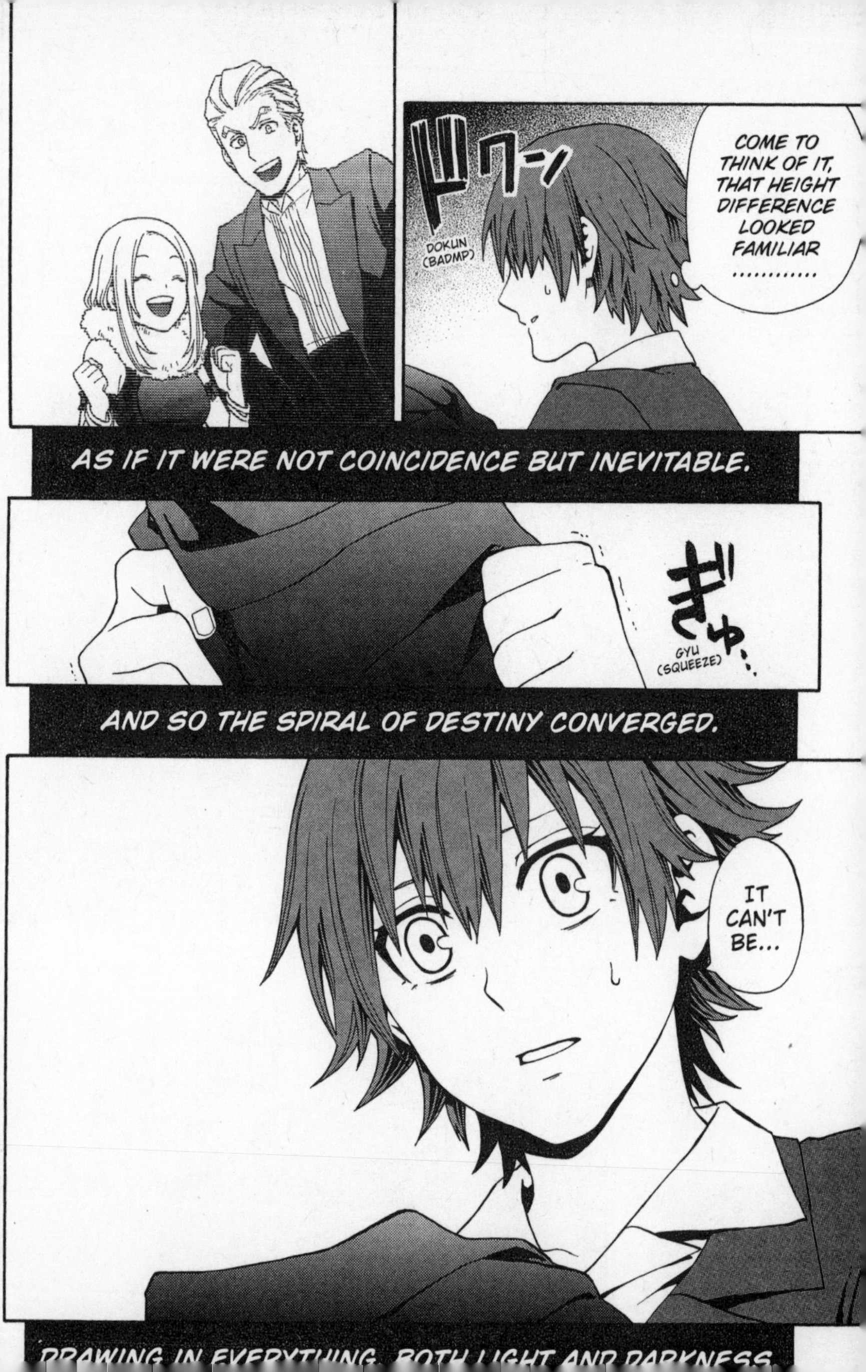
COME TO THINK OF IT, THAT HEIGHT DIFFERENCE LOOKED FAMILIAR …………
DOKUN (BADMP)
AS IF IT WERE NOT COINCIDENCE BUT INEVITABLE.
GYU (SQUEEZE)
AND SO THE SPIRAL OF DESTINY CONVERGED.
IT CAN'T BE...
DRAWING IN EVERYTHING, BOTH LIGHT AND DARKNESS.

#16 Day 2

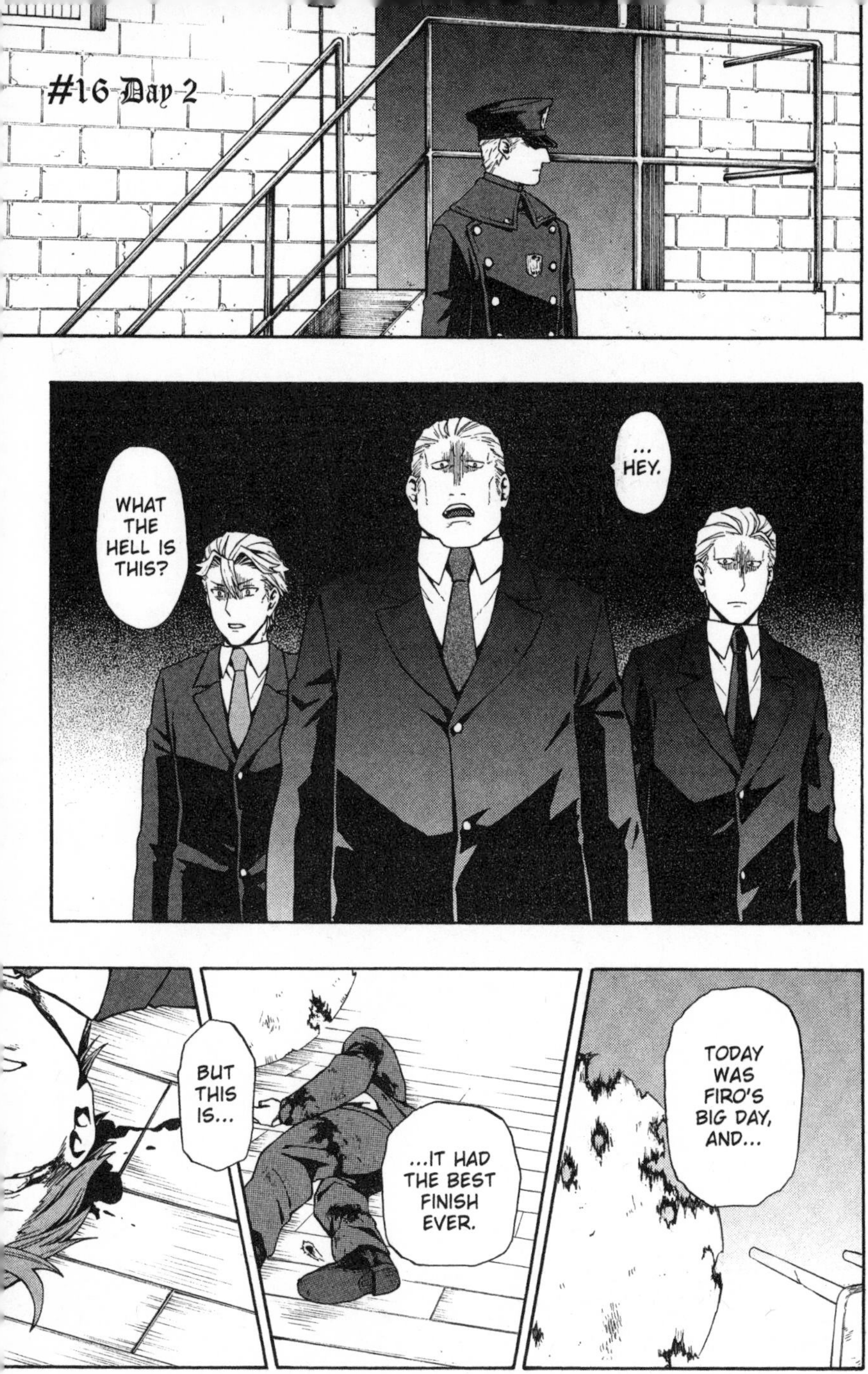
...HEY.
WHAT THE HELL IS THIS?
TODAY WAS FIRO'S BIG DAY, AND...
BUT THIS IS...
...IT HAD THE BEST FINISH EVER.

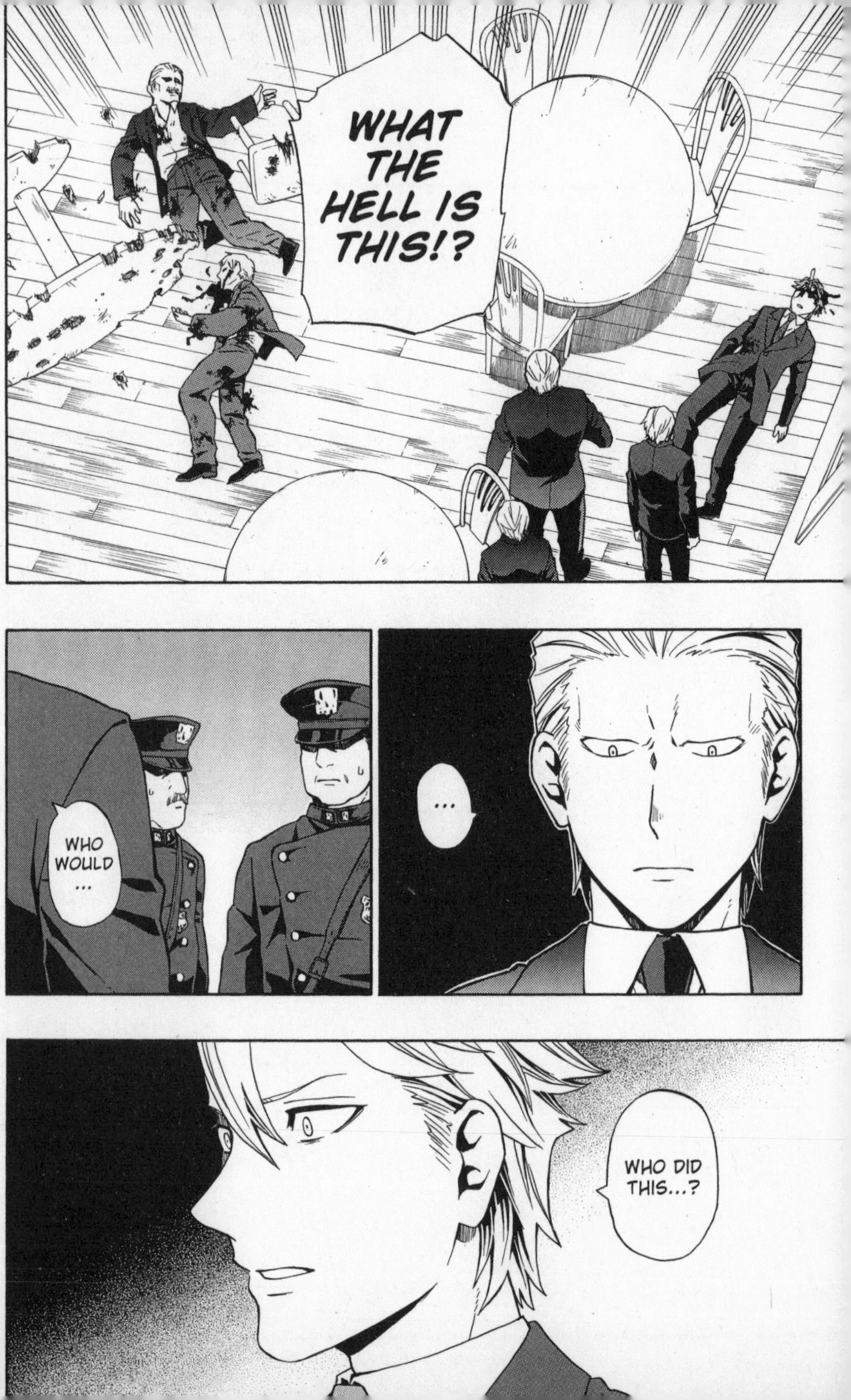
WHAT THE HELL IS THIS!?
...
WHO WOULD ...
WHO DID THIS...?

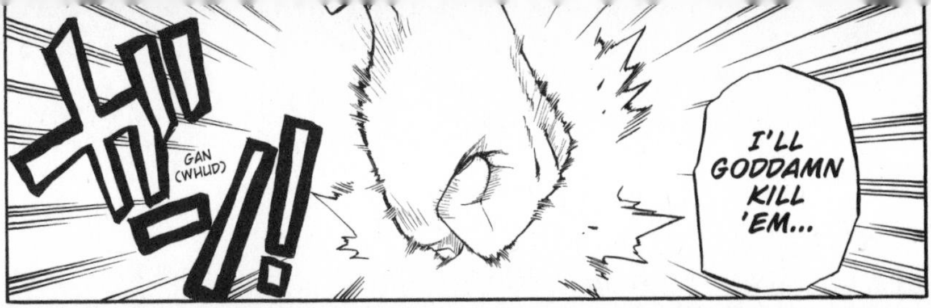
I'LL GODDAMN KILL 'EM...
GAN (WHUD)

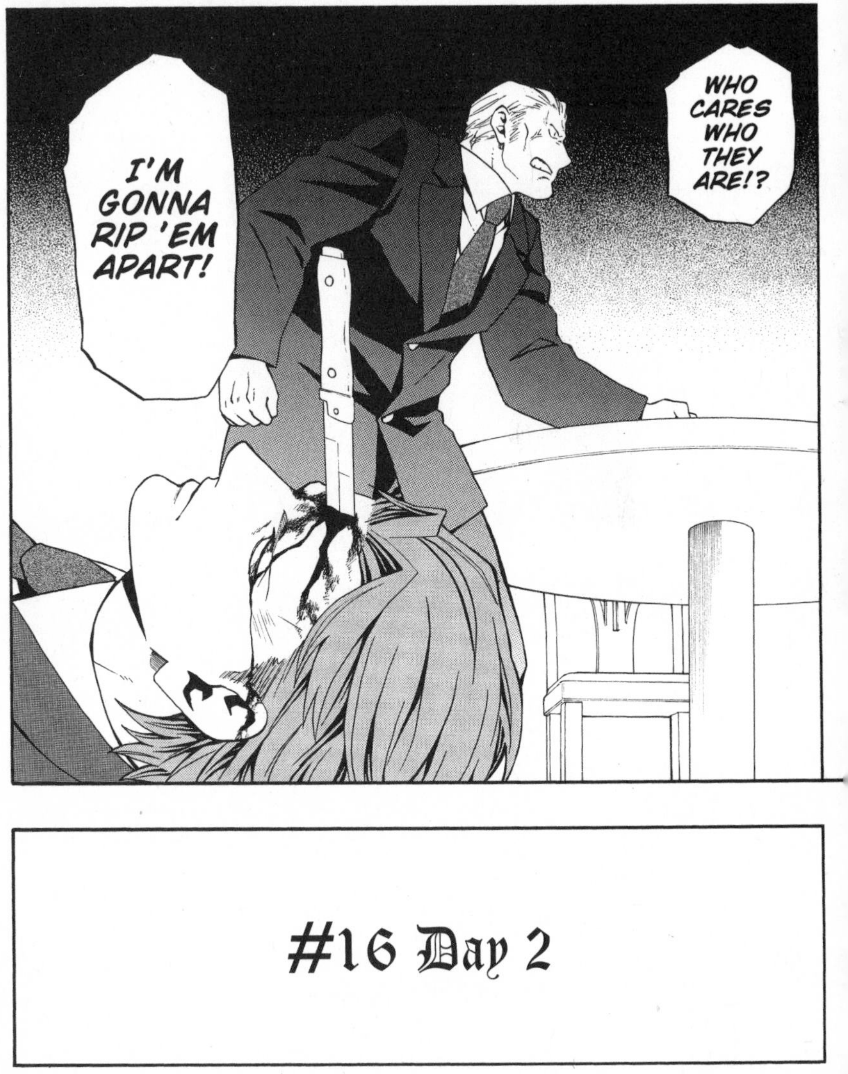
WHO CARES WHO THEY ARE!?
I'M GONNA RIP 'EM APART!

#16 Day 2

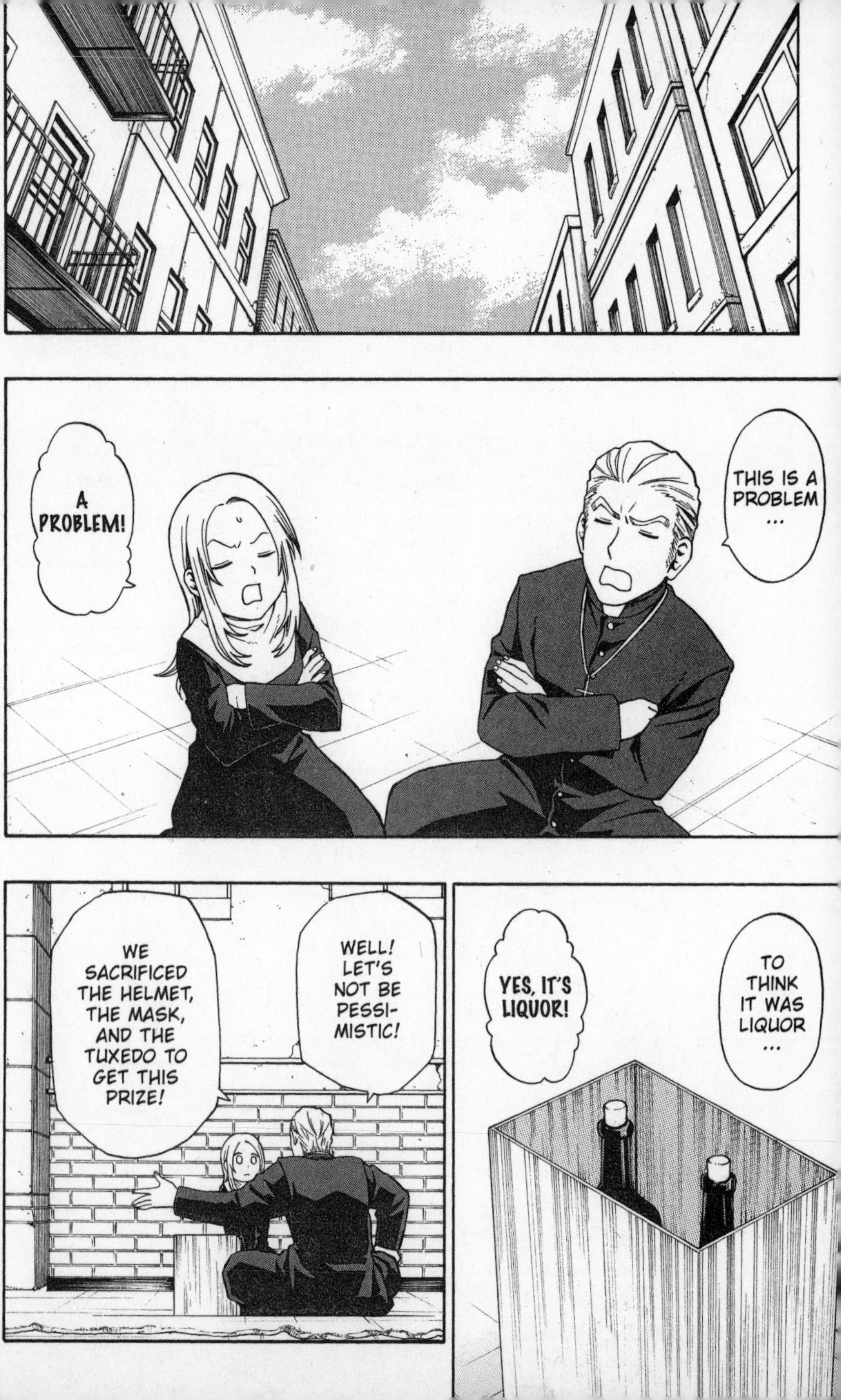
THIS IS A PROBLEM ...
A PROBLEM!
TO THINK IT WAS LIQUOR ...
YES, IT'S LIQUOR!
WELL! LET'S NOT BE PESSI-MISTIC!
WE SACRIFICED THE HELMET, THE MASK, AND THE TUXEDO TO GET THIS PRIZE!

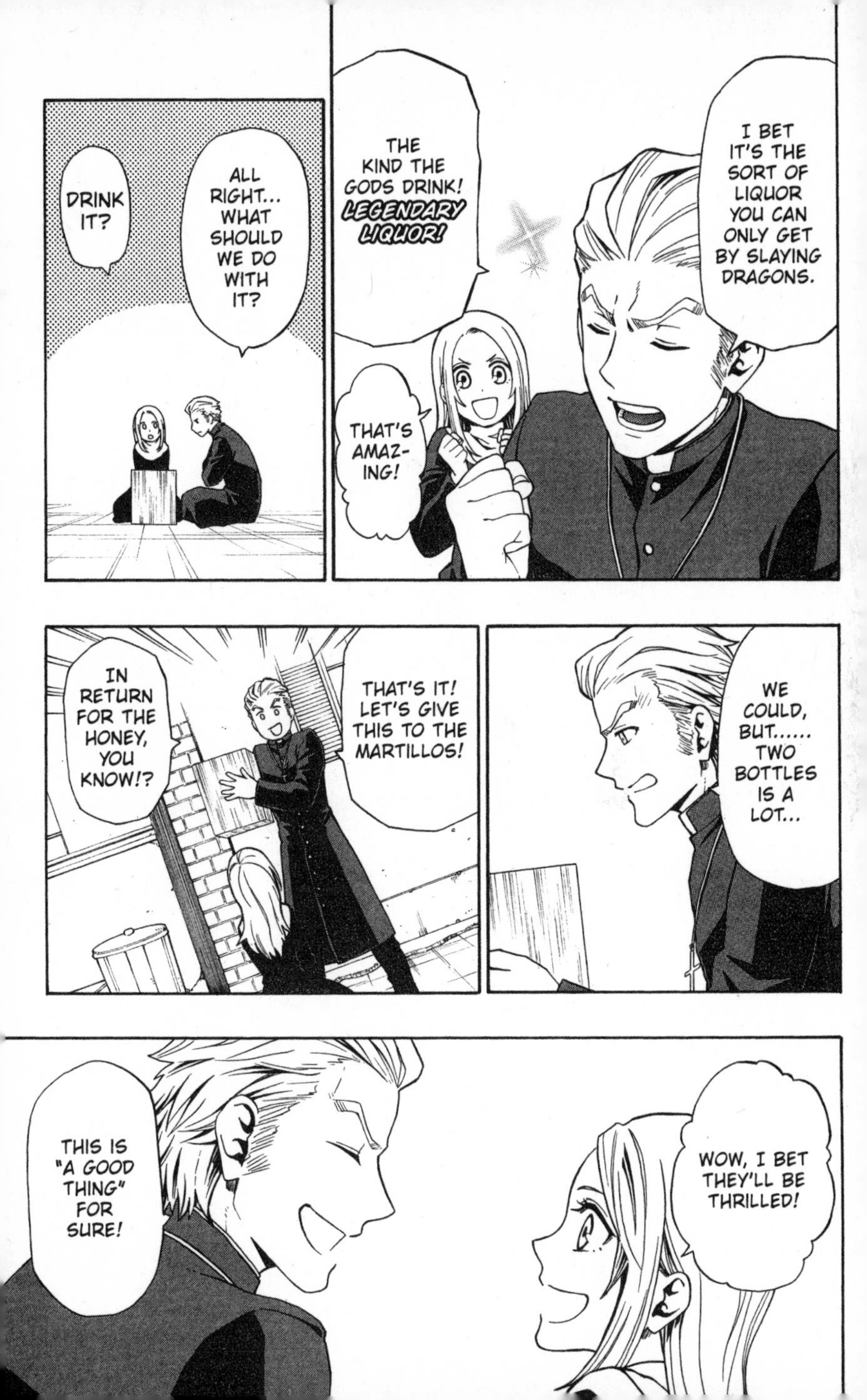
I BET IT'S THE SORT OF LIQUOR YOU CAN ONLY GET BY SLAYING DRAGONS.
THE KIND THE GODS DRINK! LEGENDARY LIQUOR!
THAT'S AMAZ-ING!
ALL RIGHT... WHAT SHOULD WE DO WITH IT?
DRINK IT?
WE COULD, BUT...... TWO BOTTLES IS A LOT...
THAT'S IT! LET'S GIVE THIS TO THE MARTILLOS!
IN RETURN FOR THE HONEY, YOU KNOW!?
WOW, I BET THEY'LL BE THRILLED!
THIS IS "A GOOD THING" FOR SURE!

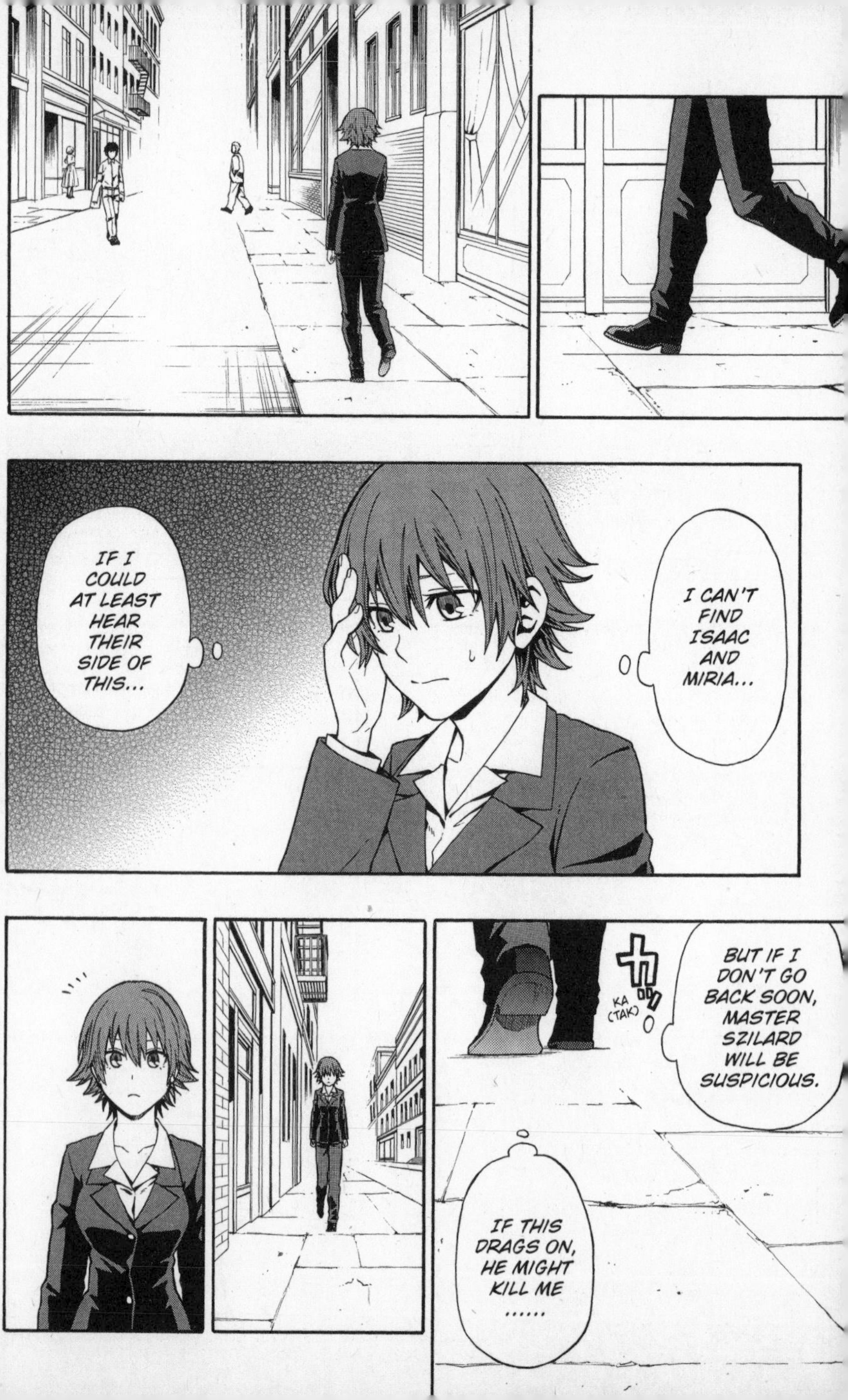
I CAN'T FIND ISAAC AND MIRIA...
IF I COULD AT LEAST HEAR THEIR SIDE OF THIS...
BUT IF I DON'T GO BACK SOON, MASTER SZILARD WILL BE SUSPICIOUS.
KA (TAK)
IF THIS DRAGS ON, HE MIGHT KILL ME ......

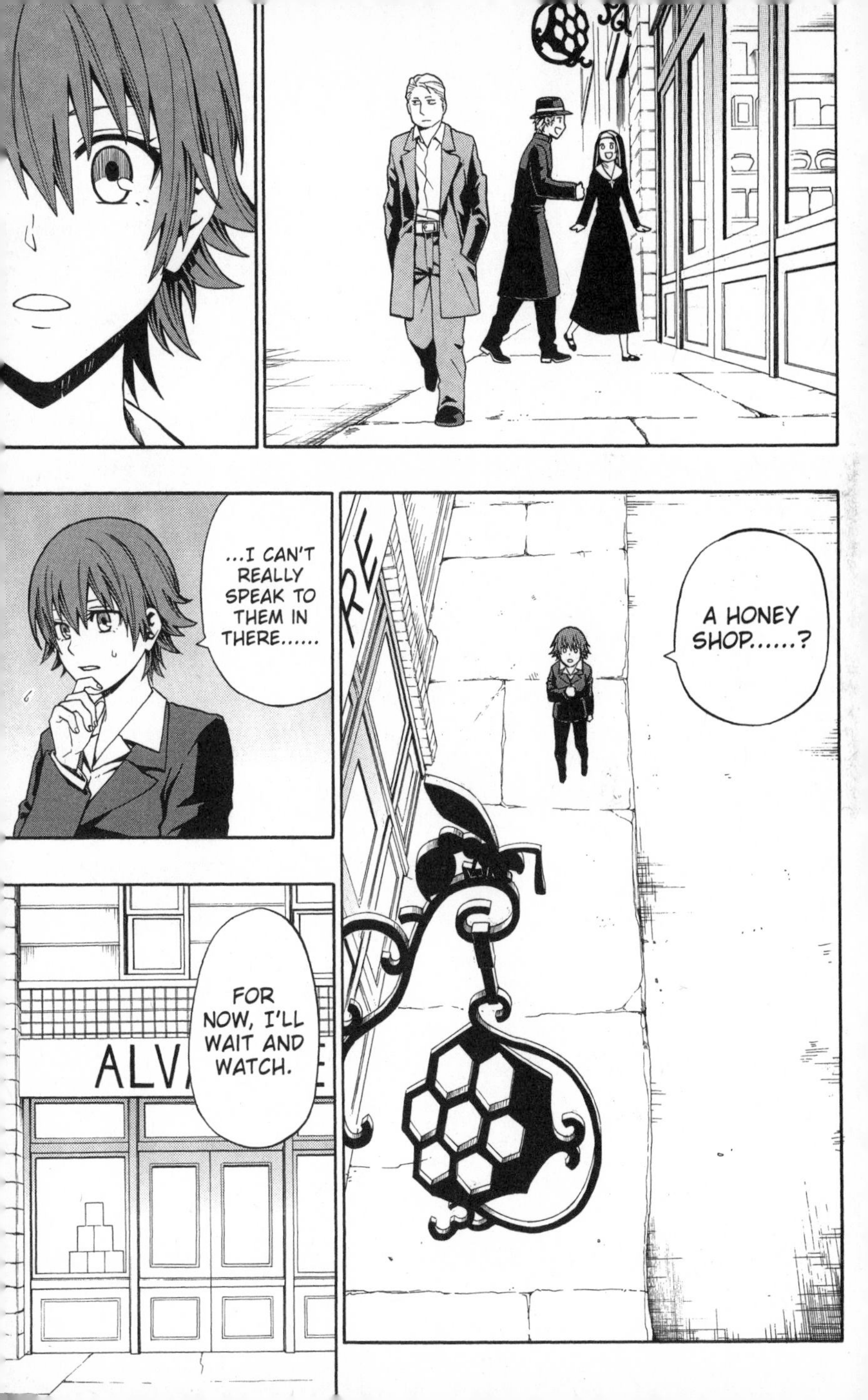
A HONEY SHOP......?
...I CAN'T REALLY SPEAK TO THEM IN THERE......
FOR NOW, I'LL WAIT AND WATCH.
ALVA

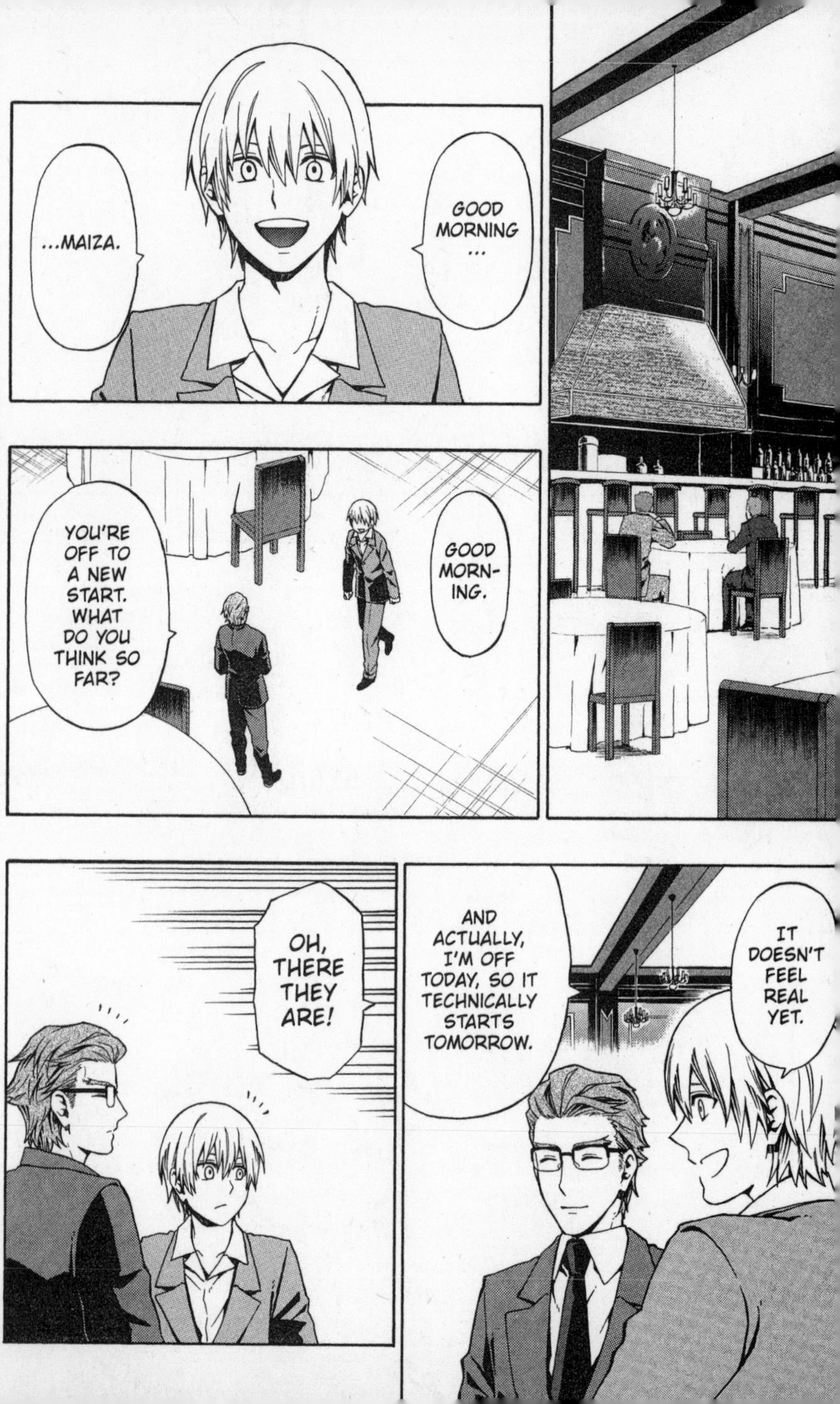
GOOD MORNING ...
...MAIZA.
GOOD MORN-ING.
YOU'RE OFF TO A NEW START. WHAT DO YOU THINK SO FAR?
IT DOESN'T FEEL REAL YET.
AND ACTUALLY, I'M OFF TODAY, SO IT TECHNICALLY STARTS TOMORROW.
OH, THERE THEY ARE!

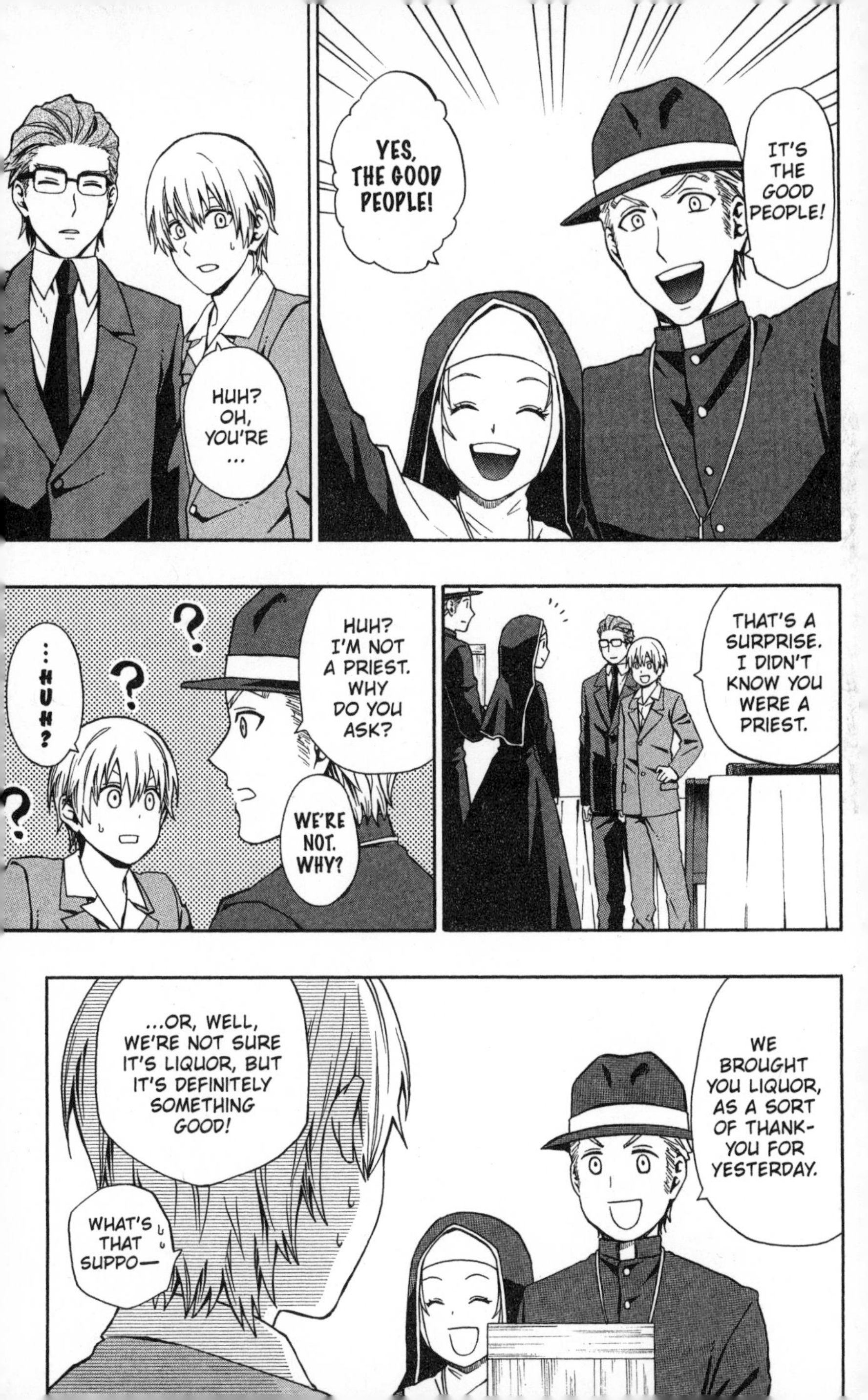
IT'S THE GOOD PEOPLE!
YES, THE GOOD PEOPLE!
HUH? OH, YOU'RE ...
THAT'S A SURPRISE. I DIDN'T KNOW YOU WERE A PRIEST.
HUH? I'M NOT A PRIEST. WHY DO YOU ASK?
WE'RE NOT. WHY?
...HUH?
WE BROUGHT YOU LIQUOR, AS A SORT OF THANK-YOU FOR YESTERDAY.
...OR, WELL, WE'RE NOT SURE IT'S LIQUOR, BUT IT'S DEFINITELY SOMETHING GOOD!
WHAT'S THAT SUPPO—

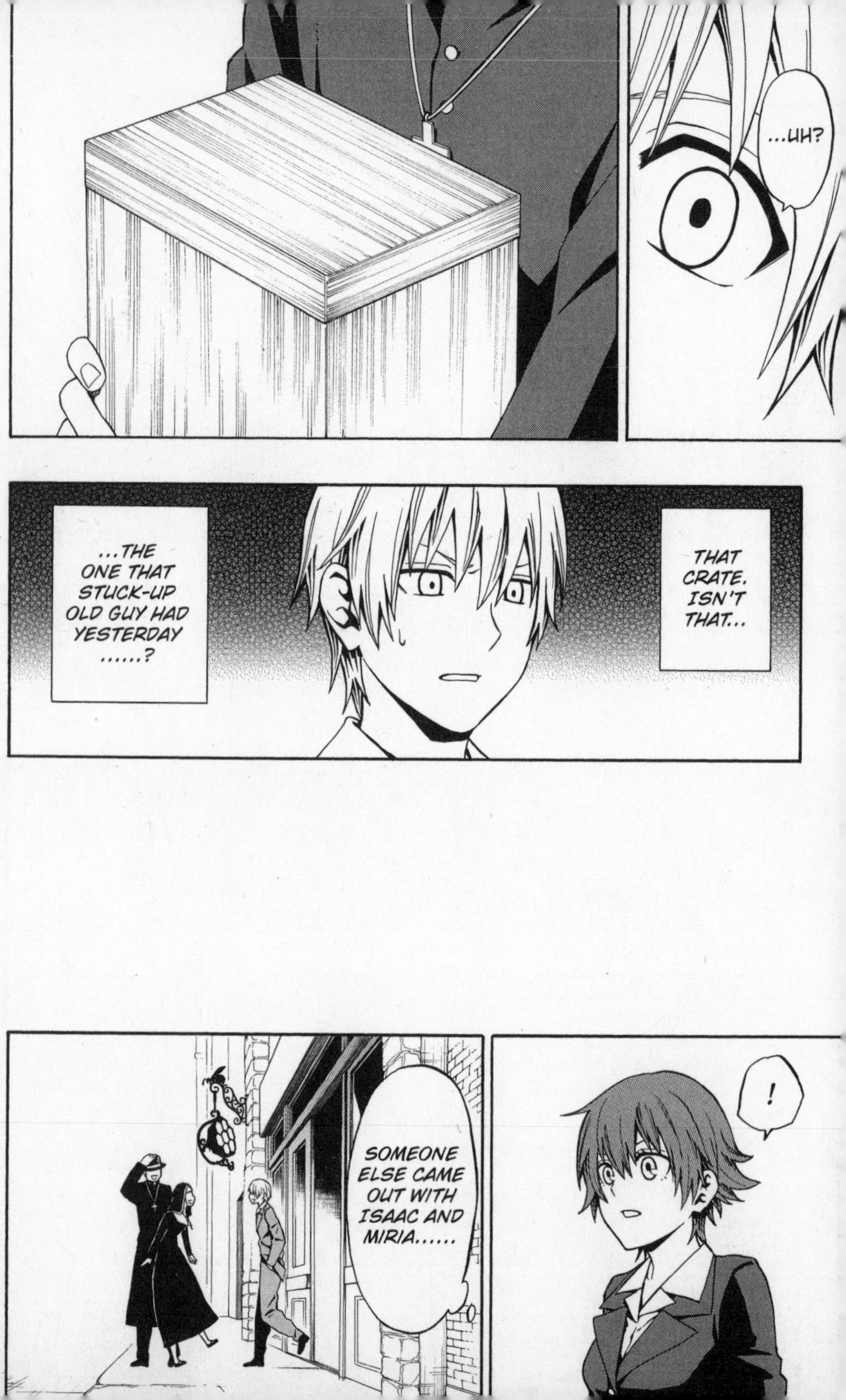
...UH?
THAT CRATE. ISN'T THAT...
...THE ONE THAT STUCK-UP OLD GUY HAD YESTERDAY ......?
!
SOMEONE ELSE CAME OUT WITH ISAAC AND MIRIA......

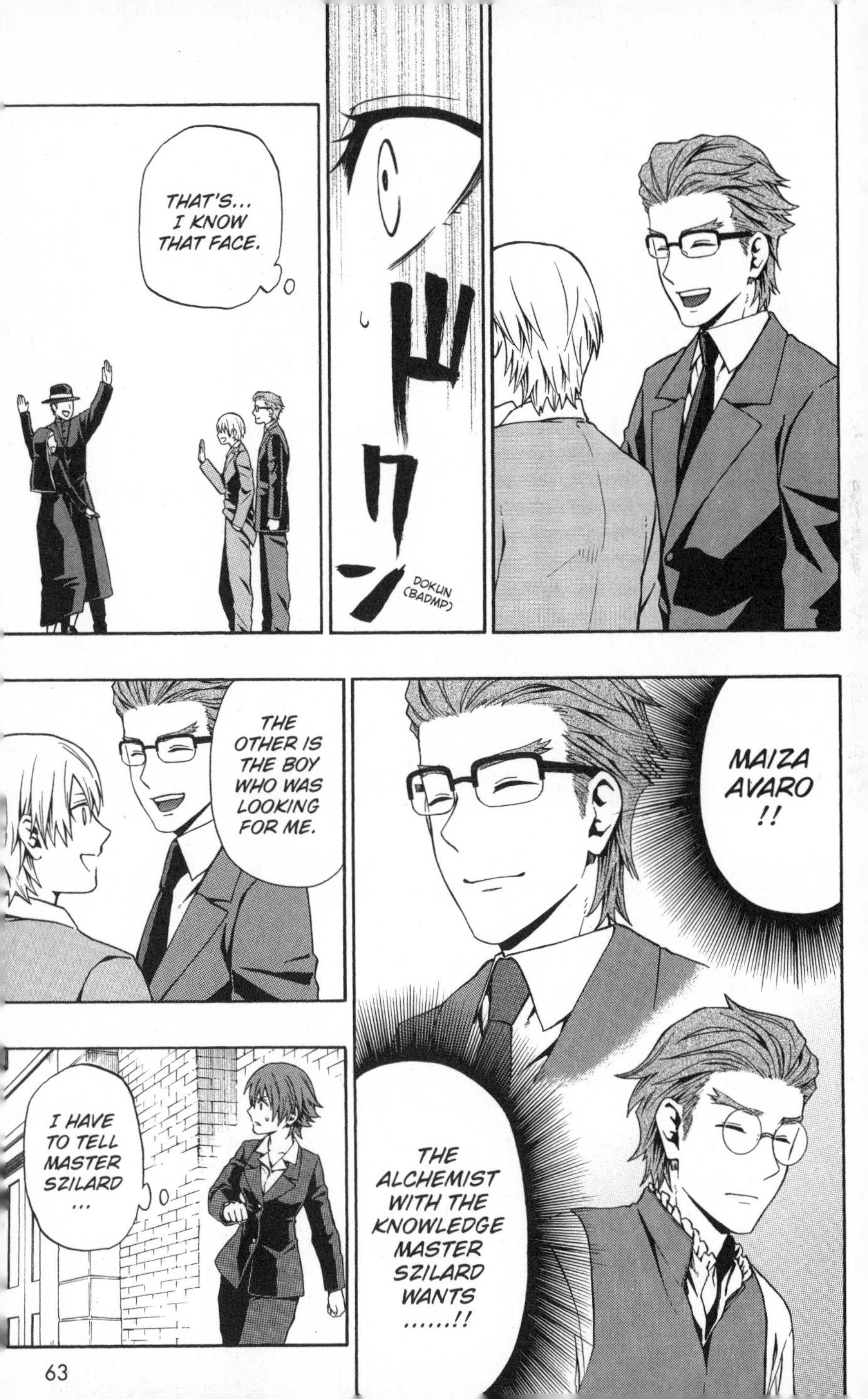
ドクン
DOKUN (BADMP)
THAT'S... I KNOW THAT FACE.
MAIZA AVARO !!
THE ALCHEMIST WITH THE KNOWLEDGE MASTER SZILARD WANTS ......!!
THE OTHER IS THE BOY WHO WAS LOOKING FOR ME.
I HAVE TO TELL MASTER SZILARD ...

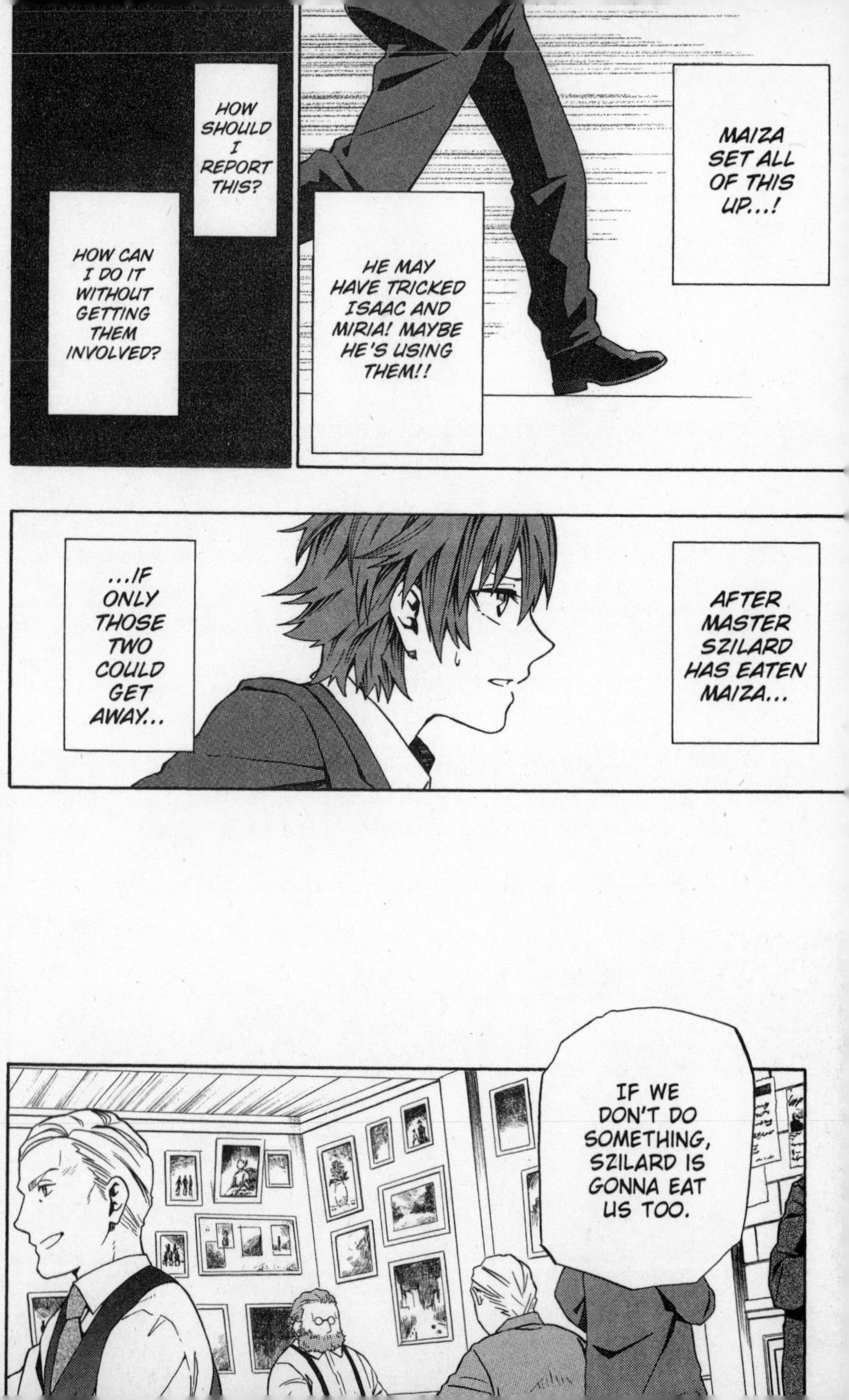
MAIZA SET ALL OF THIS UP...!
HE MAY HAVE TRICKED ISAAC AND MIRIA! MAYBE HE'S USING THEM!!
HOW SHOULD I REPORT THIS?
HOW CAN I DO IT WITHOUT GETTING THEM INVOLVED?
AFTER MASTER SZILARD HAS EATEN MAIZA...
...IF ONLY THOSE TWO COULD GET AWAY...
IF WE DON'T DO SOMETHING, SZILARD IS GONNA EAT US TOO.

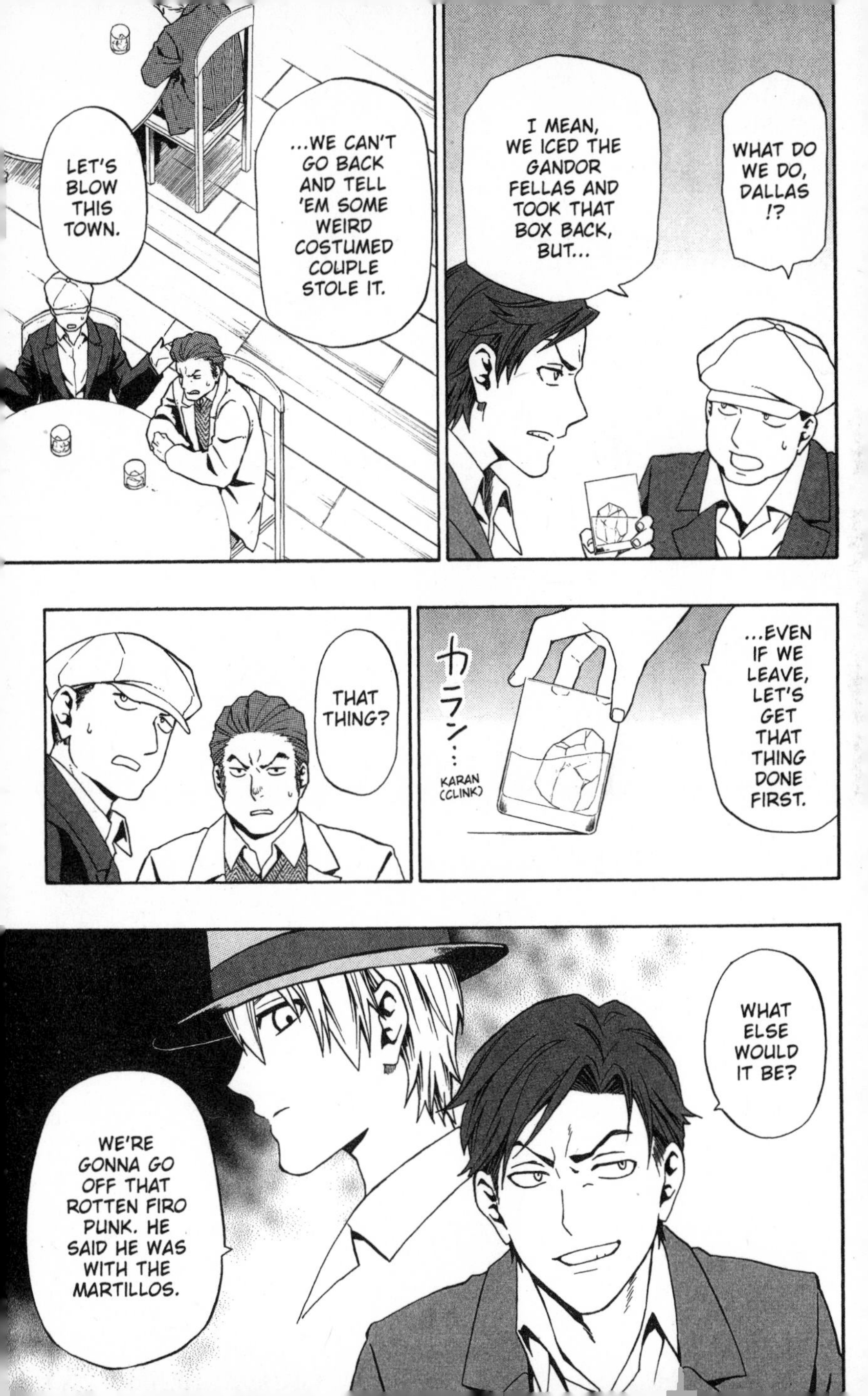
WHAT DO WE DO, DALLAS !?
I MEAN, WE ICED THE GANDOR FELLAS AND TOOK THAT BOX BACK, BUT...
...WE CAN'T GO BACK AND TELL 'EM SOME WEIRD COSTUMED COUPLE STOLE IT.
LET'S BLOW THIS TOWN.
...EVEN IF WE LEAVE, LET'S GET THAT THING DONE FIRST.
カラン…
KARAN (CLINK)
THAT THING?
WHAT ELSE WOULD IT BE?
WE'RE GONNA GO OFF THAT ROTTEN FIRO PUNK. HE SAID HE WAS WITH THE MARTILLOS.

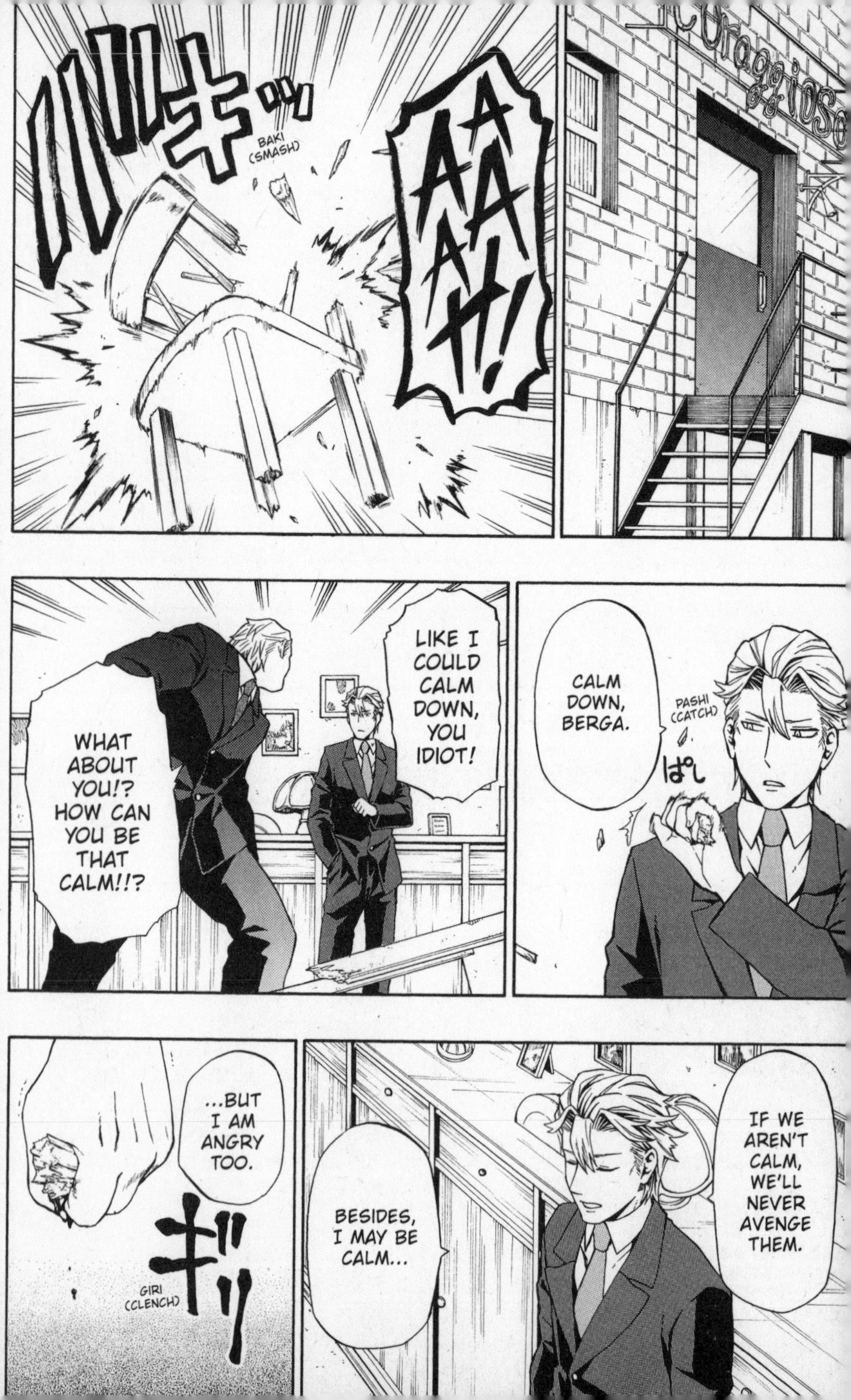
AAAAH!!
BAKI (SMASH)
CALM DOWN, BERGA.
PASHI (CATCH)
ぱし
LIKE I COULD CALM DOWN, YOU IDIOT!
WHAT ABOUT YOU!? HOW CAN YOU BE THAT CALM!!?
IF WE AREN'T CALM, WE'LL NEVER AVENGE THEM.
BESIDES, I MAY BE CALM...
...BUT I AM ANGRY TOO.
ギリ
GIRI (CLENCH)

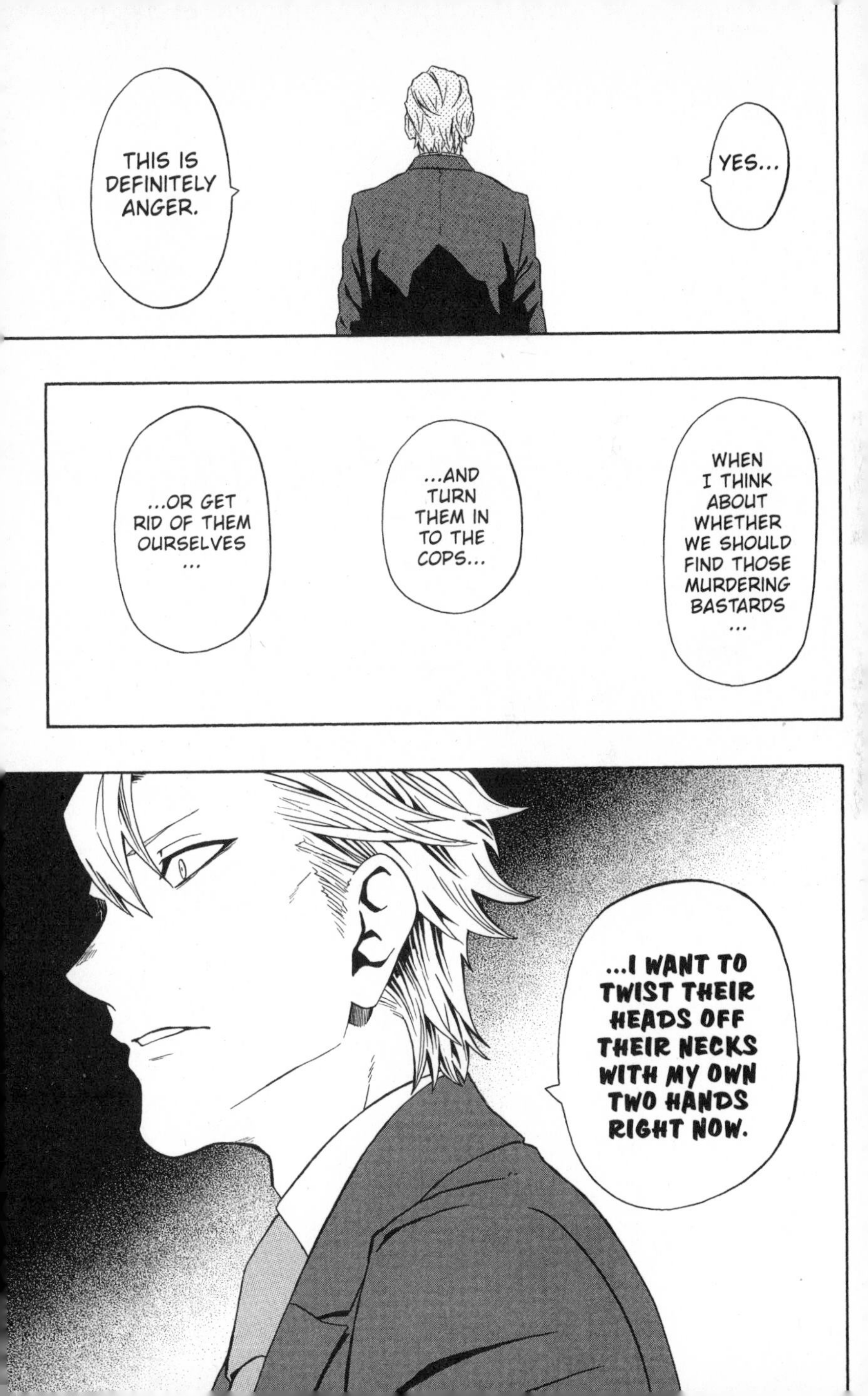
YES...
THIS IS DEFINITELY ANGER.
WHEN I THINK ABOUT WHETHER WE SHOULD FIND THOSE MURDERING BASTARDS...
...AND TURN THEM IN TO THE COPS...
...OR GET RID OF THEM OURSELVES...
...I WANT TO TWIST THEIR HEADS OFF THEIR NECKS WITH MY OWN TWO HANDS RIGHT NOW.

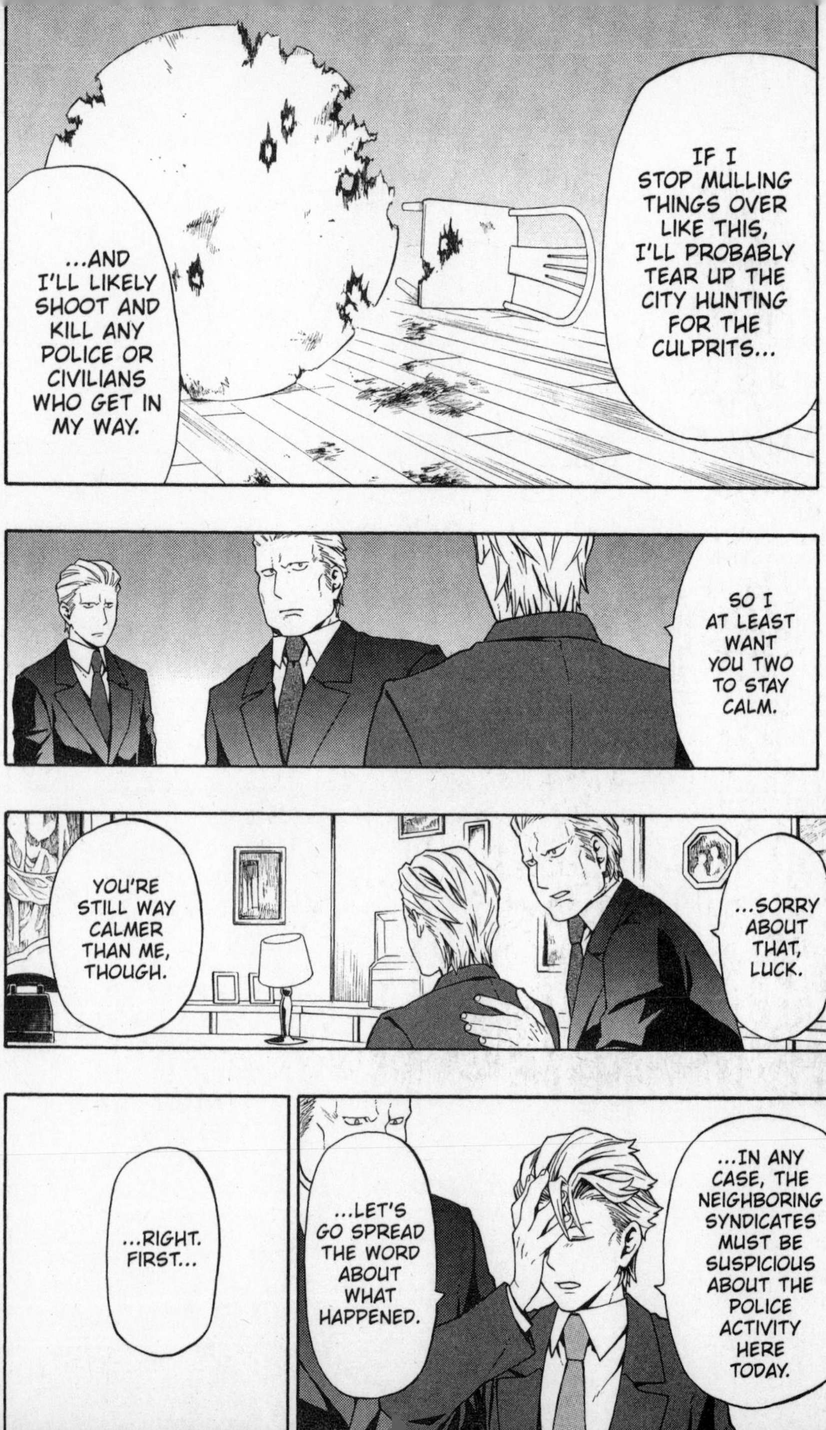
IF I STOP MULLING THINGS OVER LIKE THIS, I'LL PROBABLY TEAR UP THE CITY HUNTING FOR THE CULPRITS...
...AND I'LL LIKELY SHOOT AND KILL ANY POLICE OR CIVILIANS WHO GET IN MY WAY.
SO I AT LEAST WANT YOU TWO TO STAY CALM.
...SORRY ABOUT THAT, LUCK.
YOU'RE STILL WAY CALMER THAN ME, THOUGH.
...IN ANY CASE, THE NEIGHBORING SYNDICATES MUST BE SUSPICIOUS ABOUT THE POLICE ACTIVITY HERE TODAY.
...LET'S GO SPREAD THE WORD ABOUT WHAT HAPPENED.
...RIGHT. FIRST...

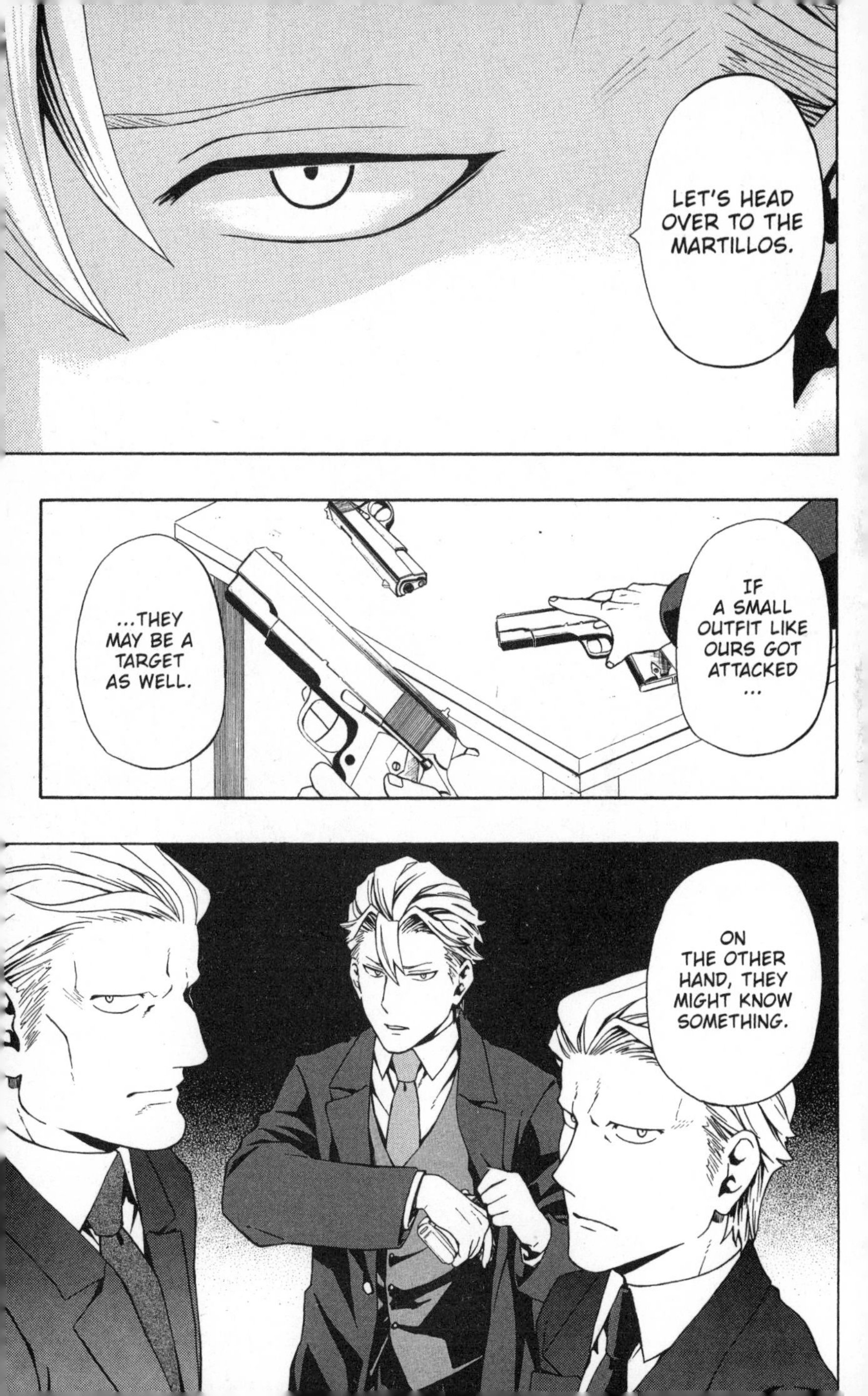
LET'S HEAD OVER TO THE MARTILLOS.
IF A SMALL OUTFIT LIKE OURS GOT ATTACKED ...
...THEY MAY BE A TARGET AS WELL.
ON THE OTHER HAND, THEY MIGHT KNOW SOMETHING.

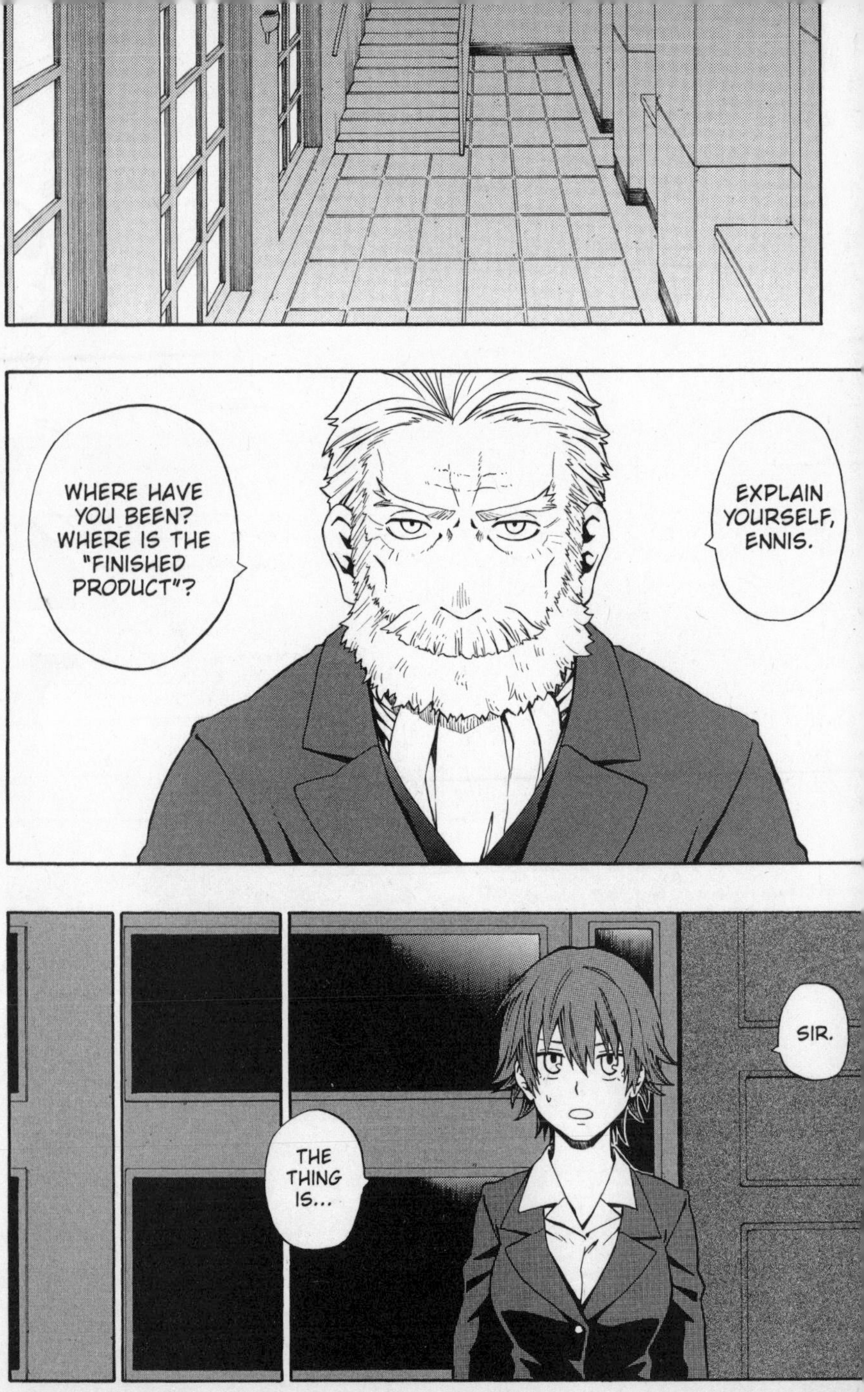
EXPLAIN YOURSELF, ENNIS.
WHERE HAVE YOU BEEN? WHERE IS THE "FINISHED PRODUCT"?
SIR.
THE THING IS...

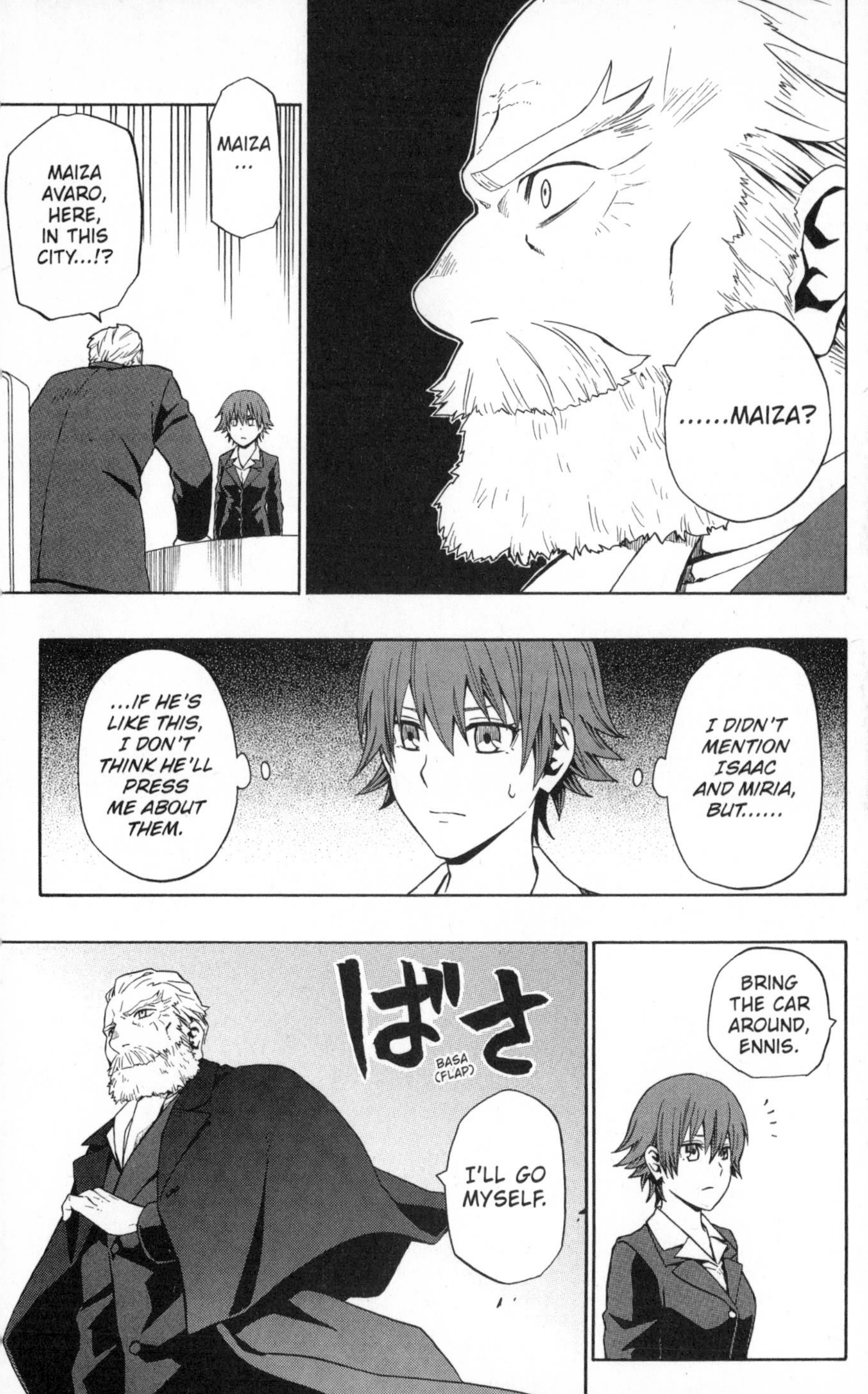
......MAIZA?
MAIZA ...
MAIZA AVARO, HERE, IN THIS CITY...!?
I DIDN'T MENTION ISAAC AND MIRIA, BUT......
...IF HE'S LIKE THIS, I DON'T THINK HE'LL PRESS ME ABOUT THEM.
BRING THE CAR AROUND, ENNIS.
ばさ
BASA (FLAP)
I'LL GO MYSELF.

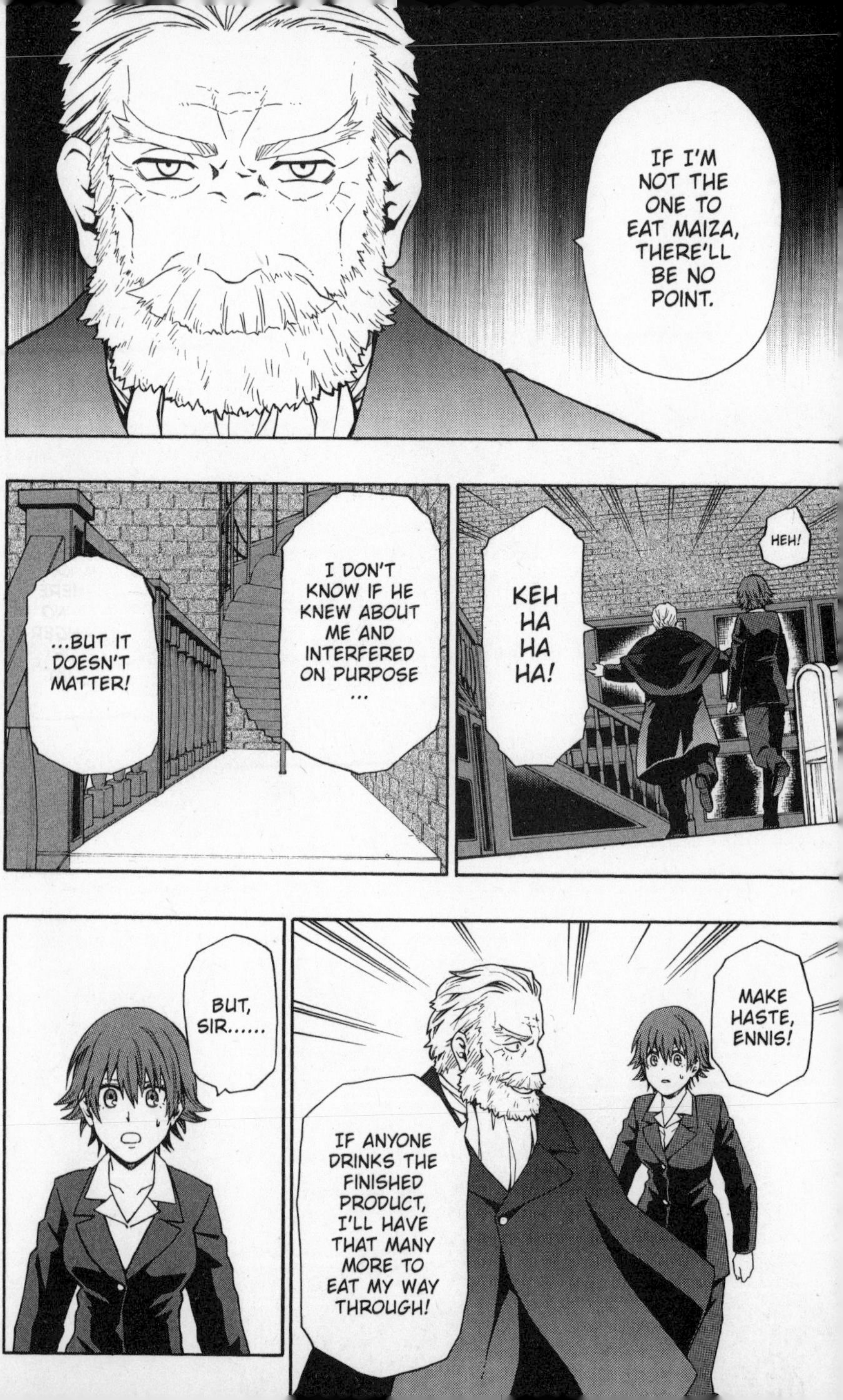
IF I'M NOT THE ONE TO EAT MAIZA, THERE'LL BE NO POINT.
HEH!
KEH HA HA HA!
I DON'T KNOW IF HE KNEW ABOUT ME AND INTERFERED ON PURPOSE ...
...BUT IT DOESN'T MATTER!
MAKE HASTE, ENNIS!
IF ANYONE DRINKS THE FINISHED PRODUCT, I'LL HAVE THAT MANY MORE TO EAT MY WAY THROUGH!
BUT, SIR......

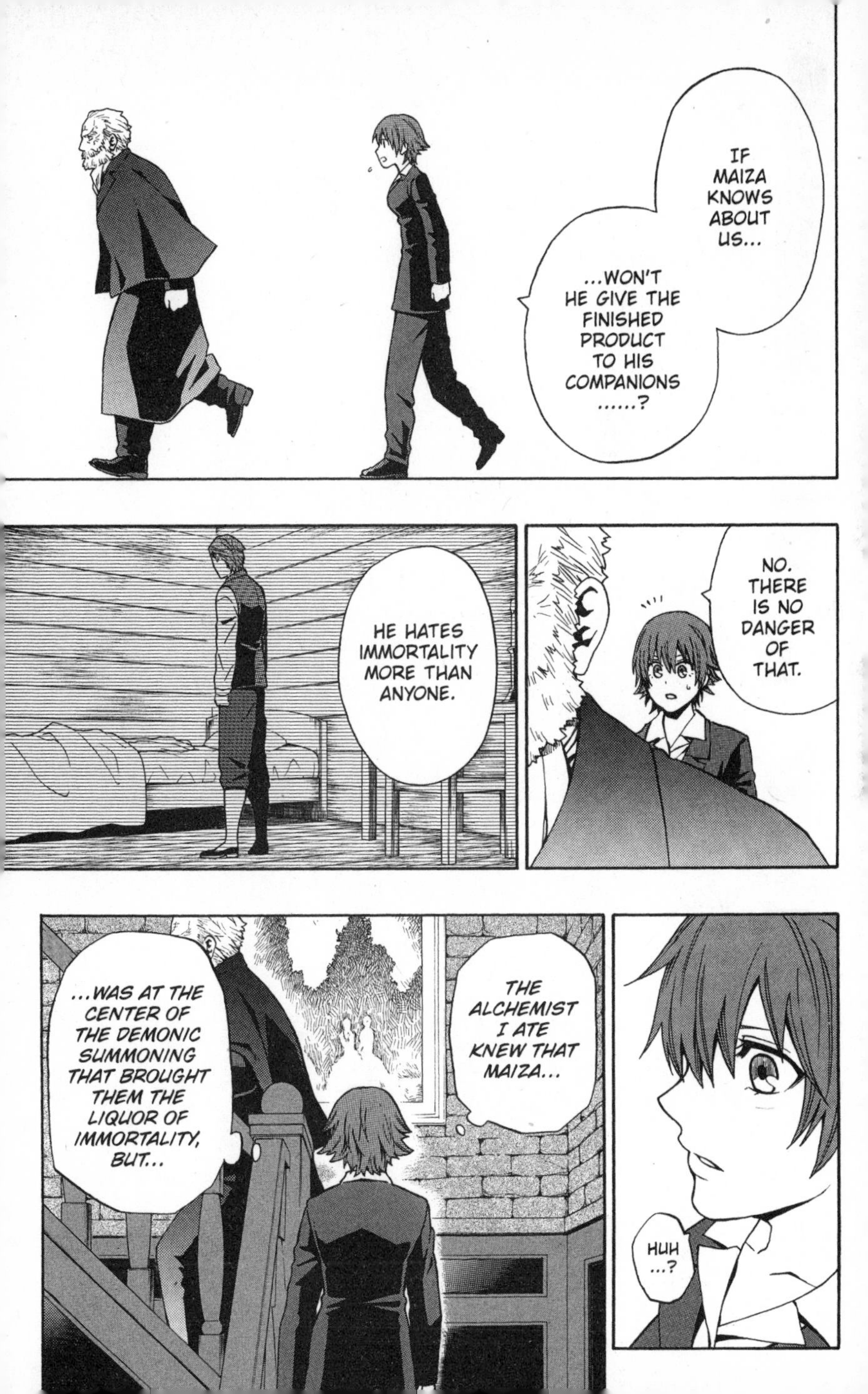
IF MAIZA KNOWS ABOUT US...
...WON'T HE GIVE THE FINISHED PRODUCT TO HIS COMPANIONS ......?
NO. THERE IS NO DANGER OF THAT.
HE HATES IMMORTALITY MORE THAN ANYONE.
HUH ...?
THE ALCHEMIST I ATE KNEW THAT MAIZA...
...WAS AT THE CENTER OF THE DEMONIC SUMMONING THAT BROUGHT THEM THE LIQUOR OF IMMORTALITY, BUT...

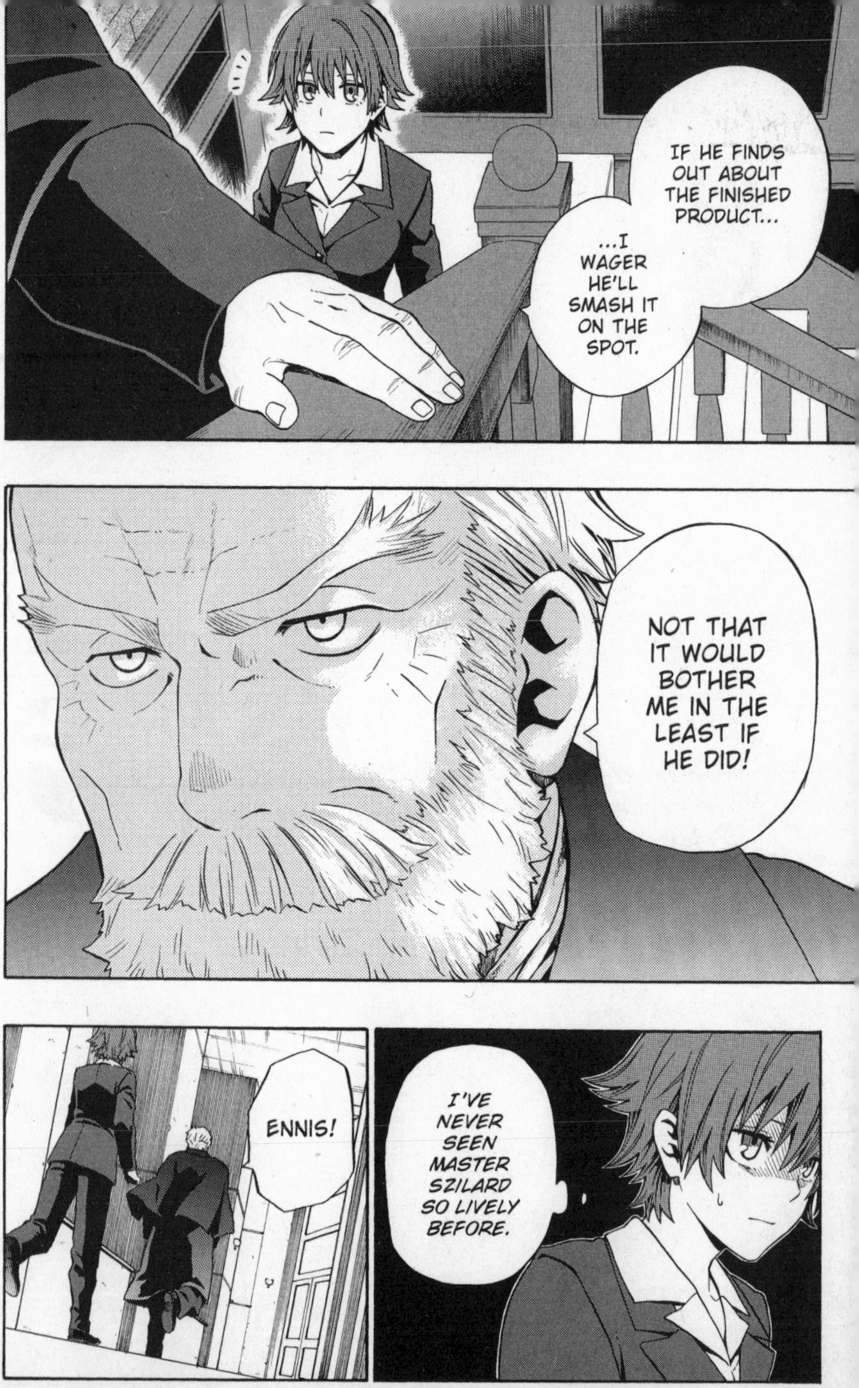
IF HE FINDS OUT ABOUT THE FINISHED PRODUCT...
...I WAGER HE'LL SMASH IT ON THE SPOT.
NOT THAT IT WOULD BOTHER ME IN THE LEAST IF HE DID!
I'VE NEVER SEEN MASTER SZILARD SO LIVELY BEFORE.
ENNIS!

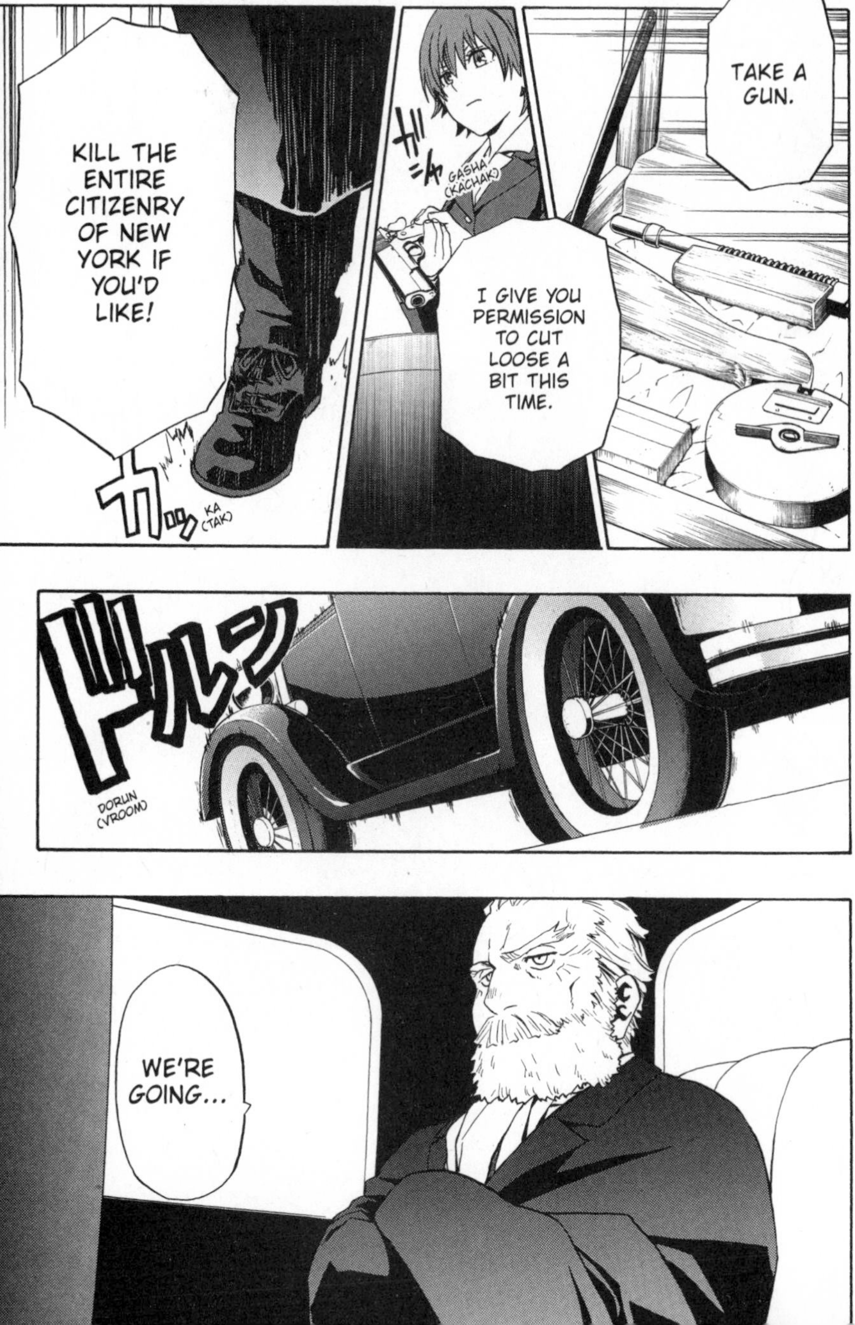
TAKE A GUN.
ガシャ
GASHA (KACHAK)
I GIVE YOU PERMISSION TO CUT LOOSE A BIT THIS TIME.
KILL THE ENTIRE CITIZENRY OF NEW YORK IF YOU'D LIKE!
カッ
KA (TAK)
ドルン
DORUN (VROOM)
WE'RE GOING...

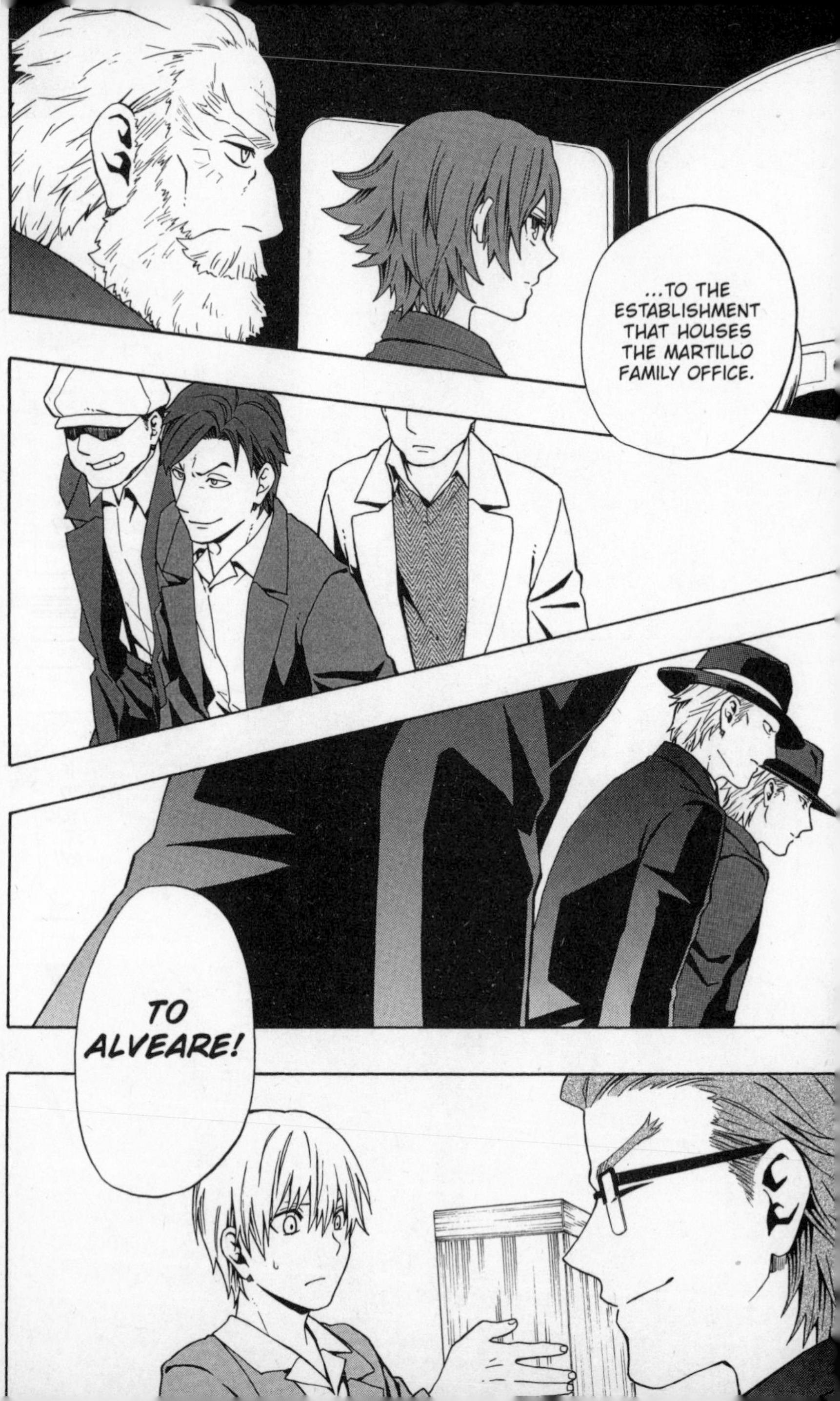
...TO THE ESTABLISHMENT THAT HOUSES THE MARTILLO FAMILY OFFICE.
TO ALVEARE!

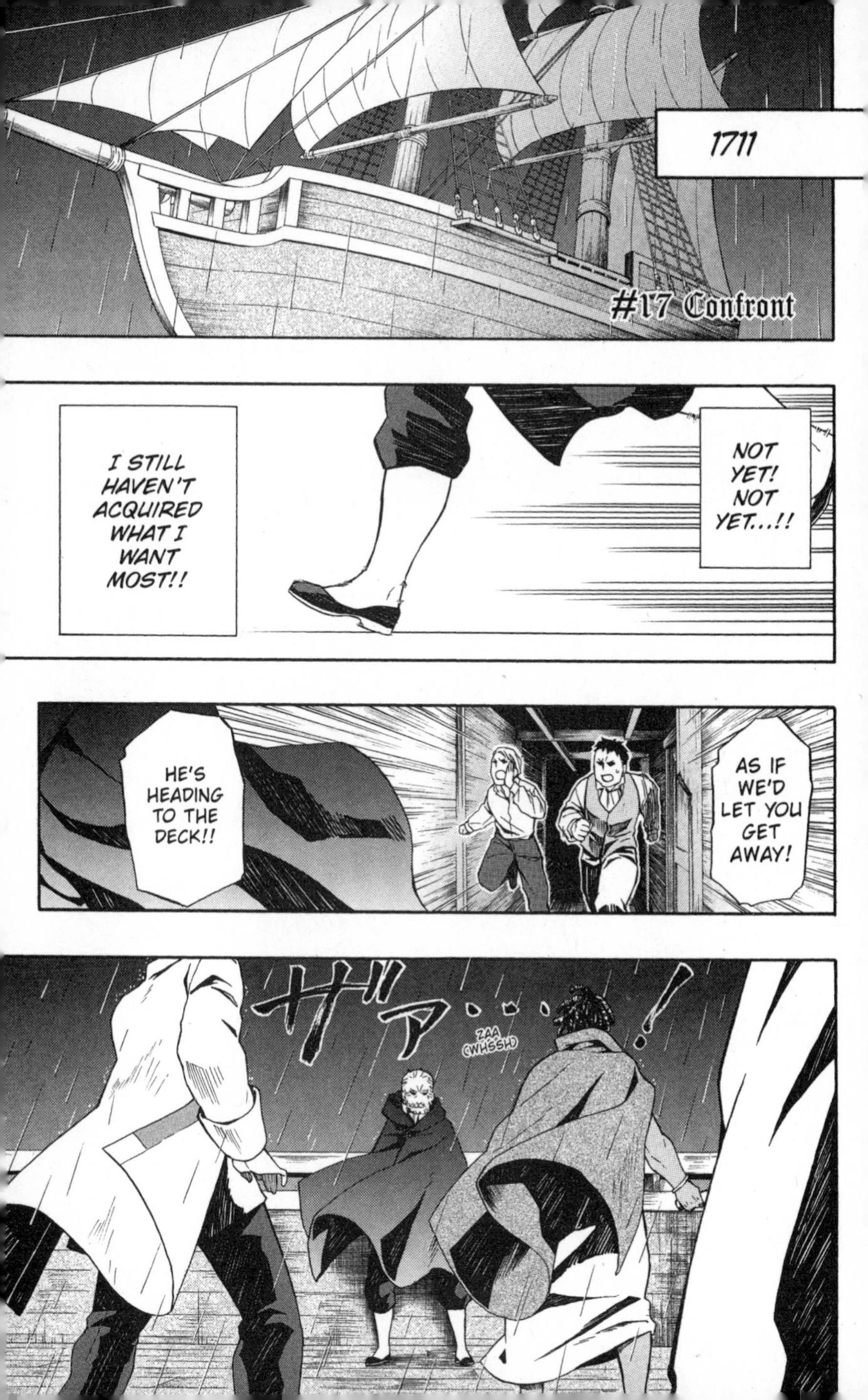
1711
#17 Confront
NOT YET! NOT YET...!!
I STILL HAVEN'T ACQUIRED WHAT I WANT MOST!!
AS IF WE'D LET YOU GET AWAY!
HE'S HEADING TO THE DECK!!
ザア…!
ZAA (WHSSH)

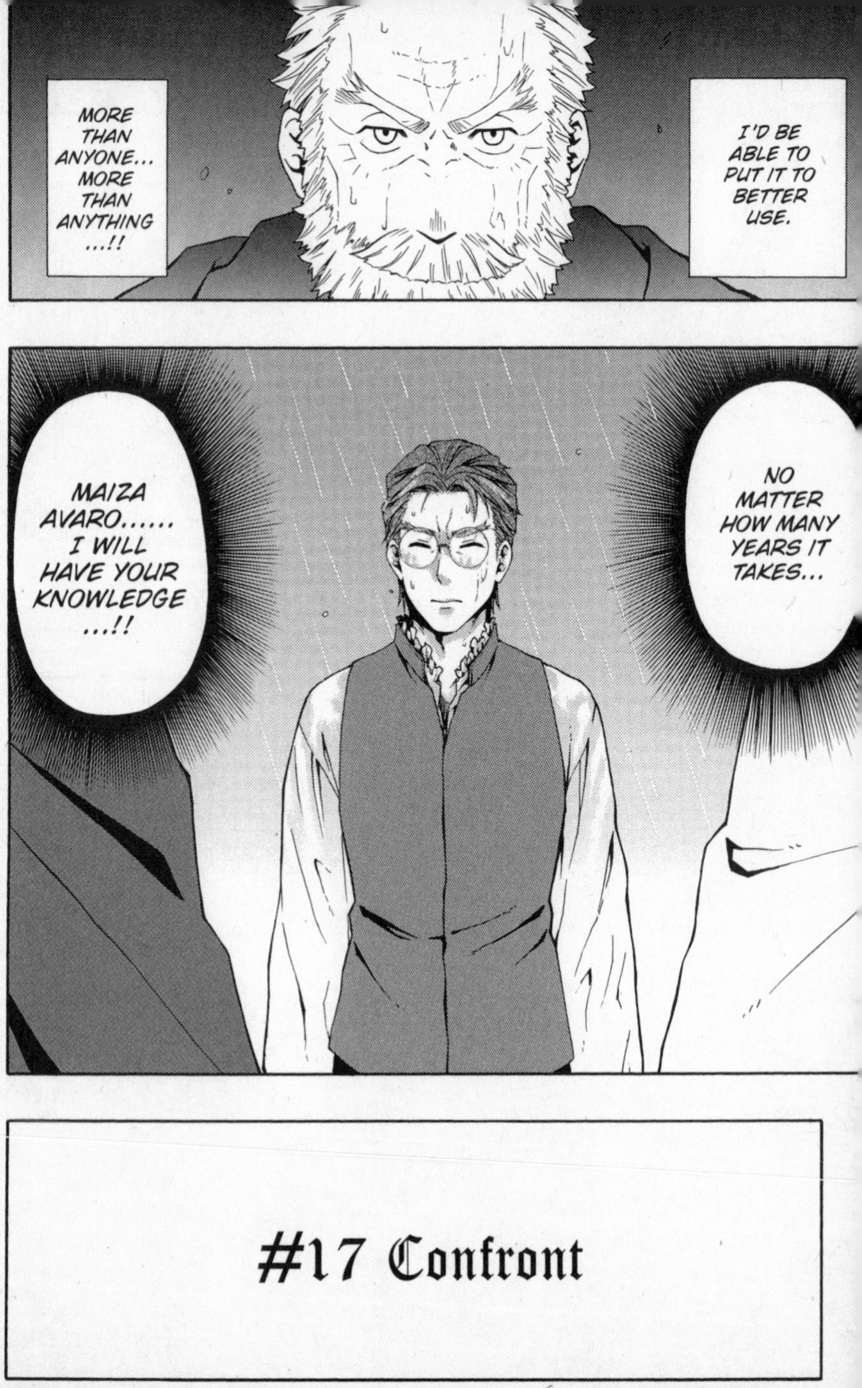
I'D BE ABLE TO PUT IT TO BETTER USE.
MORE THAN ANYONE... MORE THAN ANYTHING ...!!
NO MATTER HOW MANY YEARS IT TAKES...
MAIZA AVARO...... I WILL HAVE YOUR KNOWLEDGE ...!!

#17 Confront

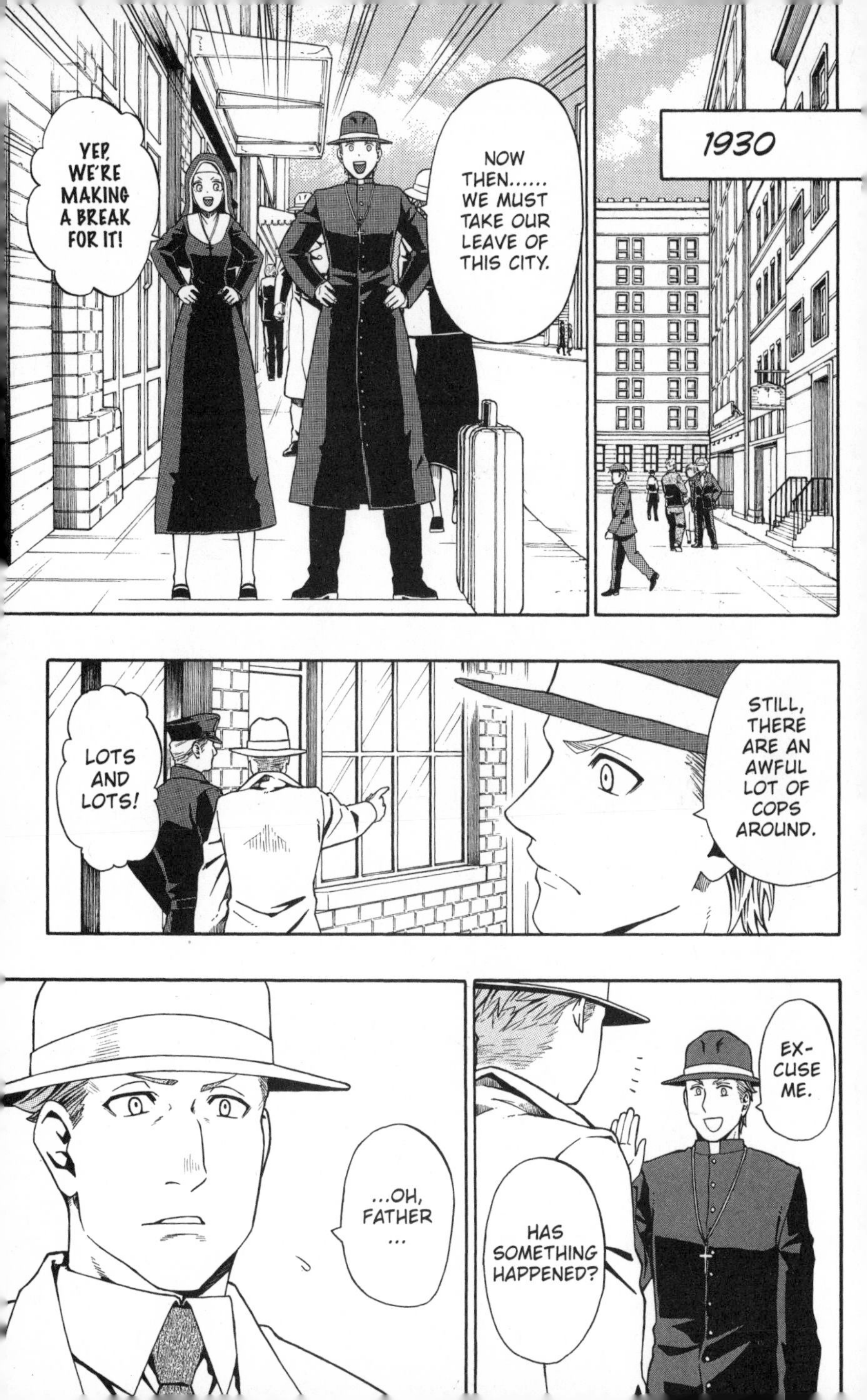
1930
NOW THEN...... WE MUST TAKE OUR LEAVE OF THIS CITY.
YEP, WE'RE MAKING A BREAK FOR IT!
STILL, THERE ARE AN AWFUL LOT OF COPS AROUND.
LOTS AND LOTS!
EX-CUSE ME.
HAS SOMETHING HAPPENED?
...OH, FATHER...

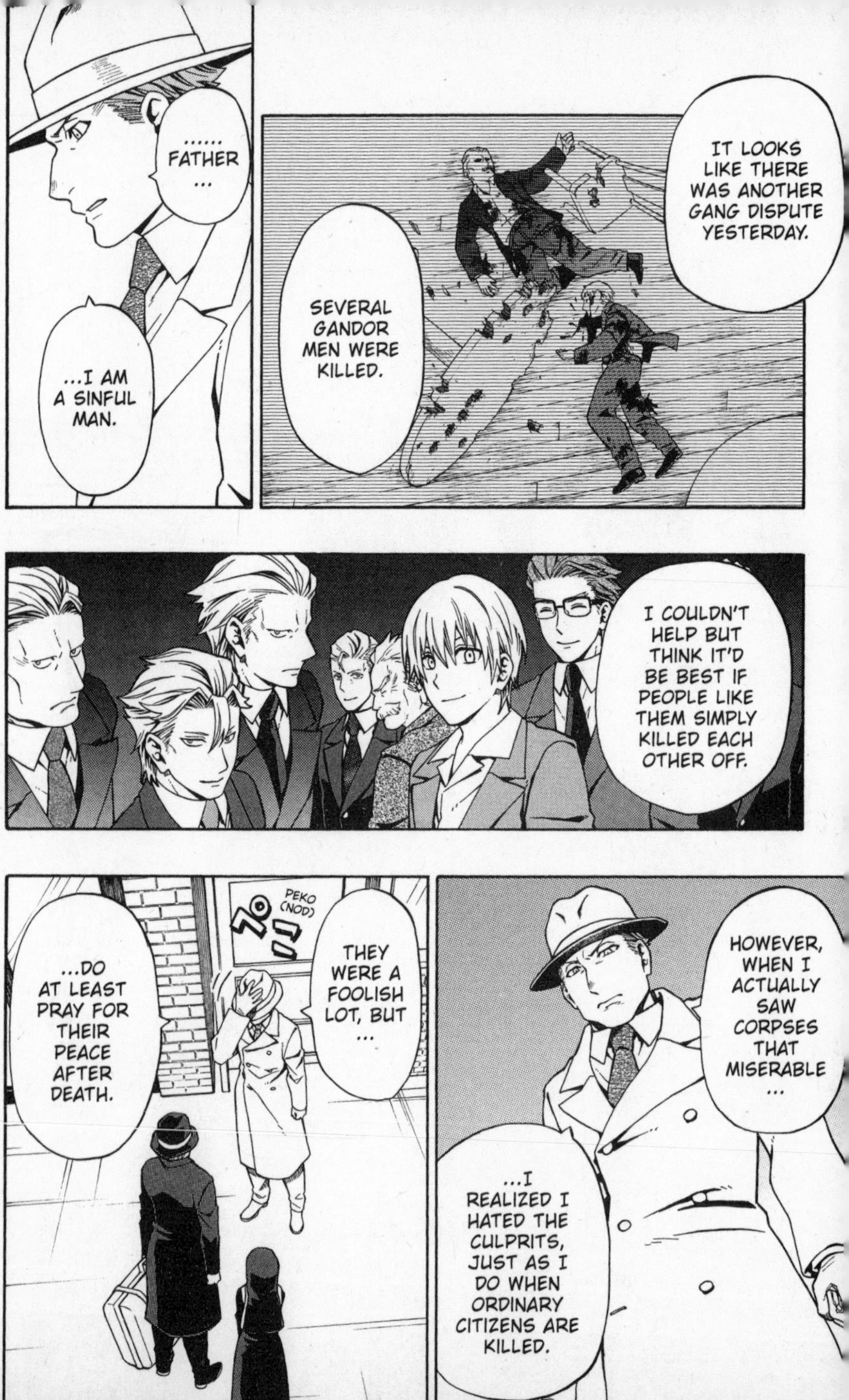
IT LOOKS LIKE THERE WAS ANOTHER GANG DISPUTE YESTERDAY.
SEVERAL GANDOR MEN WERE KILLED.
......FATHER...
...I AM A SINFUL MAN.
I COULDN'T HELP BUT THINK IT'D BE BEST IF PEOPLE LIKE THEM SIMPLY KILLED EACH OTHER OFF.
HOWEVER, WHEN I ACTUALLY SAW CORPSES THAT MISERABLE...
...I REALIZED I HATED THE CULPRITS, JUST AS I DO WHEN ORDINARY CITIZENS ARE KILLED.
PEKO (NOD)
THEY WERE A FOOLISH LOT, BUT...
...DO AT LEAST PRAY FOR THEIR PEACE AFTER DEATH.

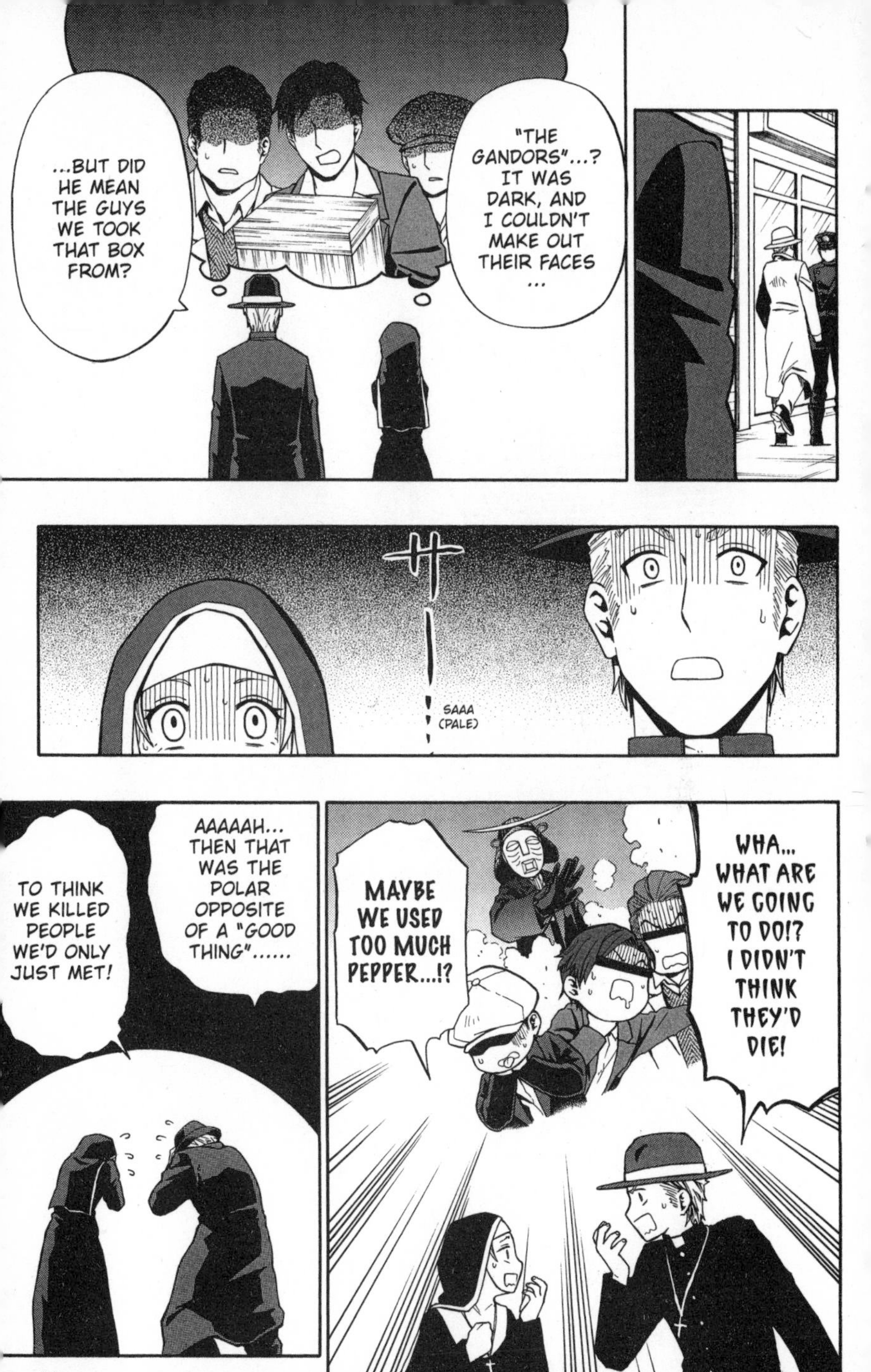
"THE GANDORS"...? IT WAS DARK, AND I COULDN'T MAKE OUT THEIR FACES...
...BUT DID HE MEAN THE GUYS WE TOOK THAT BOX FROM?
SAAA (PALE)
WHA... WHAT ARE WE GOING TO DO!? I DIDN'T THINK THEY'D DIE!
MAYBE WE USED TOO MUCH PEPPER...!?
AAAAAH... THEN THAT WAS THE POLAR OPPOSITE OF A "GOOD THING"......
TO THINK WE KILLED PEOPLE WE'D ONLY JUST MET!

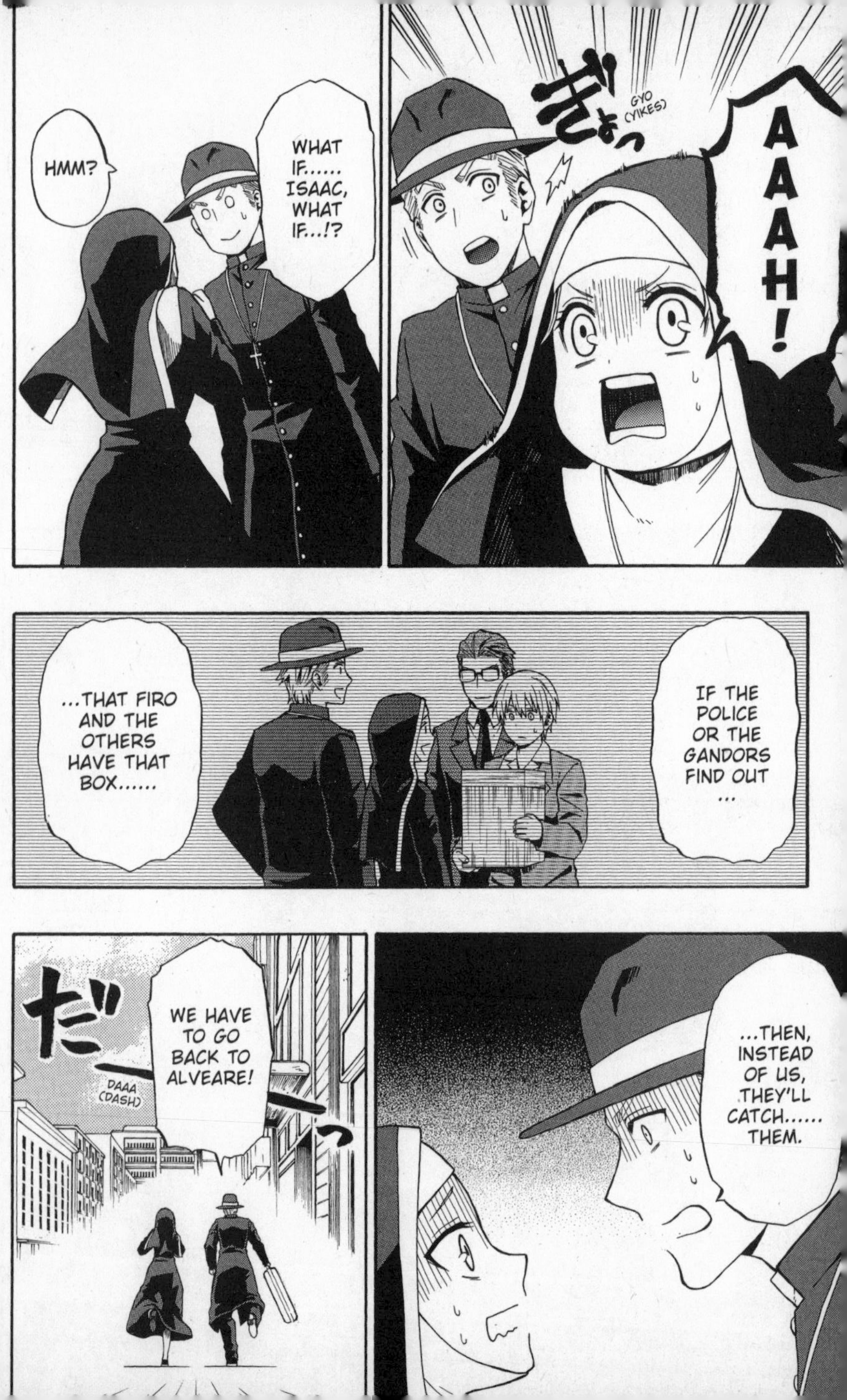
GYO (YIKES)
AAAH!
WHAT IF...... ISAAC, WHAT IF...!?
HMM?
IF THE POLICE OR THE GANDORS FIND OUT ...
...THAT FIRO AND THE OTHERS HAVE THAT BOX......
...THEN, INSTEAD OF US, THEY'LL CATCH...... THEM.
WE HAVE TO GO BACK TO ALVEARE!
DAAA (DASH)

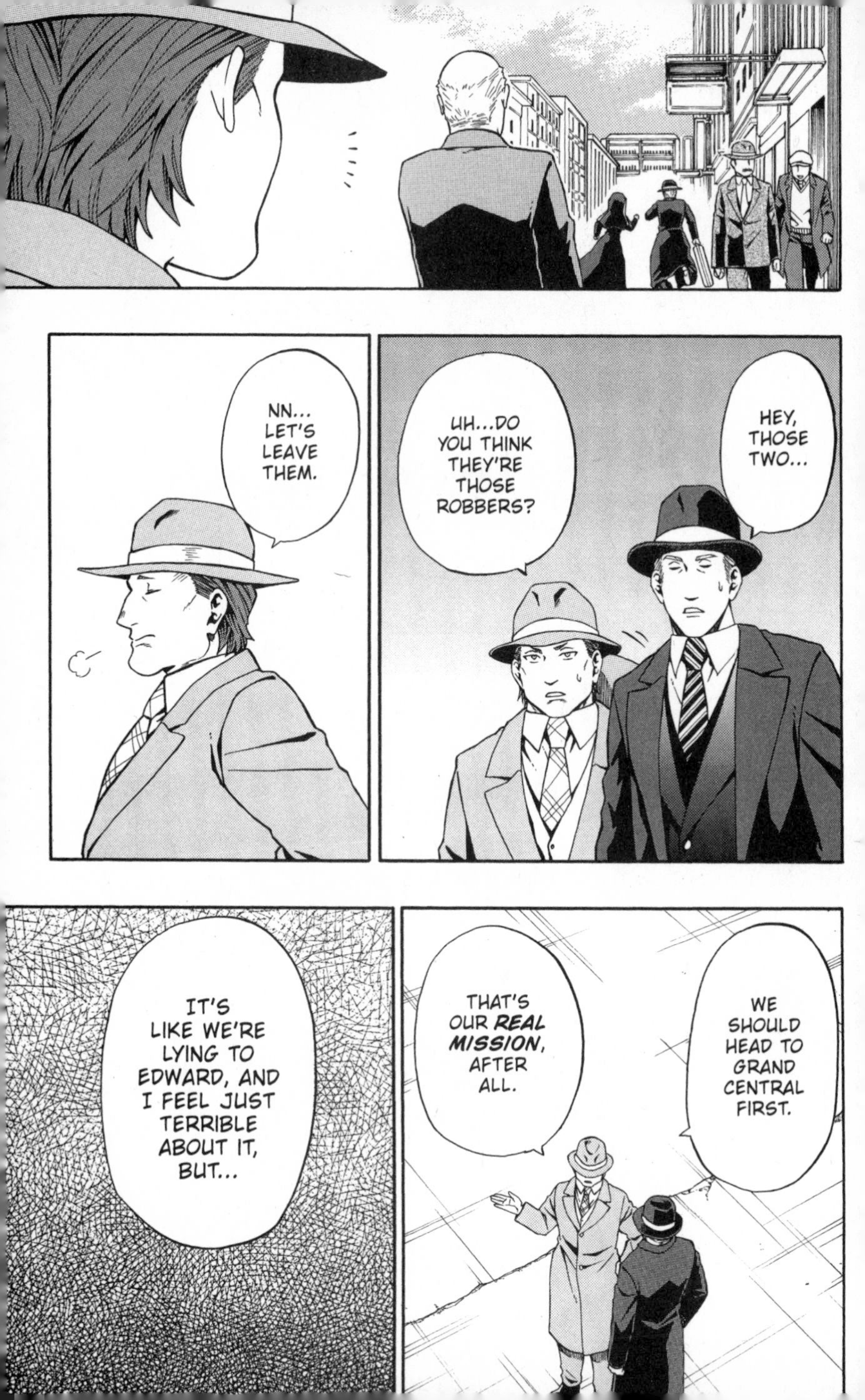
HEY, THOSE TWO...
UH...DO YOU THINK THEY'RE THOSE ROBBERS?
NN... LET'S LEAVE THEM.
WE SHOULD HEAD TO GRAND CENTRAL FIRST.
THAT'S OUR REAL MISSION, AFTER ALL.
IT'S LIKE WE'RE LYING TO EDWARD, AND I FEEL JUST TERRIBLE ABOUT IT, BUT...

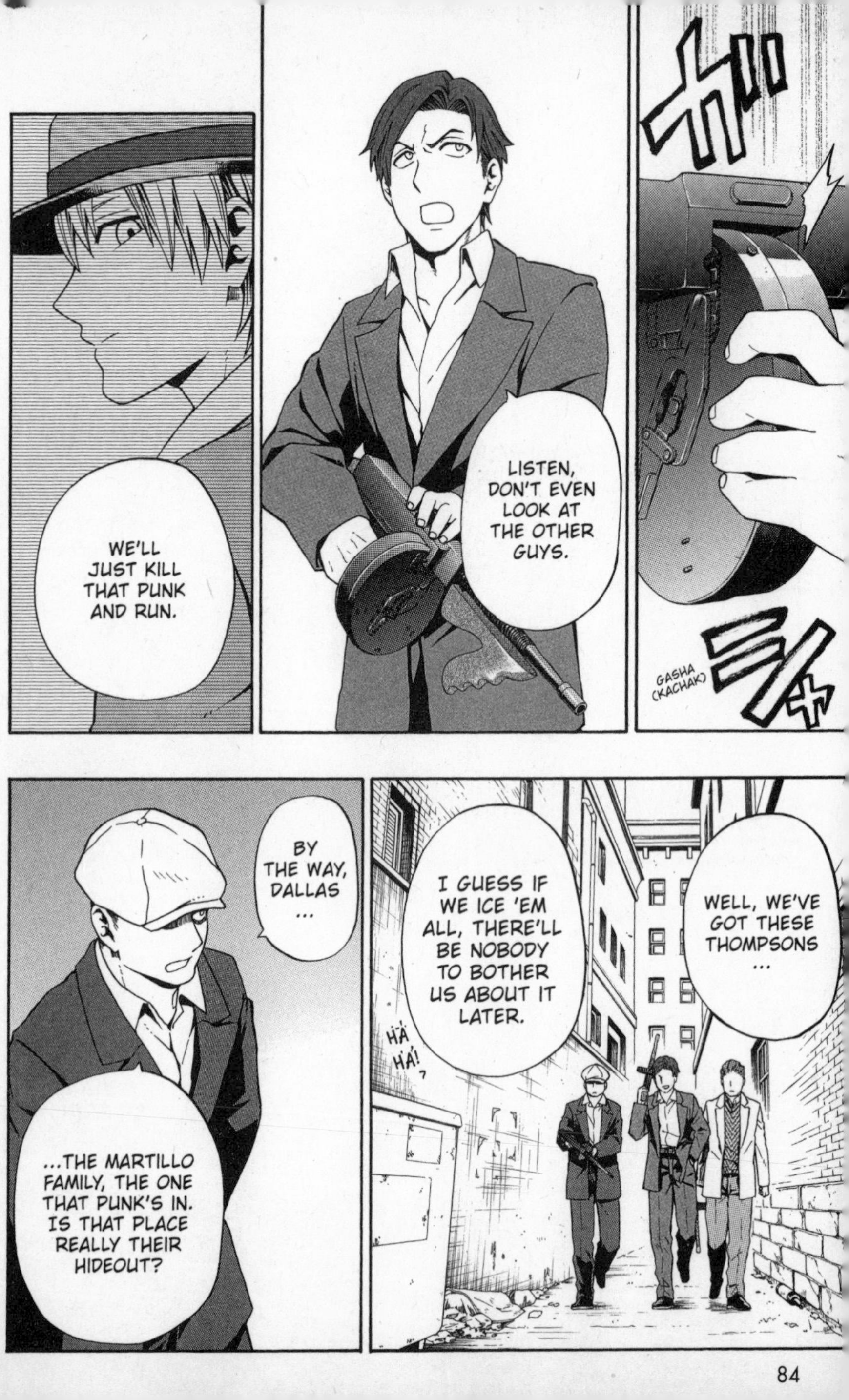
GASHA (KACHAK)
LISTEN, DON'T EVEN LOOK AT THE OTHER GUYS.
WE'LL JUST KILL THAT PUNK AND RUN.
WELL, WE'VE GOT THESE THOMPSONS ...
I GUESS IF WE ICE 'EM ALL, THERE'LL BE NOBODY TO BOTHER US ABOUT IT LATER.
HA HA!
BY THE WAY, DALLAS ...
...THE MARTILLO FAMILY, THE ONE THAT PUNK'S IN. IS THAT PLACE REALLY THEIR HIDEOUT?

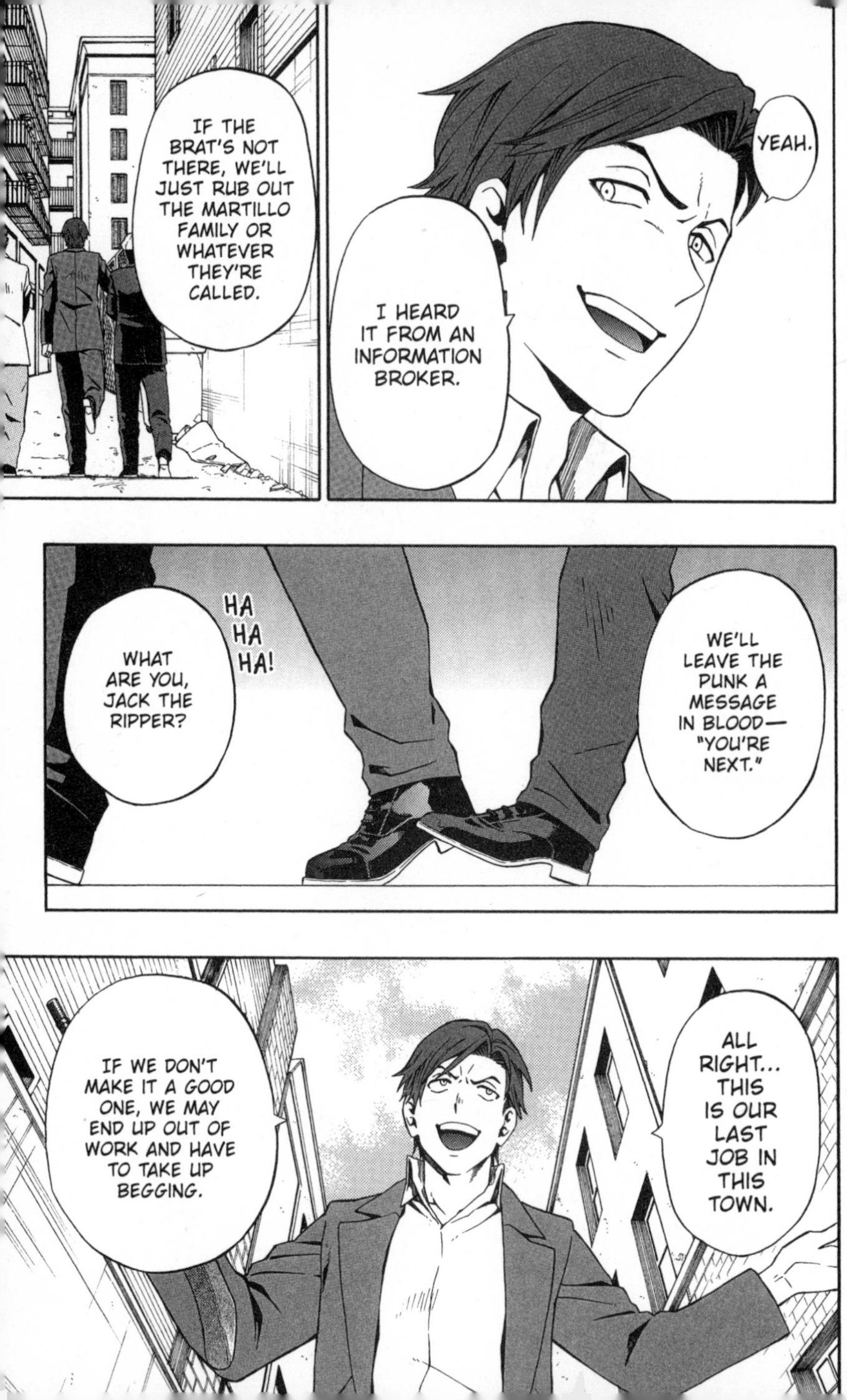
YEAH.
I HEARD IT FROM AN INFORMATION BROKER.
IF THE BRAT'S NOT THERE, WE'LL JUST RUB OUT THE MARTILLO FAMILY OR WHATEVER THEY'RE CALLED.
WE'LL LEAVE THE PUNK A MESSAGE IN BLOOD—"YOU'RE NEXT."
HA HA HA!
WHAT ARE YOU, JACK THE RIPPER?
ALL RIGHT... THIS IS OUR LAST JOB IN THIS TOWN.
IF WE DON'T MAKE IT A GOOD ONE, WE MAY END UP OUT OF WORK AND HAVE TO TAKE UP BEGGING.

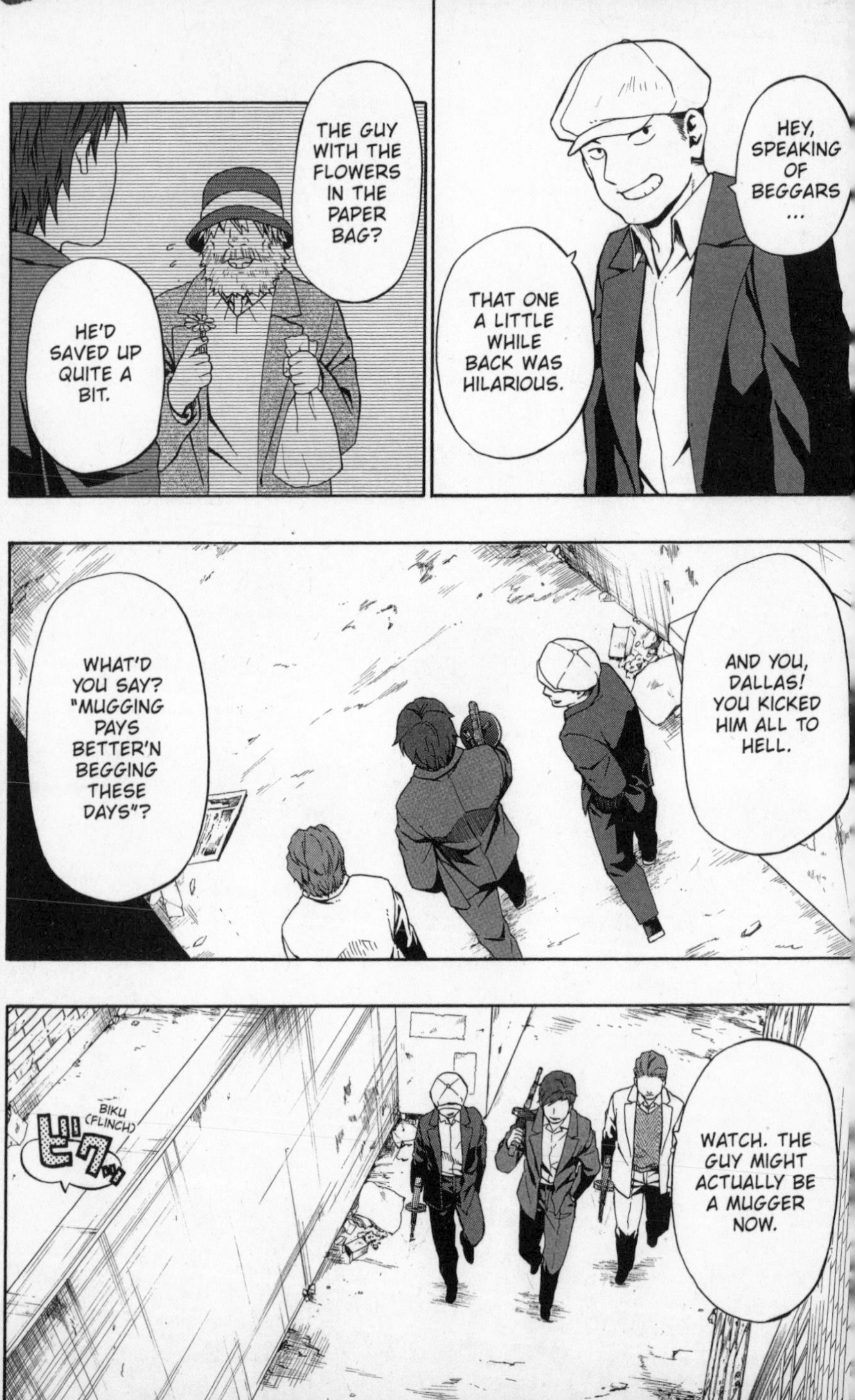
HEY, SPEAKING OF BEGGARS ...
THAT ONE A LITTLE WHILE BACK WAS HILARIOUS.
THE GUY WITH THE FLOWERS IN THE PAPER BAG?
HE'D SAVED UP QUITE A BIT.
AND YOU, DALLAS! YOU KICKED HIM ALL TO HELL.
WHAT'D YOU SAY? "MUGGING PAYS BETTER'N BEGGING THESE DAYS"?
WATCH. THE GUY MIGHT ACTUALLY BE A MUGGER NOW.
BIKU (FLINCH)

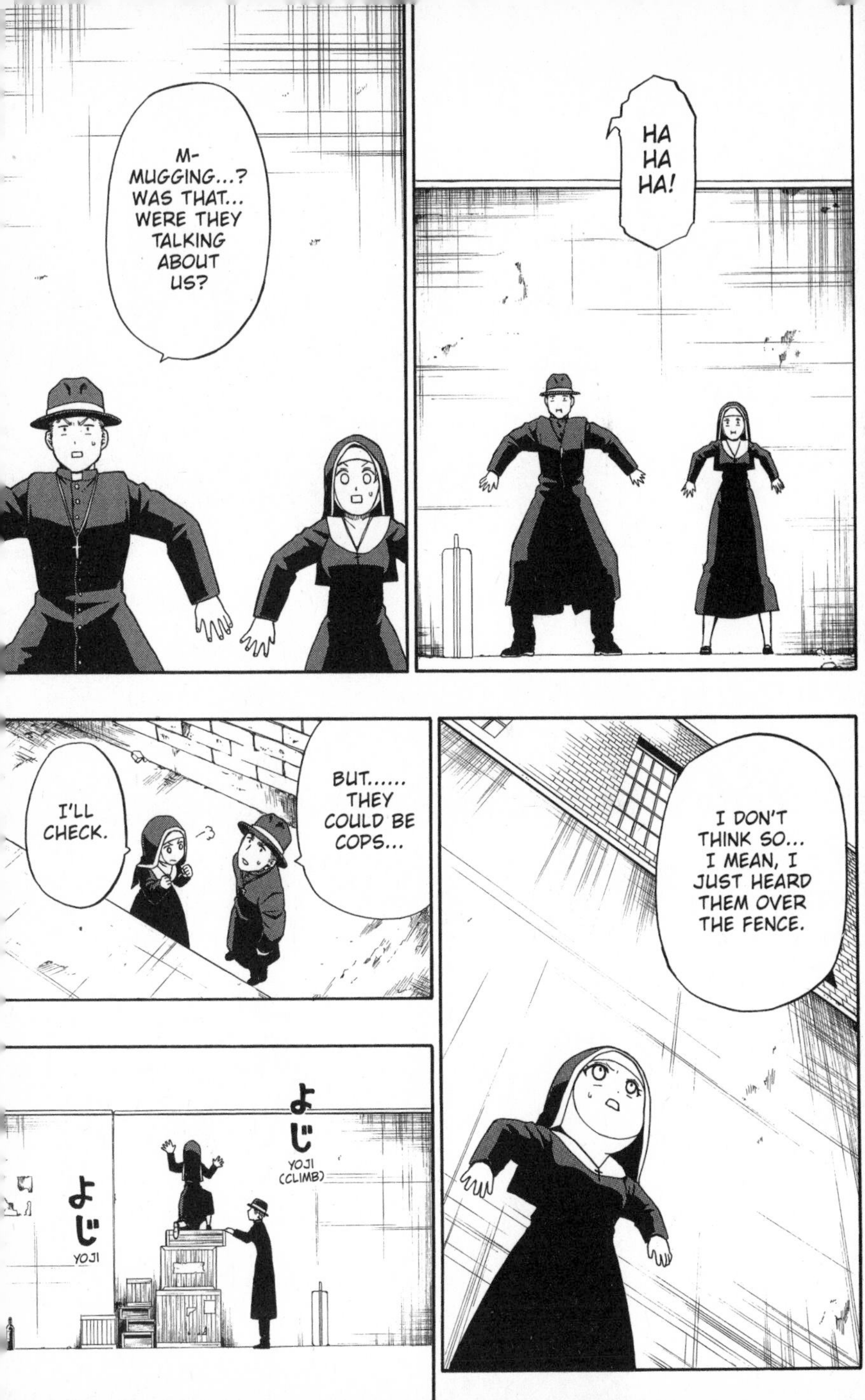
HA HA HA!
M-MUGGING...? WAS THAT... WERE THEY TALKING ABOUT US?
I DON'T THINK SO... I MEAN, I JUST HEARD THEM OVER THE FENCE.
BUT...... THEY COULD BE COPS...
I'LL CHECK.
よじ
YOJI (CLIMB)
よじ
YOJI

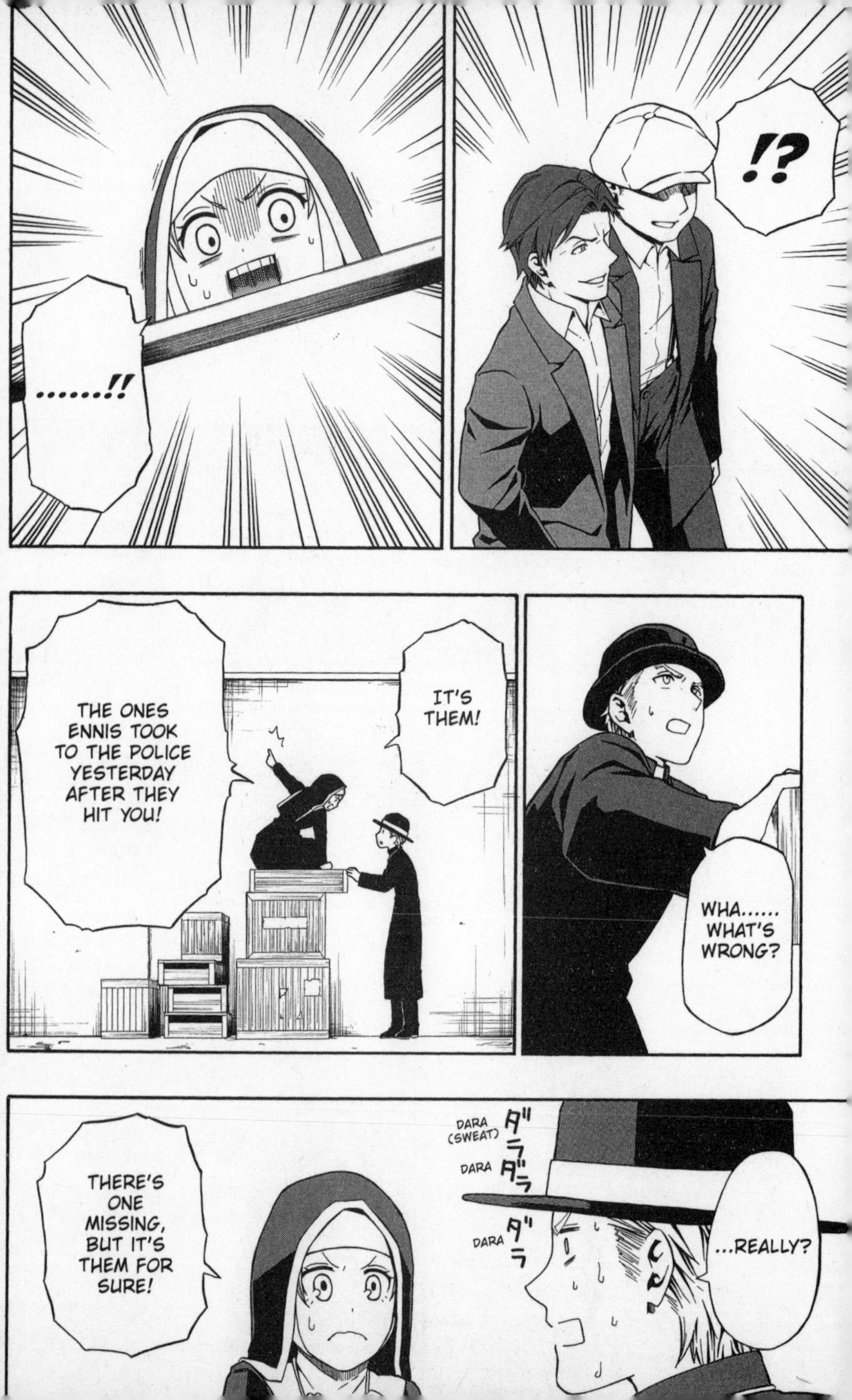
!?
......!!
WHA...... WHAT'S WRONG?
IT'S THEM!
THE ONES ENNIS TOOK TO THE POLICE YESTERDAY AFTER THEY HIT YOU!
DARA (SWEAT)
DARA
DARA
...REALLY?
THERE'S ONE MISSING, BUT IT'S THEM FOR SURE!

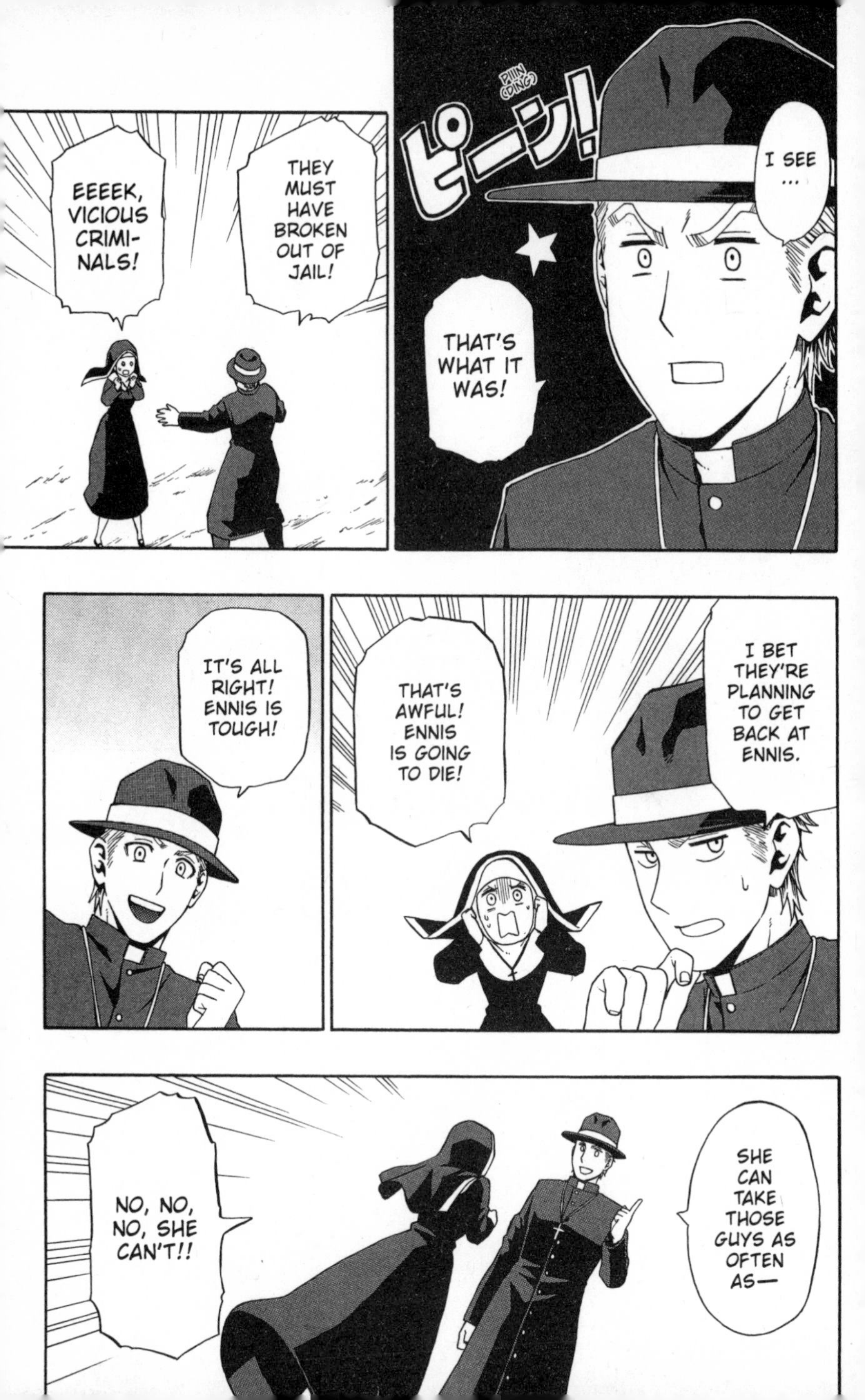
ピーン!
PIIIN (DING)
I SEE ...
THAT'S WHAT IT WAS!
THEY MUST HAVE BROKEN OUT OF JAIL!
EEEEK, VICIOUS CRIMI-NALS!
I BET THEY'RE PLANNING TO GET BACK AT ENNIS.
THAT'S AWFUL! ENNIS IS GOING TO DIE!
IT'S ALL RIGHT! ENNIS IS TOUGH!
SHE CAN TAKE THOSE GUYS AS OFTEN AS—
NO, NO, NO, SHE CAN'T!!

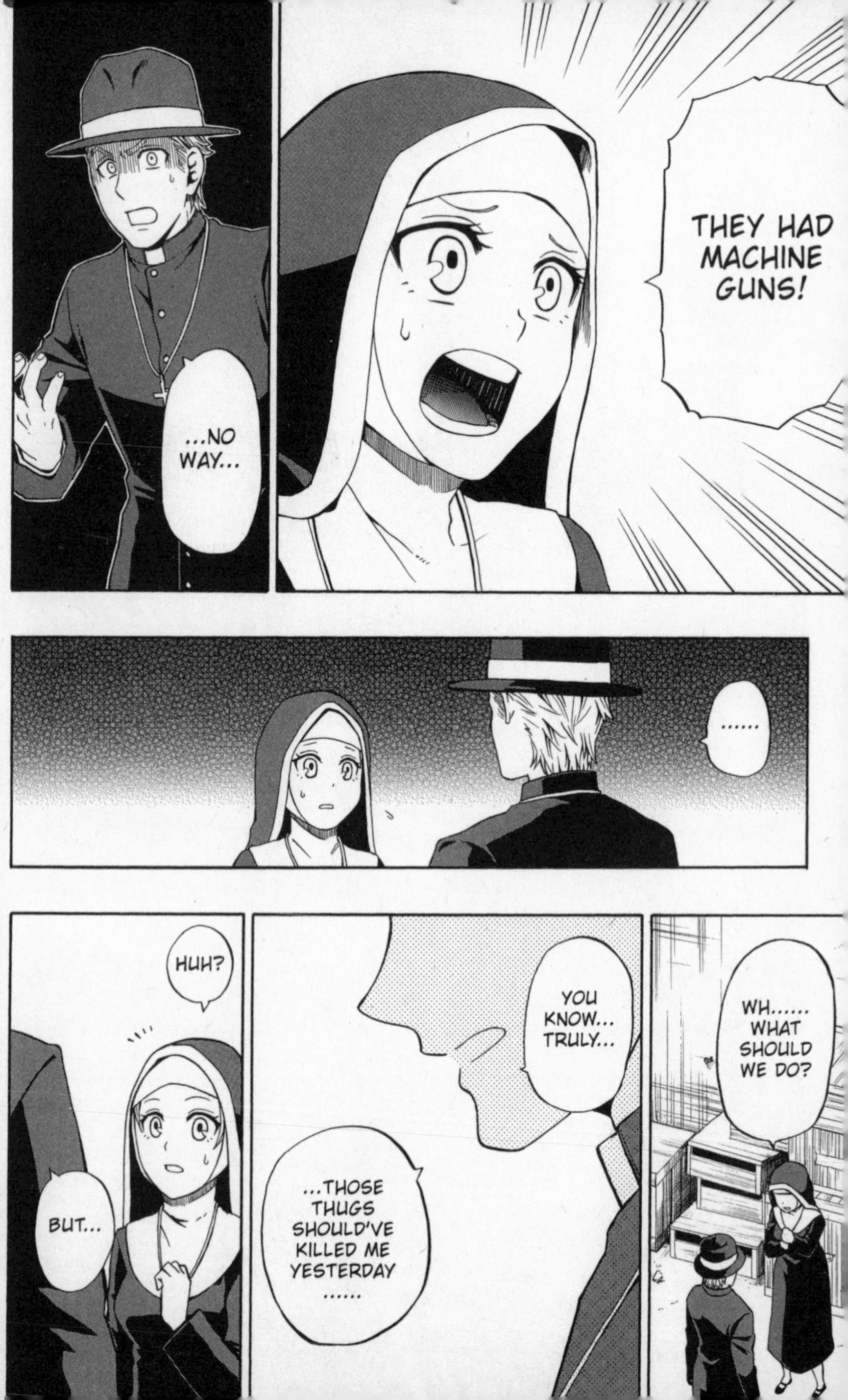
THEY HAD MACHINE GUNS!
...NO WAY...
......
WH...... WHAT SHOULD WE DO?
YOU KNOW... TRULY...
...THOSE THUGS SHOULD'VE KILLED ME YESTERDAY ......
HUH?
BUT...

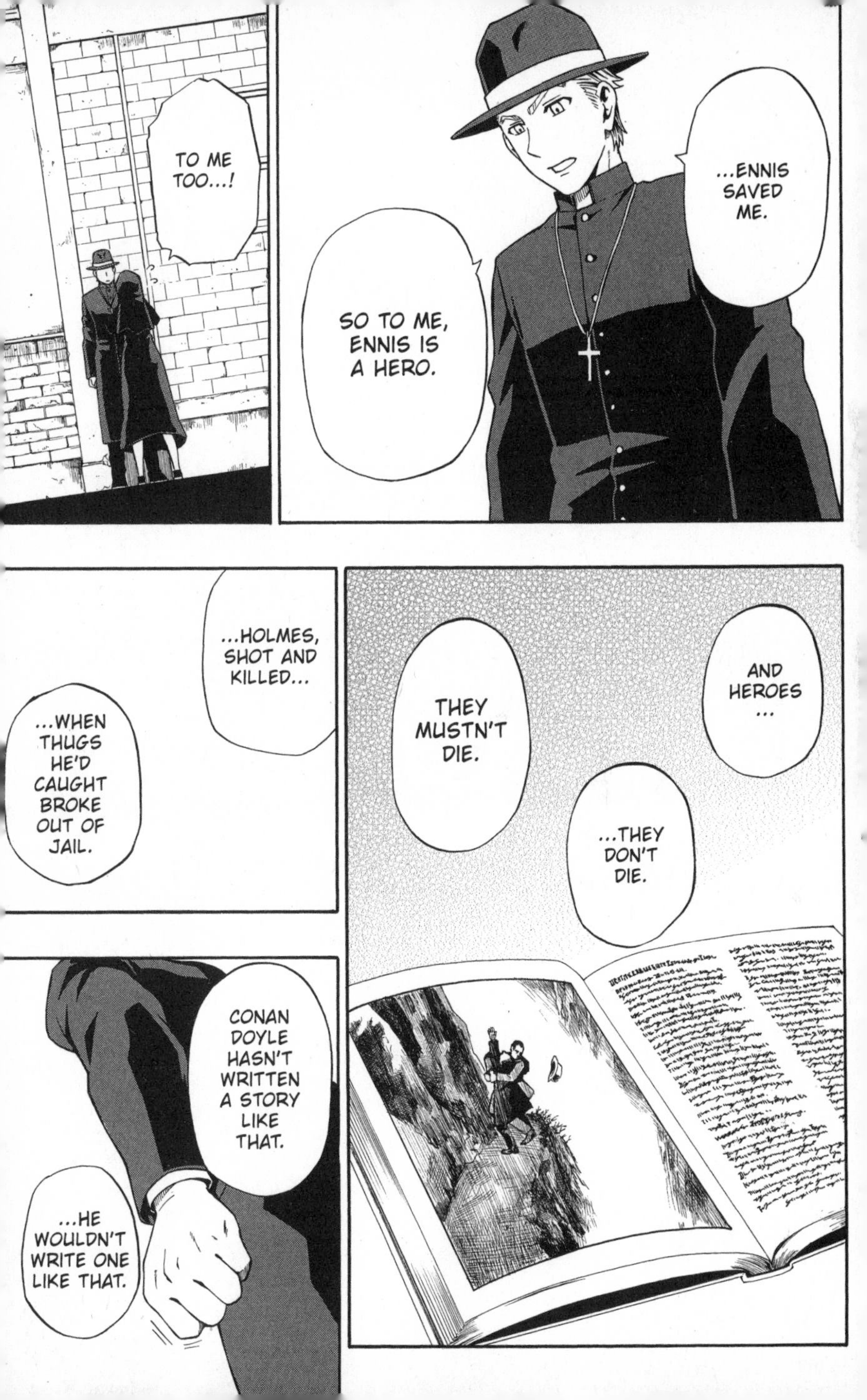
...ENNIS SAVED ME.
SO TO ME, ENNIS IS A HERO.
TO ME TOO...!
AND HEROES...
THEY MUSTN'T DIE.
...THEY DON'T DIE.
...HOLMES, SHOT AND KILLED...
...WHEN THUGS HE'D CAUGHT BROKE OUT OF JAIL.
CONAN DOYLE HASN'T WRITTEN A STORY LIKE THAT.
...HE WOULDN'T WRITE ONE LIKE THAT.

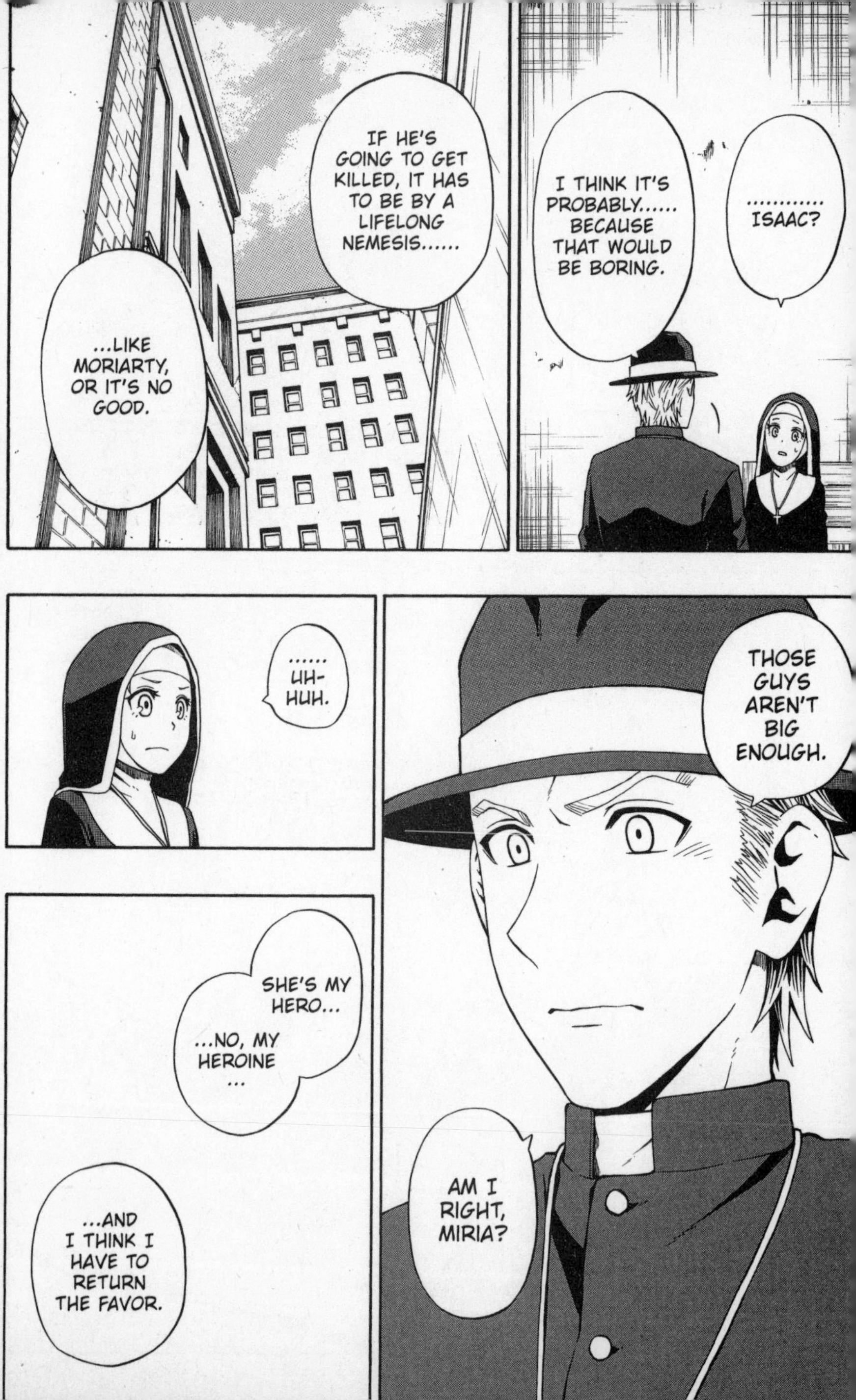
.... ISAAC?
I THINK IT'S PROBABLY...... BECAUSE THAT WOULD BE BORING.
IF HE'S GOING TO GET KILLED, IT HAS TO BE BY A LIFELONG NEMESIS......
...LIKE MORIARTY, OR IT'S NO GOOD.
THOSE GUYS AREN'T BIG ENOUGH.
AM I RIGHT, MIRIA?
...... UH-HUH.
SHE'S MY HERO...
...NO, MY HEROINE ...
...AND I THINK I HAVE TO RETURN THE FAVOR.

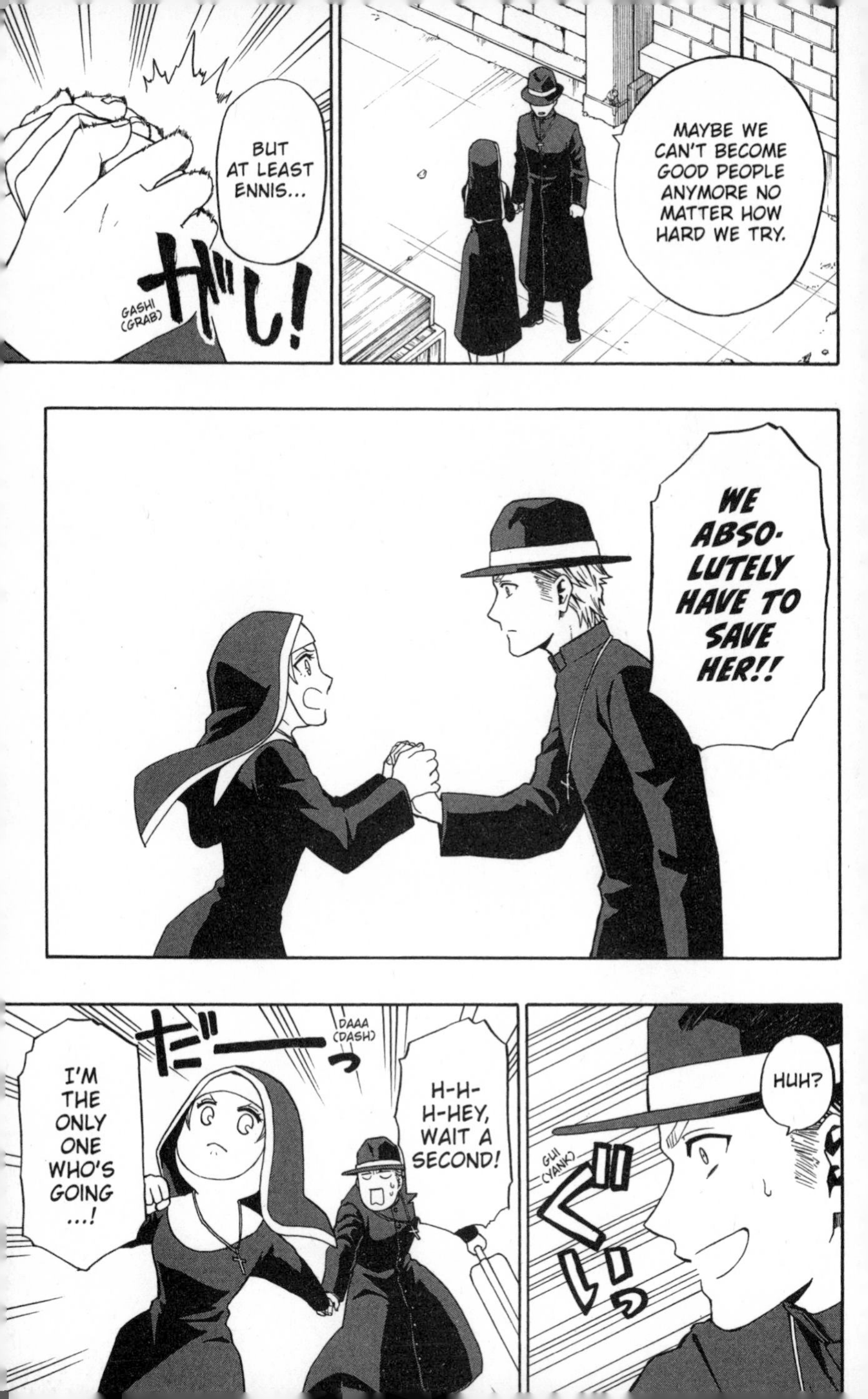
MAYBE WE CAN'T BECOME GOOD PEOPLE ANYMORE NO MATTER HOW HARD WE TRY.
BUT AT LEAST ENNIS...
GASHI (GRAB)
WE ABSO-LUTELY HAVE TO SAVE HER!!
HUH?
GUI (YANK)
DAAA (DASH)
H-H-H-HEY, WAIT A SECOND!
I'M THE ONLY ONE WHO'S GOING...!

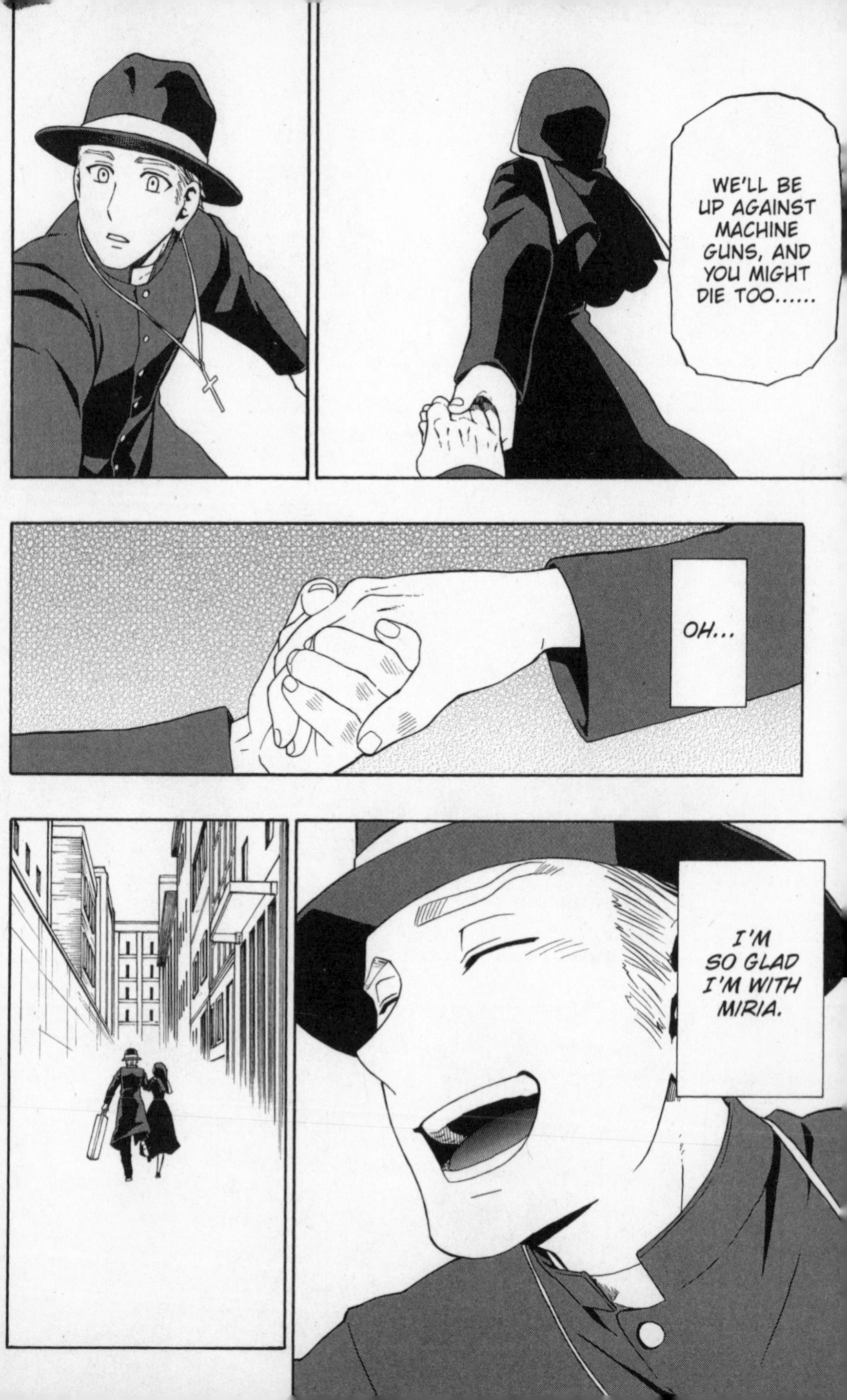
WE'LL BE UP AGAINST MACHINE GUNS, AND YOU MIGHT DIE TOO......
OH...
I'M SO GLAD I'M WITH MIRIA.

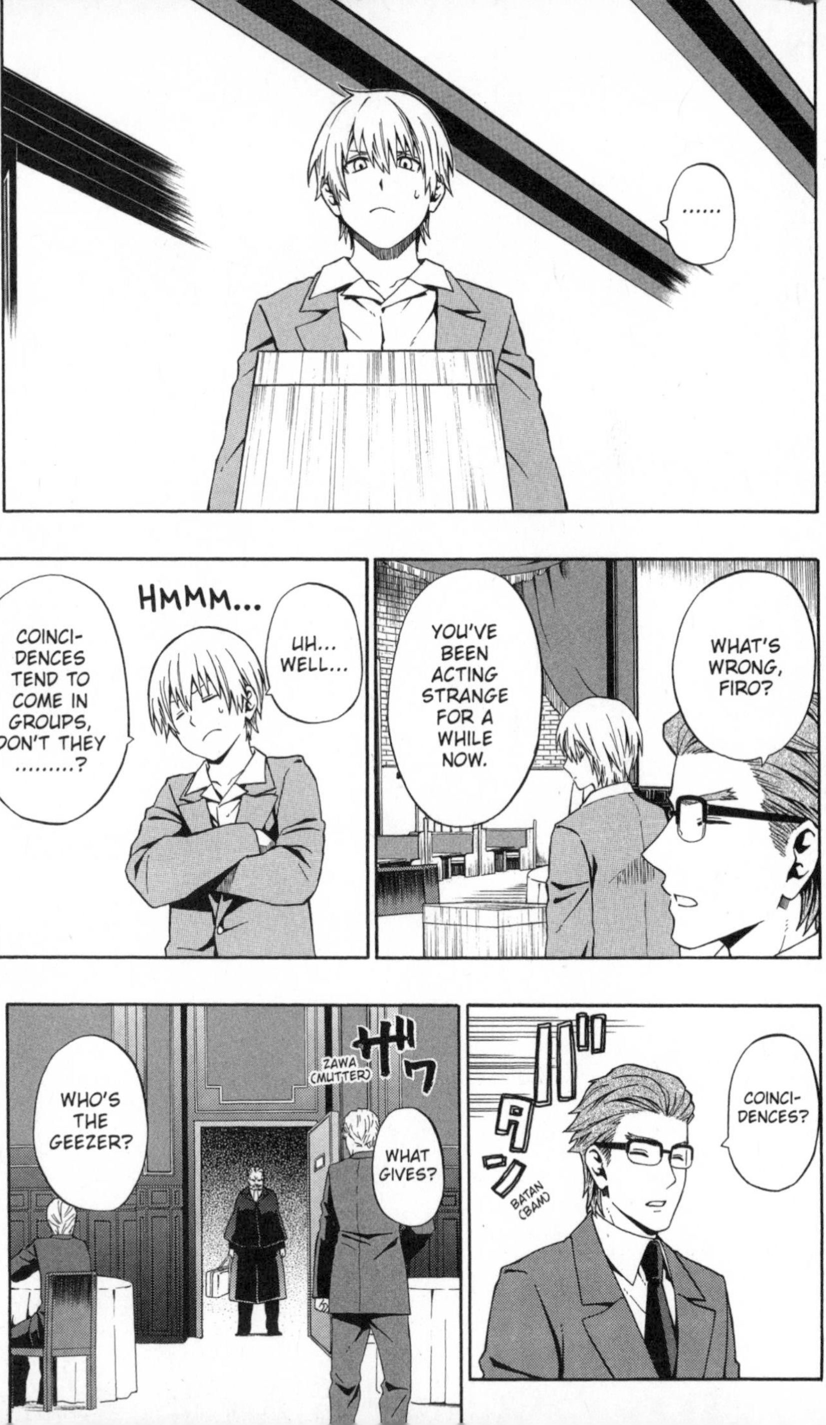
......
WHAT'S WRONG, FIRO?
YOU'VE BEEN ACTING STRANGE FOR A WHILE NOW.
UH... WELL...
HMMM...
COINCI-DENCES TEND TO COME IN GROUPS, DON'T THEY ....?
COINCI-DENCES?
BATAN (BAM)
ZAWA (MUTTER)
WHAT GIVES?
WHO'S THE GEEZER?

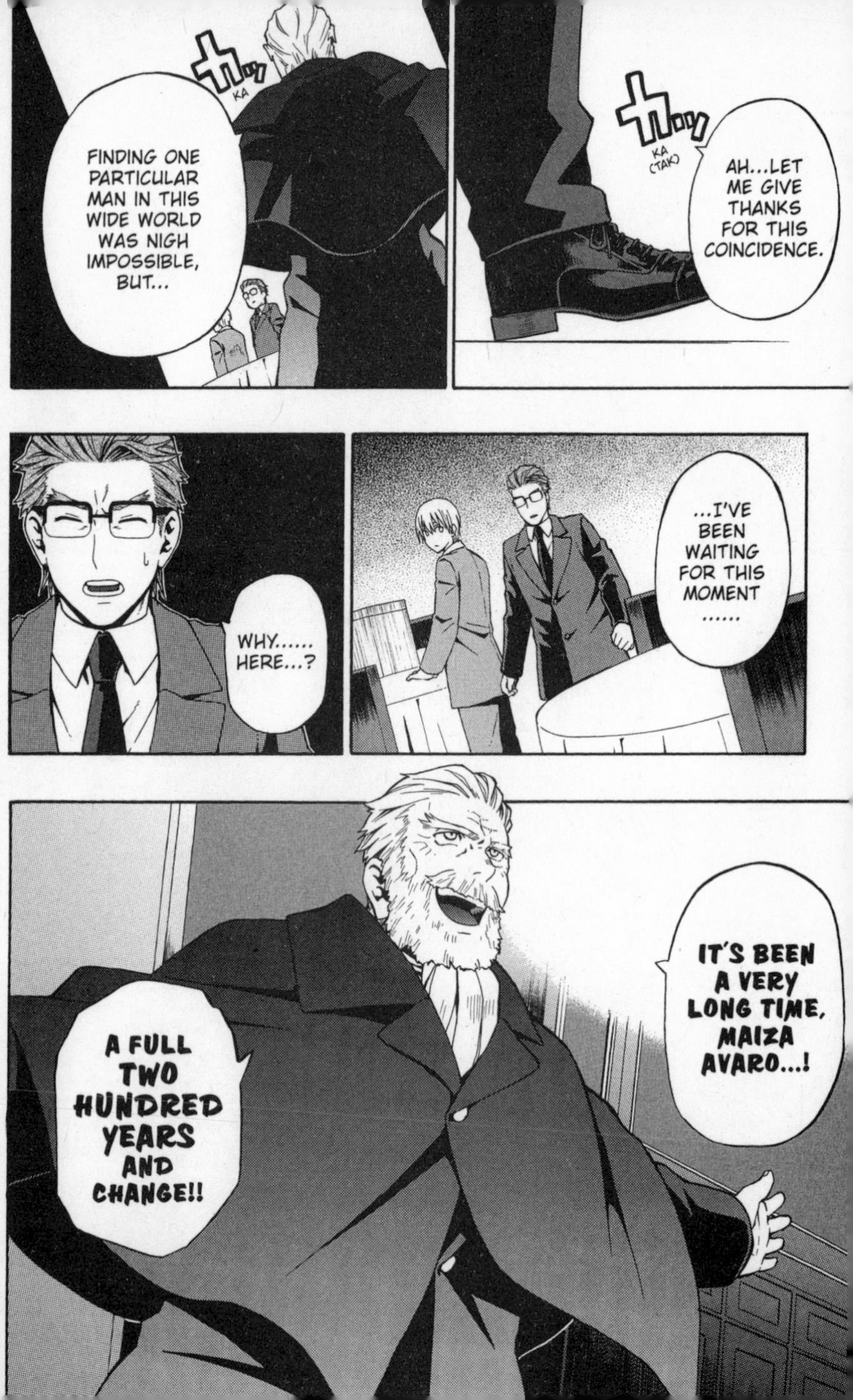
KA (TAK)
AH...LET ME GIVE THANKS FOR THIS COINCIDENCE.
KA
FINDING ONE PARTICULAR MAN IN THIS WIDE WORLD WAS NIGH IMPOSSIBLE, BUT...
...I'VE BEEN WAITING FOR THIS MOMENT ......
WHY...... HERE...?
IT'S BEEN A VERY LONG TIME, MAIZA AVARO...!
A FULL TWO HUNDRED YEARS AND CHANGE!!

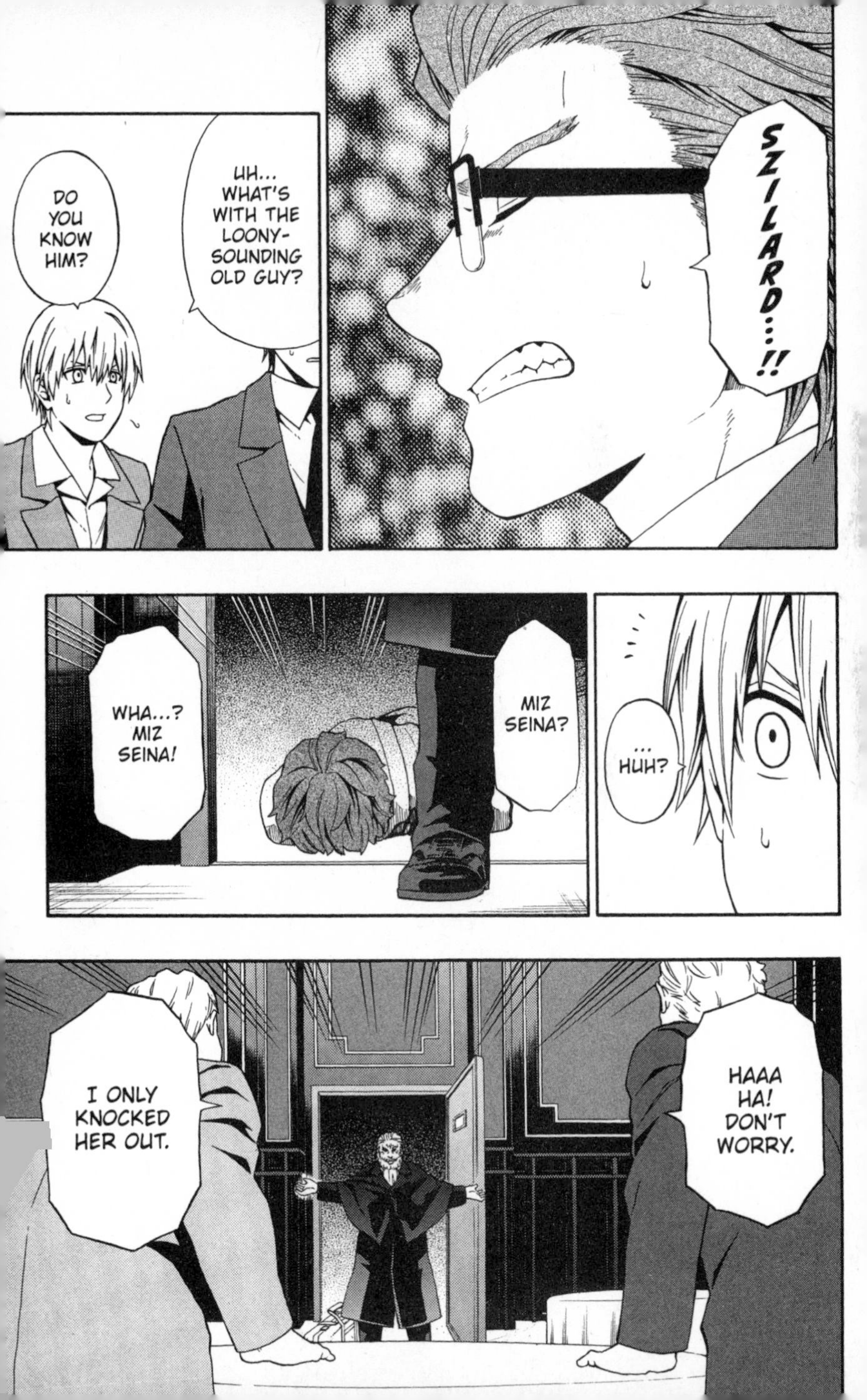
SZILARD...!!
UH... WHAT'S WITH THE LOONY-SOUNDING OLD GUY?
DO YOU KNOW HIM?
...HUH?
MIZ SEINA?
WHA...? MIZ SEINA!
HAAA HA! DON'T WORRY.
I ONLY KNOCKED HER OUT.

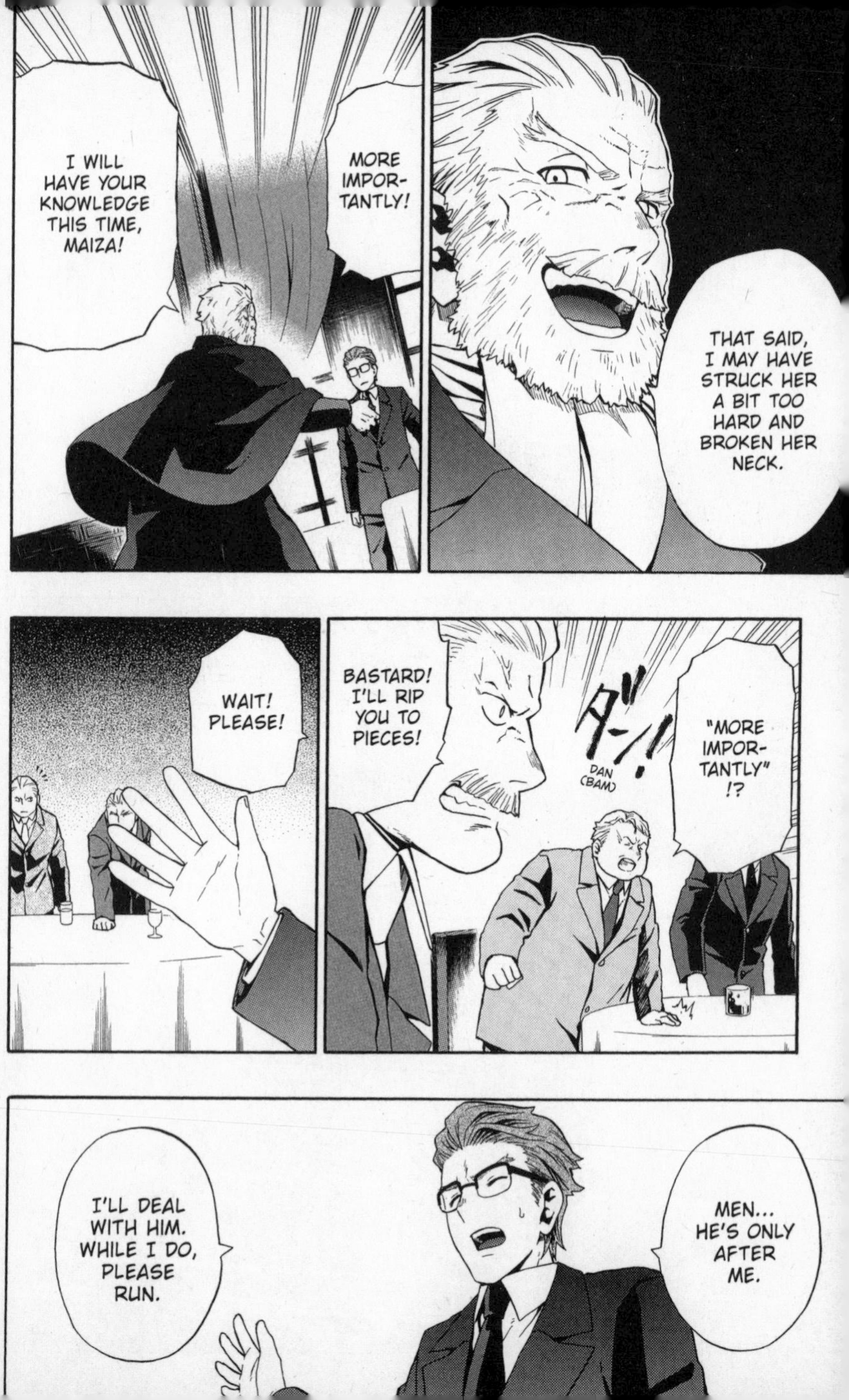
THAT SAID, I MAY HAVE STRUCK HER A BIT TOO HARD AND BROKEN HER NECK.
MORE IMPORTANTLY!
I WILL HAVE YOUR KNOWLEDGE THIS TIME, MAIZA!
"MORE IMPORTANTLY" !?
DAN (BAM)
BASTARD! I'LL RIP YOU TO PIECES!
WAIT! PLEASE!
MEN... HE'S ONLY AFTER ME.
I'LL DEAL WITH HIM. WHILE I DO, PLEASE RUN.

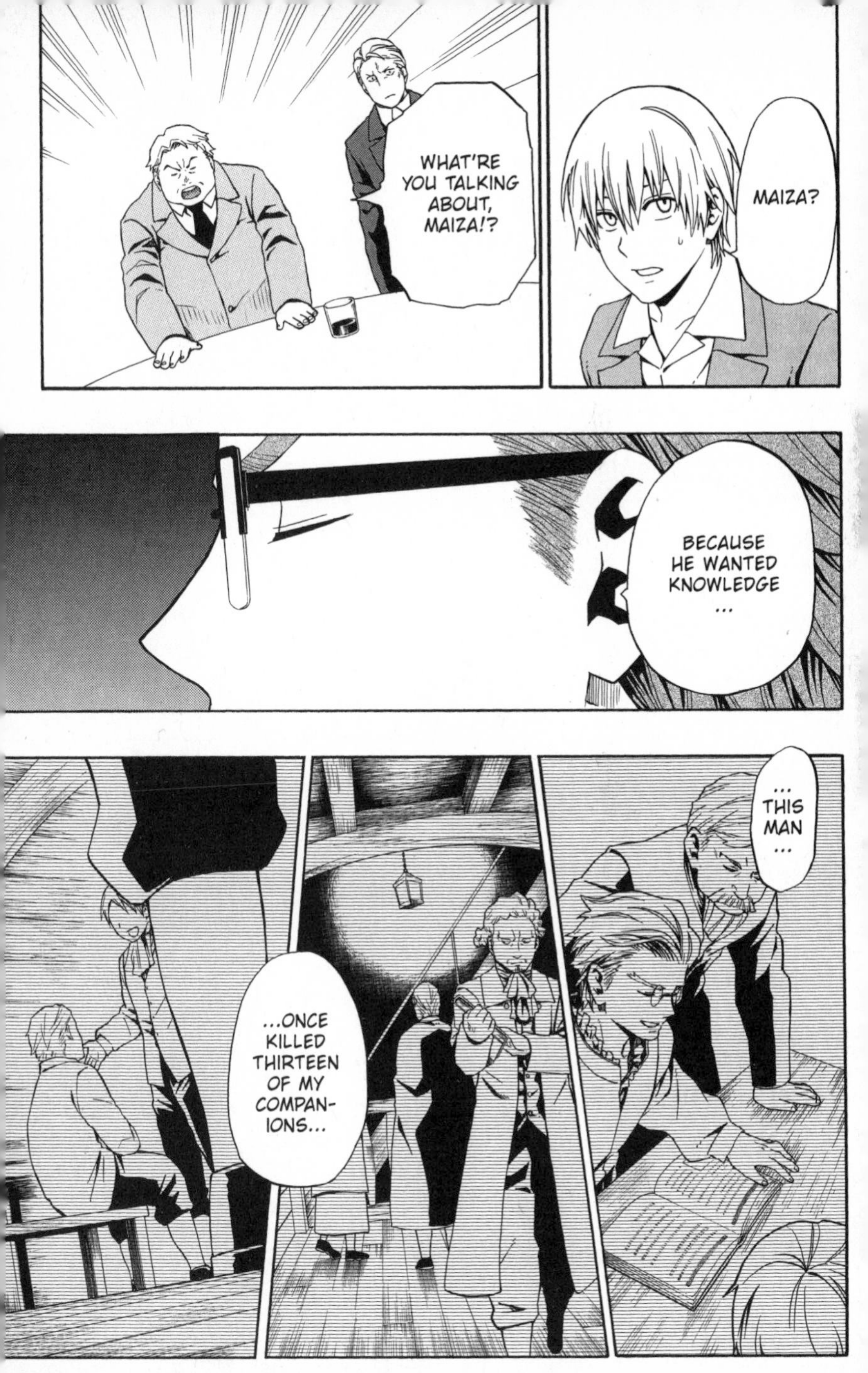
MAIZA?
WHAT'RE YOU TALKING ABOUT, MAIZA!?
BECAUSE HE WANTED KNOWLEDGE ...
... THIS MAN ...
...ONCE KILLED THIRTEEN OF MY COMPAN-IONS...

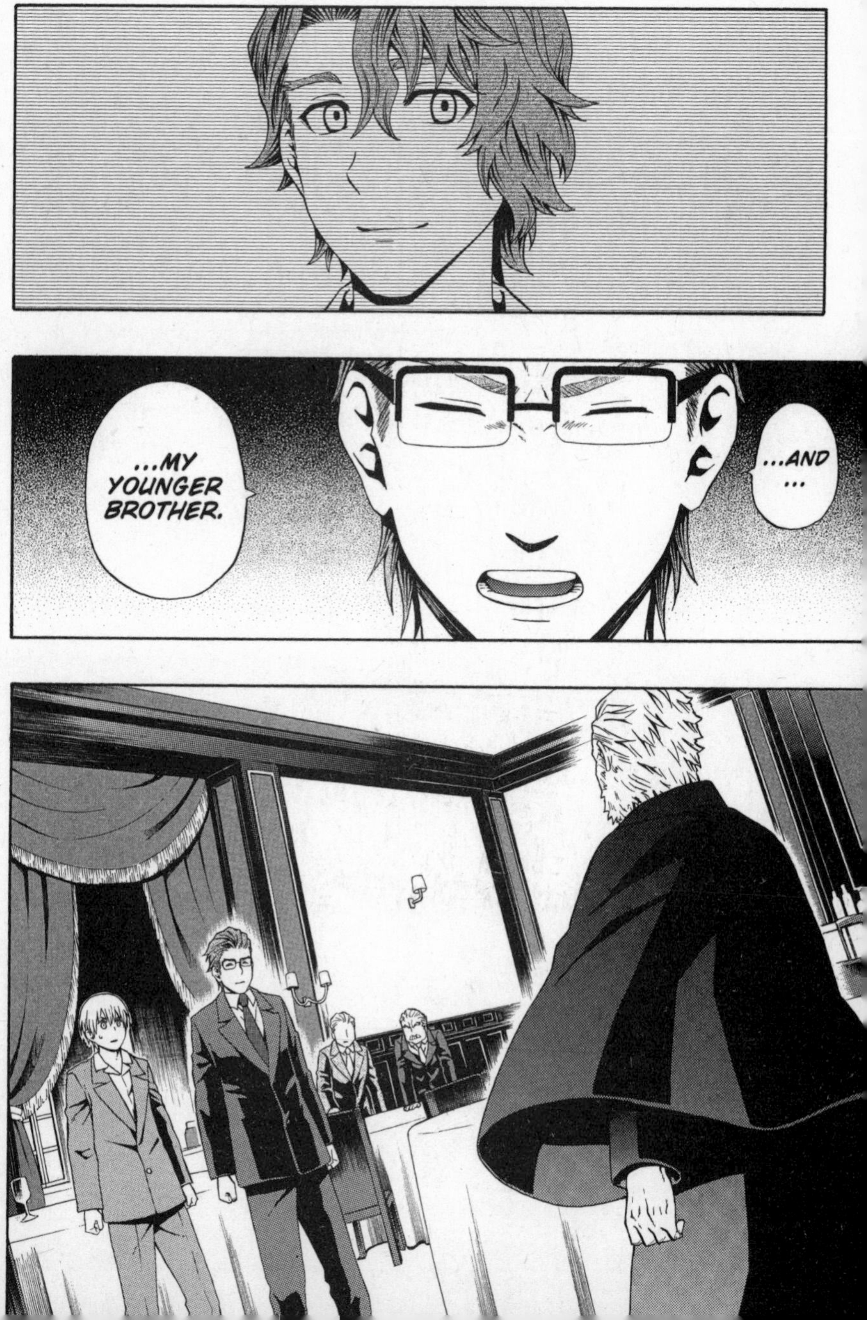
...AND ...
...MY YOUNGER BROTHER.

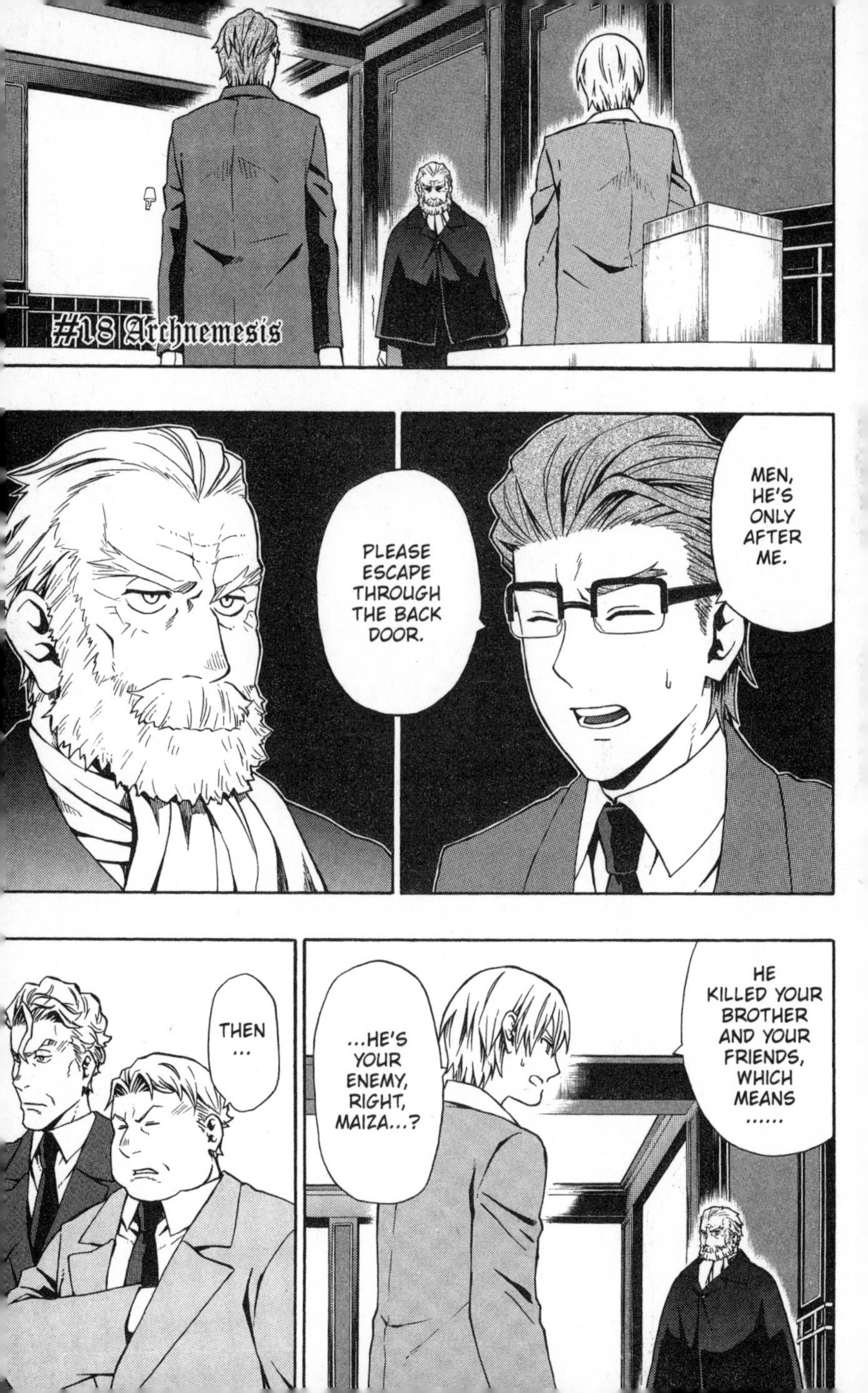
#18 Archnemesis
MEN, HE'S ONLY AFTER ME.
PLEASE ESCAPE THROUGH THE BACK DOOR.
HE KILLED YOUR BROTHER AND YOUR FRIENDS, WHICH MEANS ......
...HE'S YOUR ENEMY, RIGHT, MAIZA...?
THEN ...

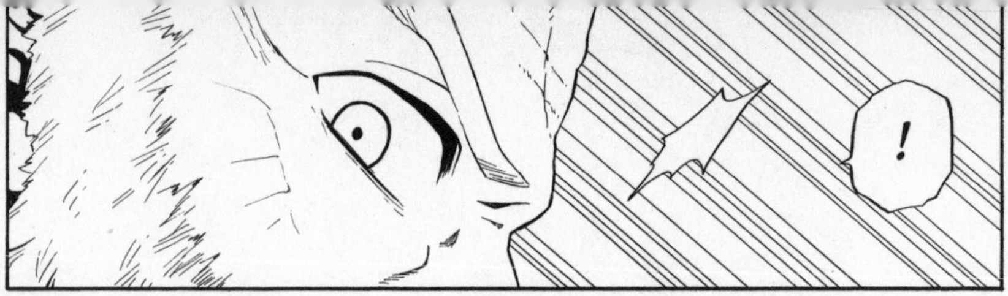
!

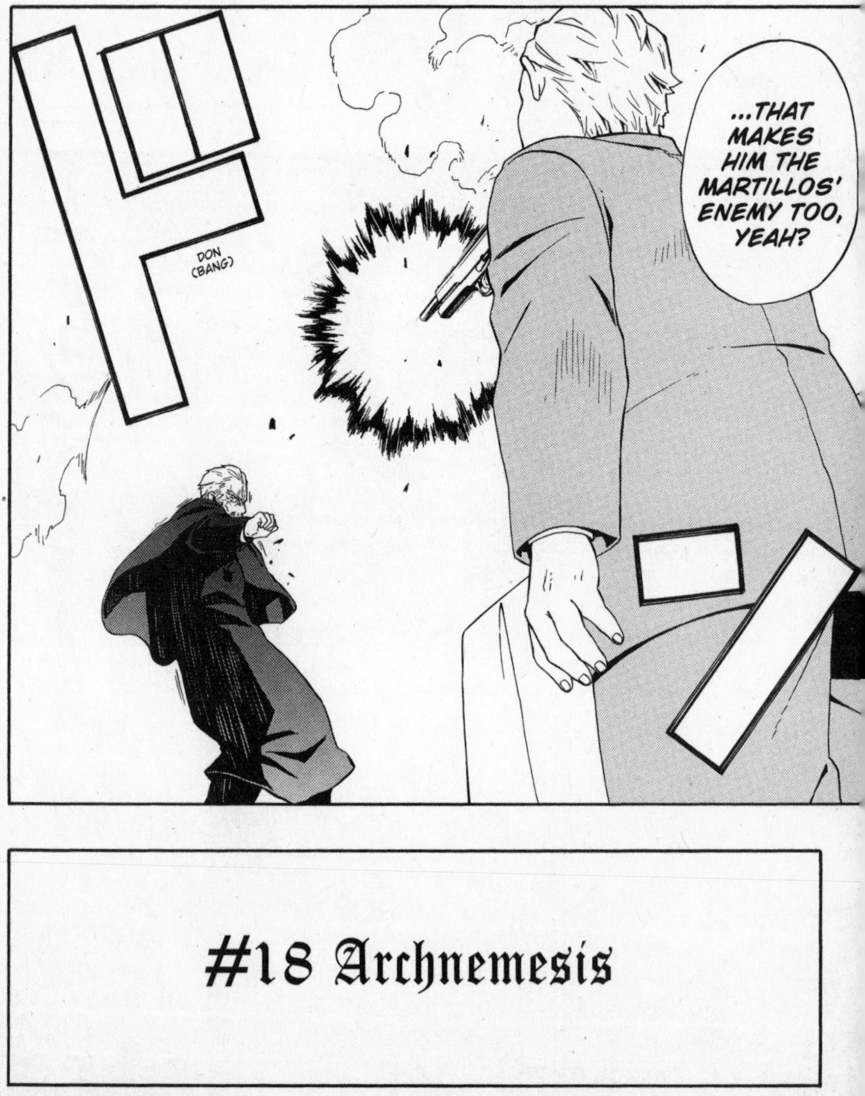
...THAT MAKES HIM THE MARTILLOS' ENEMY TOO, YEAH?
DON (BANG)

#18 Archnemesis

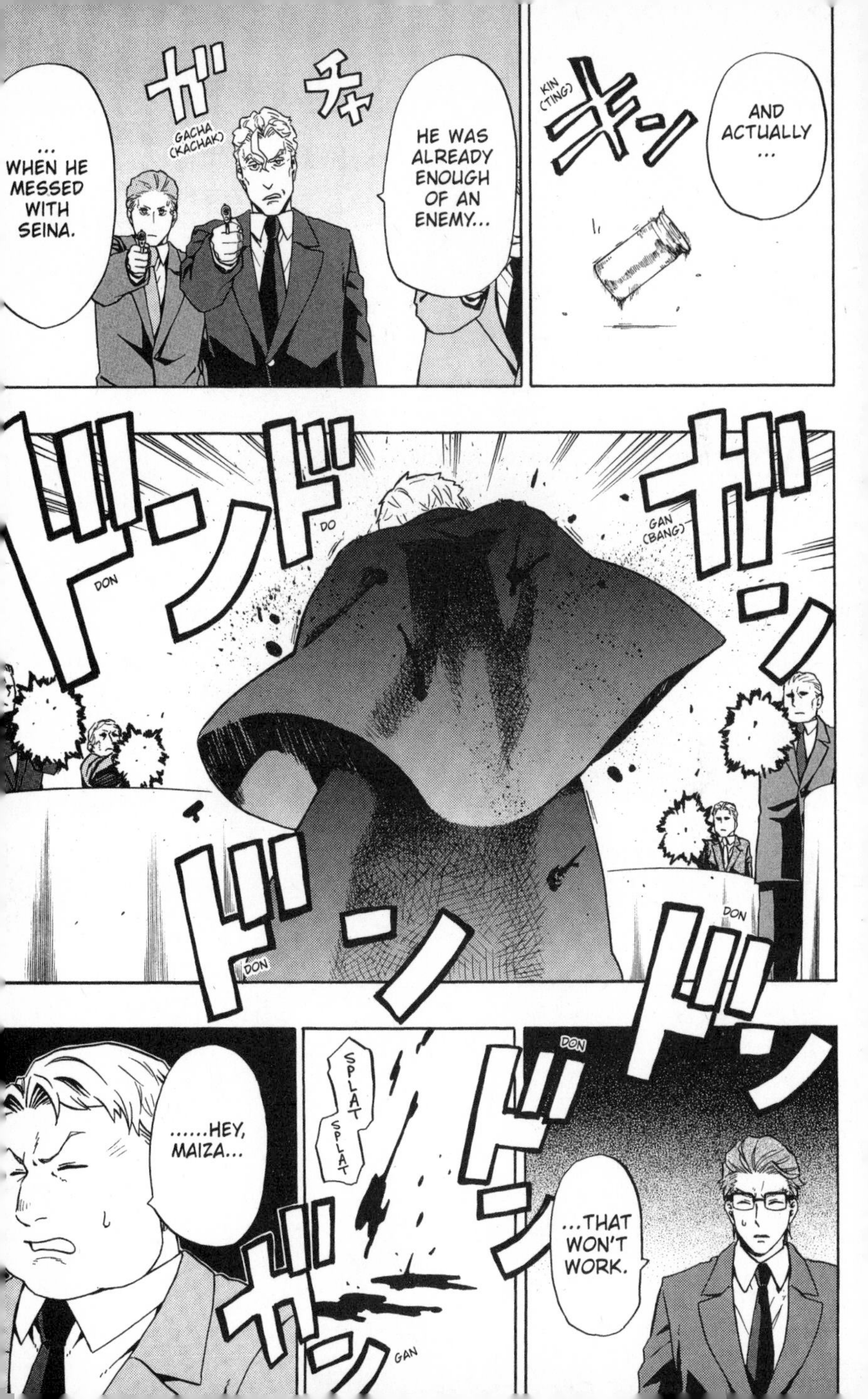
KIN (TING)
AND ACTUALLY ...
HE WAS ALREADY ENOUGH OF AN ENEMY...
GACHA (KACHAK)
... WHEN HE MESSED WITH SEINA.
GAN (BANG)
DO
DON
DON
DON
DON
...THAT WON'T WORK.
SPLAT SPLAT
GAN
......HEY, MAIZA...

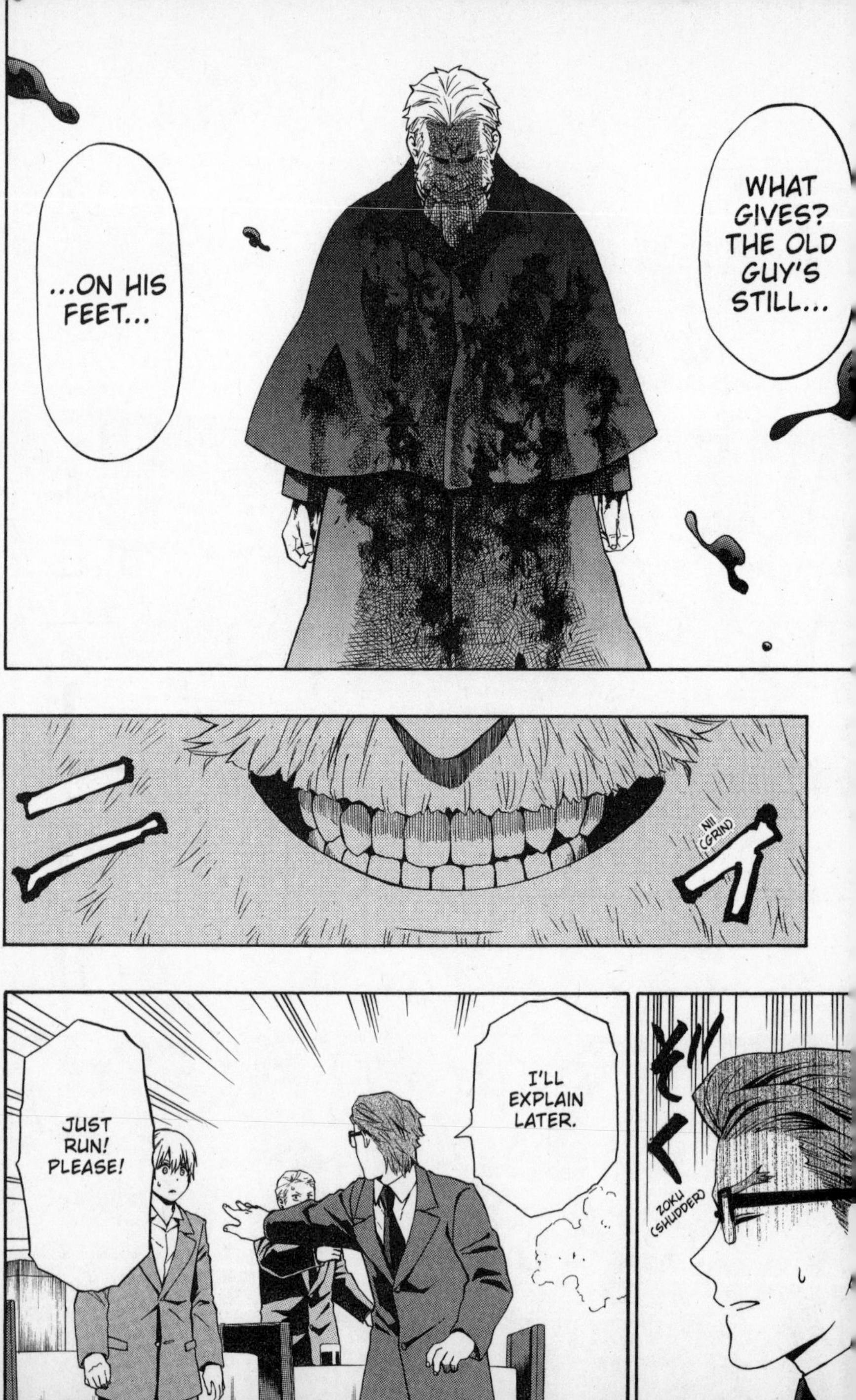
WHAT GIVES? THE OLD GUY'S STILL...
...ON HIS FEET...
NII (GRIN)
ZOKU (SHUDDER)
I'LL EXPLAIN LATER.
JUST RUN! PLEASE!

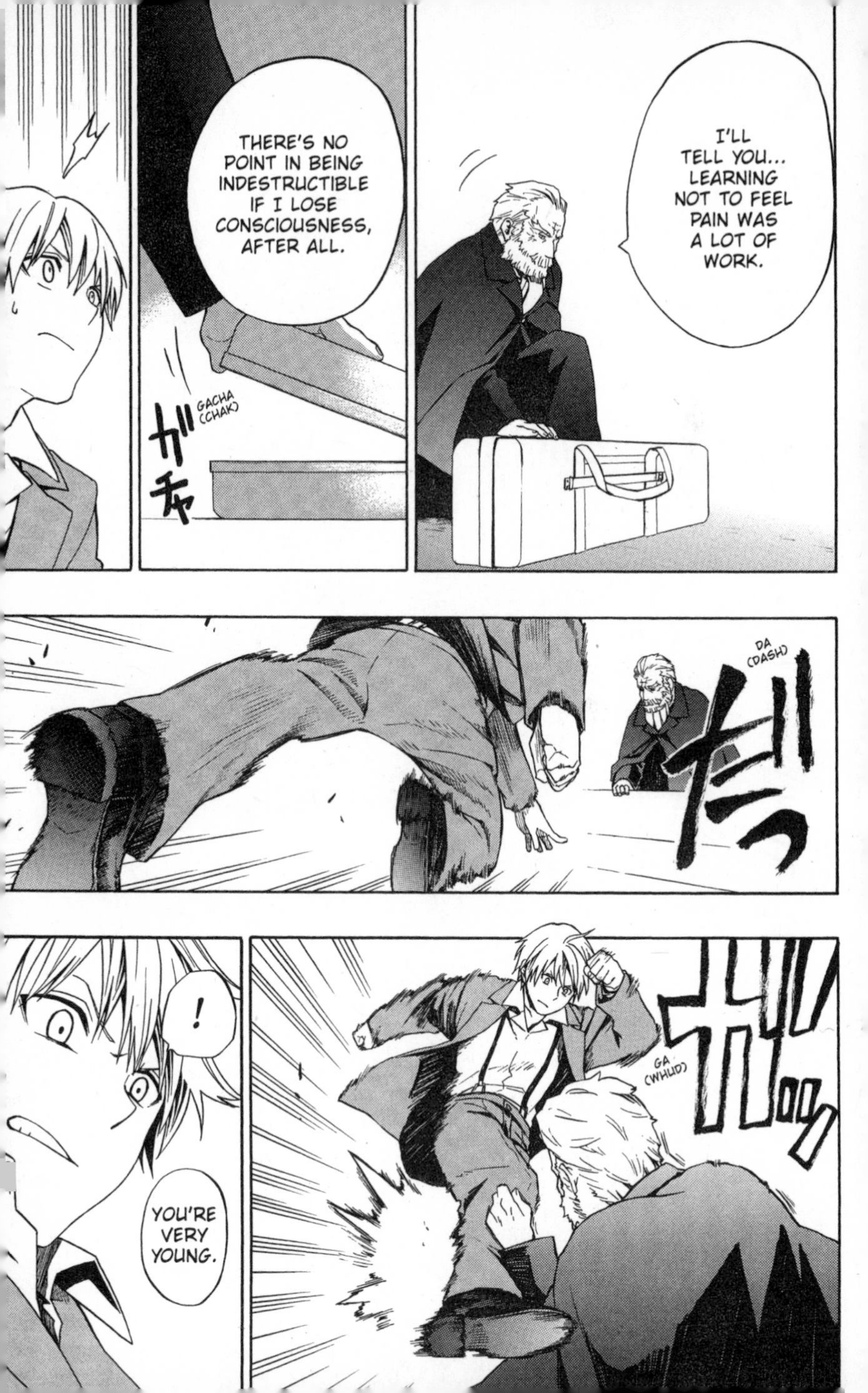
I'LL TELL YOU... LEARNING NOT TO FEEL PAIN WAS A LOT OF WORK.
THERE'S NO POINT IN BEING INDESTRUCTIBLE IF I LOSE CONSCIOUSNESS, AFTER ALL.
ガチャ
GACHA (CHAK)
ダッ
DA (DASH)
ガッ
GA (WHUD)
!
YOU'RE VERY YOUNG.

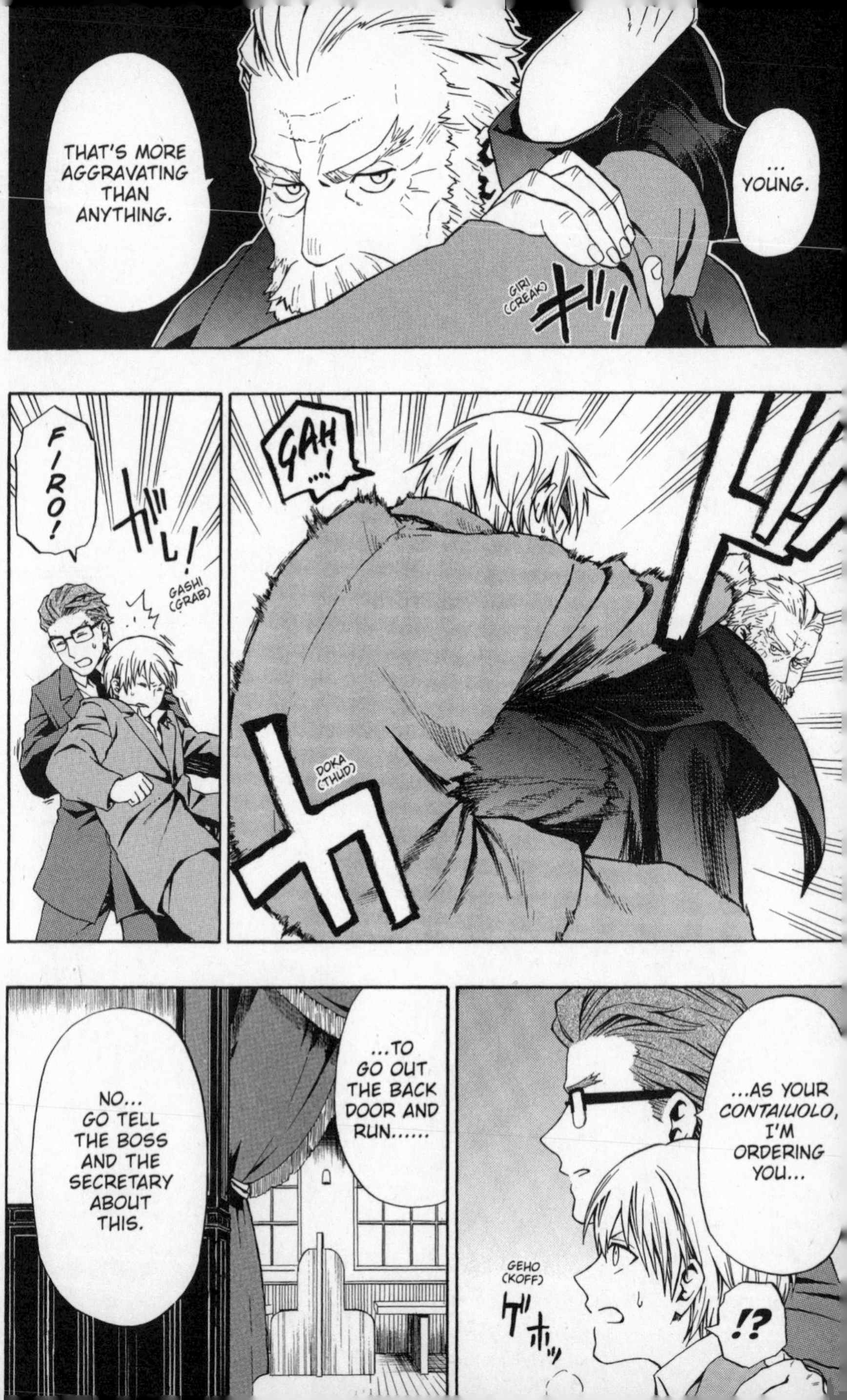
...
YOUNG.
THAT'S MORE AGGRAVATING THAN ANYTHING.
GIRI (CREAK)
GAH...!
DOKA (THUD)
FIRO!
GASHI (GRAB)
...AS YOUR CONTAIUOLO, I'M ORDERING YOU...
!?
GEHO (KOFF)
...TO GO OUT THE BACK DOOR AND RUN......
NO... GO TELL THE BOSS AND THE SECRETARY ABOUT THIS.

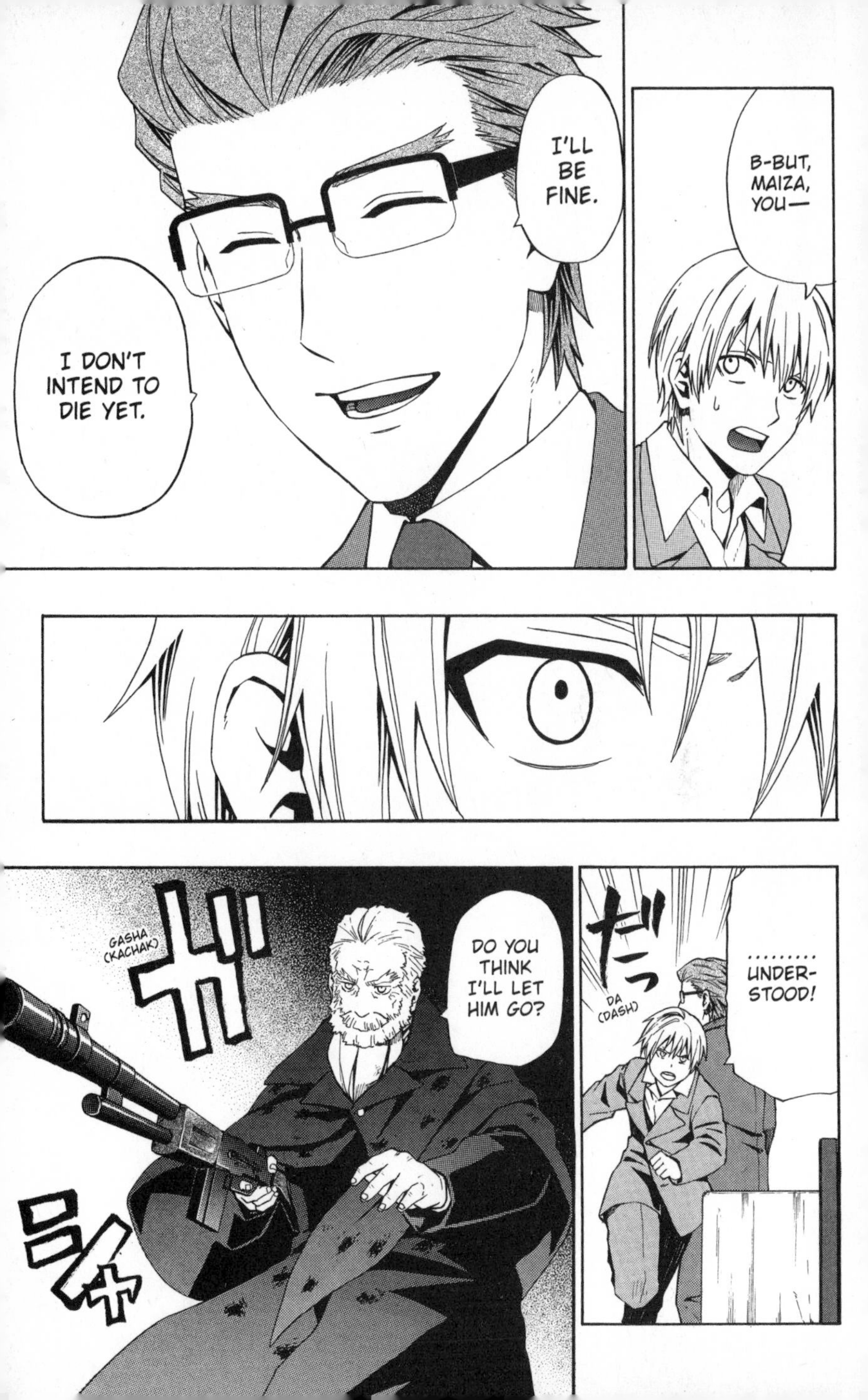
B-BUT, MAIZA, YOU—
I'LL BE FINE.
I DON'T INTEND TO DIE YET.
....
UNDER-STOOD!
だっ
DA (DASH)
DO YOU THINK I'LL LET HIM GO?
GASHA (KACHAK)

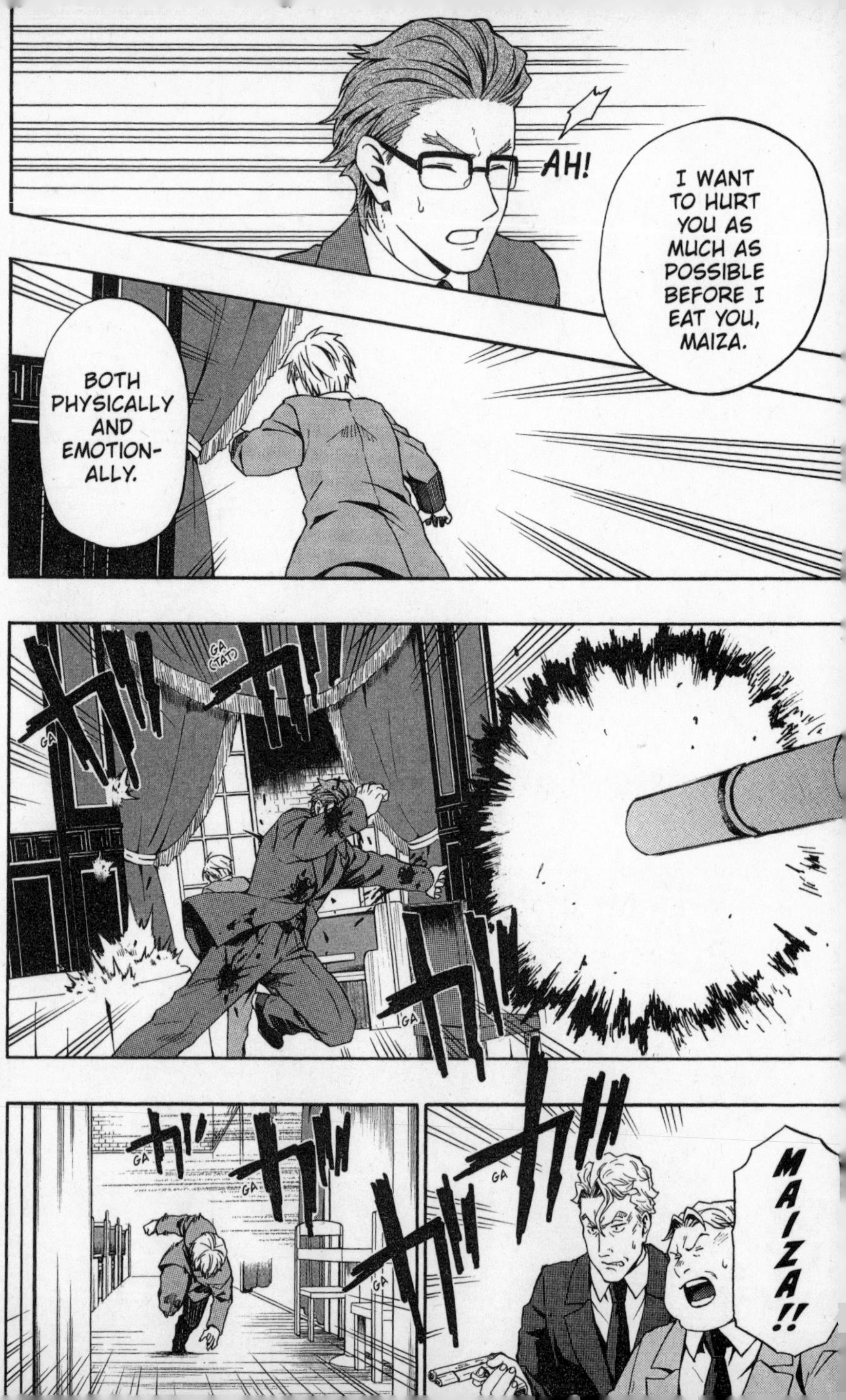
I WANT TO HURT YOU AS MUCH AS POSSIBLE BEFORE I EAT YOU, MAIZA.
AH!
BOTH PHYSICALLY AND EMOTION-ALLY.
GA (TAT)
GA
GA
MAIZA!!
GA
GA
GA
GA

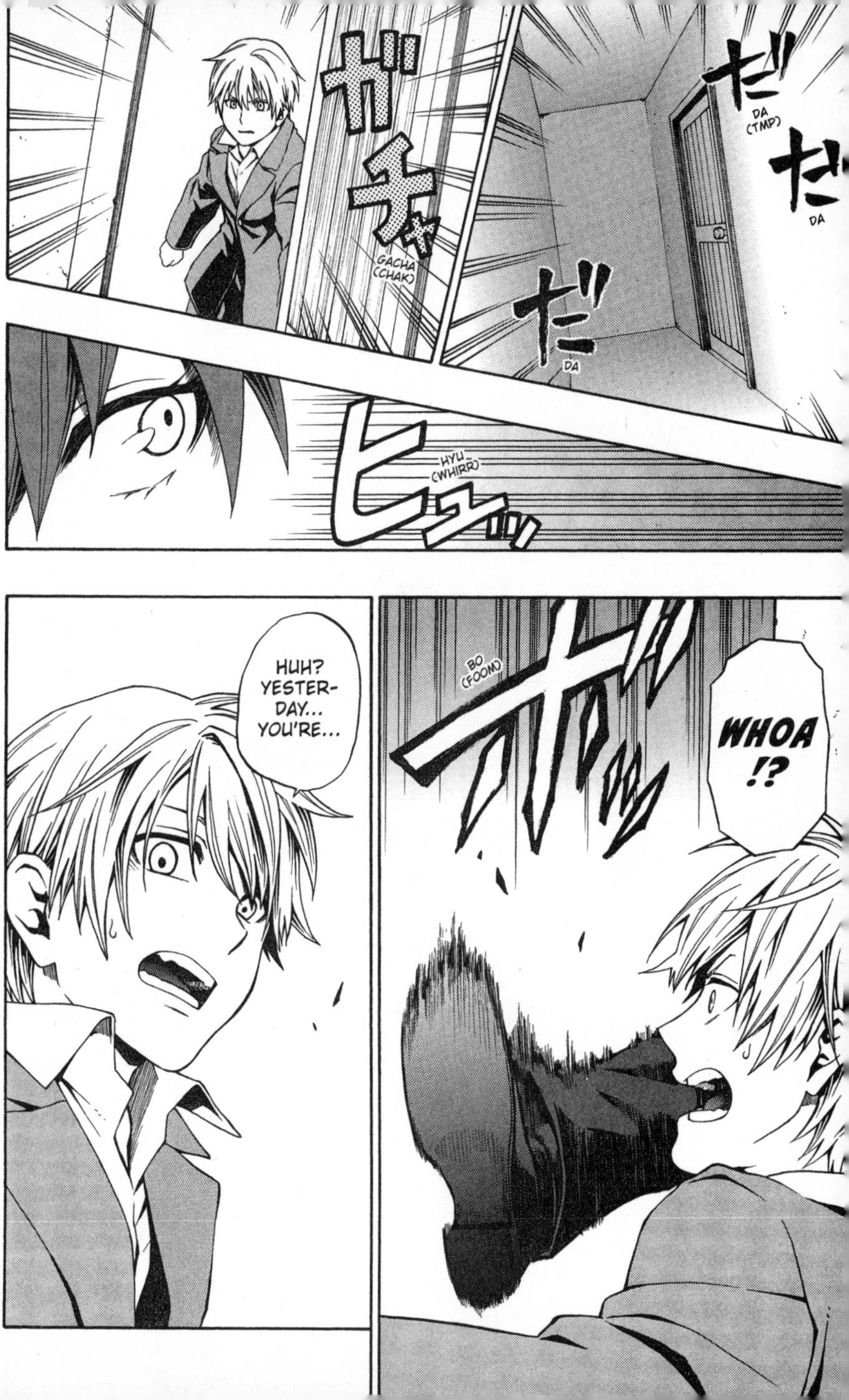
DA (TMP)
DA
DA
GACHA (CHAK)
HYU (WHIRR)
BO (FOOM)
WHOA !?
HUH? YESTER-DAY... YOU'RE...

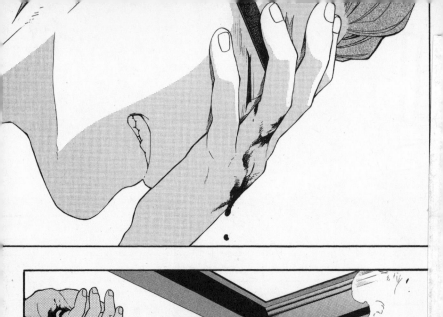

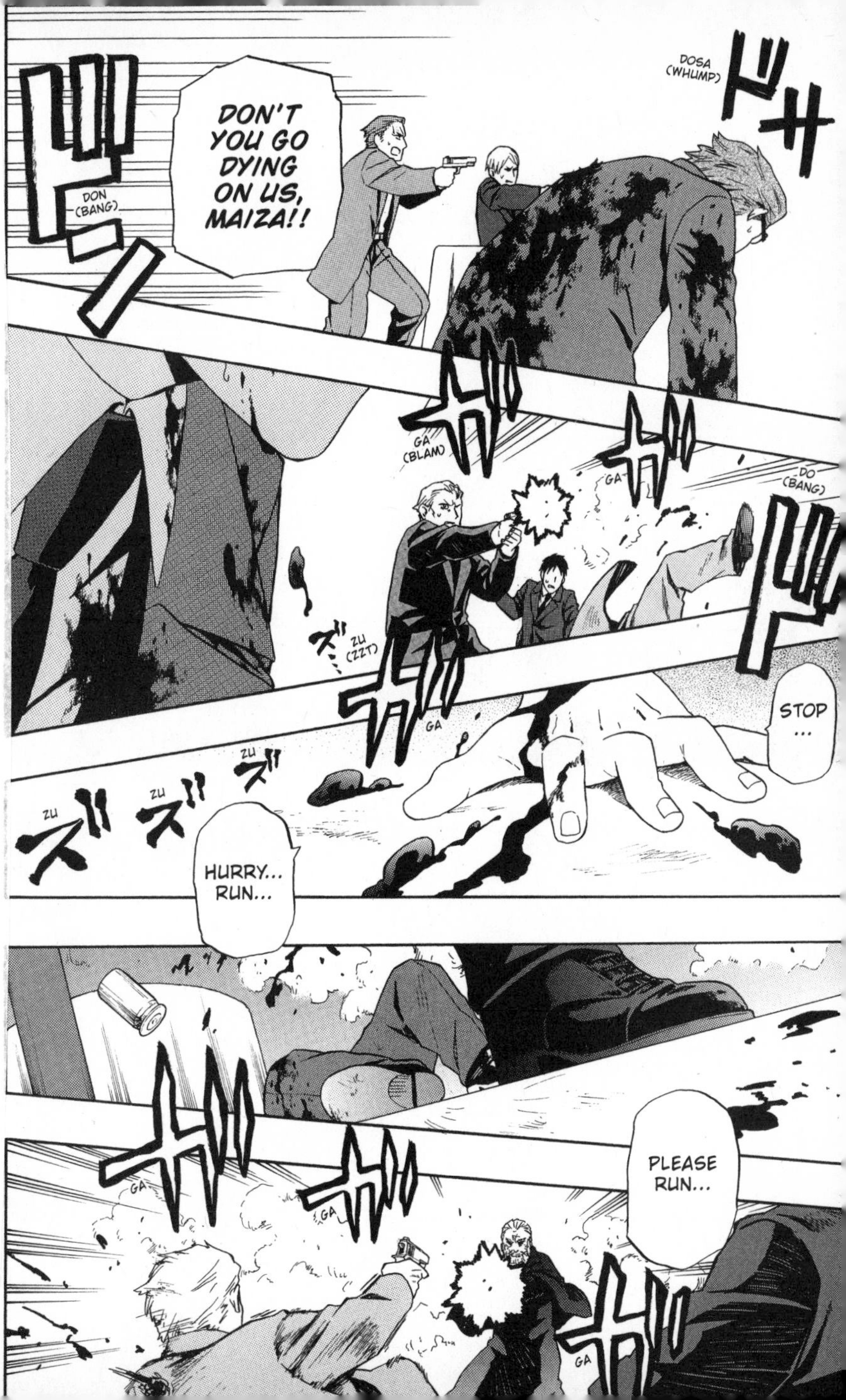
DOSA (WHUMP)
DON'T YOU GO DYING ON US, MAIZA!!
DON (BANG)
DO (BANG)
GA
GA (BLAM)
ZU (ZZT)
GA
STOP...
ZU
ZU
ZU
HURRY... RUN...
PLEASE RUN...
GA
GA
GA

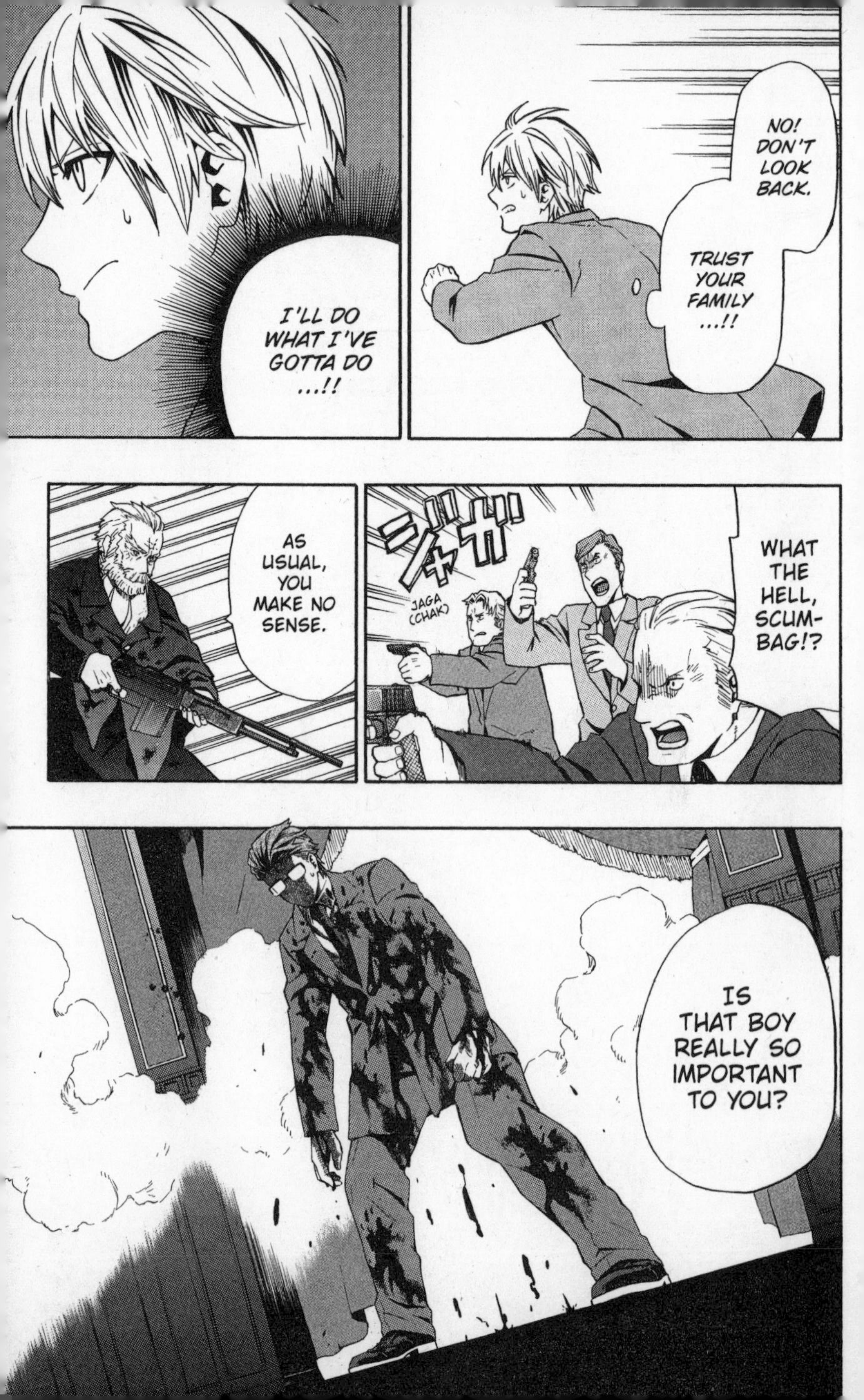

NO! DON'T LOOK BACK.
TRUST YOUR FAMILY ...!!
I'LL DO WHAT I'VE GOTTA DO ...!!
WHAT THE HELL, SCUM-BAG!?
ジャガ
JAGA (CHAK)
AS USUAL, YOU MAKE NO SENSE.
IS THAT BOY REALLY SO IMPORTANT TO YOU?

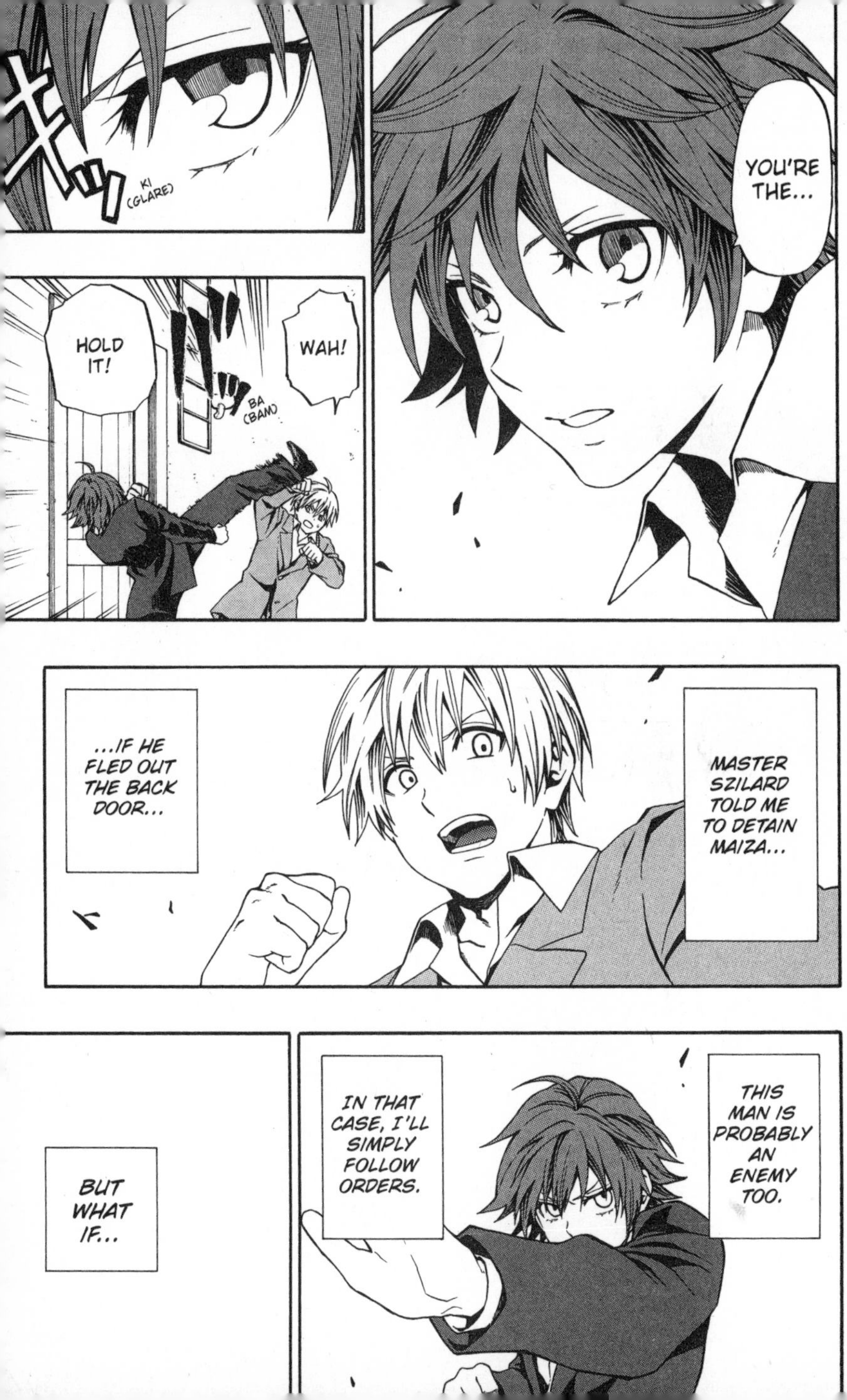
YOU'RE THE...
KI (GLARE)
WAH!
BA (BAM)
HOLD IT!
MASTER SZILARD TOLD ME TO DETAIN MAIZA...
...IF HE FLED OUT THE BACK DOOR...
THIS MAN IS PROBABLY AN ENEMY TOO.
IN THAT CASE, I'LL SIMPLY FOLLOW ORDERS.
BUT WHAT IF...

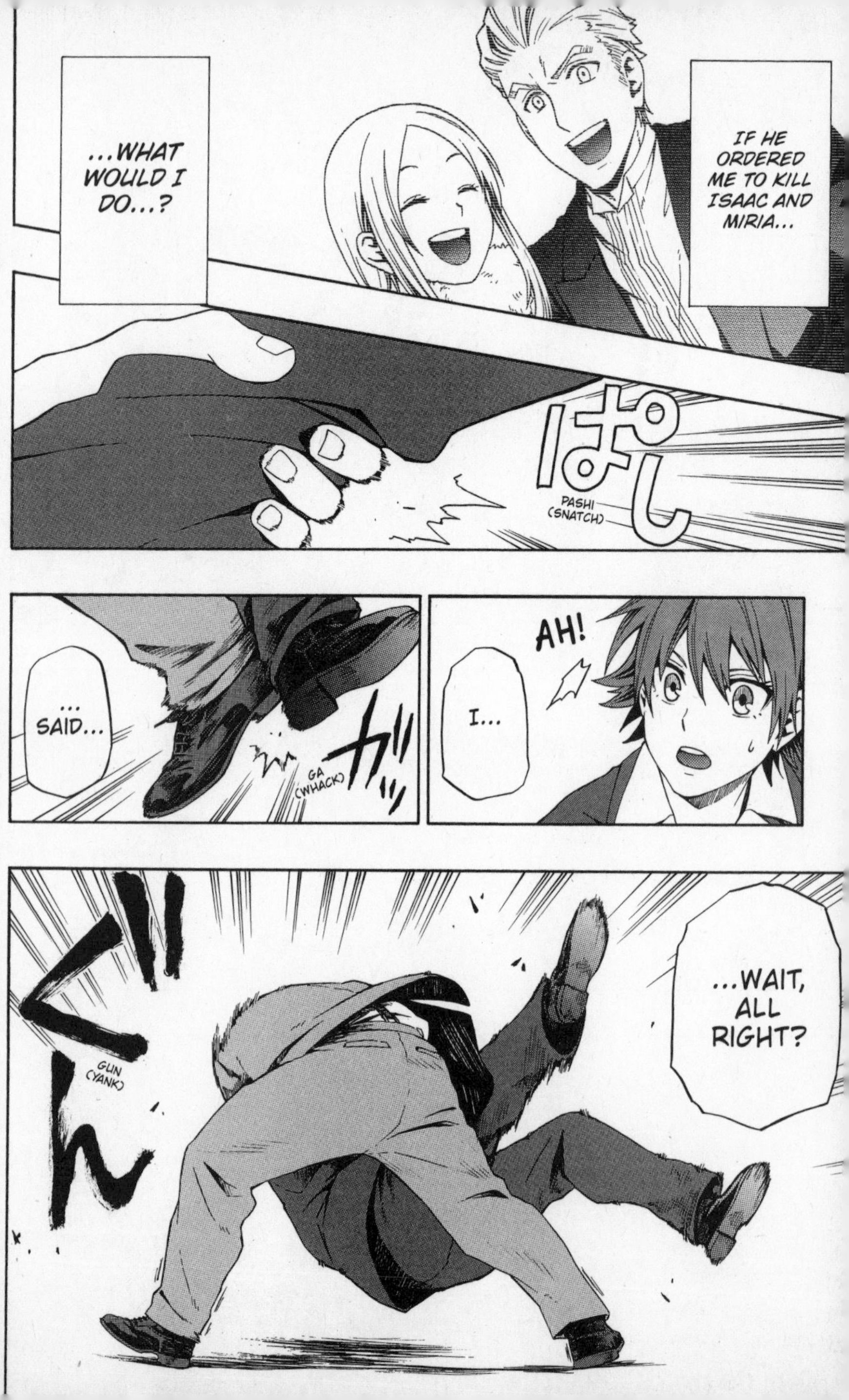
IF HE ORDERED ME TO KILL ISAAC AND MIRIA...
...WHAT WOULD I DO...?
ぱし
PASHI (SNATCH)
AH!
I...
... SAID...
ガッ
GA (WHACK)
...WAIT, ALL RIGHT?
ぐん
GUN (YANK)

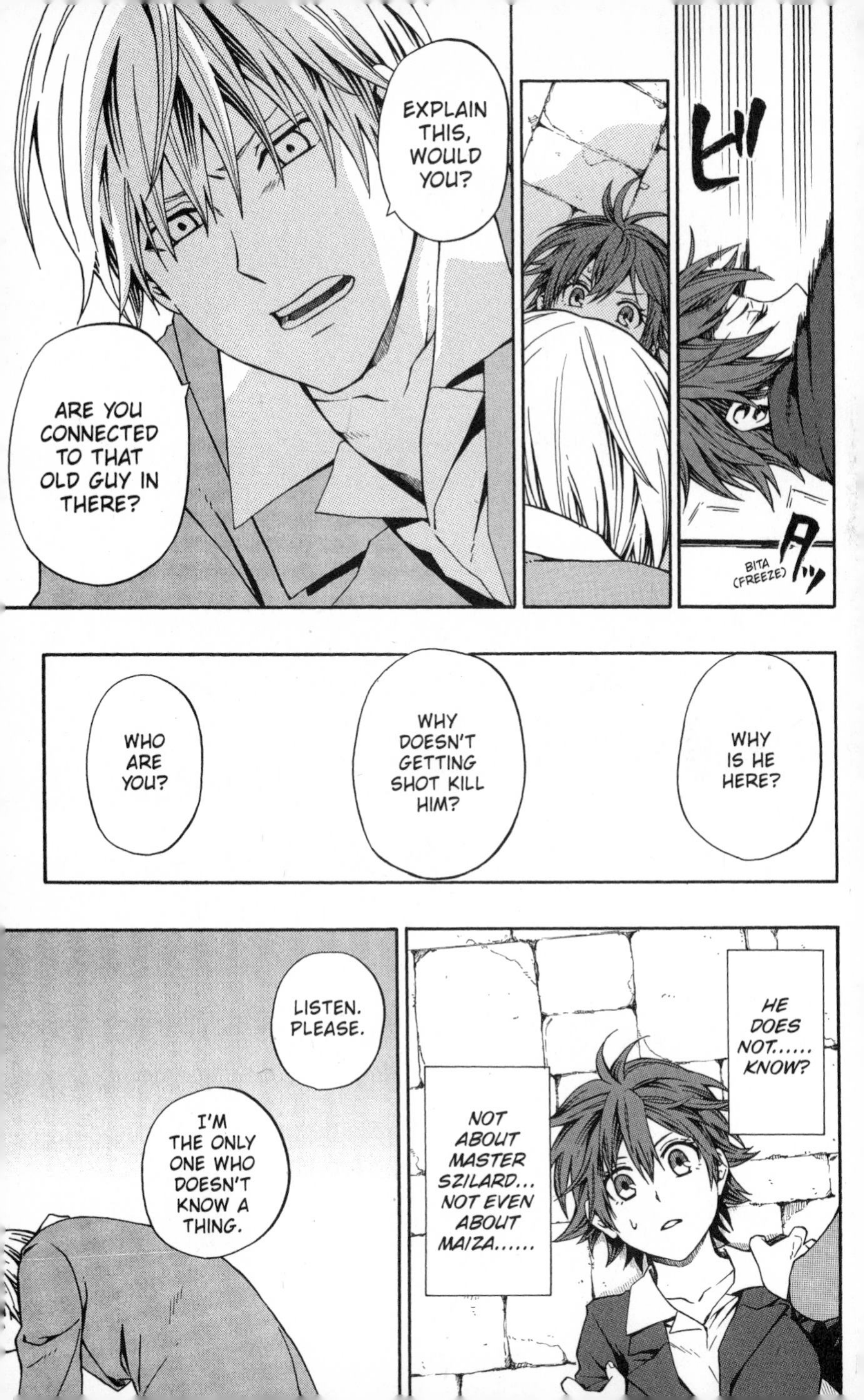
BITA (FREEZE)
EXPLAIN THIS, WOULD YOU?
ARE YOU CONNECTED TO THAT OLD GUY IN THERE?
WHY IS HE HERE?
WHY DOESN'T GETTING SHOT KILL HIM?
WHO ARE YOU?
HE DOES NOT...... KNOW?
NOT ABOUT MASTER SZILARD... NOT EVEN ABOUT MAIZA......
LISTEN. PLEASE.
I'M THE ONLY ONE WHO DOESN'T KNOW A THING.

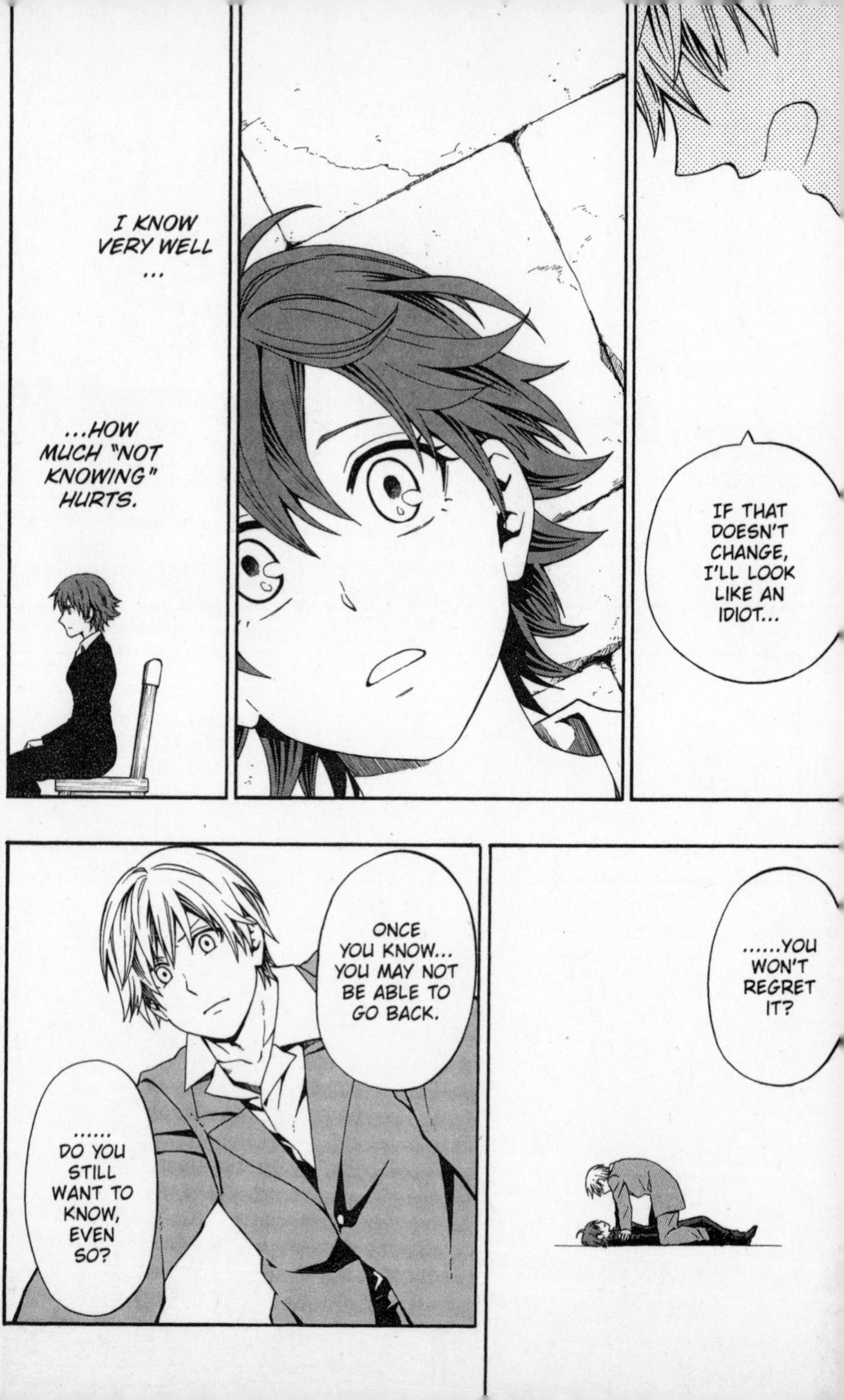
IF THAT DOESN'T CHANGE, I'LL LOOK LIKE AN IDIOT...
I KNOW VERY WELL ...
...HOW MUCH "NOT KNOWING" HURTS.
......YOU WON'T REGRET IT?
ONCE YOU KNOW... YOU MAY NOT BE ABLE TO GO BACK.
...... DO YOU STILL WANT TO KNOW, EVEN SO?

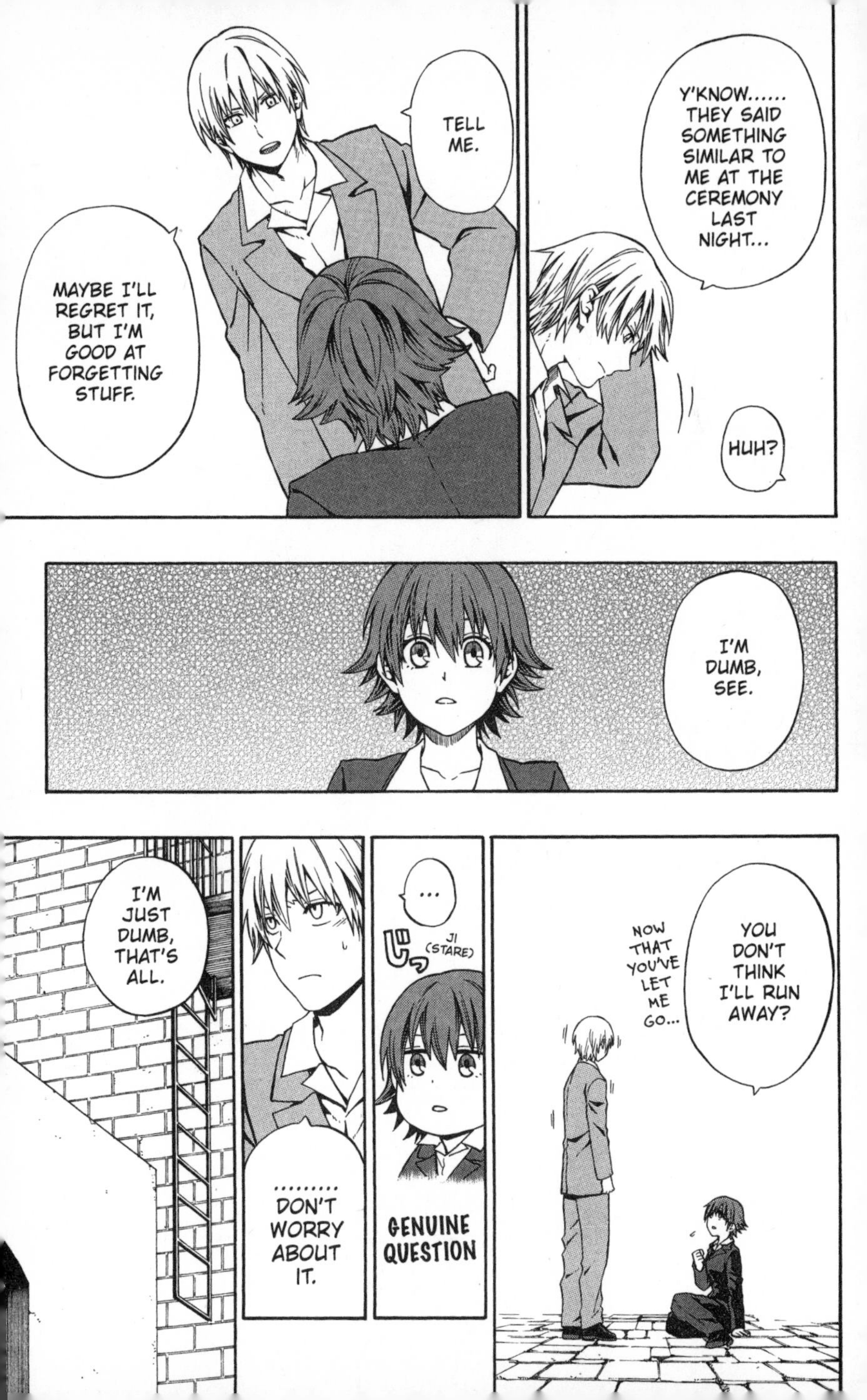
Y'KNOW...... THEY SAID SOMETHING SIMILAR TO ME AT THE CEREMONY LAST NIGHT...
HUH?
TELL ME.
MAYBE I'LL REGRET IT, BUT I'M GOOD AT FORGETTING STUFF.
I'M DUMB, SEE.
YOU DON'T THINK I'LL RUN AWAY?
NOW THAT YOU'VE LET ME GO...
...
JI (STARE)
GENUINE QUESTION
.... DON'T WORRY ABOUT IT.
I'M JUST DUMB, THAT'S ALL.

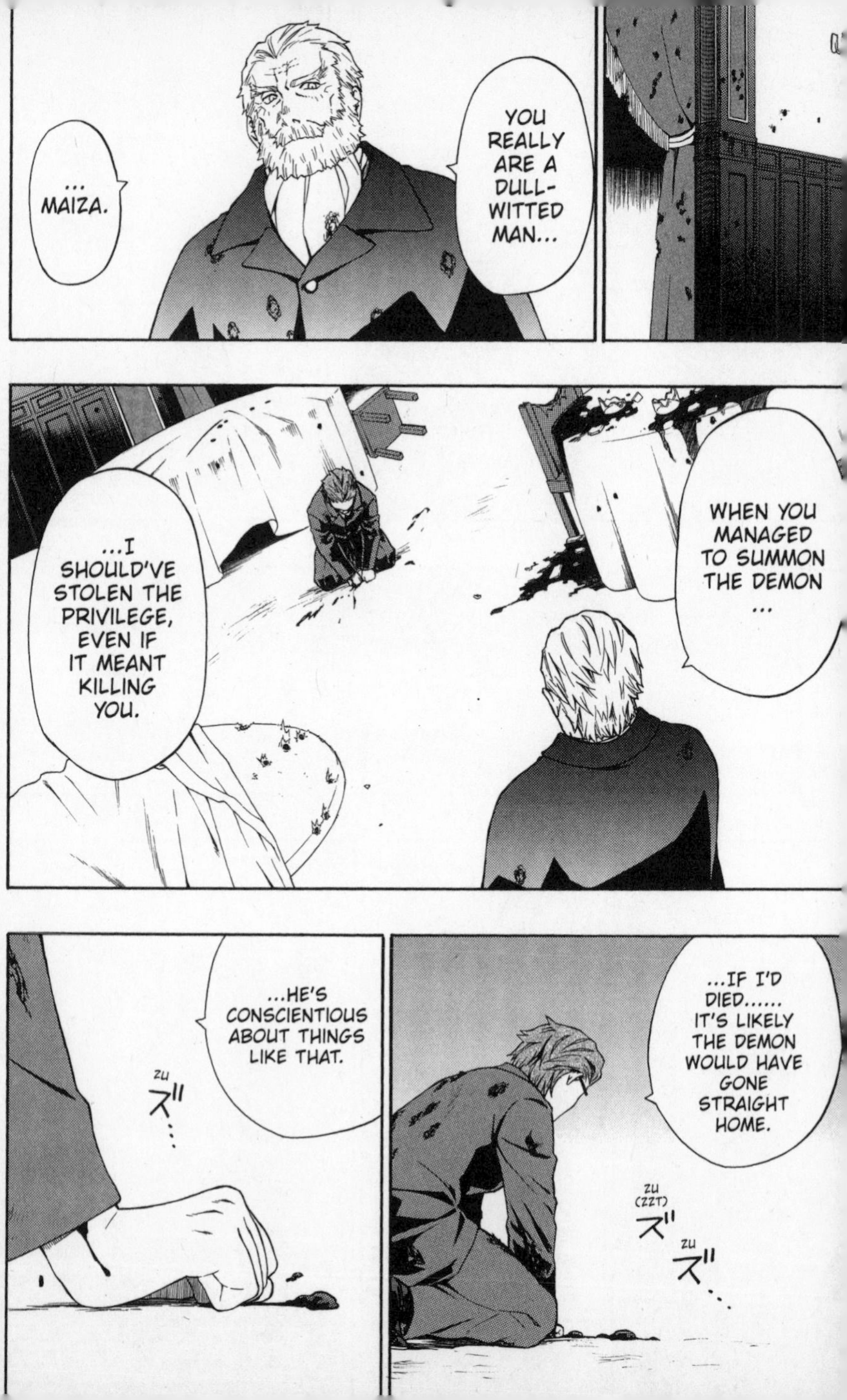
YOU REALLY ARE A DULL-WITTED MAN...
... MAIZA.
WHEN YOU MANAGED TO SUMMON THE DEMON ...
...I SHOULD'VE STOLEN THE PRIVILEGE, EVEN IF IT MEANT KILLING YOU.
...IF I'D DIED...... IT'S LIKELY THE DEMON WOULD HAVE GONE STRAIGHT HOME.
ZU (ZZT) ズ
ZU ズ...
...HE'S CONSCIENTIOUS ABOUT THINGS LIKE THAT.
ZU ズ...

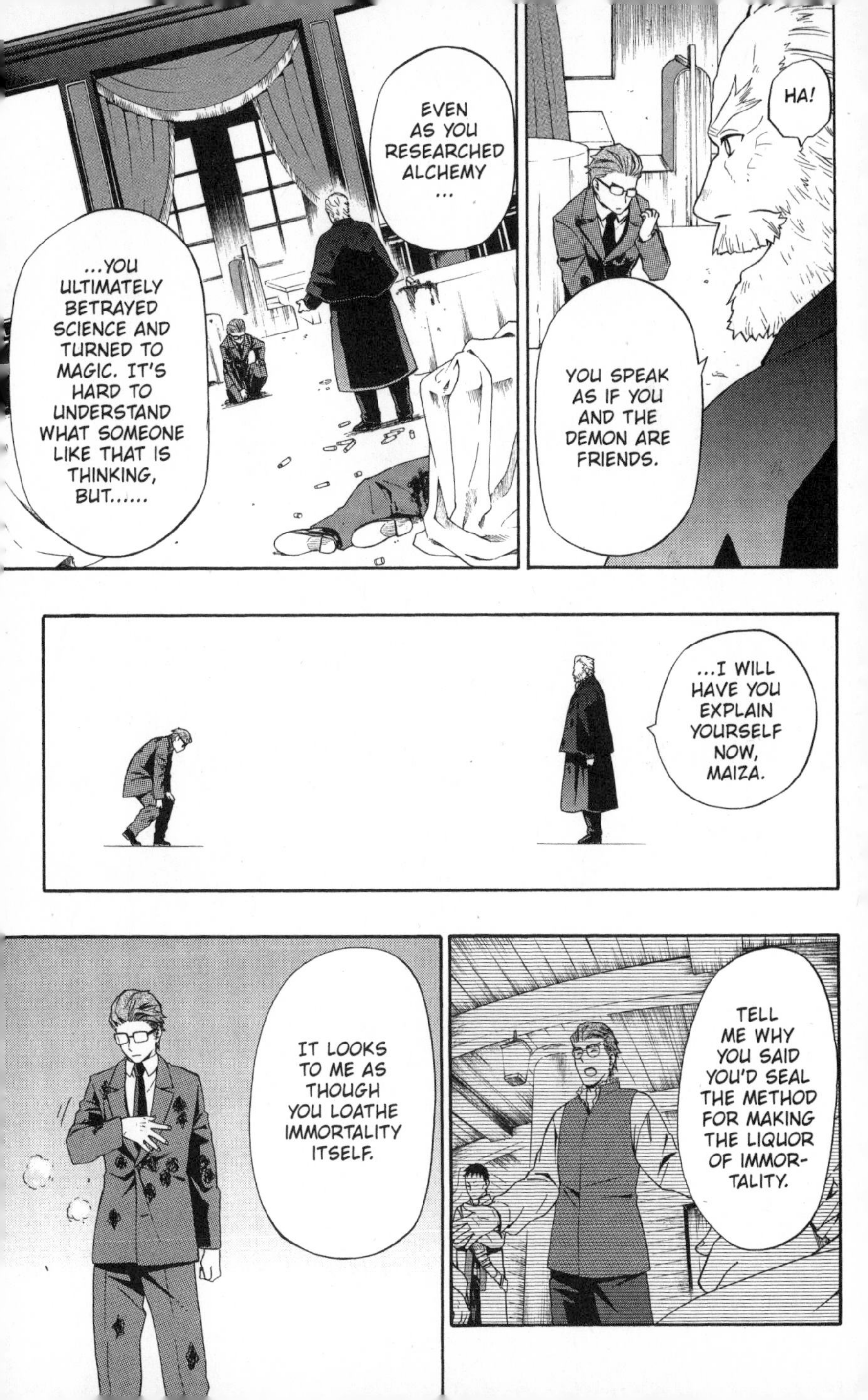
HA!
YOU SPEAK AS IF YOU AND THE DEMON ARE FRIENDS.
EVEN AS YOU RESEARCHED ALCHEMY ...
...YOU ULTIMATELY BETRAYED SCIENCE AND TURNED TO MAGIC. IT'S HARD TO UNDERSTAND WHAT SOMEONE LIKE THAT IS THINKING, BUT......
...I WILL HAVE YOU EXPLAIN YOURSELF NOW, MAIZA.
TELL ME WHY YOU SAID YOU'D SEAL THE METHOD FOR MAKING THE LIQUOR OF IMMORTALITY.
IT LOOKS TO ME AS THOUGH YOU LOATHE IMMORTALITY ITSELF.

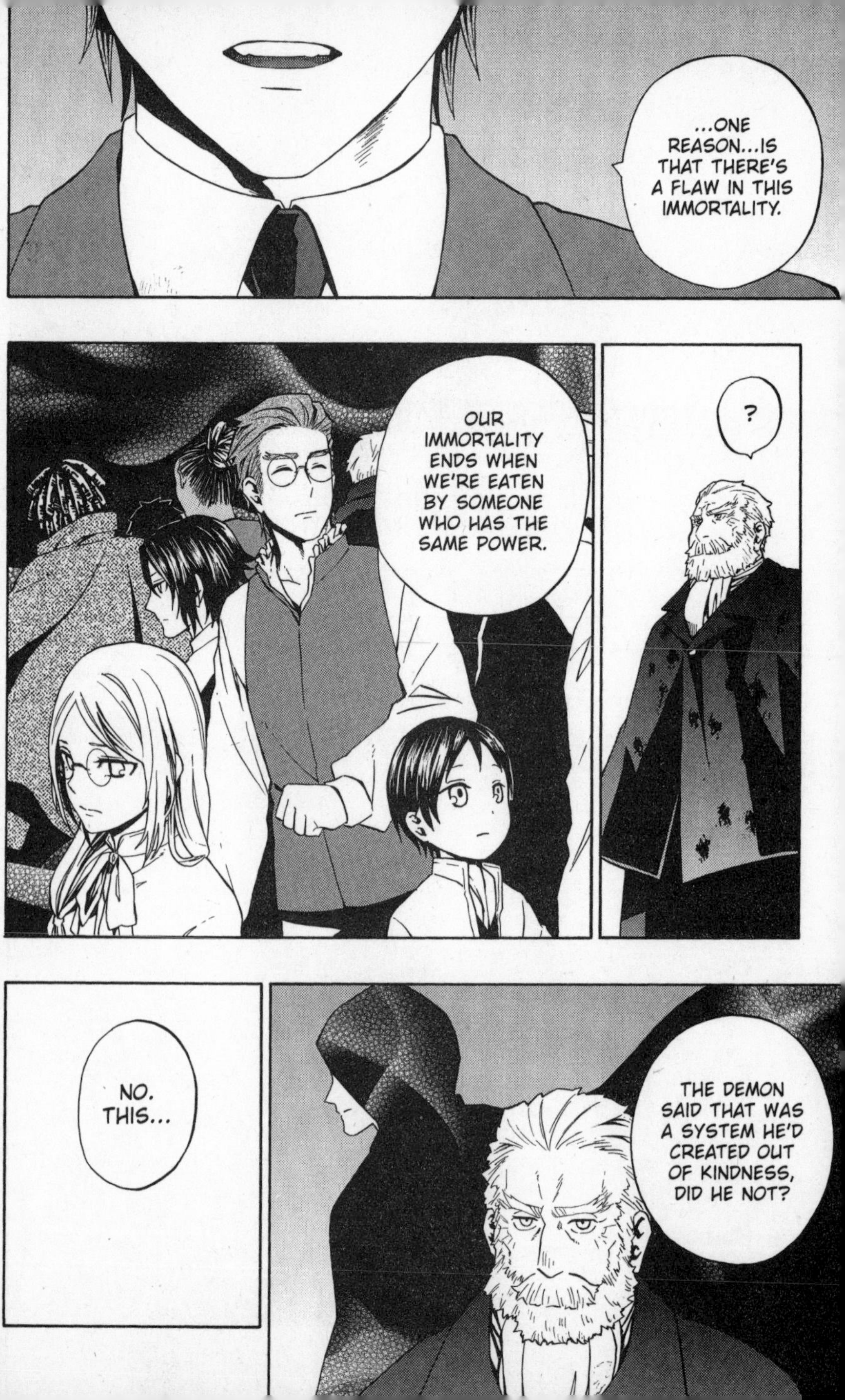
...ONE REASON...IS THAT THERE'S A FLAW IN THIS IMMORTALITY.
?
OUR IMMORTALITY ENDS WHEN WE'RE EATEN BY SOMEONE WHO HAS THE SAME POWER.
THE DEMON SAID THAT WAS A SYSTEM HE'D CREATED OUT OF KINDNESS, DID HE NOT?
NO. THIS...

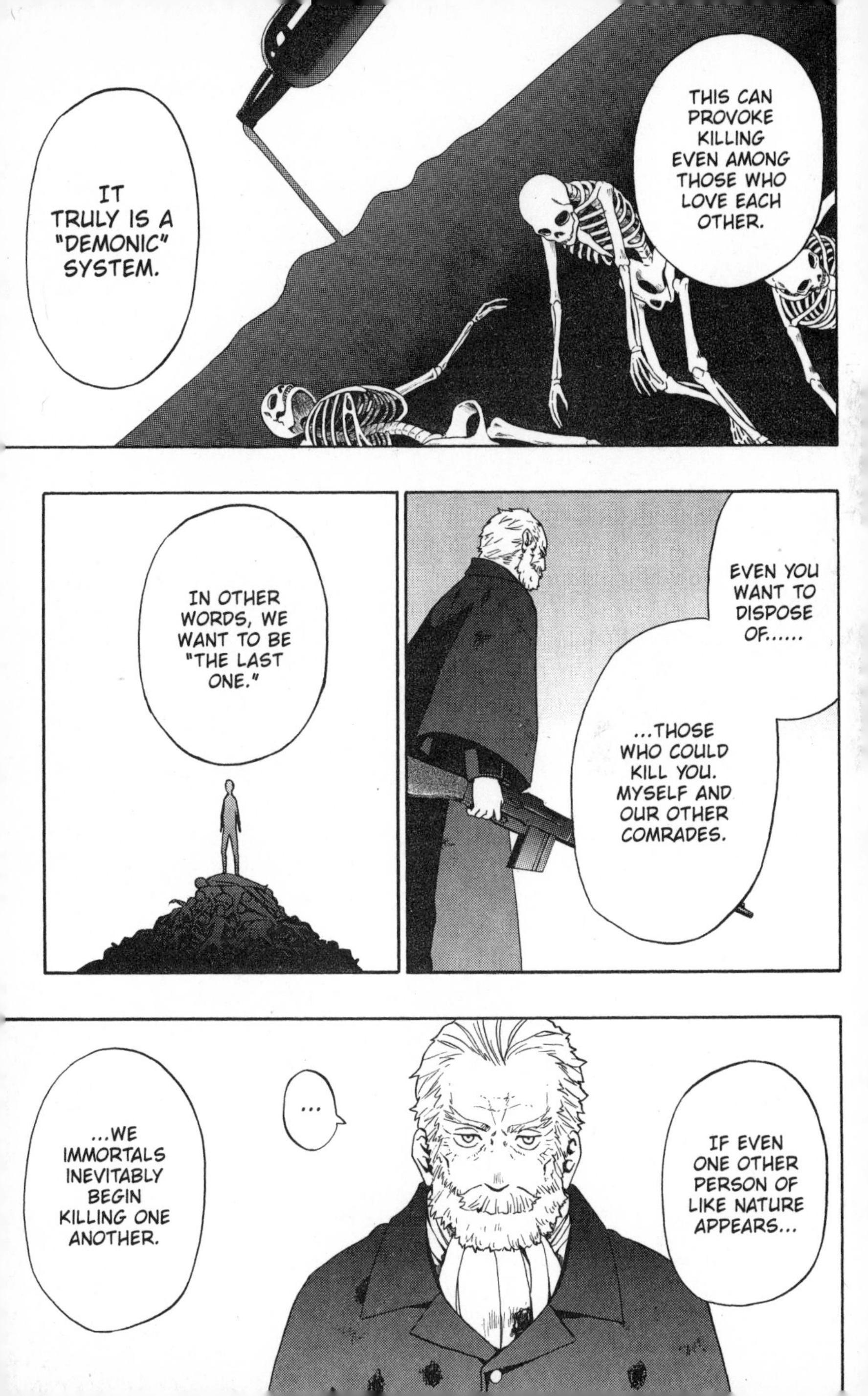
THIS CAN PROVOKE KILLING EVEN AMONG THOSE WHO LOVE EACH OTHER.
IT TRULY IS A "DEMONIC" SYSTEM.
EVEN YOU WANT TO DISPOSE OF......
...THOSE WHO COULD KILL YOU. MYSELF AND OUR OTHER COMRADES.
IN OTHER WORDS, WE WANT TO BE "THE LAST ONE."
IF EVEN ONE OTHER PERSON OF LIKE NATURE APPEARS...
...
...WE IMMORTALS INEVITABLY BEGIN KILLING ONE ANOTHER.

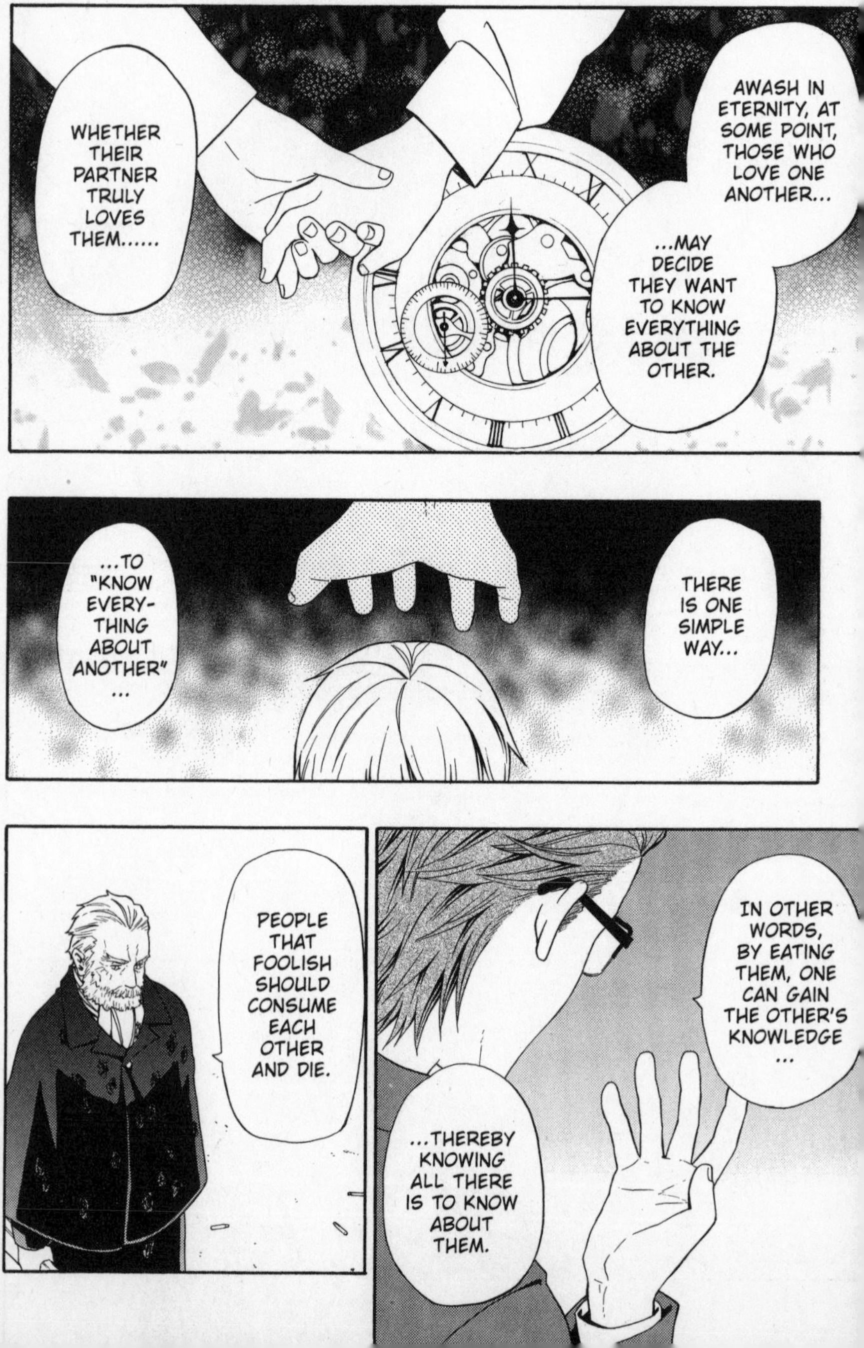
AWASH IN ETERNITY, AT SOME POINT, THOSE WHO LOVE ONE ANOTHER...
...MAY DECIDE THEY WANT TO KNOW EVERYTHING ABOUT THE OTHER.
WHETHER THEIR PARTNER TRULY LOVES THEM......
THERE IS ONE SIMPLE WAY...
...TO "KNOW EVERY-THING ABOUT ANOTHER"...
IN OTHER WORDS, BY EATING THEM, ONE CAN GAIN THE OTHER'S KNOWLEDGE...
...THEREBY KNOWING ALL THERE IS TO KNOW ABOUT THEM.
PEOPLE THAT FOOLISH SHOULD CONSUME EACH OTHER AND DIE.

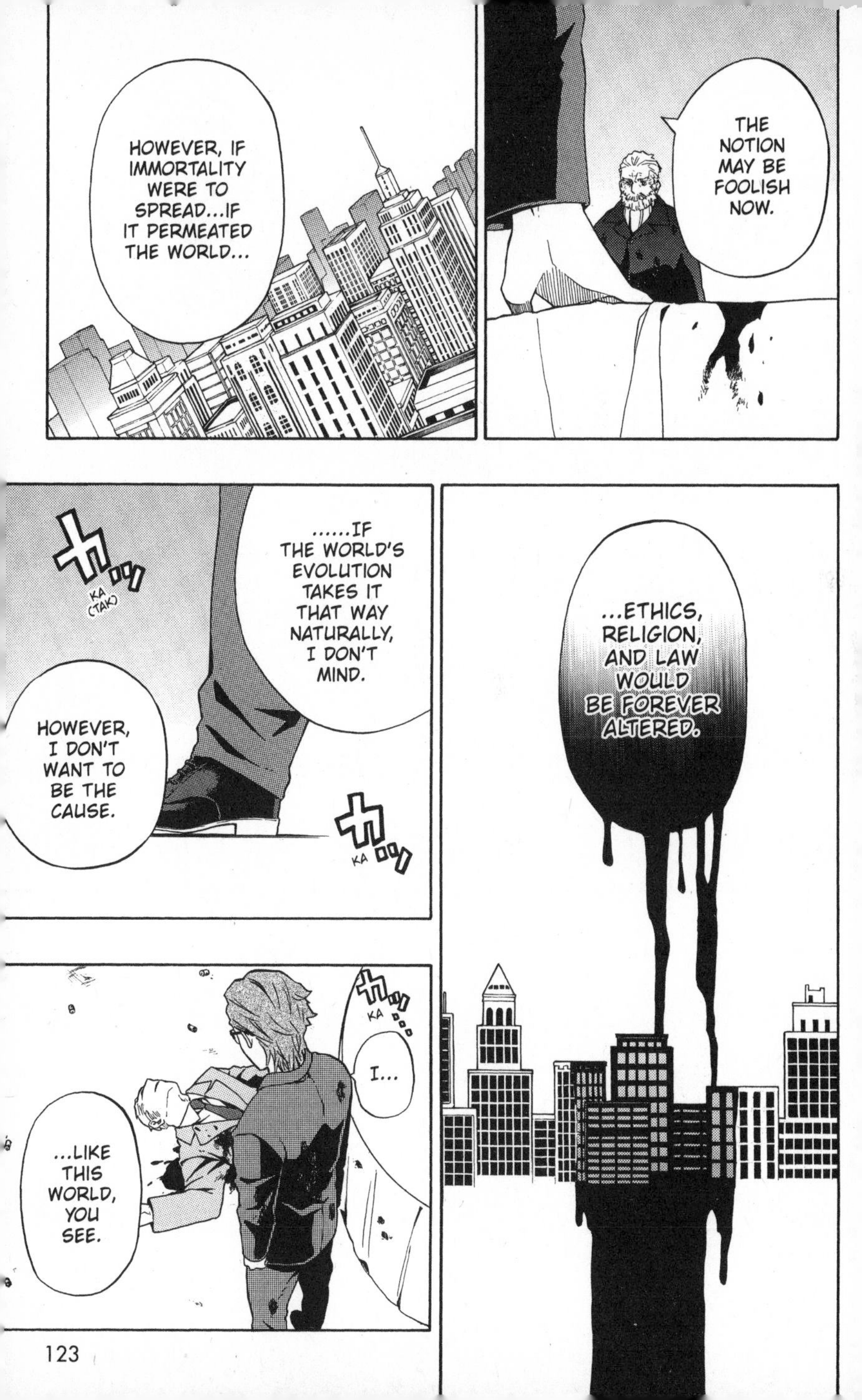
THE NOTION MAY BE FOOLISH NOW.
HOWEVER, IF IMMORTALITY WERE TO SPREAD...IF IT PERMEATED THE WORLD...
...ETHICS, RELIGION, AND LAW WOULD BE FOREVER ALTERED.
......IF THE WORLD'S EVOLUTION TAKES IT THAT WAY NATURALLY, I DON'T MIND.
KA (TAK)
HOWEVER, I DON'T WANT TO BE THE CAUSE.
KA
KA
I...
...LIKE THIS WORLD, YOU SEE.

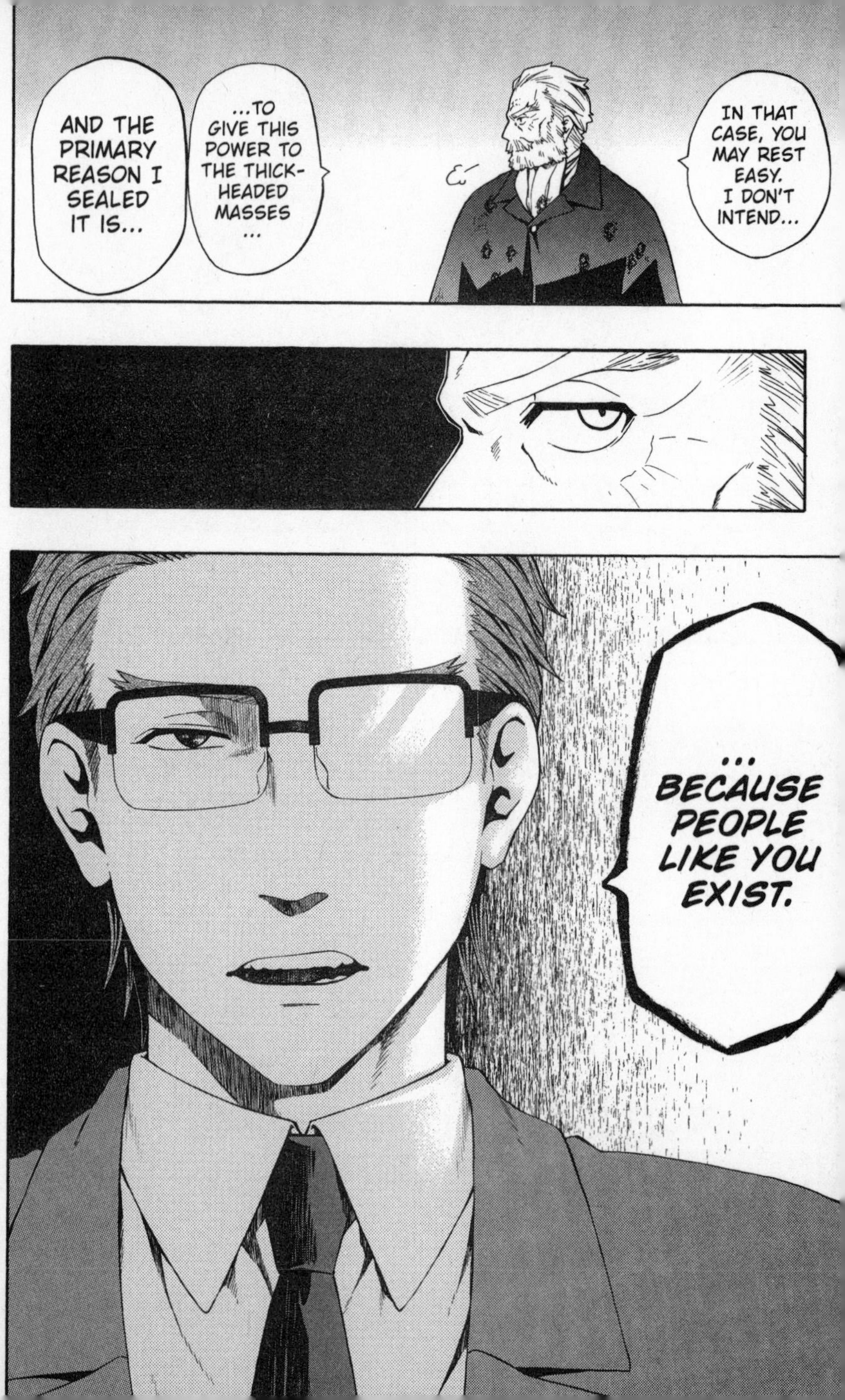
IN THAT CASE, YOU MAY REST EASY. I DON'T INTEND...
...TO GIVE THIS POWER TO THE THICK-HEADED MASSES...
AND THE PRIMARY REASON I SEALED IT IS...
...BECAUSE PEOPLE LIKE YOU EXIST.

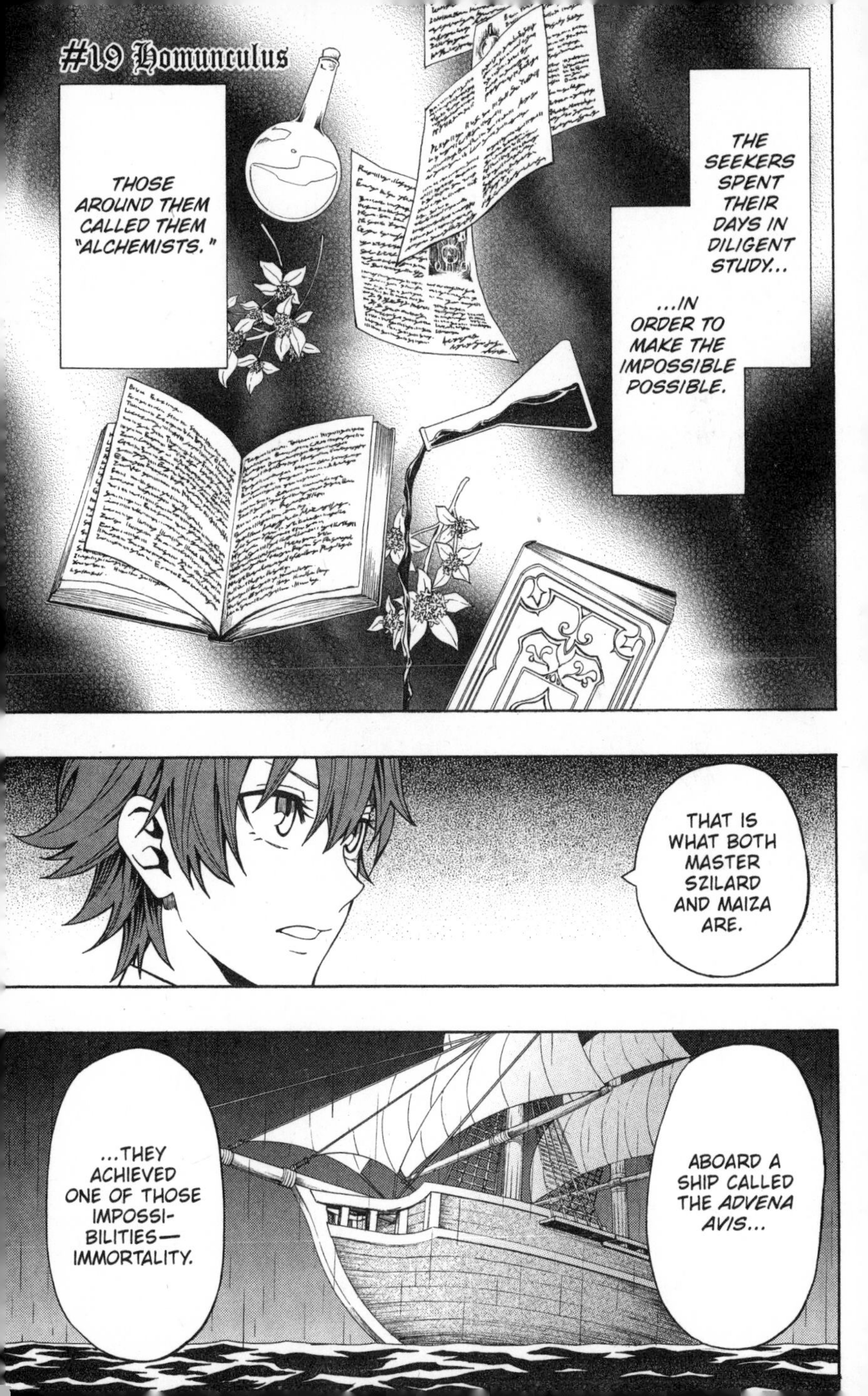
#19 Homunculus
THE SEEKERS SPENT THEIR DAYS IN DILIGENT STUDY...
...IN ORDER TO MAKE THE IMPOSSIBLE POSSIBLE.
THOSE AROUND THEM CALLED THEM "ALCHEMISTS."
THAT IS WHAT BOTH MASTER SZILARD AND MAIZA ARE.
ABOARD A SHIP CALLED THE *ADVENA AVIS*...
...THEY ACHIEVED ONE OF THOSE IMPOSSI-BILITIES—IMMORTALITY.

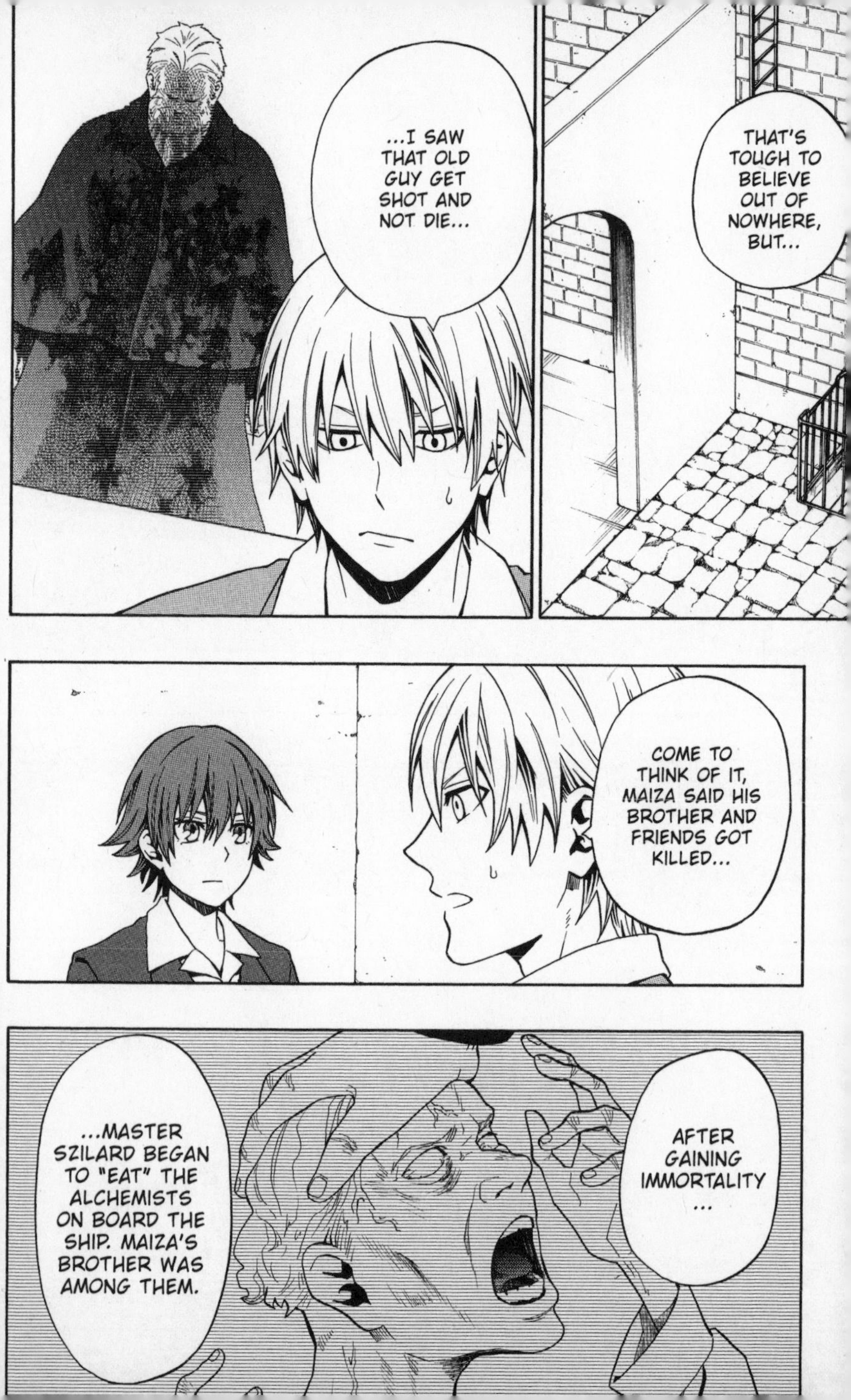
THAT'S TOUGH TO BELIEVE OUT OF NOWHERE, BUT...
...I SAW THAT OLD GUY GET SHOT AND NOT DIE...
COME TO THINK OF IT, MAIZA SAID HIS BROTHER AND FRIENDS GOT KILLED...
AFTER GAINING IMMORTALITY...
...MASTER SZILARD BEGAN TO "EAT" THE ALCHEMISTS ON BOARD THE SHIP. MAIZA'S BROTHER WAS AMONG THEM.

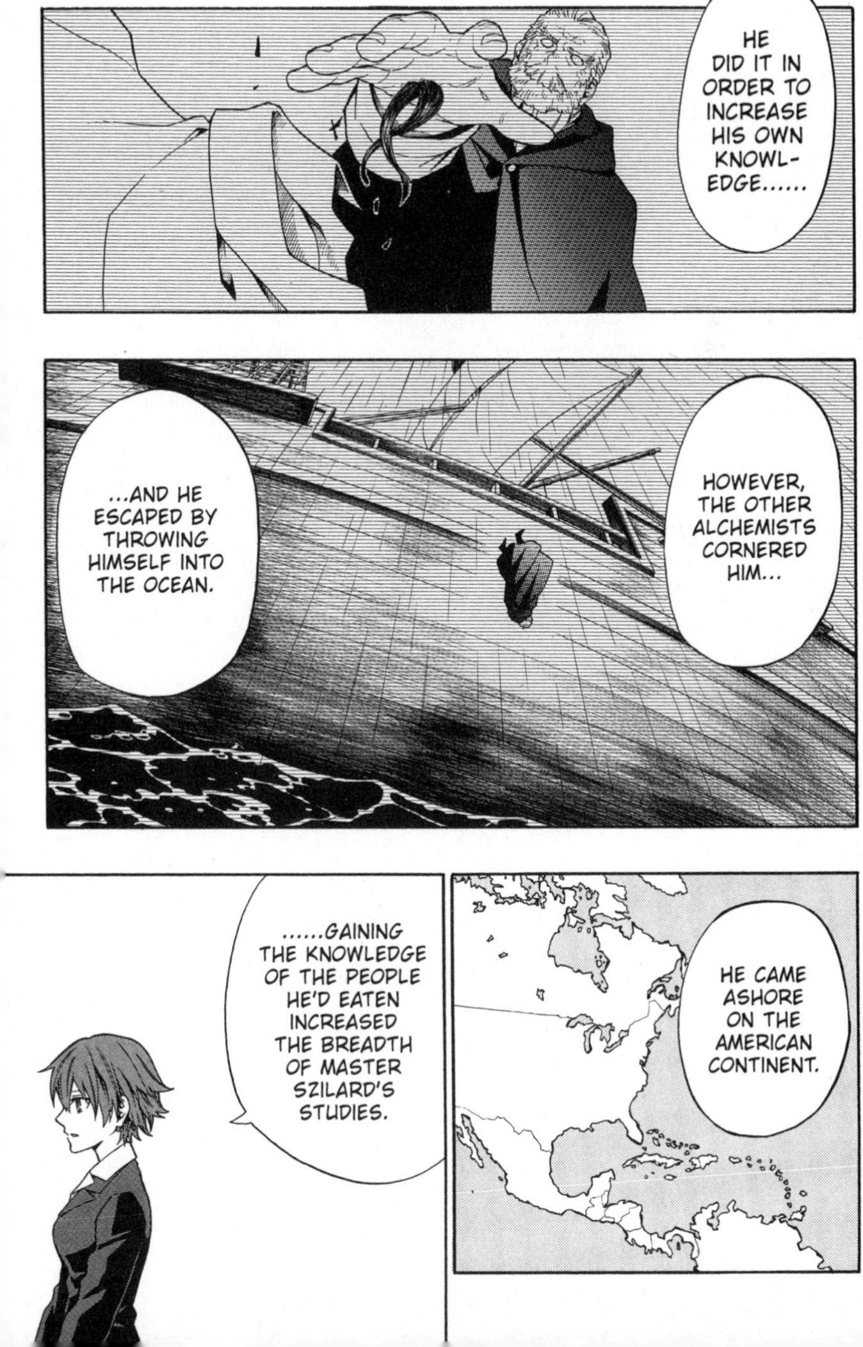
HE DID IT IN ORDER TO INCREASE HIS OWN KNOWL-EDGE......
HOWEVER, THE OTHER ALCHEMISTS CORNERED HIM...
...AND HE ESCAPED BY THROWING HIMSELF INTO THE OCEAN.
HE CAME ASHORE ON THE AMERICAN CONTINENT.
......GAINING THE KNOWLEDGE OF THE PEOPLE HE'D EATEN INCREASED THE BREADTH OF MASTER SZILARD'S STUDIES.

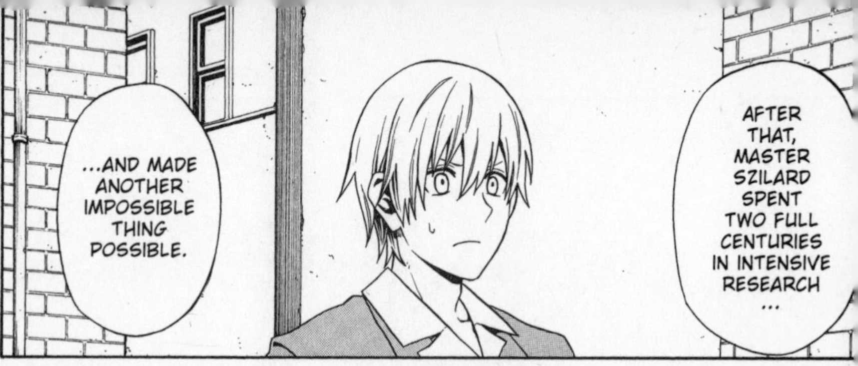
AFTER THAT, MASTER SZILARD SPENT TWO FULL CENTURIES IN INTENSIVE RESEARCH...
...AND MADE ANOTHER IMPOSSIBLE THING POSSIBLE.

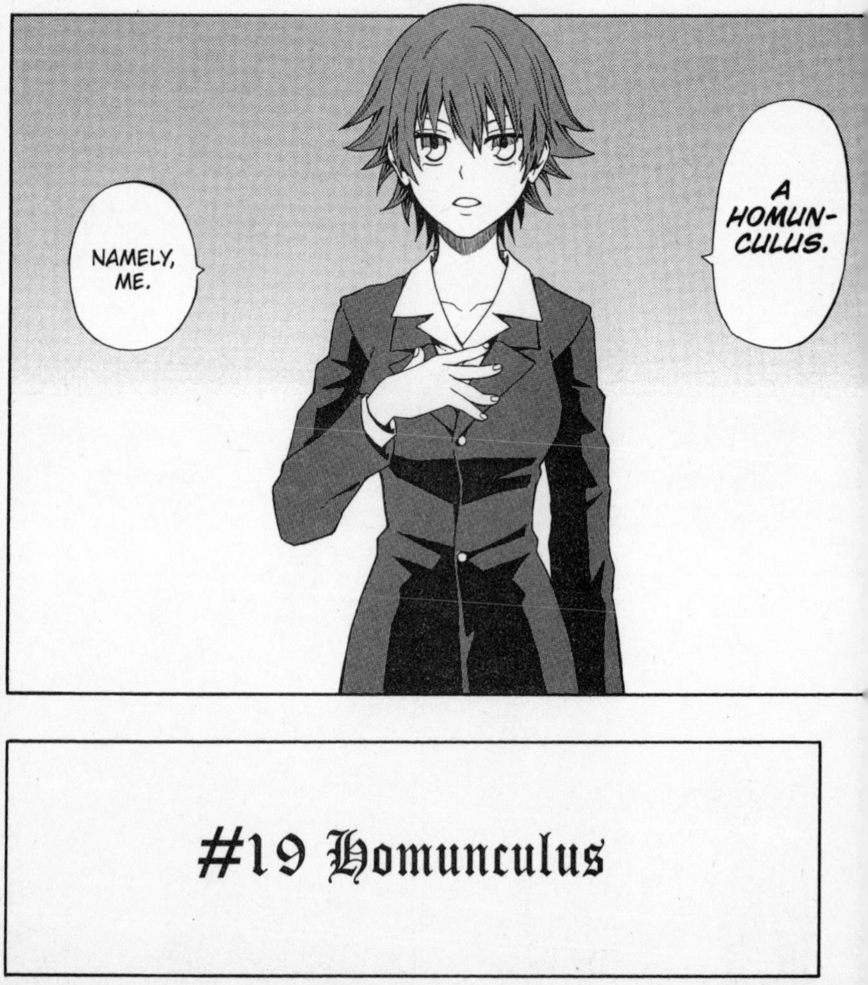
A HOMUNCULUS.
NAMELY, ME.

#19 Homunculus

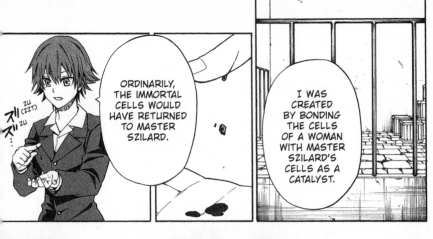

I WAS CREATED BY BONDING THE CELLS OF A WOMAN WITH MASTER SZILARD'S CELLS AS A CATALYST.
ORDINARILY, THE IMMORTAL CELLS WOULD HAVE RETURNED TO MASTER SZILARD.
ズ ZU (ZZZT)
ズ ZU...
HOWEVER, POSSIBLY BECAUSE HE USED THE FAILED LIQUOR AS A CULTURE...
...I GREW UNTIL I WAS THE SAME AGE AS MY FEMALE DONOR.
THEN, AS MY PHYSICAL NATURE WAS THE SAME AS MASTER SZILARD'S, I STOPPED GROWING.
UH...
IN OTHER WORDS ?

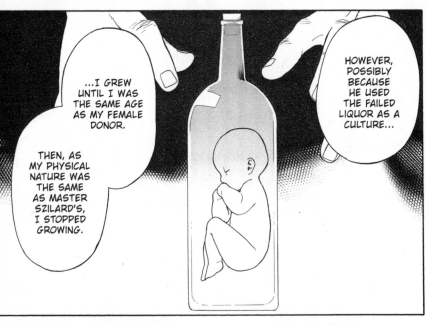

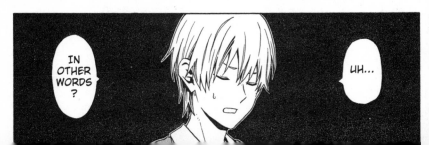

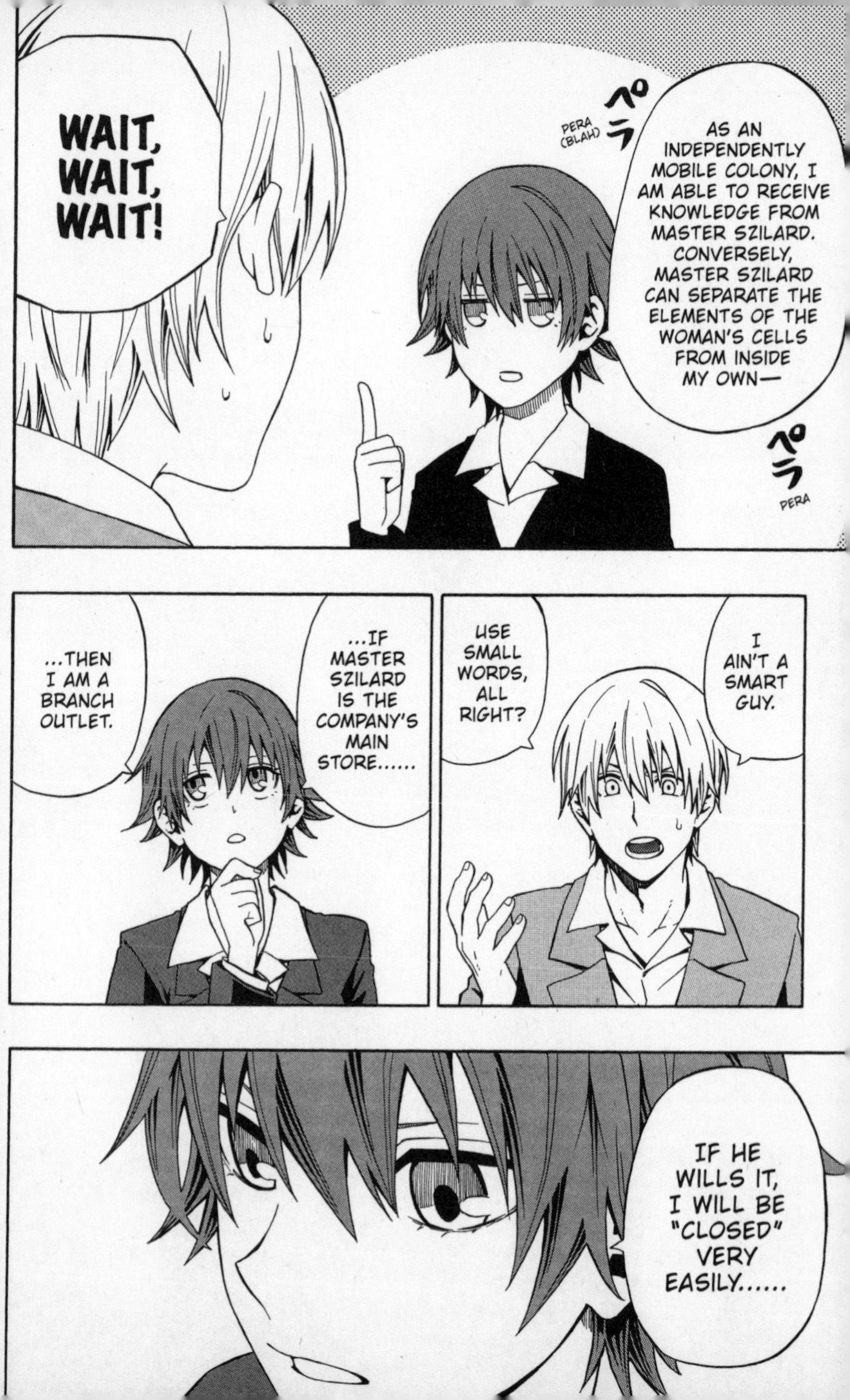
ペラ
PERA (BLAH)
AS AN INDEPENDENTLY MOBILE COLONY, I AM ABLE TO RECEIVE KNOWLEDGE FROM MASTER SZILARD. CONVERSELY, MASTER SZILARD CAN SEPARATE THE ELEMENTS OF THE WOMAN'S CELLS FROM INSIDE MY OWN—
ペラ
PERA
WAIT, WAIT, WAIT!
I AIN'T A SMART GUY.
USE SMALL WORDS, ALL RIGHT?
...IF MASTER SZILARD IS THE COMPANY'S MAIN STORE......
...THEN I AM A BRANCH OUTLET.
IF HE WILLS IT, I WILL BE "CLOSED" VERY EASILY......

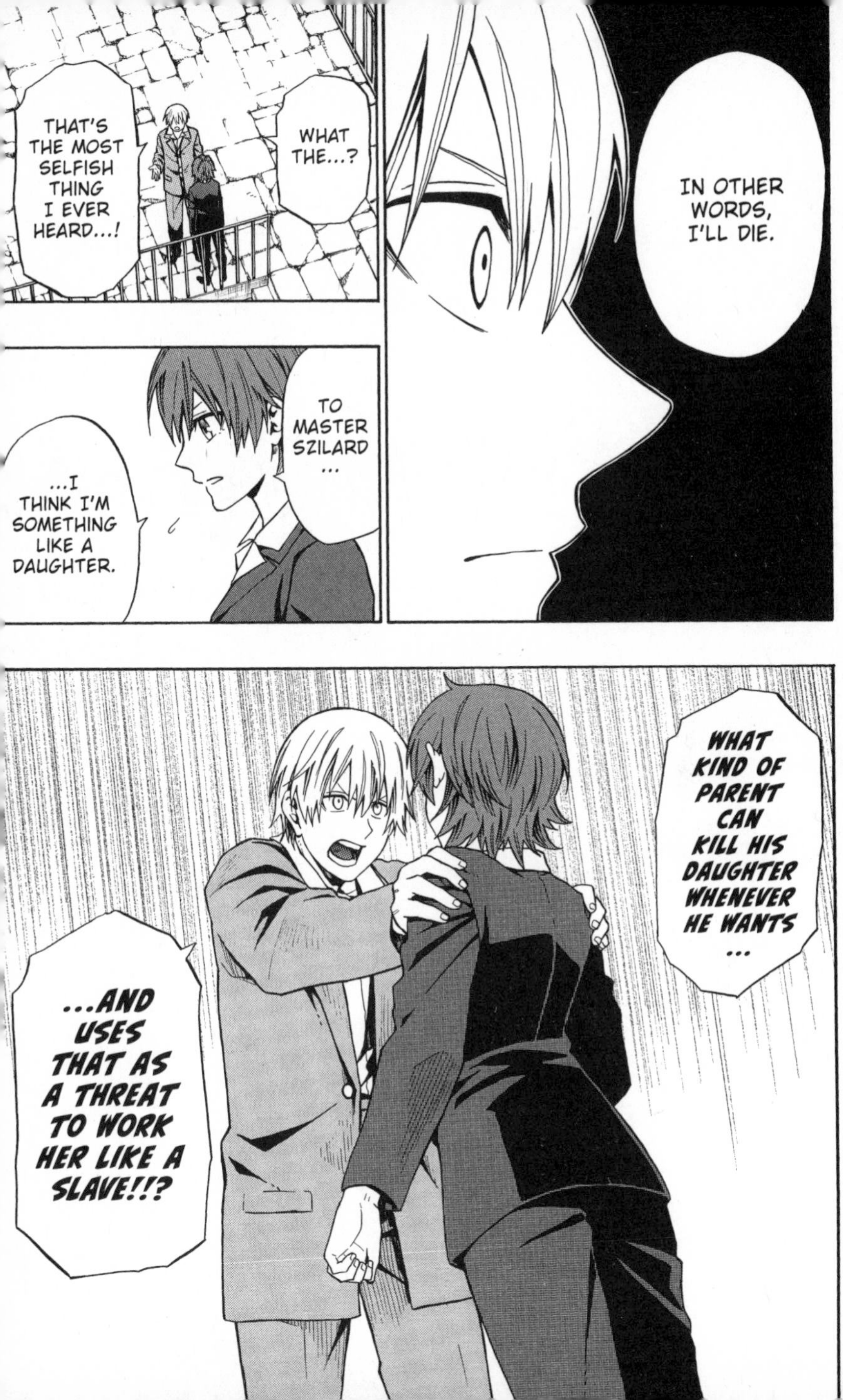
IN OTHER WORDS, I'LL DIE.
WHAT THE...?
THAT'S THE MOST SELFISH THING I EVER HEARD...!
TO MASTER SZILARD...
...I THINK I'M SOMETHING LIKE A DAUGHTER.
WHAT KIND OF PARENT CAN KILL HIS DAUGHTER WHENEVER HE WANTS...
...AND USES THAT AS A THREAT TO WORK HER LIKE A SLAVE!!?

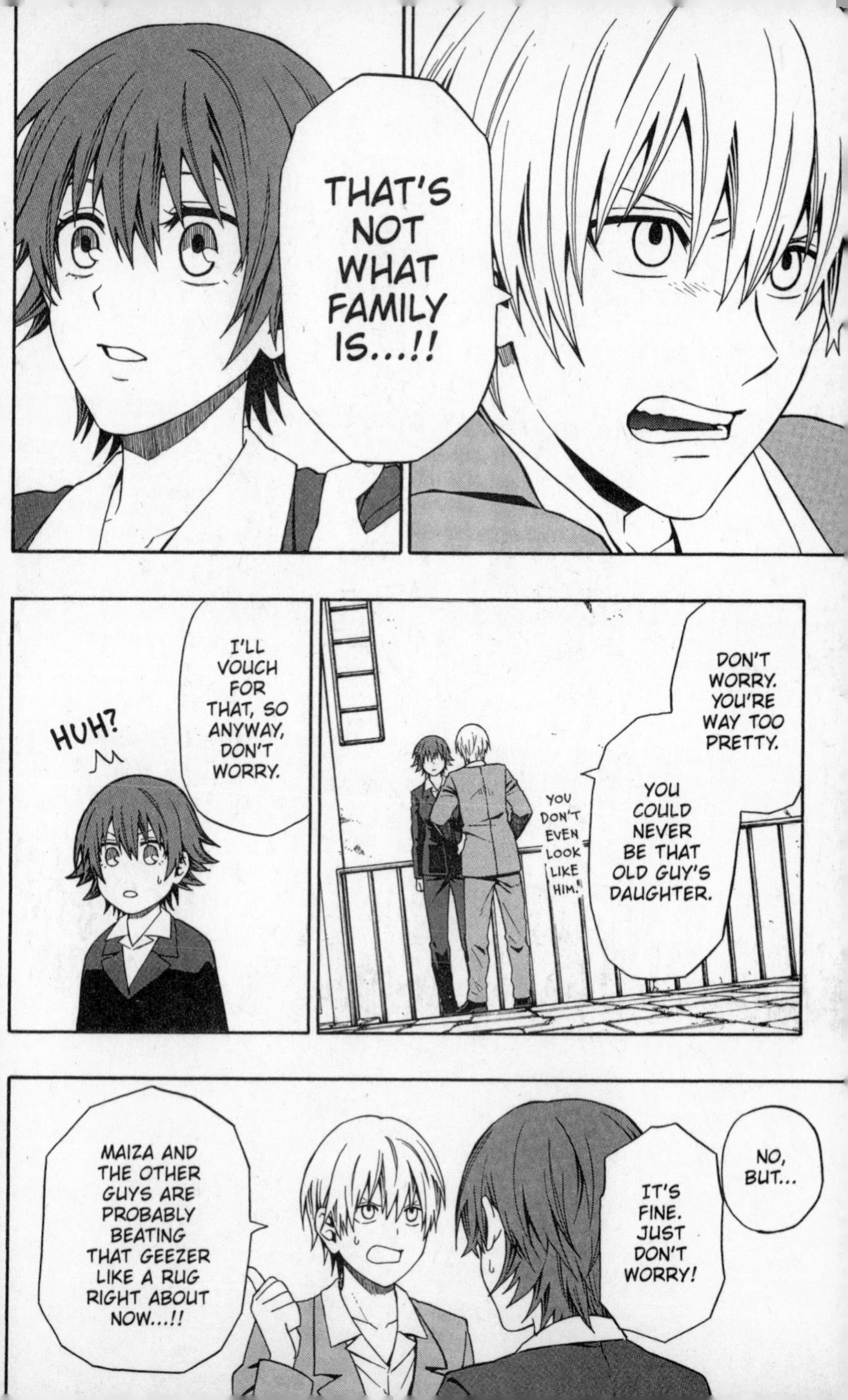
THAT'S NOT WHAT FAMILY IS...!!
DON'T WORRY. YOU'RE WAY TOO PRETTY.
YOU COULD NEVER BE THAT OLD GUY'S DAUGHTER.
YOU DON'T EVEN LOOK LIKE HIM.
I'LL VOUCH FOR THAT, SO ANYWAY, DON'T WORRY.
HUH?
NO, BUT...
IT'S FINE. JUST DON'T WORRY!
MAIZA AND THE OTHER GUYS ARE PROBABLY BEATING THAT GEEZER LIKE A RUG RIGHT ABOUT NOW...!!

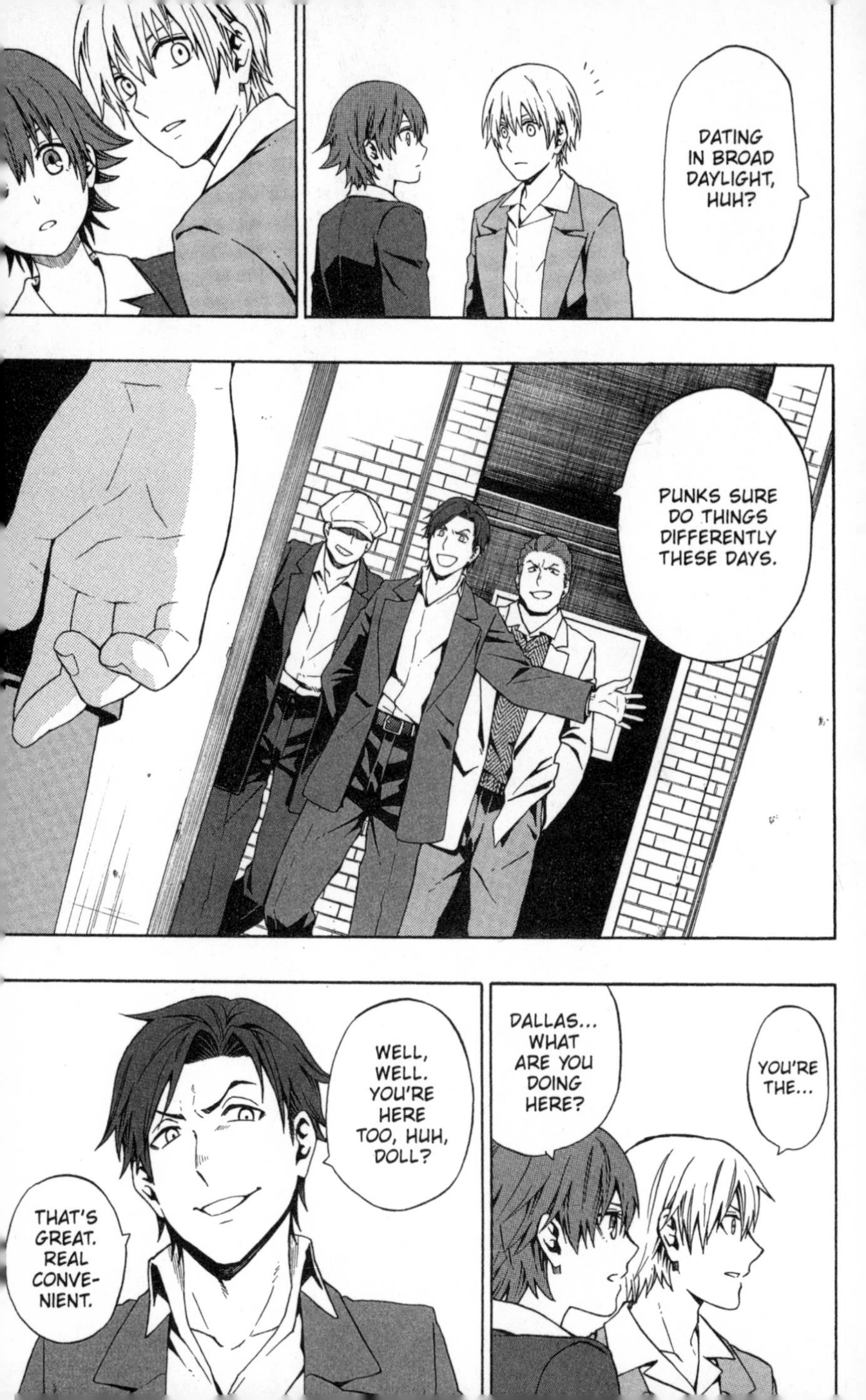
DATING IN BROAD DAYLIGHT, HUH?
PUNKS SURE DO THINGS DIFFERENTLY THESE DAYS.
YOU'RE THE...
DALLAS... WHAT ARE YOU DOING HERE?
WELL, WELL. YOU'RE HERE TOO, HUH, DOLL?
THAT'S GREAT. REAL CONVE-NIENT.

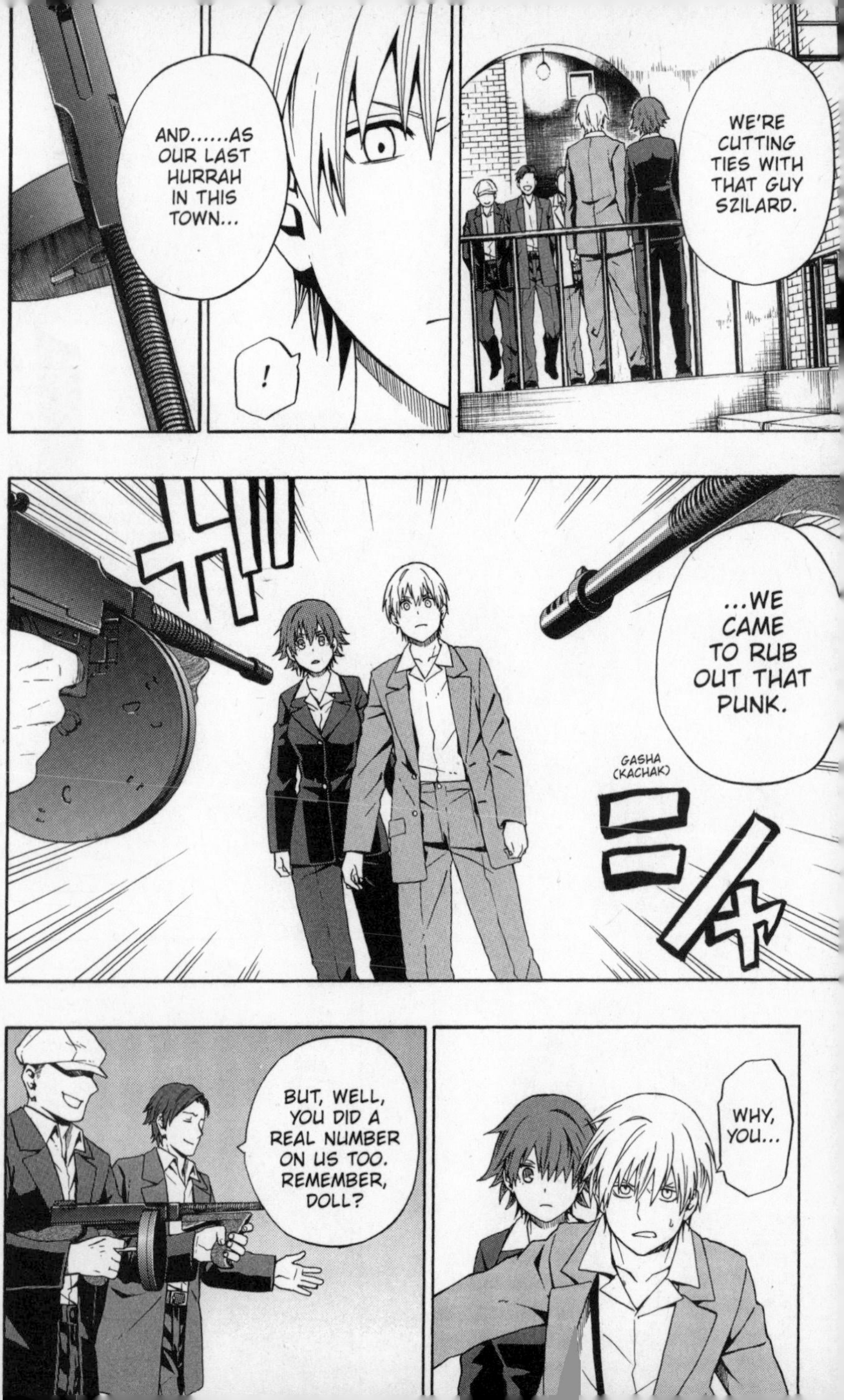
WE'RE CUTTING TIES WITH THAT GUY SZILARD.
!
AND......AS OUR LAST HURRAH IN THIS TOWN...
...WE CAME TO RUB OUT THAT PUNK.
GASHA (KACHAK)
WHY, YOU...
BUT, WELL, YOU DID A REAL NUMBER ON US TOO. REMEMBER, DOLL?

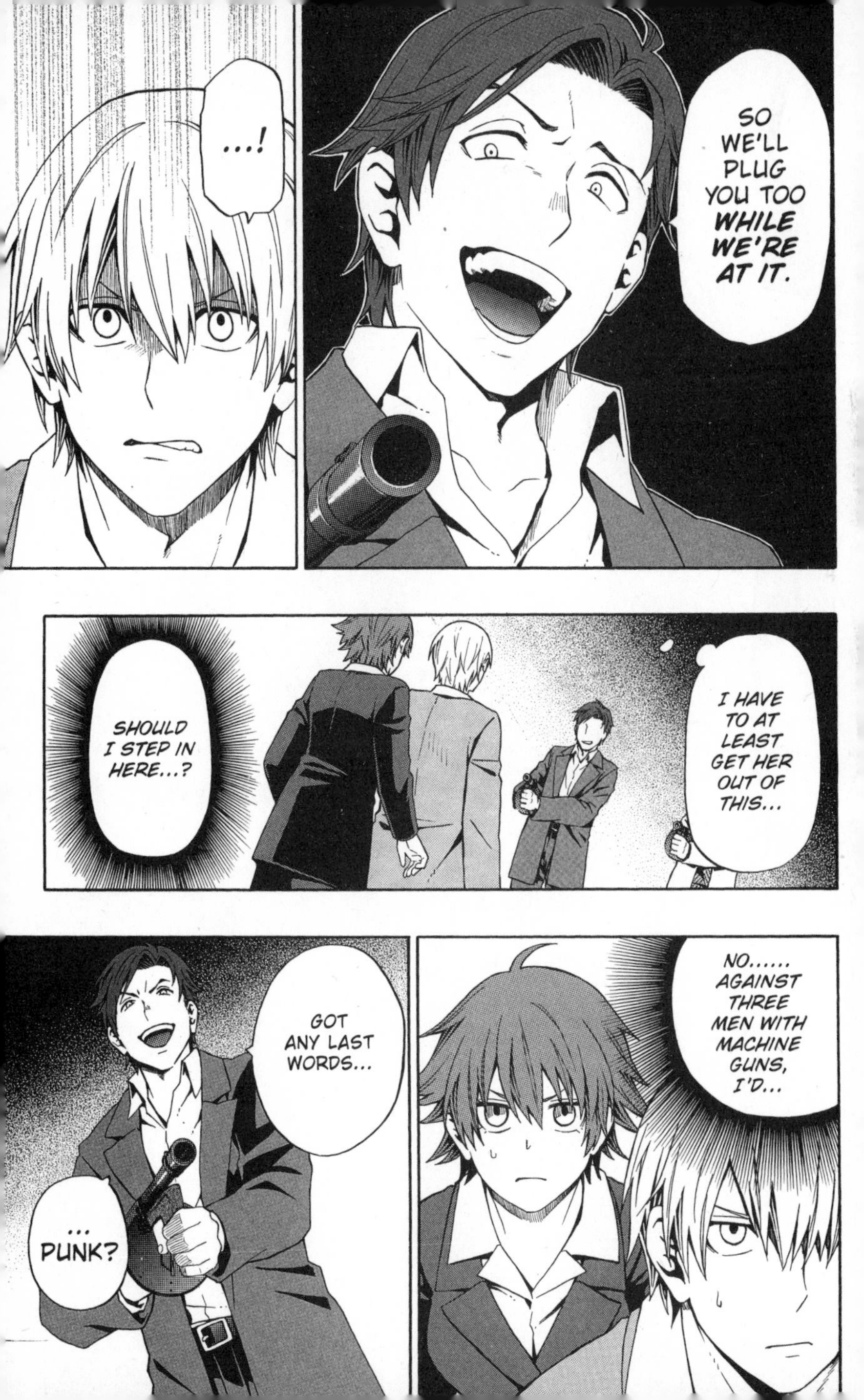
SO WE'LL PLUG YOU TOO WHILE WE'RE AT IT.
...!
I HAVE TO AT LEAST GET HER OUT OF THIS...
SHOULD I STEP IN HERE...?
NO...... AGAINST THREE MEN WITH MACHINE GUNS, I'D...
GOT ANY LAST WORDS...
... PUNK?

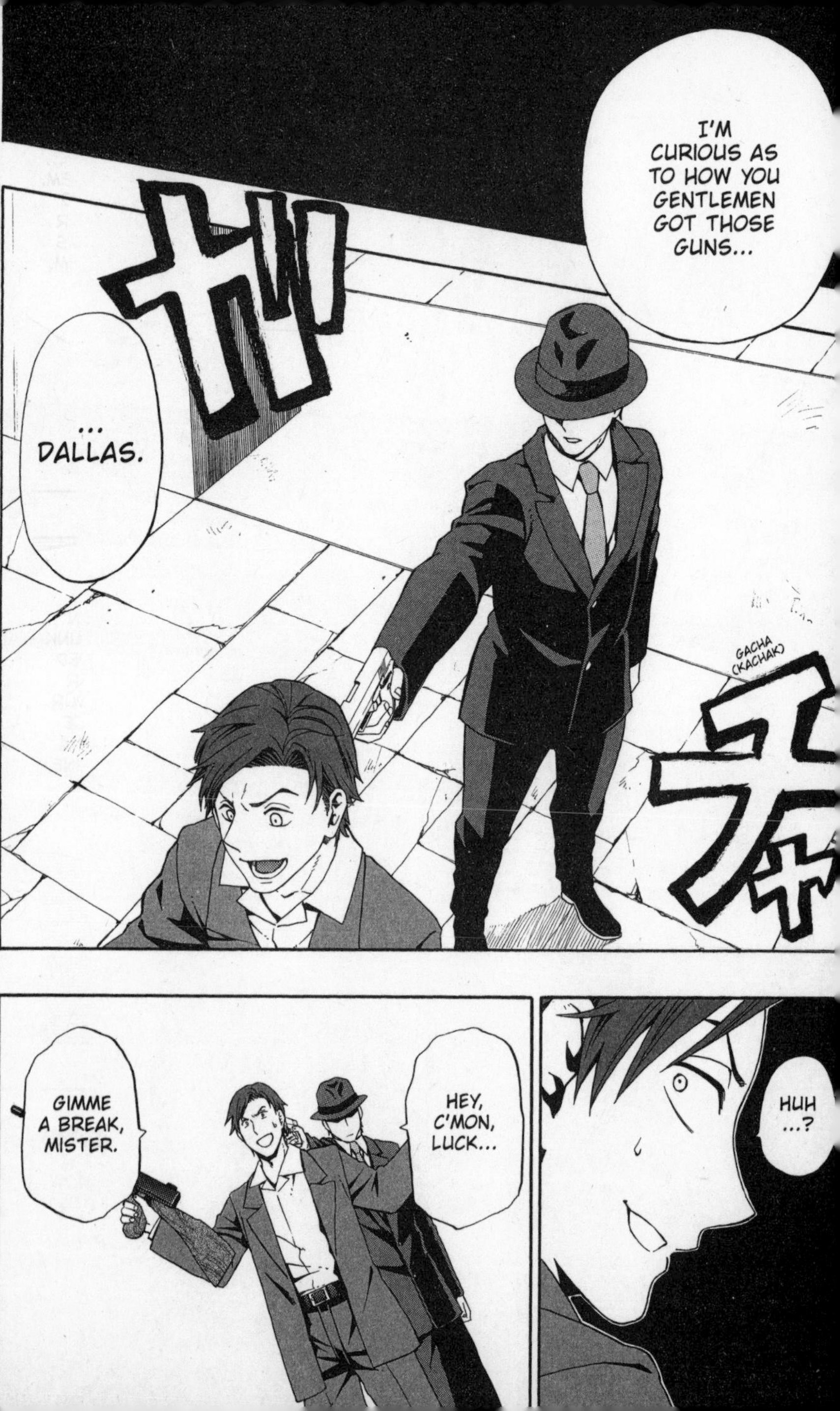
I'M CURIOUS AS TO HOW YOU GENTLEMEN GOT THOSE GUNS...
GACHA (KACHAK)
... DALLAS.
HUH ...?
HEY, C'MON, LUCK...
GIMME A BREAK, MISTER.

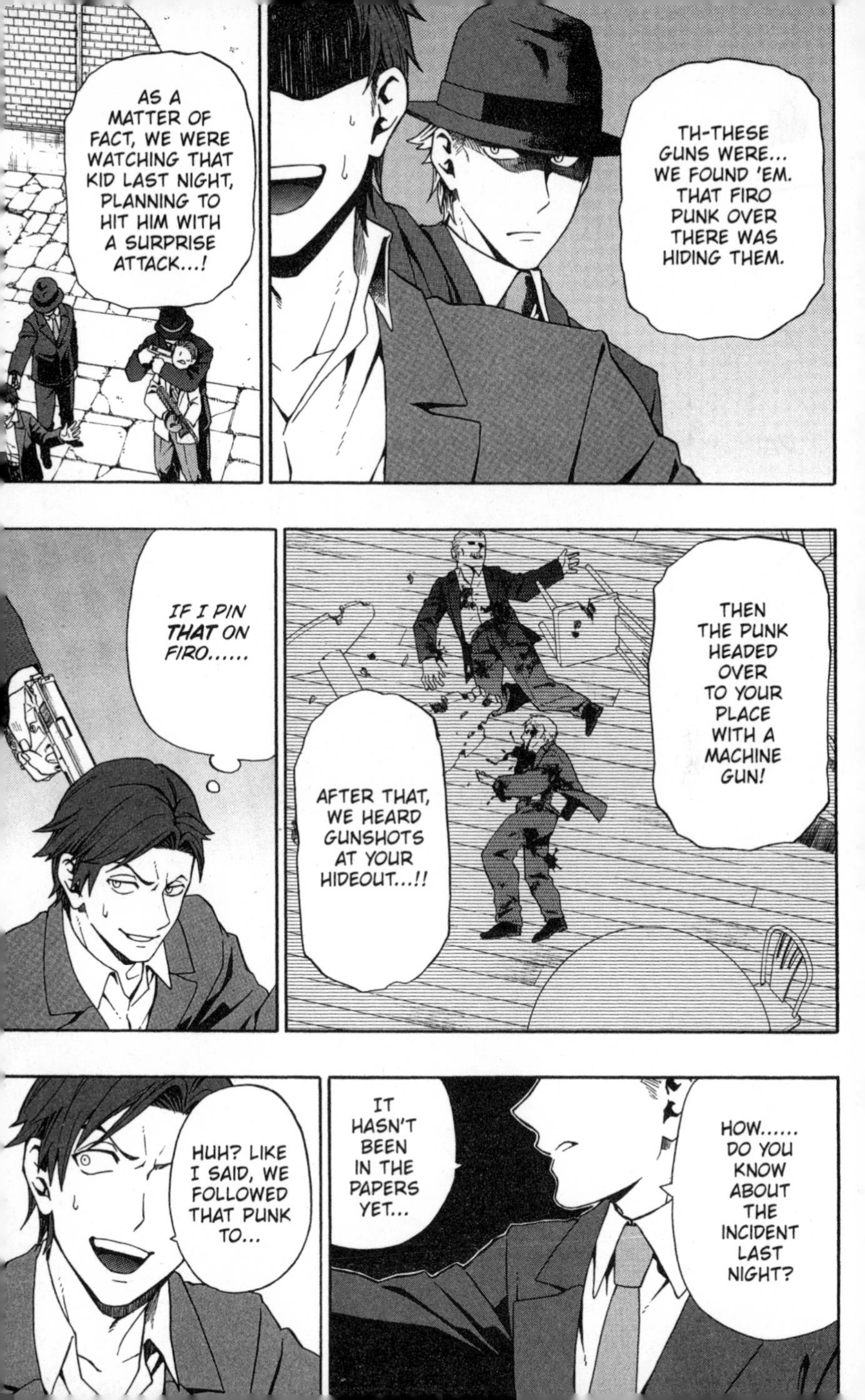
TH-THESE GUNS WERE... WE FOUND 'EM. THAT FIRO PUNK OVER THERE WAS HIDING THEM.
AS A MATTER OF FACT, WE WERE WATCHING THAT KID LAST NIGHT, PLANNING TO HIT HIM WITH A SURPRISE ATTACK...!
THEN THE PUNK HEADED OVER TO YOUR PLACE WITH A MACHINE GUN!
AFTER THAT, WE HEARD GUNSHOTS AT YOUR HIDEOUT...!!
*IF I PIN **THAT** ON FIRO......*
HOW...... DO YOU KNOW ABOUT THE INCIDENT LAST NIGHT?
IT HASN'T BEEN IN THE PAPERS YET...
HUH? LIKE I SAID, WE FOLLOWED THAT PUNK TO...

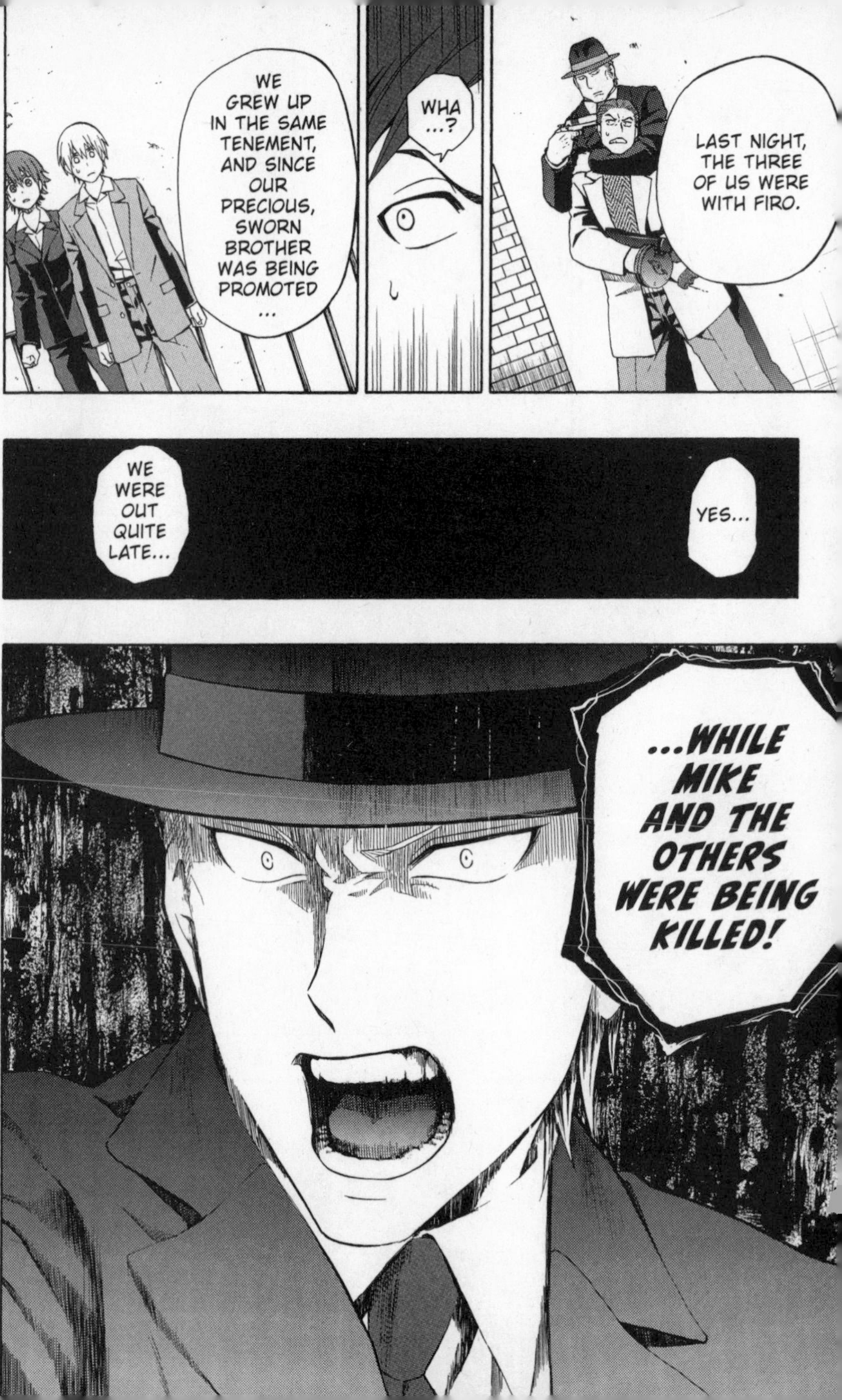
LAST NIGHT, THE THREE OF US WERE WITH FIRO.
WHA ...?
WE GREW UP IN THE SAME TENEMENT, AND SINCE OUR PRECIOUS, SWORN BROTHER WAS BEING PROMOTED ...
YES...
WE WERE OUT QUITE LATE...
...WHILE MIKE AND THE OTHERS WERE BEING KILLED!

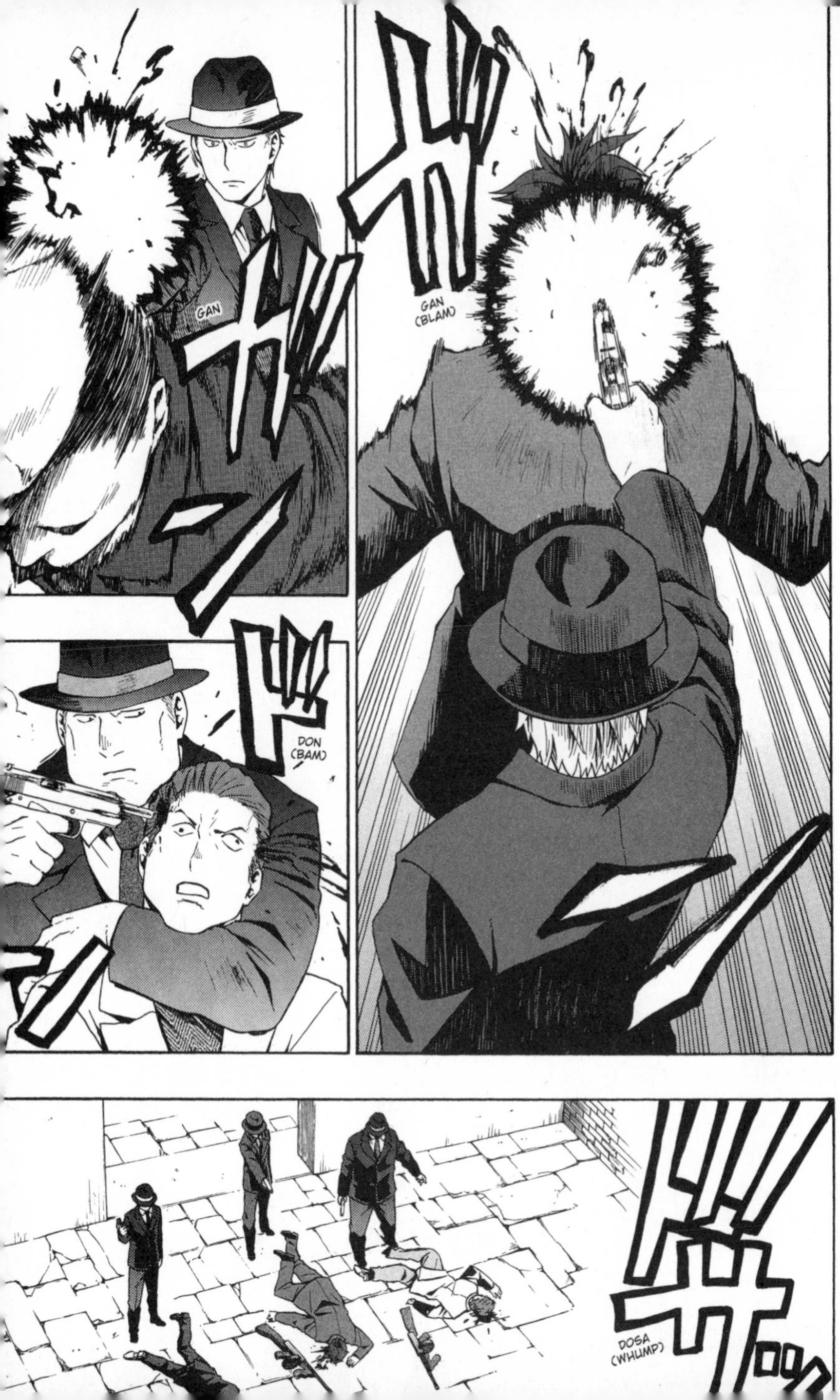
GAN
(BLAM)
GAN
DON
(BAM)
DOSA
(WHUMP)

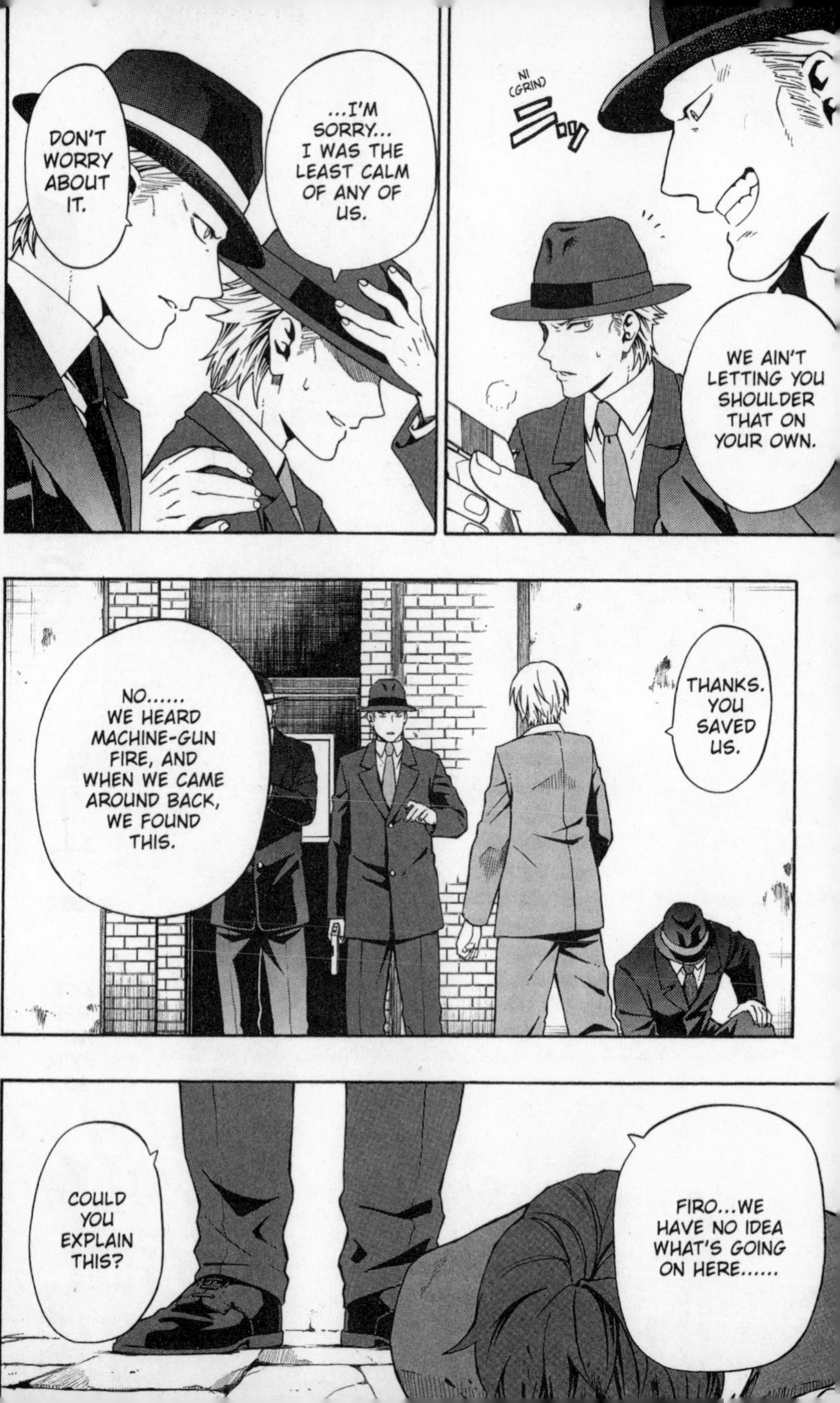
NI (GRIND)
WE AIN'T LETTING YOU SHOULDER THAT ON YOUR OWN.
...I'M SORRY... I WAS THE LEAST CALM OF ANY OF US.
DON'T WORRY ABOUT IT.
THANKS. YOU SAVED US.
NO...... WE HEARD MACHINE-GUN FIRE, AND WHEN WE CAME AROUND BACK, WE FOUND THIS.
FIRO...WE HAVE NO IDEA WHAT'S GOING ON HERE......
COULD YOU EXPLAIN THIS?

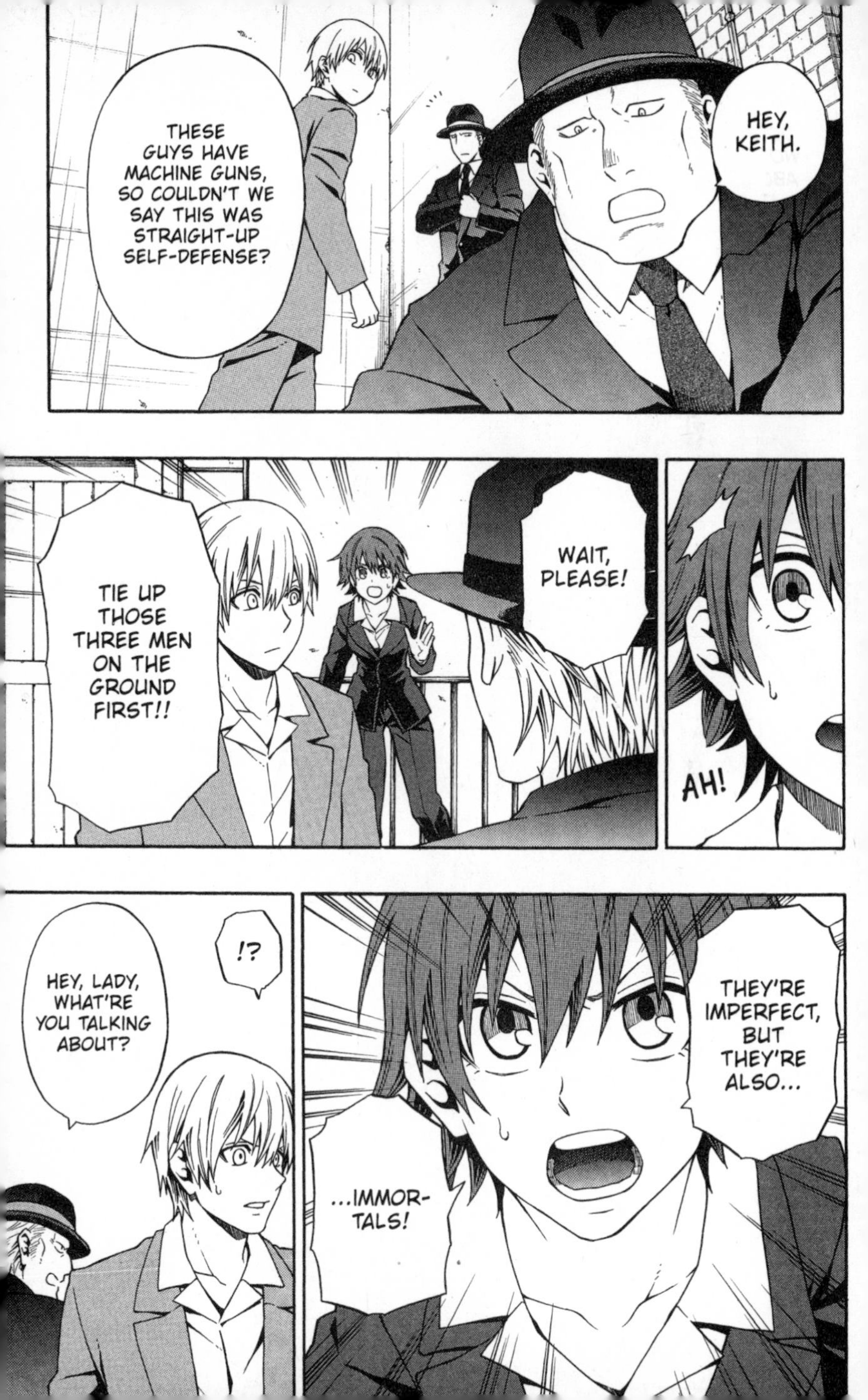
HEY, KEITH.
THESE GUYS HAVE MACHINE GUNS, SO COULDN'T WE SAY THIS WAS STRAIGHT-UP SELF-DEFENSE?
AH!
WAIT, PLEASE!
TIE UP THOSE THREE MEN ON THE GROUND FIRST!!
THEY'RE IMPERFECT, BUT THEY'RE ALSO...
...IMMOR-TALS!
!?
HEY, LADY, WHAT'RE YOU TALKING ABOUT?

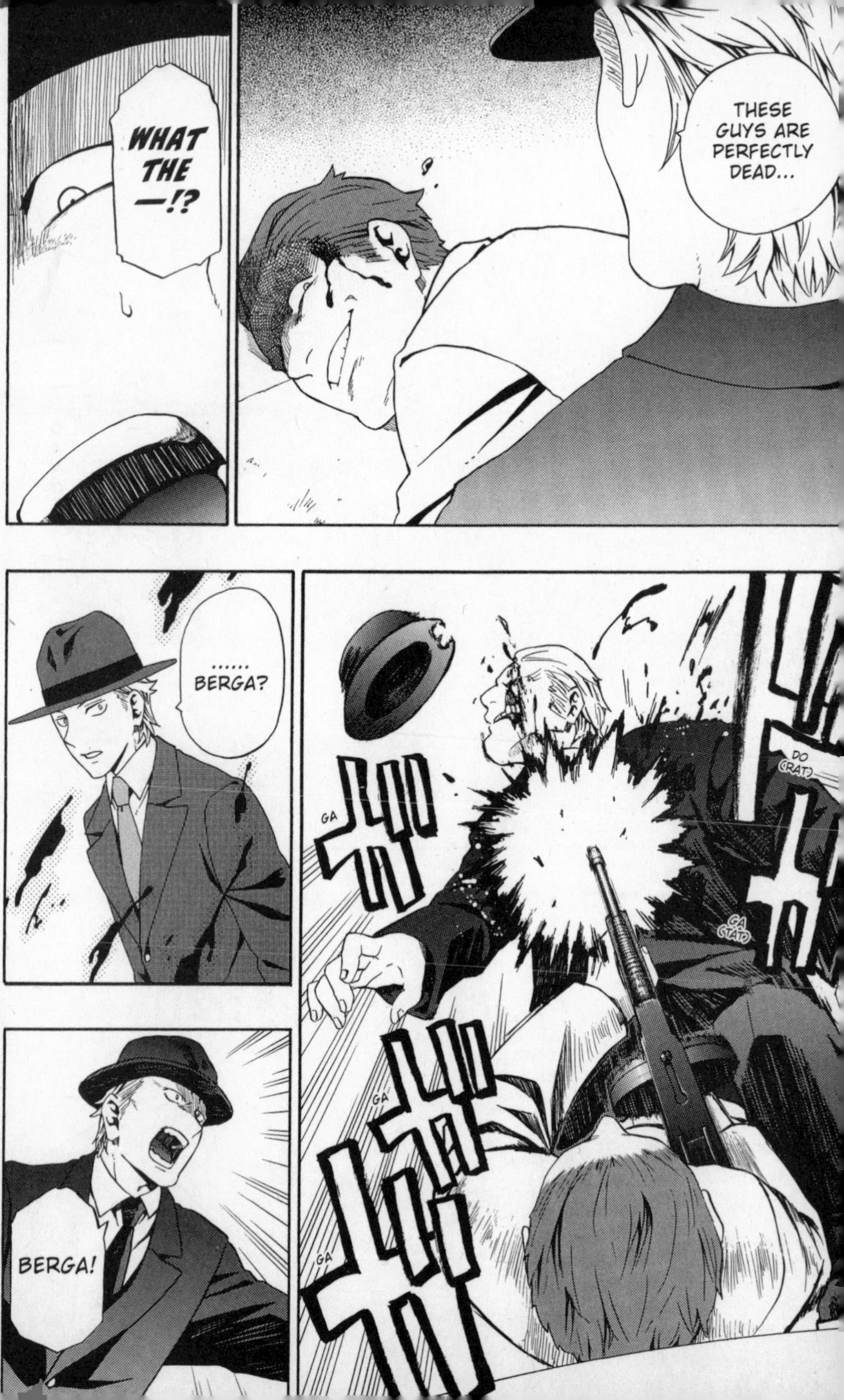
THESE GUYS ARE PERFECTLY DEAD...
WHAT THE—!?
DO (RAT)
GA
GA (TAT)
GA
GA
......BERGA?
BERGA!

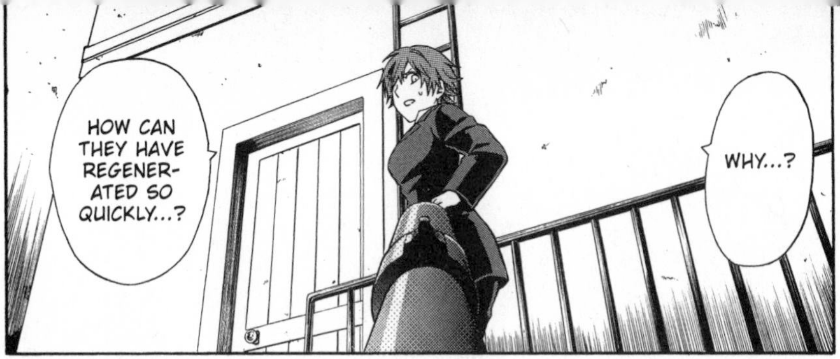
WHY...?
HOW CAN THEY HAVE REGENER-ATED SO QUICKLY...?

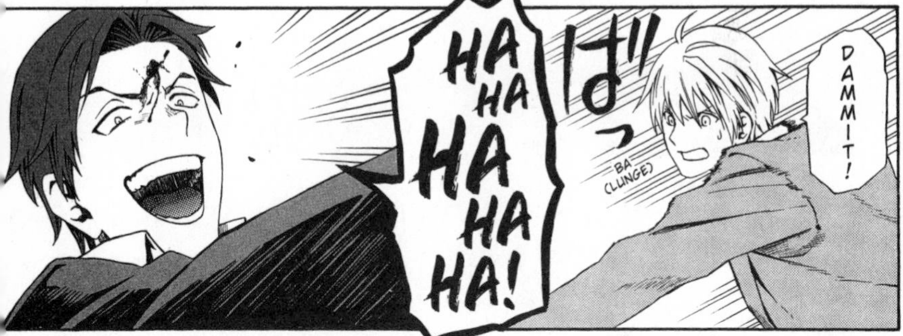
DAMMIT!
ばっ
BA (LUNGE)
HA HA HA HA HA HA HA!

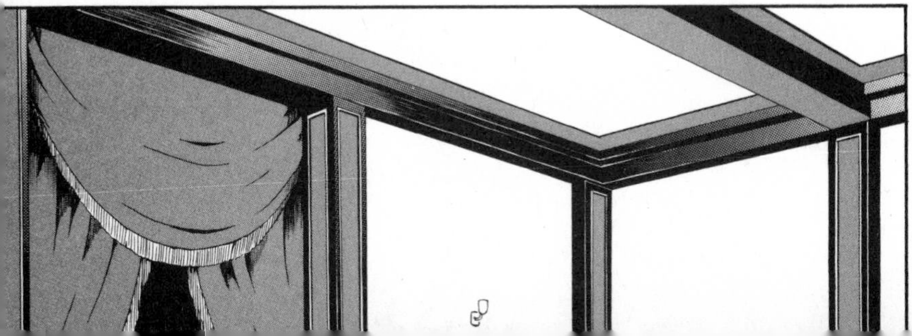

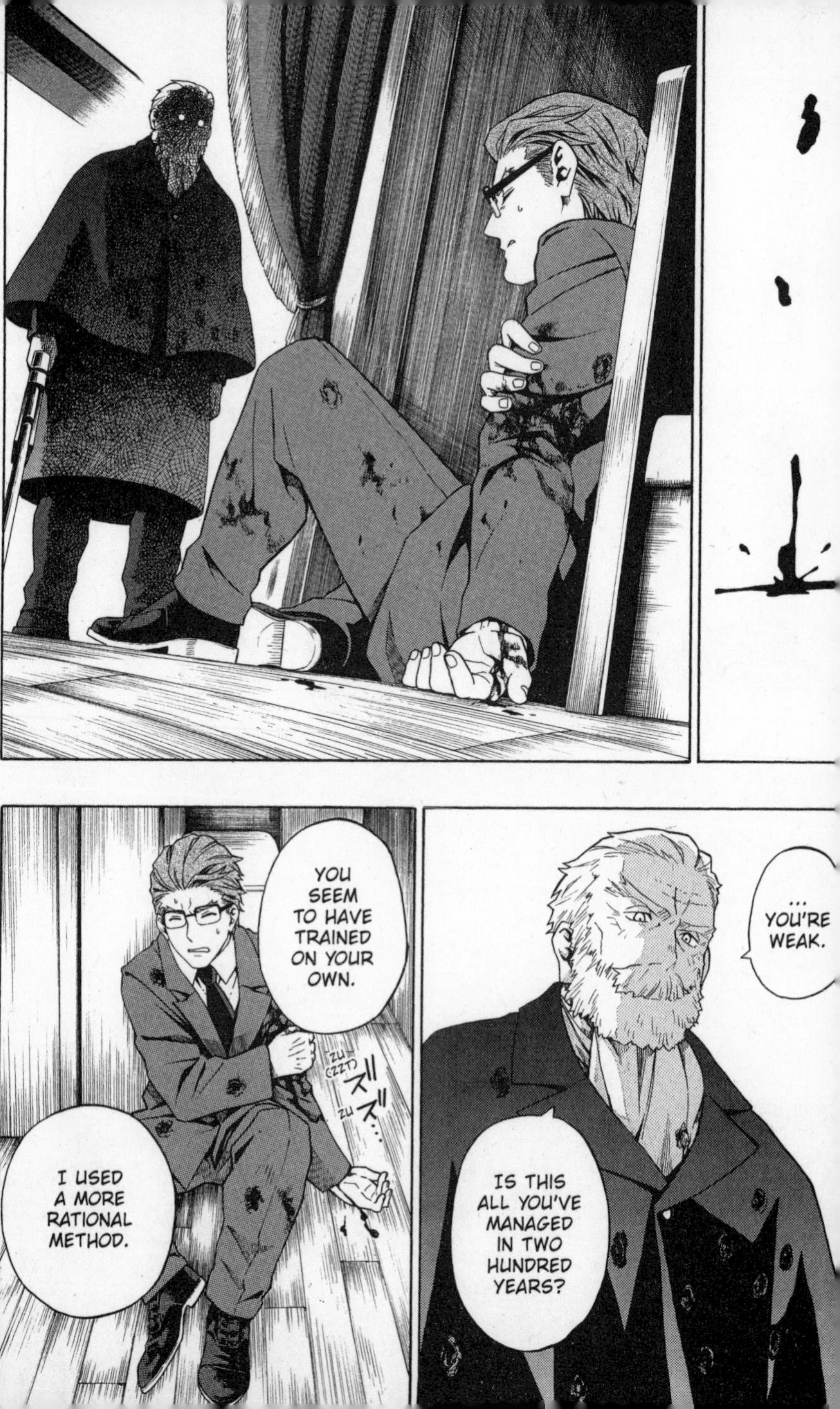
... YOU'RE WEAK.
IS THIS ALL YOU'VE MANAGED IN TWO HUNDRED YEARS?
YOU SEEM TO HAVE TRAINED ON YOUR OWN.
ズズ…
ZU (ZZZT) ZU
I USED A MORE RATIONAL METHOD.

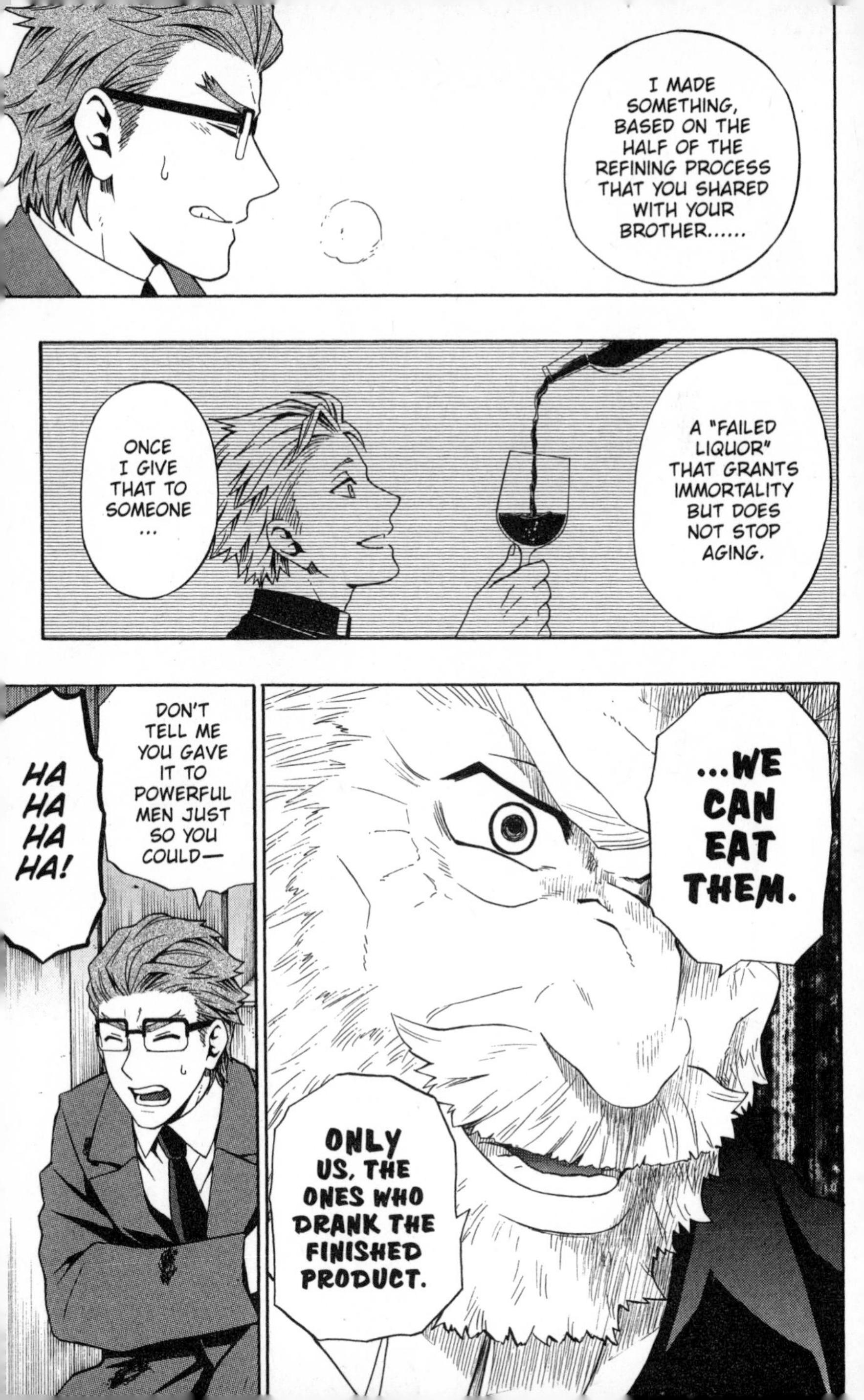
I MADE SOMETHING, BASED ON THE HALF OF THE REFINING PROCESS THAT YOU SHARED WITH YOUR BROTHER......
A "FAILED LIQUOR" THAT GRANTS IMMORTALITY BUT DOES NOT STOP AGING.
ONCE I GIVE THAT TO SOMEONE ...
...WE CAN EAT THEM.
ONLY US, THE ONES WHO DRANK THE FINISHED PRODUCT.
DON'T TELL ME YOU GAVE IT TO POWERFUL MEN JUST SO YOU COULD—
HA HA HA HA!

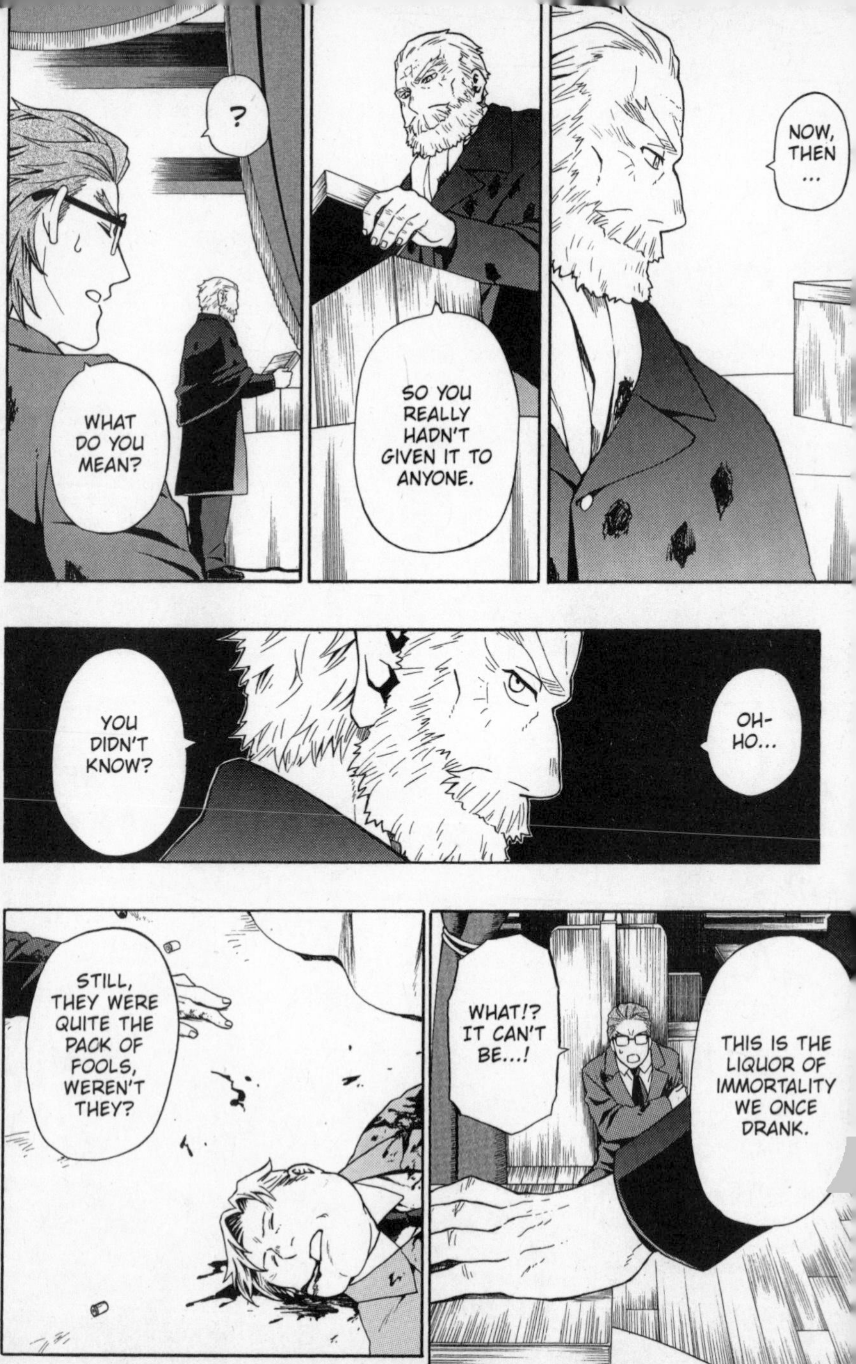
NOW, THEN ...
SO YOU REALLY HADN'T GIVEN IT TO ANYONE.
?
WHAT DO YOU MEAN?
OH-HO...
YOU DIDN'T KNOW?
THIS IS THE LIQUOR OF IMMORTALITY WE ONCE DRANK.
WHAT!? IT CAN'T BE...!
STILL, THEY WERE QUITE THE PACK OF FOOLS, WEREN'T THEY?

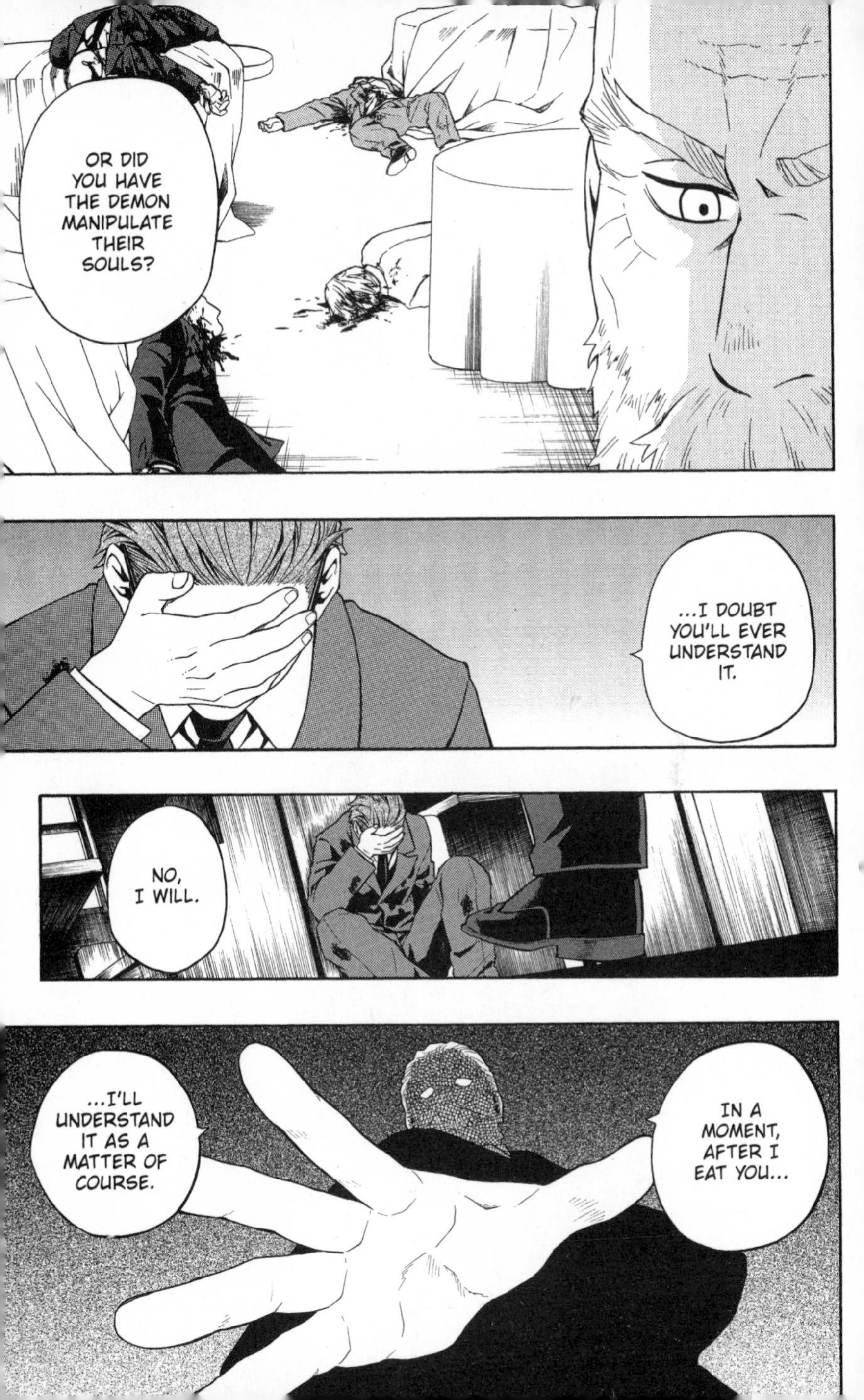
OR DID YOU HAVE THE DEMON MANIPULATE THEIR SOULS?
...I DOUBT YOU'LL EVER UNDERSTAND IT.
NO, I WILL.
IN A MOMENT, AFTER I EAT YOU...
...I'LL UNDERSTAND IT AS A MATTER OF COURSE.

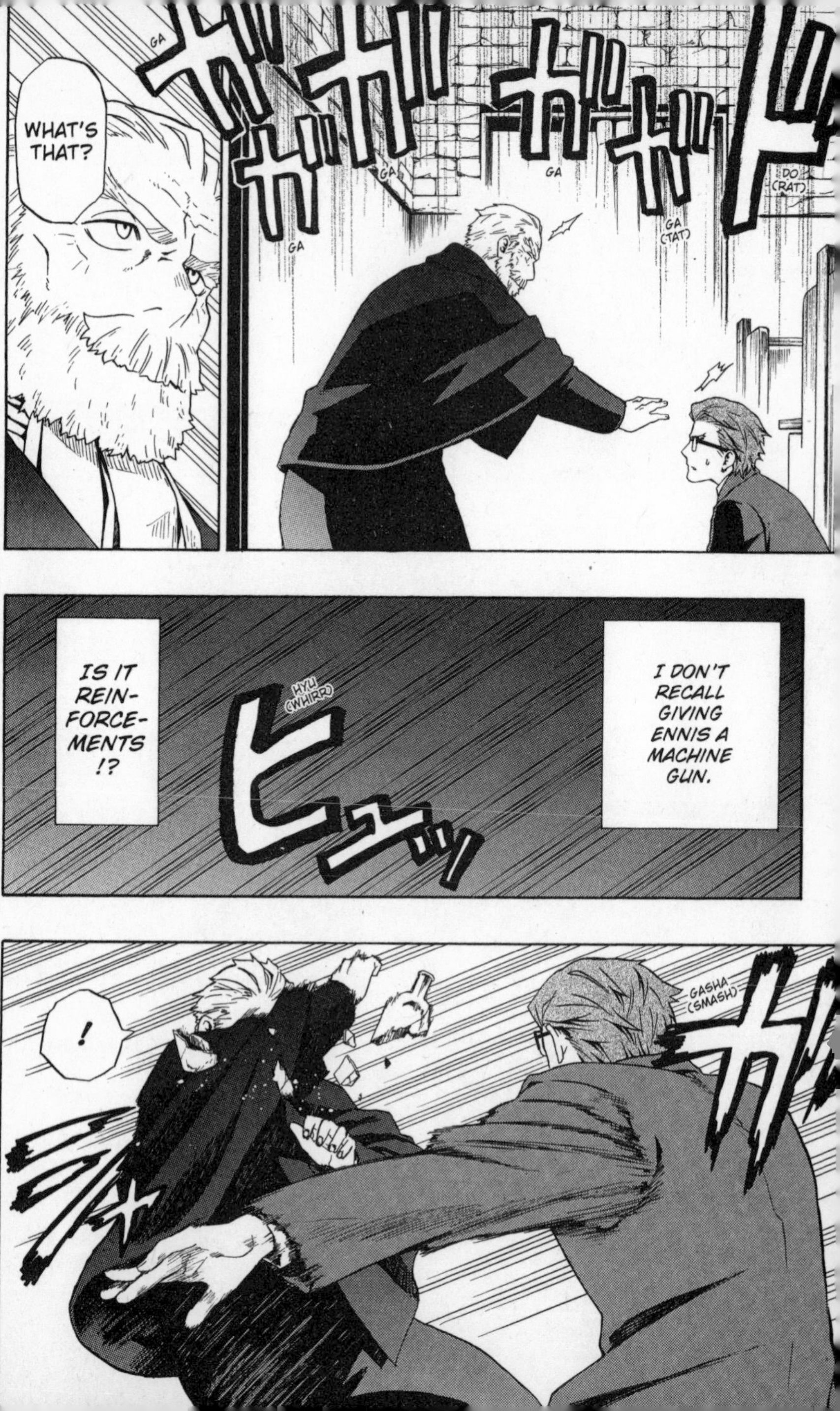
GA
GA
GA
GA
GA (TAT)
DO (RAT)
WHAT'S THAT?
I DON'T RECALL GIVING ENNIS A MACHINE GUN.
HYU (WHIRR)
IS IT REIN-FORCE-MENTS!?
GASHA (SMASH)
!

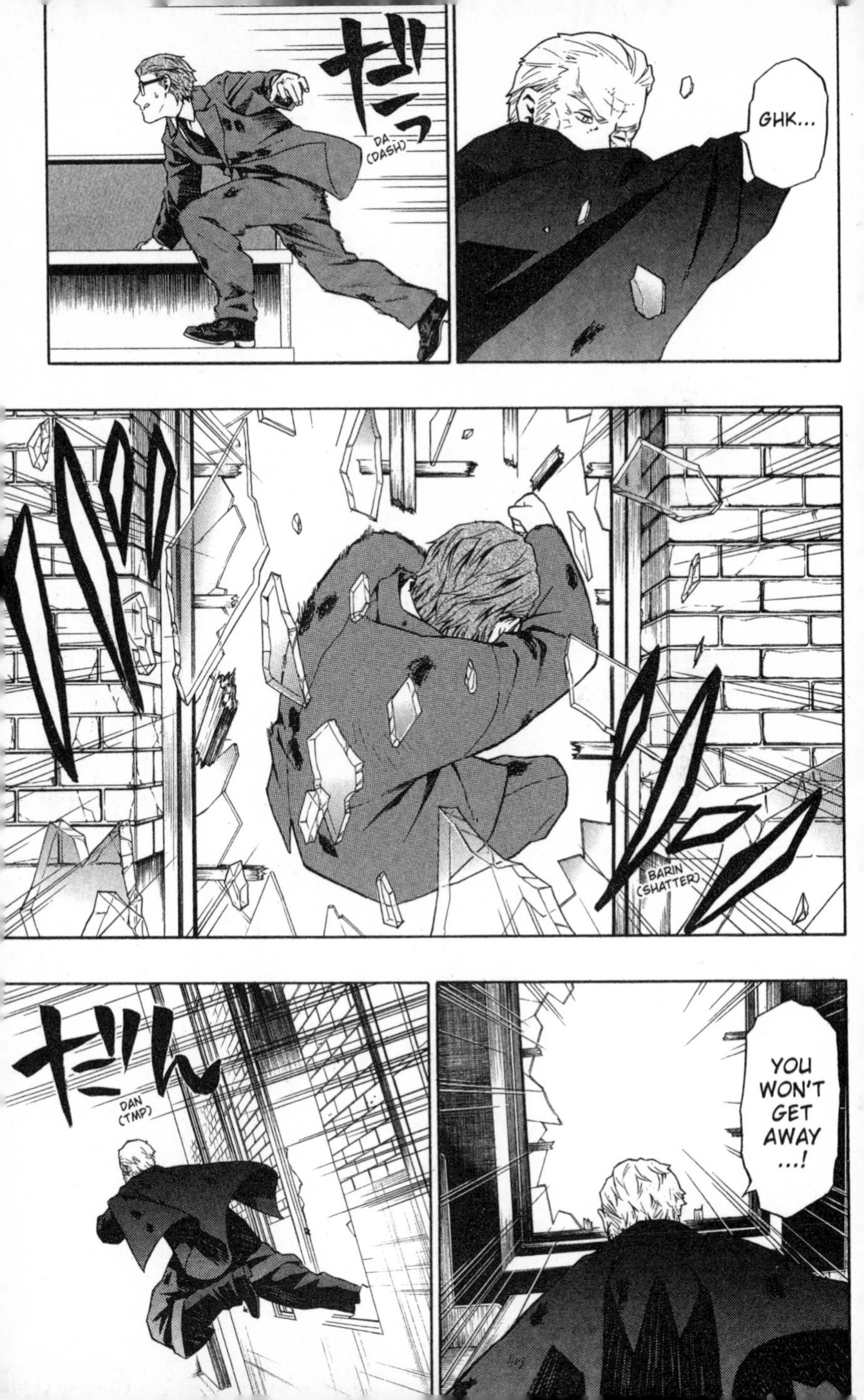
GHK...
DA (DASH)
BARIN (SHATTER)
YOU WON'T GET AWAY ...!
DAN (TMP)

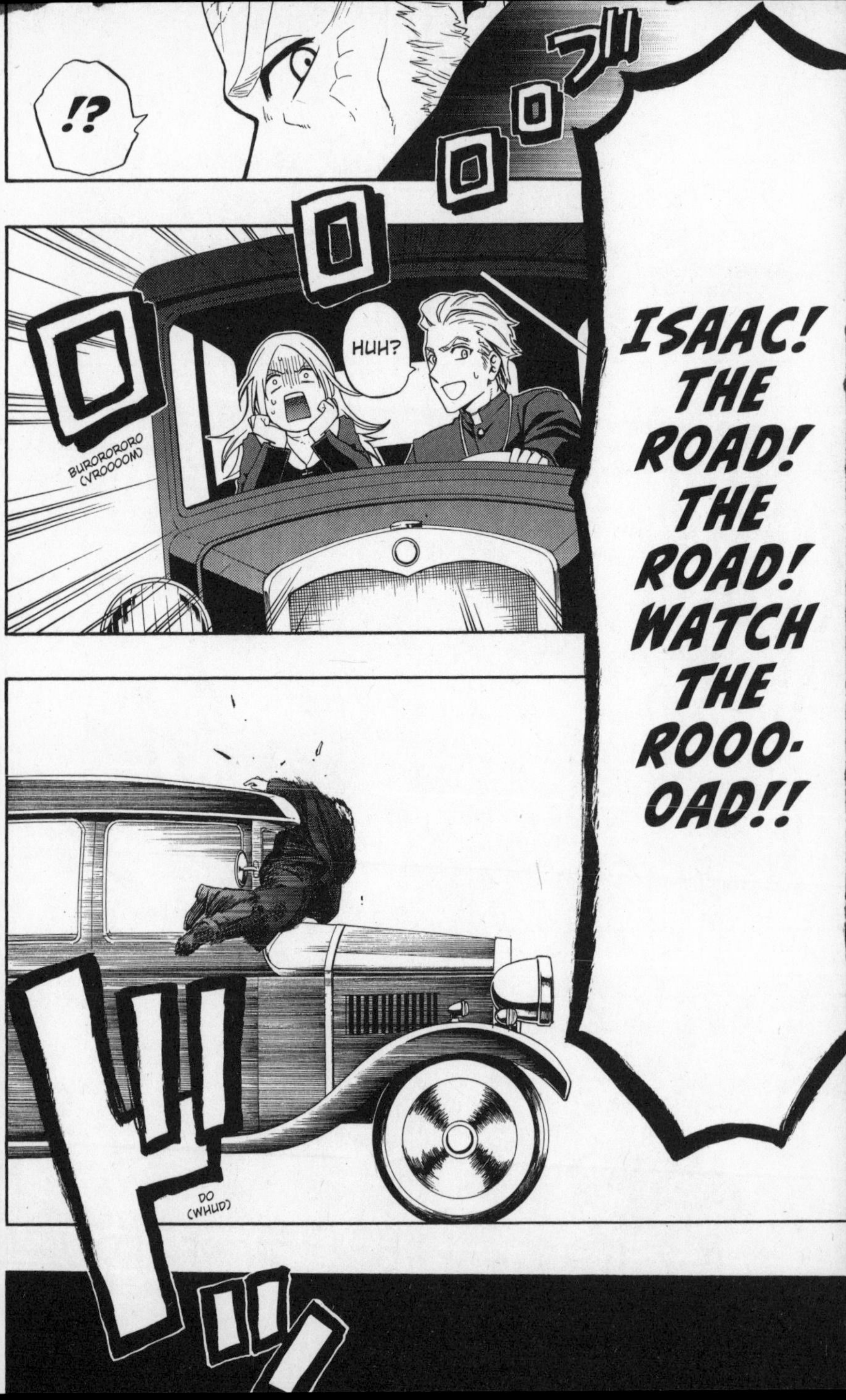
!?
ISAAC! THE ROAD! THE ROAD! WATCH THE ROOO-OAD!!
HUH?
BURORORORO
(VROOOOM)
DO
(WHUD)

#20 Intruder

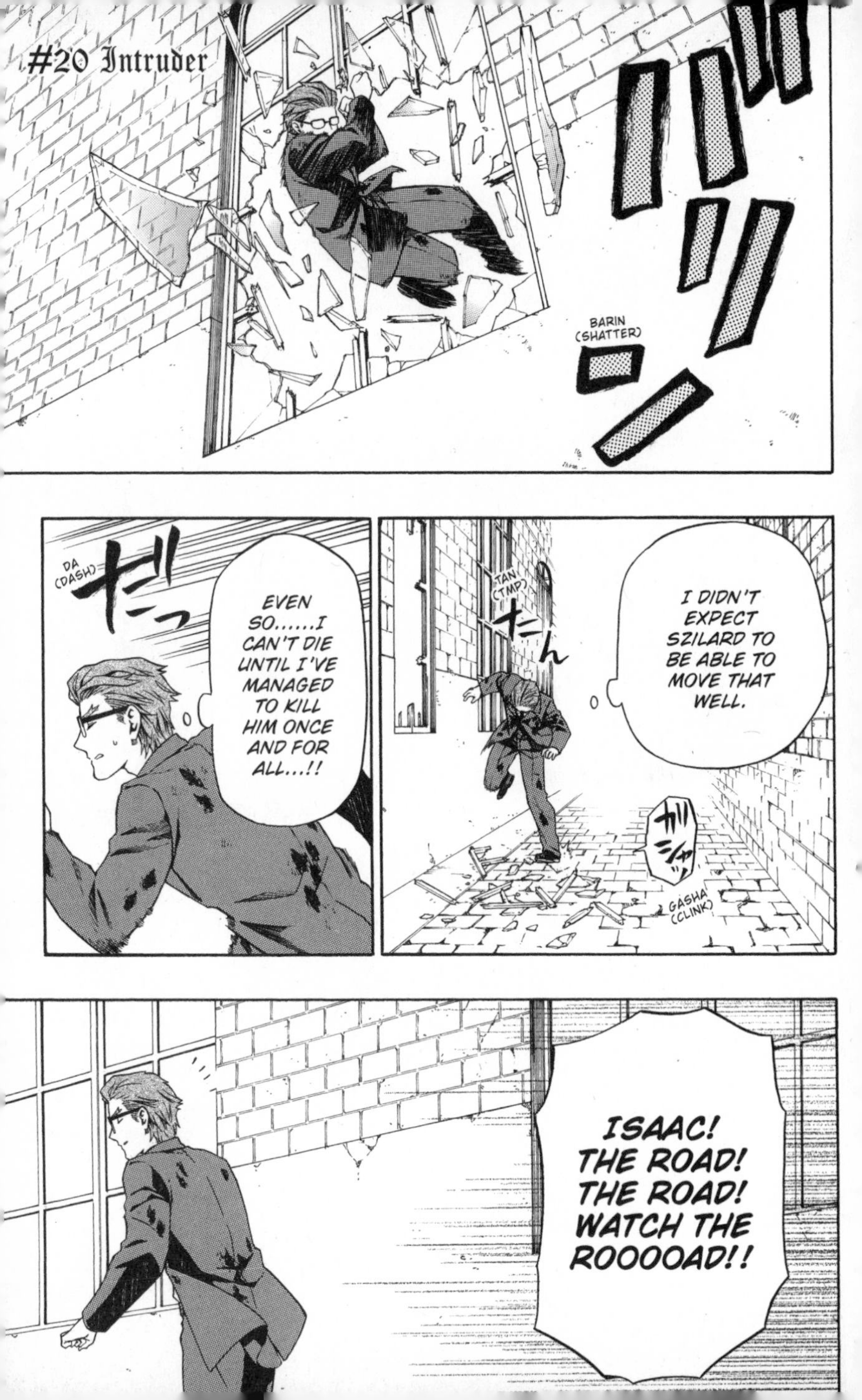
BARIN (SHATTER)
TAN (TMP)
I DIDN'T EXPECT SZILARD TO BE ABLE TO MOVE THAT WELL.
GASHA (CLINK)
DA (DASH)
EVEN SO......I CAN'T DIE UNTIL I'VE MANAGED TO KILL HIM ONCE AND FOR ALL...!!
ISAAC! THE ROAD! THE ROAD! WATCH THE ROOOOAD!!

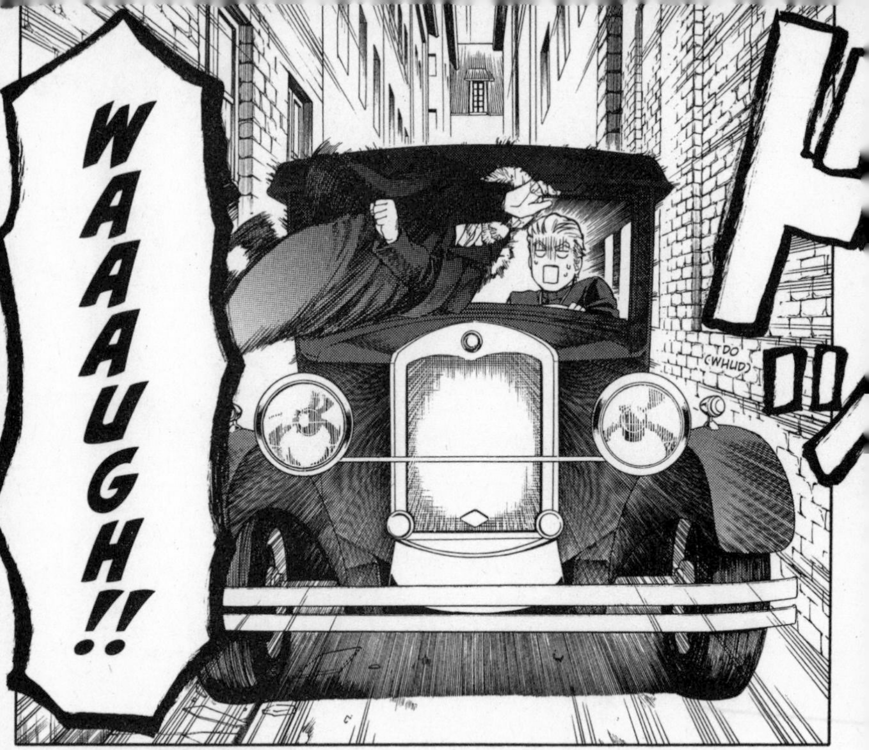
DO (WHUD)
WAAAAUGH!!

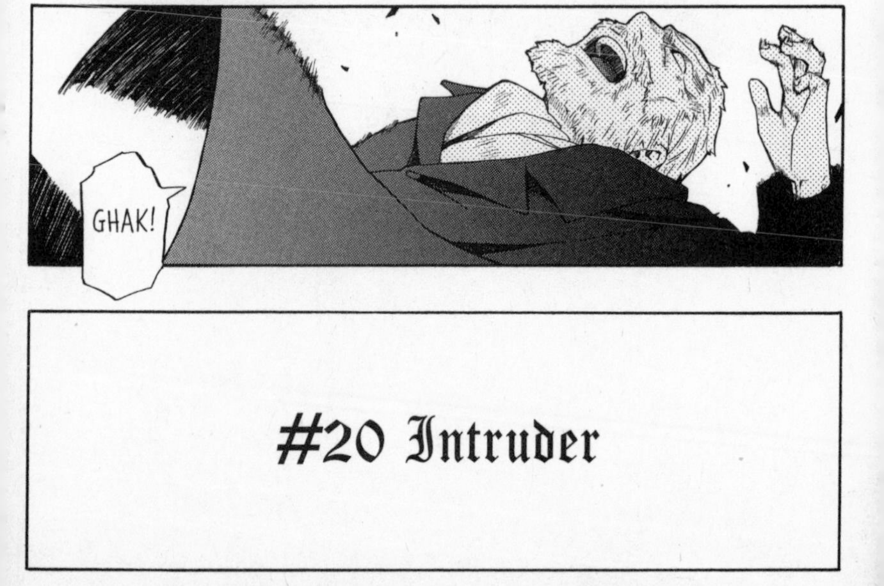
GHAK!

#20 Intruder

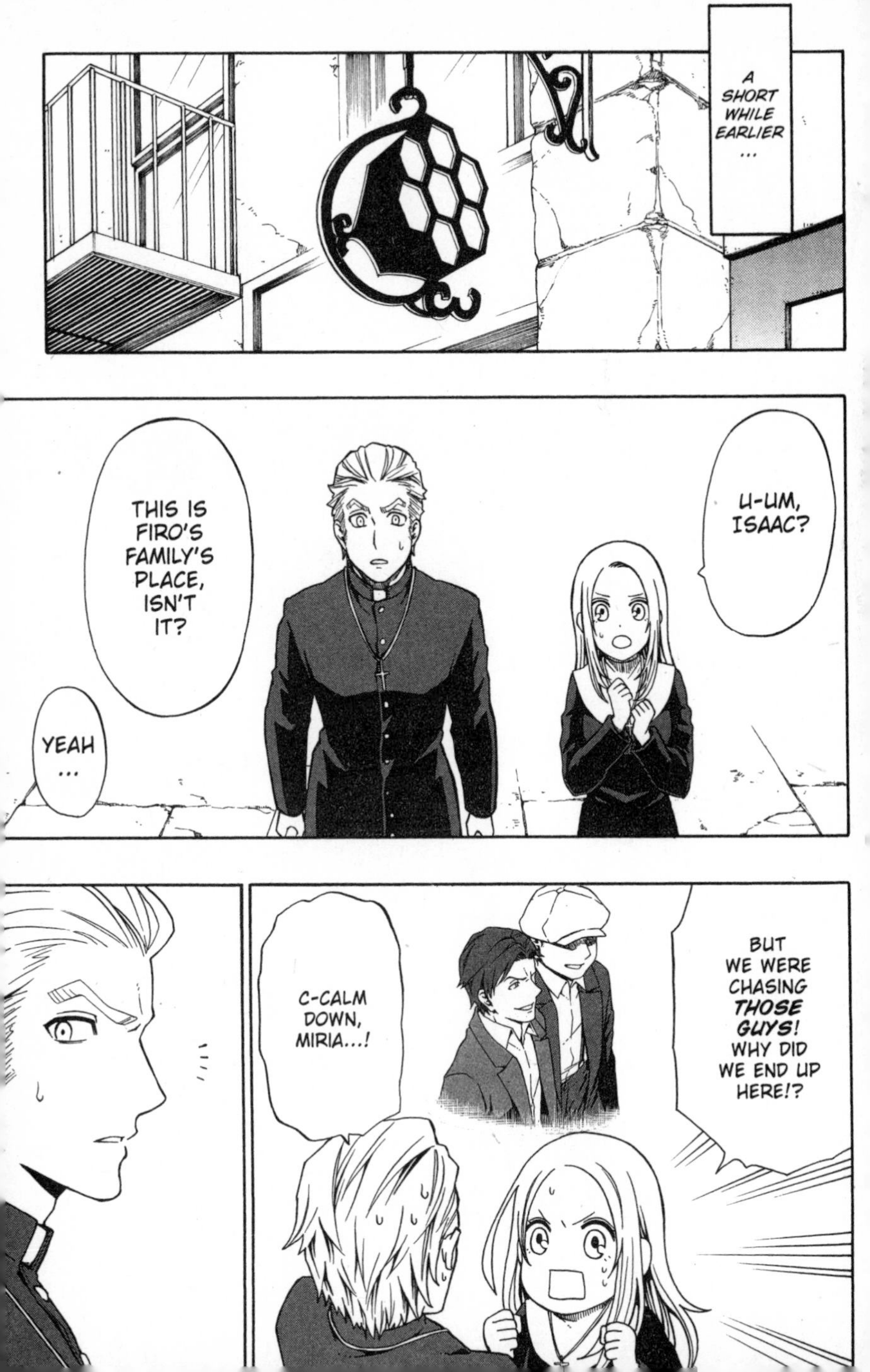
A SHORT WHILE EARLIER ...
U-UM, ISAAC?
THIS IS FIRO'S FAMILY'S PLACE, ISN'T IT?
YEAH ...
BUT WE WERE CHASING ***THOSE GUYS***! WHY DID WE END UP HERE!?
C-CALM DOWN, MIRIA...!

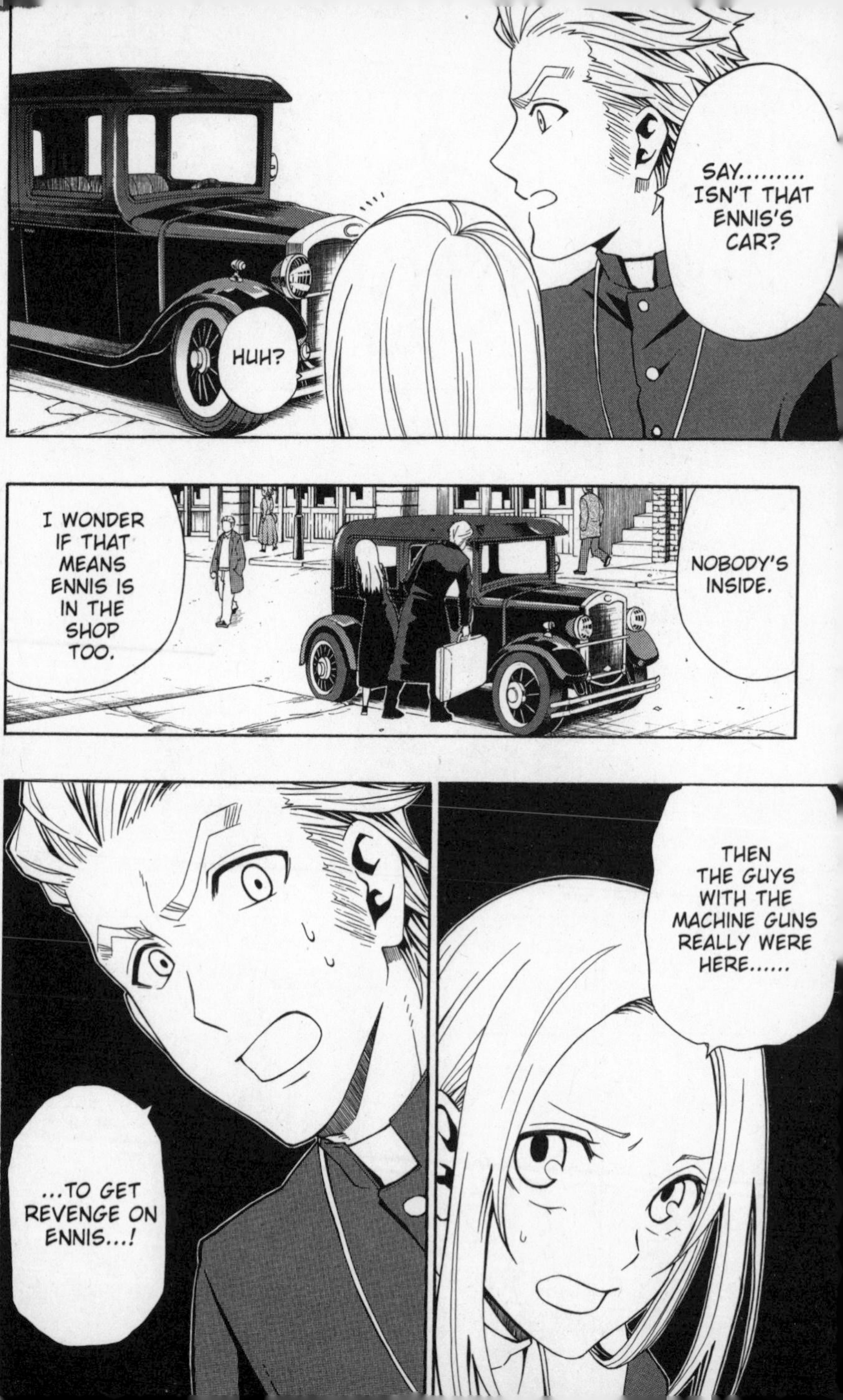
SAY......... ISN'T THAT ENNIS'S CAR?
HUH?
NOBODY'S INSIDE.
I WONDER IF THAT MEANS ENNIS IS IN THE SHOP TOO.
THEN THE GUYS WITH THE MACHINE GUNS REALLY WERE HERE......
...TO GET REVENGE ON ENNIS...!

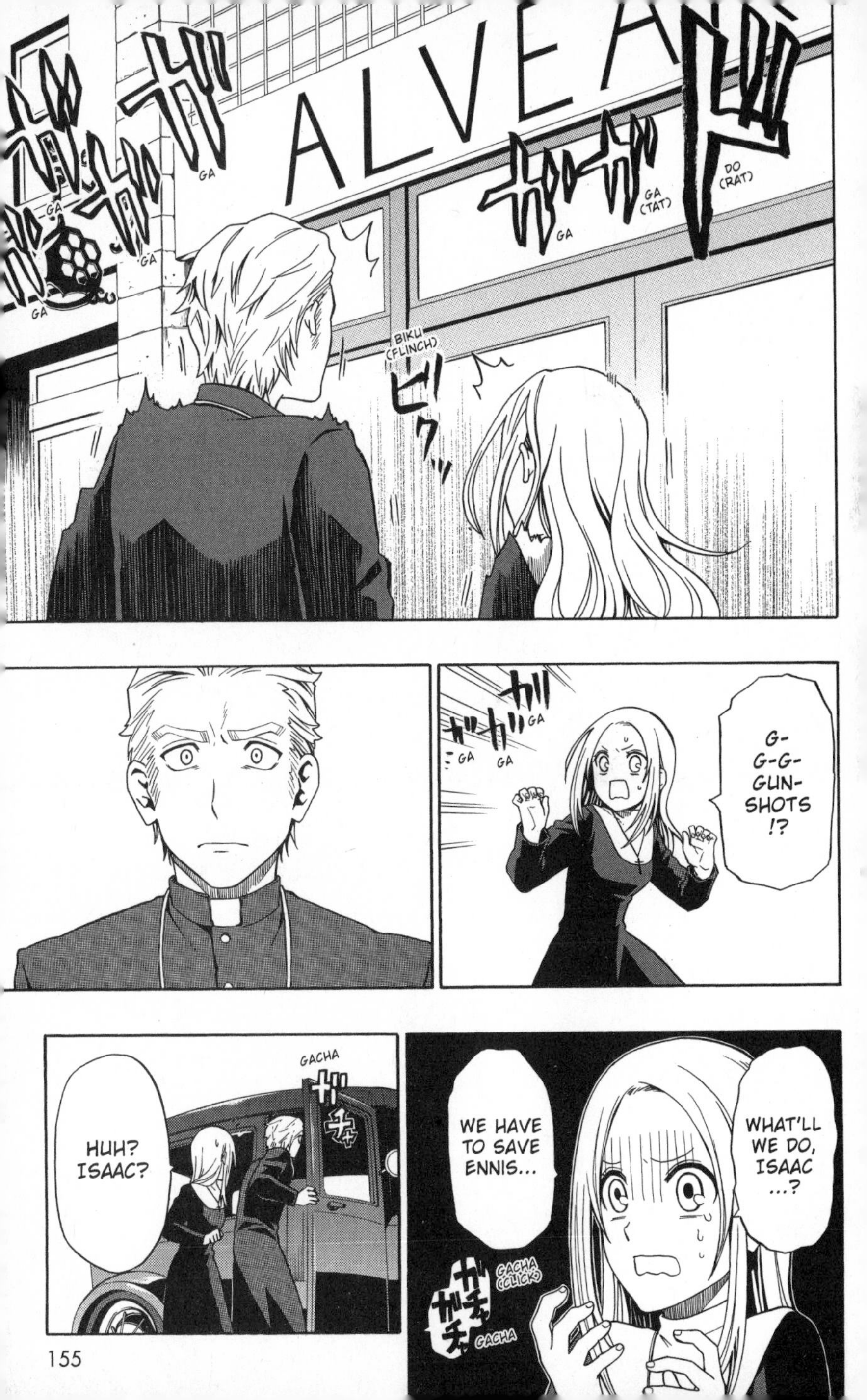
DO (RAT)
GA (TAT)
GA
GA
GA
GA
GA
BIKU (FLINCH)
GA
GA
GA
G-G-G-GUN-SHOTS!?
WHAT'LL WE DO, ISAAC ...?
WE HAVE TO SAVE ENNIS...
GACHA (CLICK)
GACHA
GACHA
HUH? ISAAC?

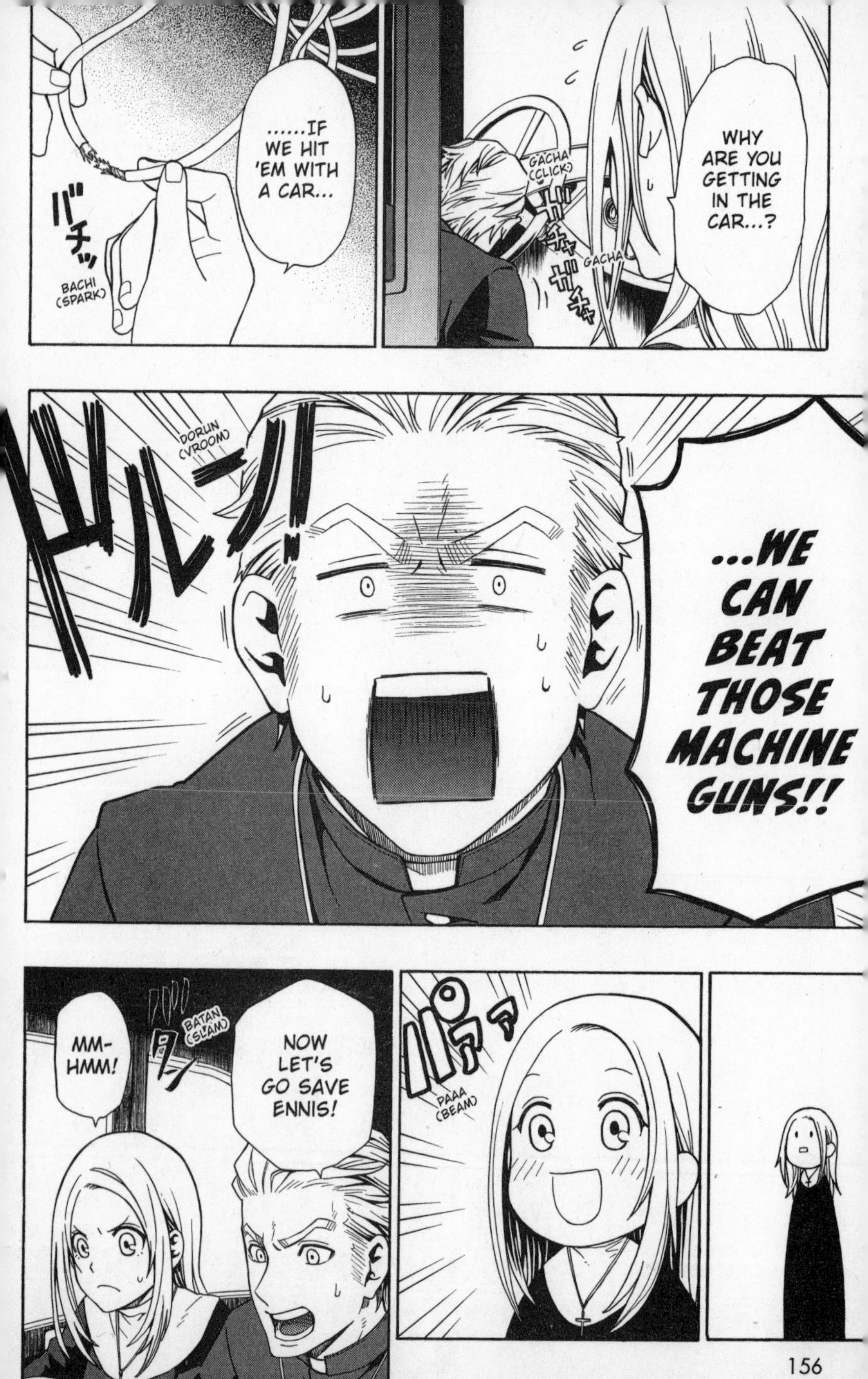
WHY ARE YOU GETTING IN THE CAR...?
GACHA (CLICK)
GACHA
......IF WE HIT 'EM WITH A CAR...
BACHI (SPARK)
...WE CAN BEAT THOSE MACHINE GUNS!!
DORUN (VROOM)
PAAA (BEAM)
NOW LET'S GO SAVE ENNIS!
BATAN (SLAM)
MM-HMM!

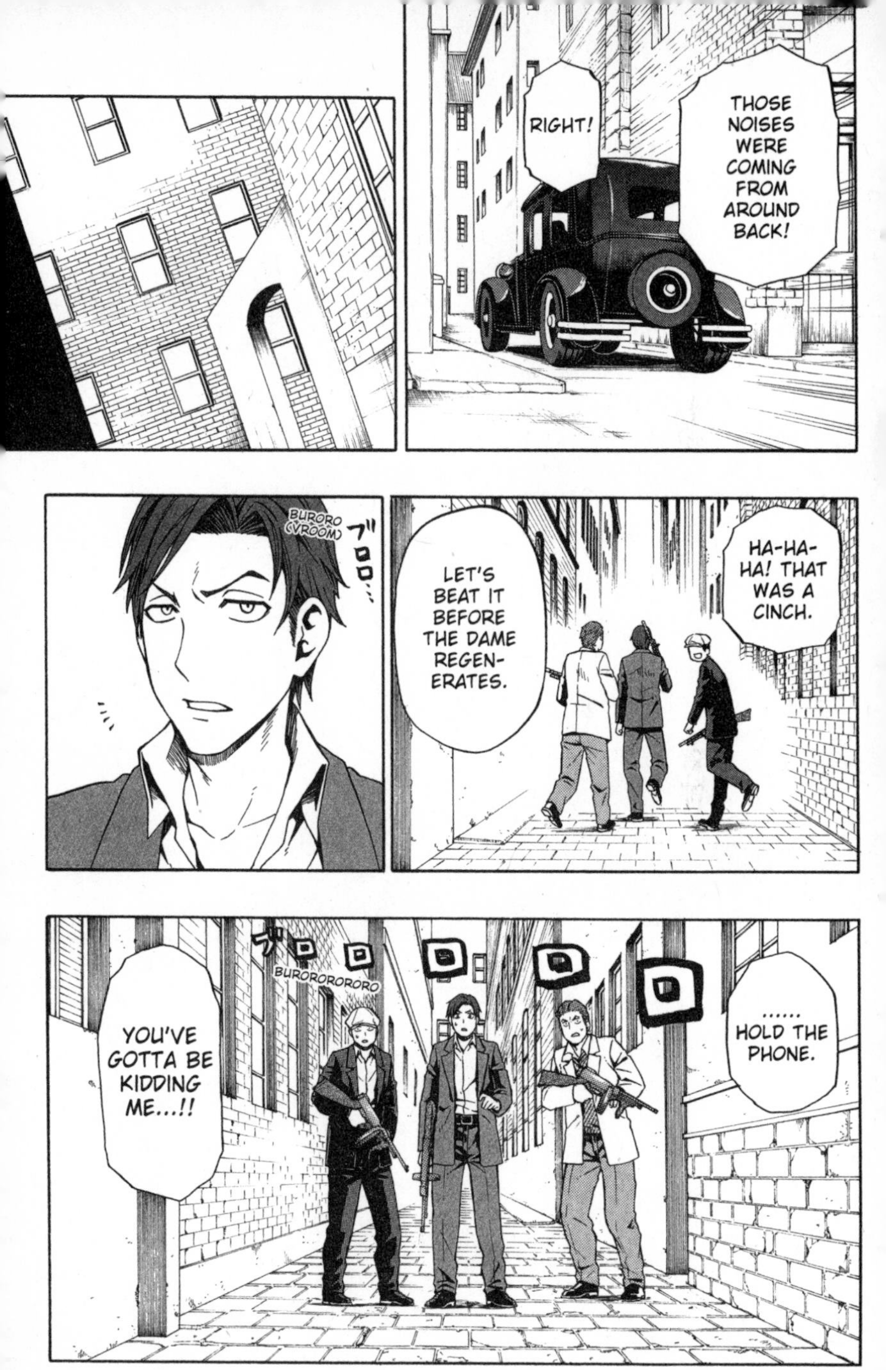
THOSE NOISES WERE COMING FROM AROUND BACK!
RIGHT!
HA-HA-HA! THAT WAS A CINCH.
LET'S BEAT IT BEFORE THE DAME REGENERATES.
BURORO (VROOM)
ブロロ…
...... HOLD THE PHONE.
ブロロロロロロ
BURORORORORO
YOU'VE GOTTA BE KIDDING ME...!!

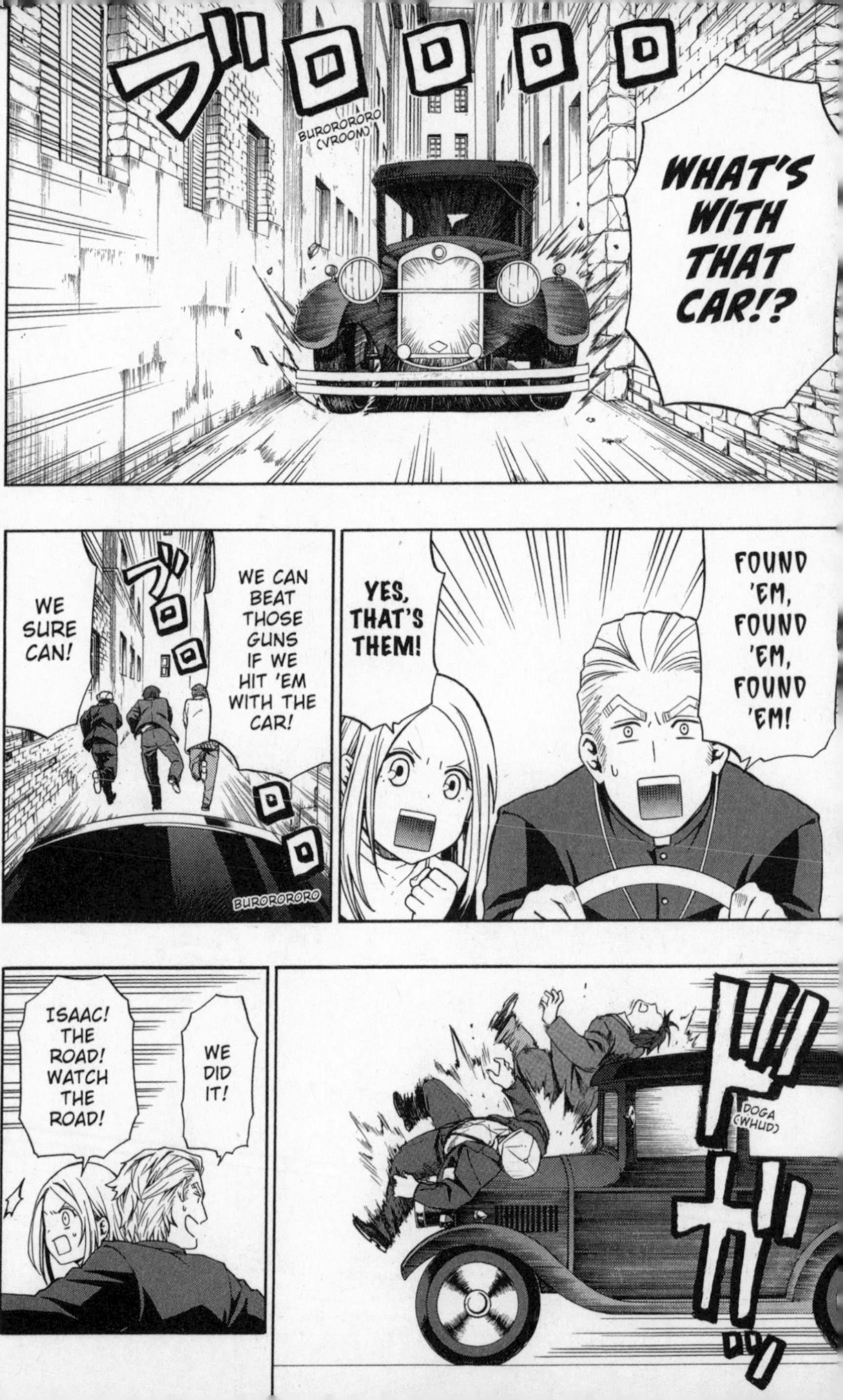
ブロロロロロ
BURORORORO (VROOM)
WHAT'S WITH THAT CAR!?
FOUND 'EM, FOUND 'EM, FOUND 'EM!
YES, THAT'S THEM!
WE CAN BEAT THOSE GUNS IF WE HIT 'EM WITH THE CAR!
WE SURE CAN!
ブロロロロ
BURORORORO
ドガッ
DOGA (WHUD)
WE DID IT!
ISAAC! THE ROAD! WATCH THE ROAD!

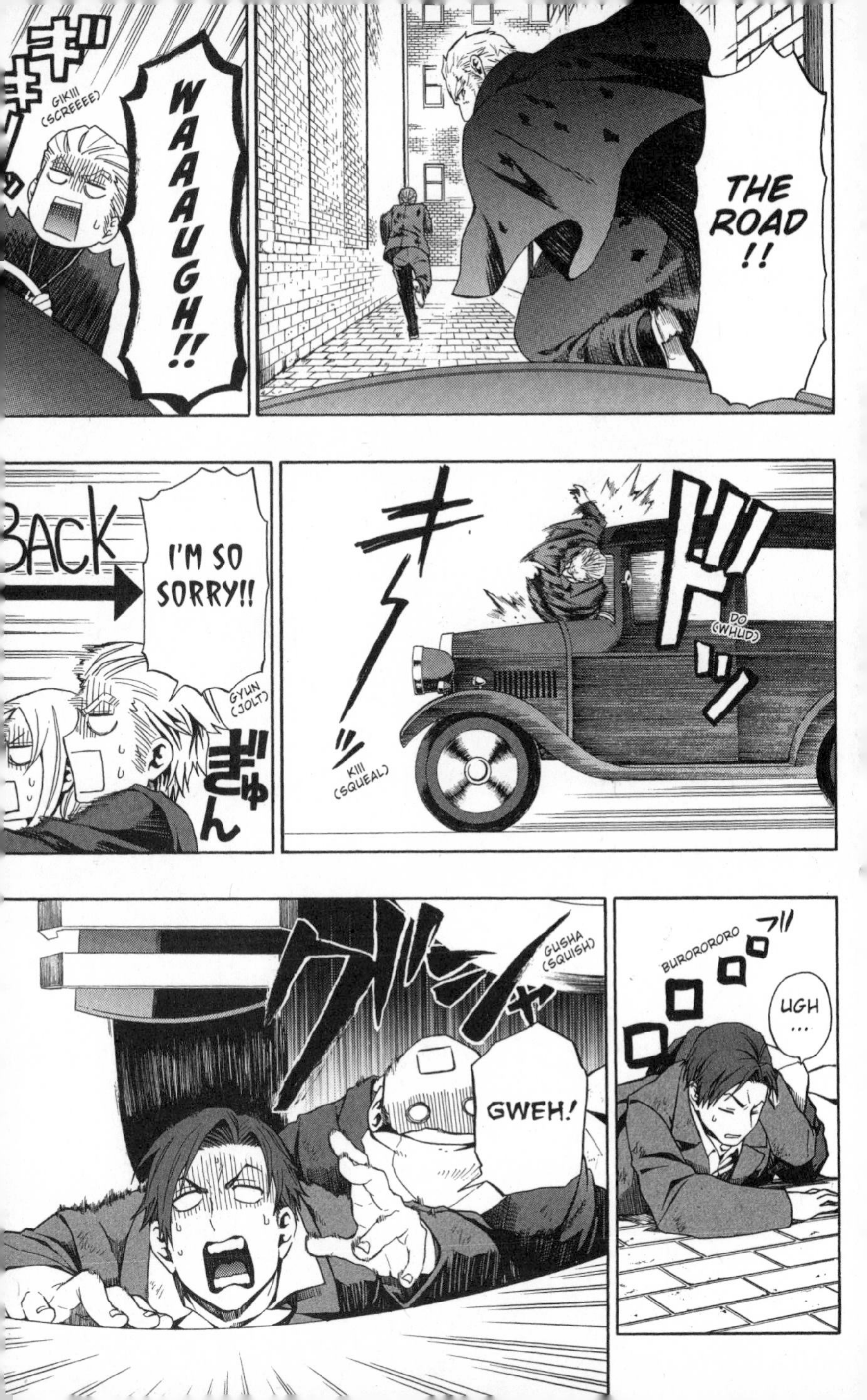
THE ROAD !!
GIKIII (SCREEEE)
WAAAAUGH!!
KIII (SQUEAL)
DO (WHUD)
BACK
I'M SO SORRY!!
GYUN (JOLT)
ぎゅん
BURORORORO
UGH ...
GUSHA (SQUISH)
GWEH!

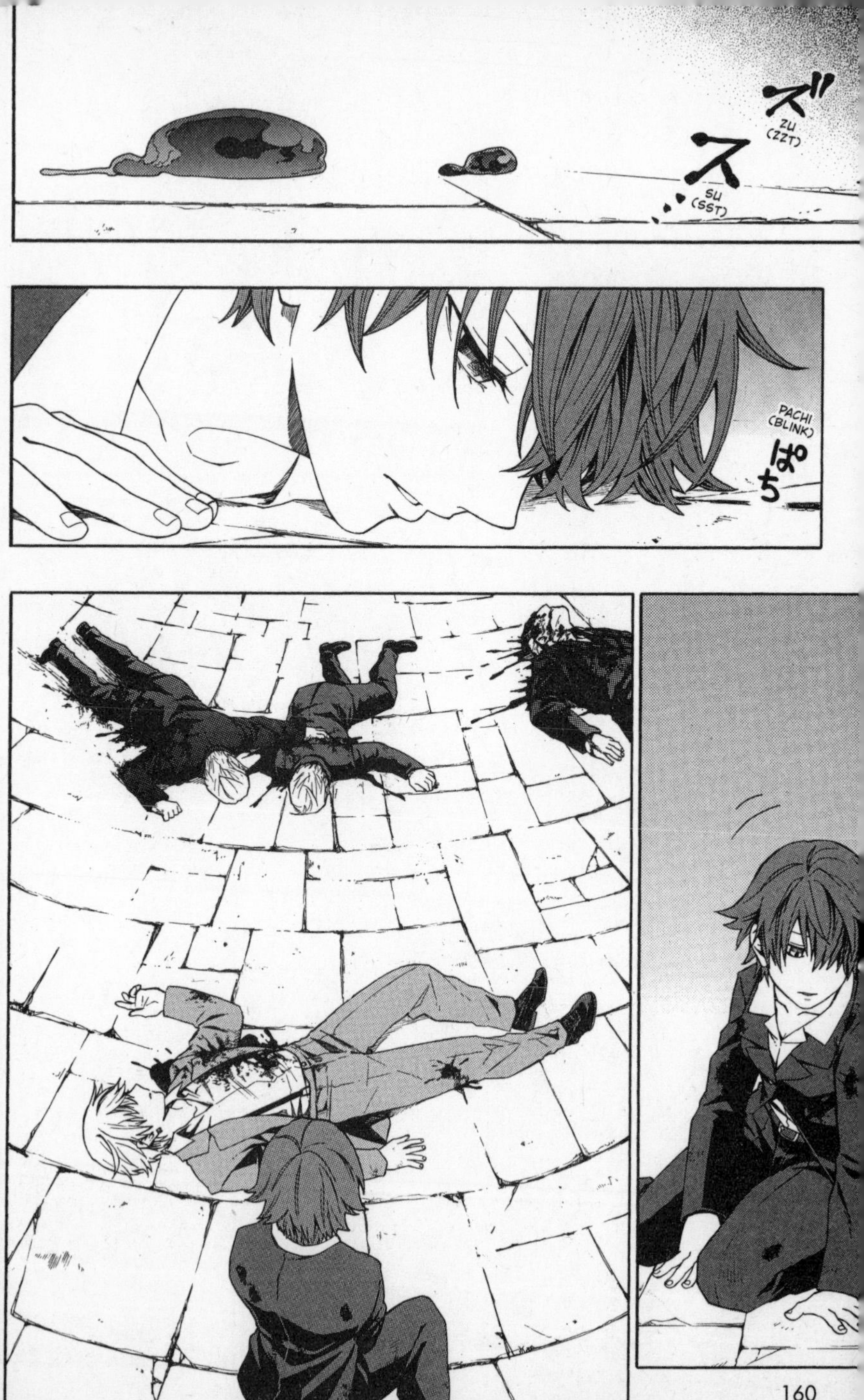
ズ
ZU (ZZT)
ス
SU (SST)
PACHI (BLINK)
ぱち

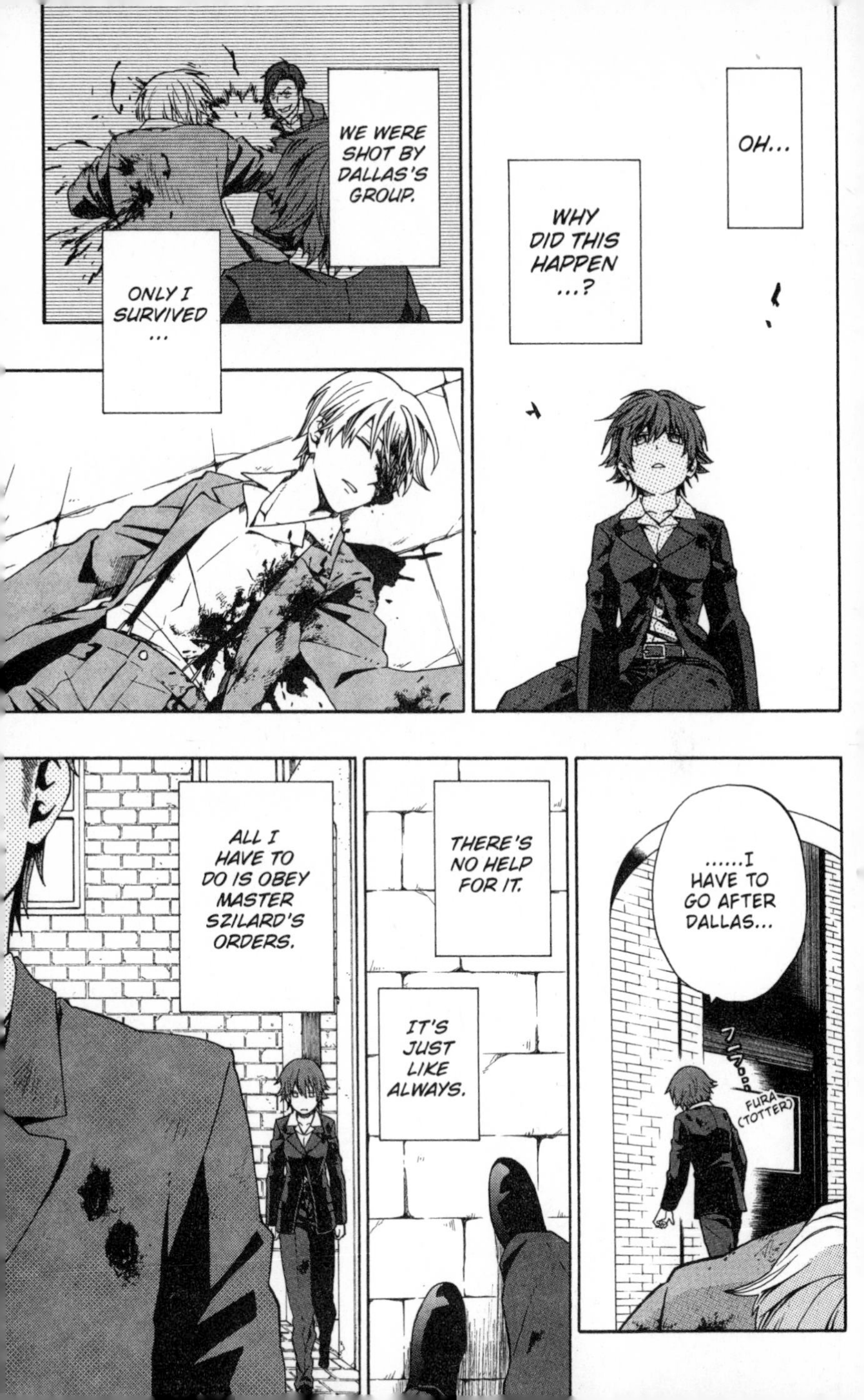
OH...
WHY DID THIS HAPPEN ...?
WE WERE SHOT BY DALLAS'S GROUP.
ONLY I SURVIVED ...
......I HAVE TO GO AFTER DALLAS...
FURA (TOTTER)
THERE'S NO HELP FOR IT.
IT'S JUST LIKE ALWAYS.
ALL I HAVE TO DO IS OBEY MASTER SZILARD'S ORDERS.

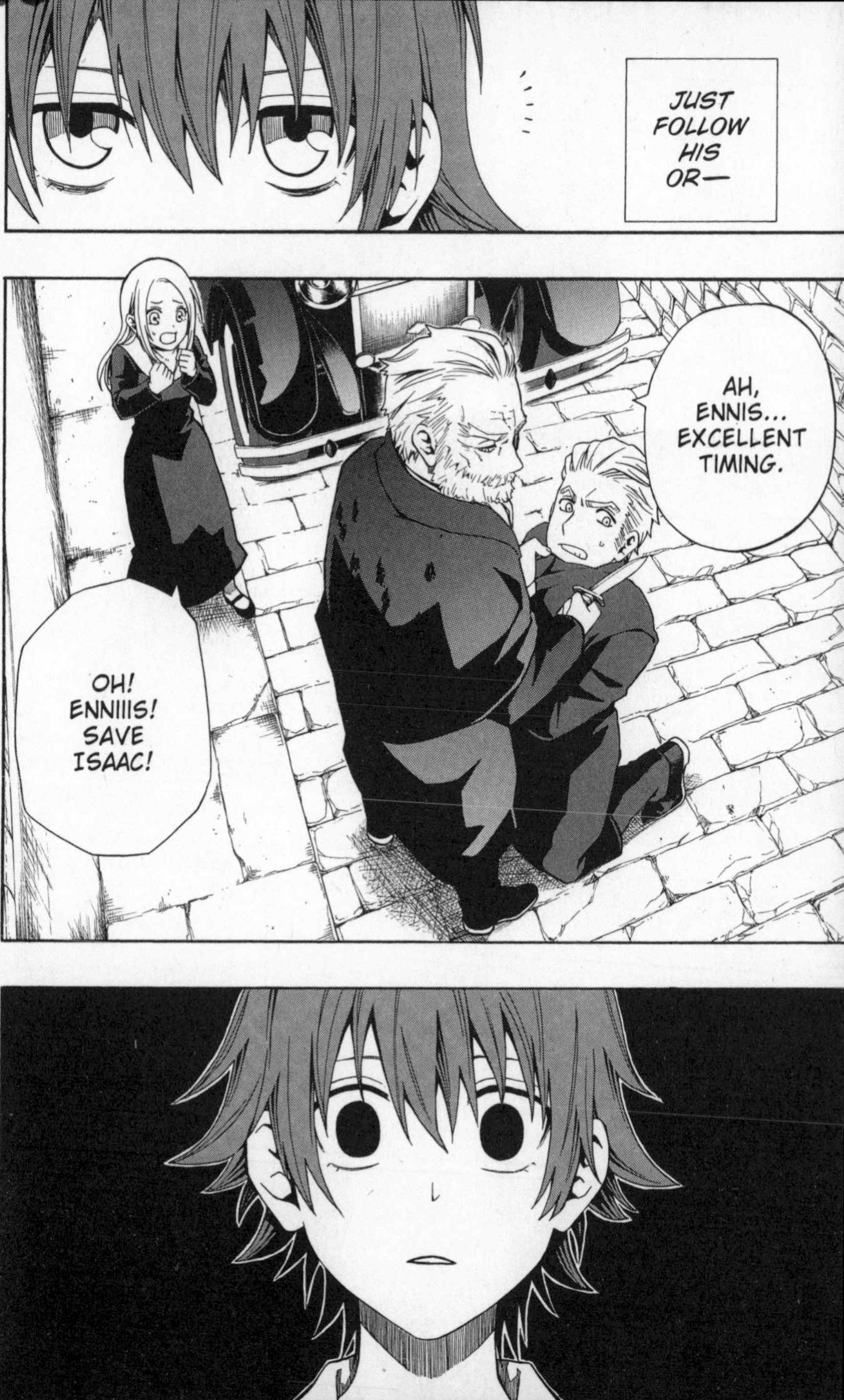
JUST FOLLOW HIS OR—
AH, ENNIS... EXCELLENT TIMING.
OH! ENNIIIS! SAVE ISAAC!

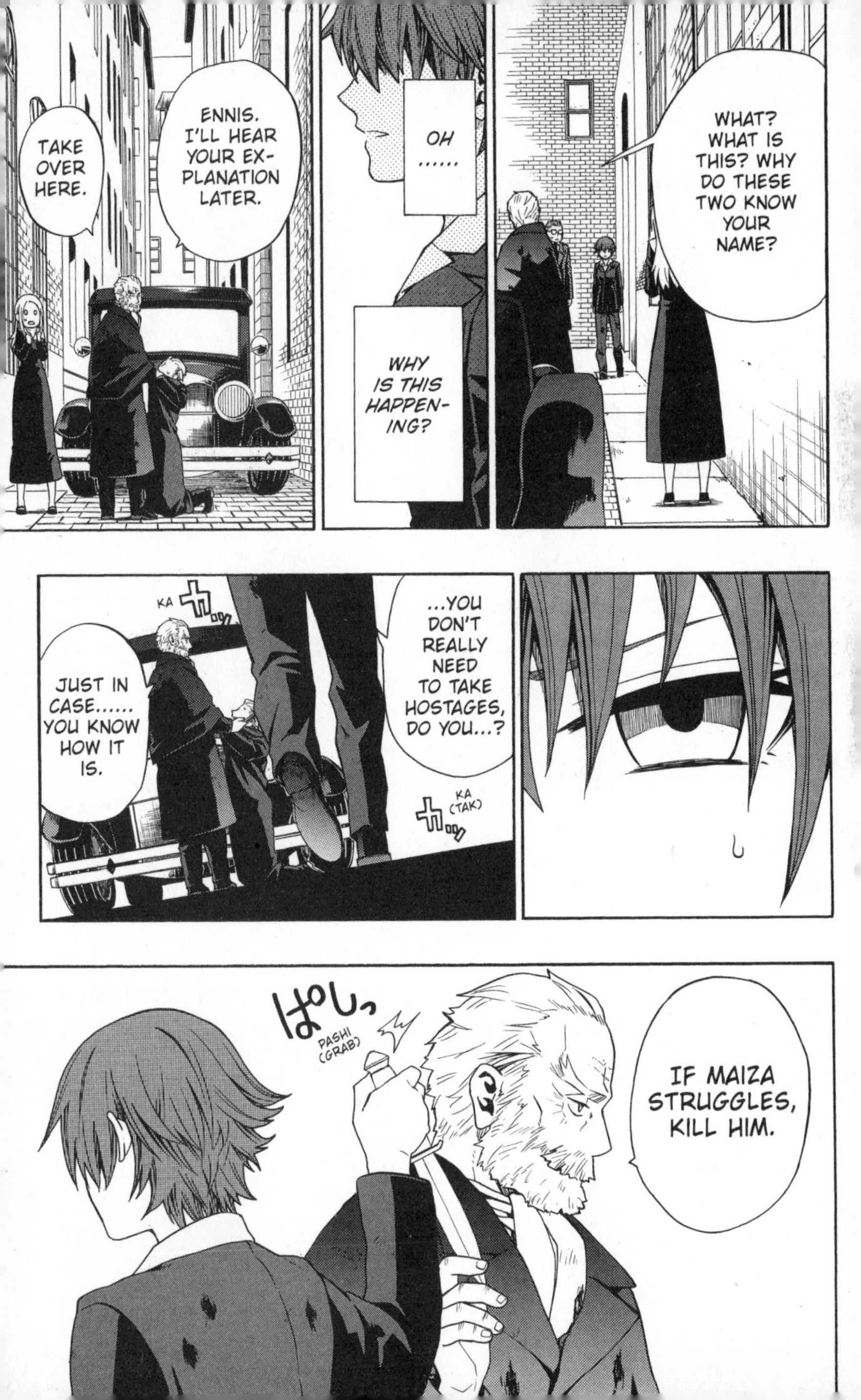
WHAT? WHAT IS THIS? WHY DO THESE TWO KNOW YOUR NAME?
OH ......
WHY IS THIS HAPPENING?
ENNIS. I'LL HEAR YOUR EXPLANATION LATER.
TAKE OVER HERE.
...YOU DON'T REALLY NEED TO TAKE HOSTAGES, DO YOU...?
KA
JUST IN CASE...... YOU KNOW HOW IT IS.
KA (TAK)
IF MAIZA STRUGGLES, KILL HIM.
ぱしっ
PASHI (GRAB)

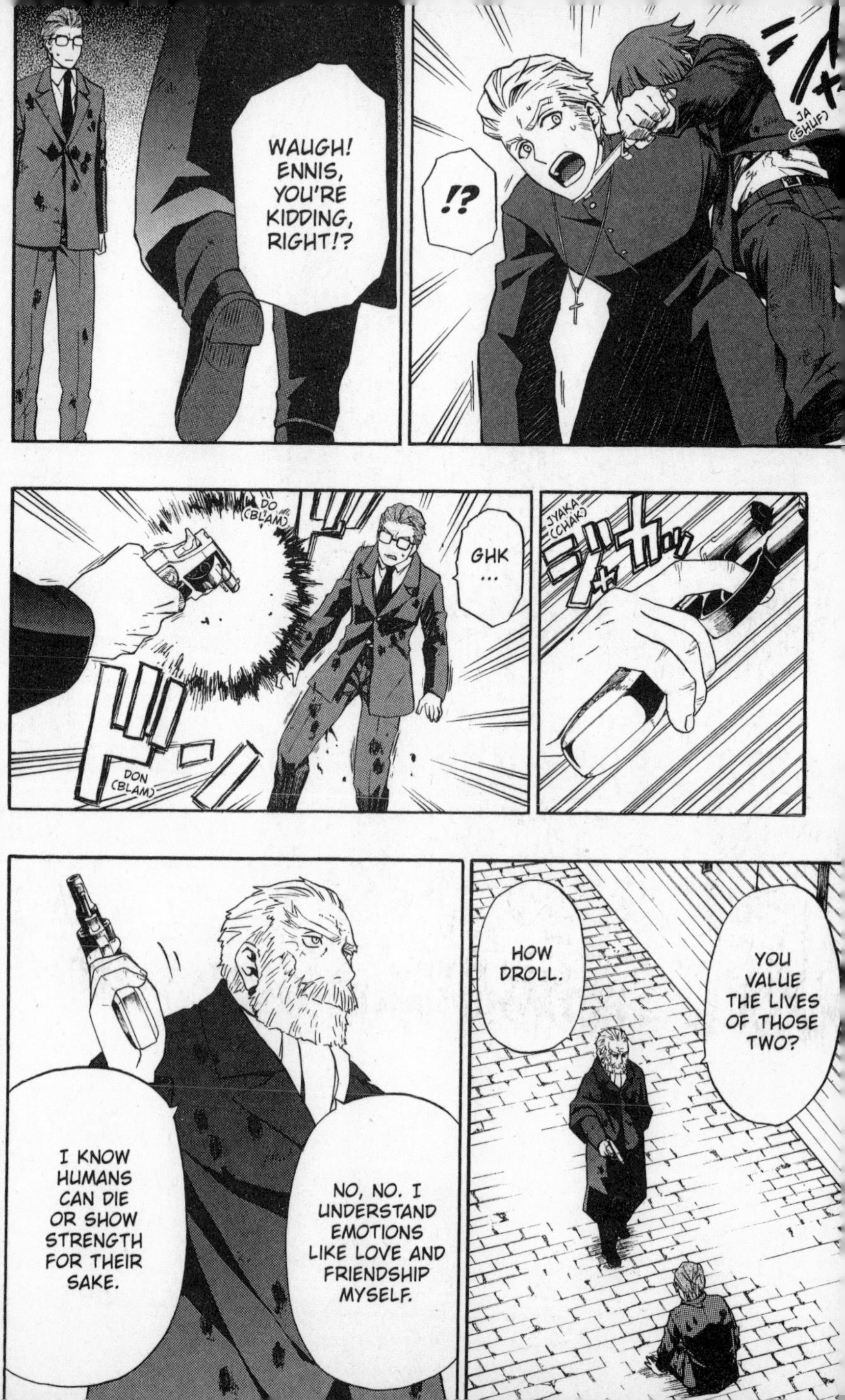
JA (SHUF)
!?
WAUGH! ENNIS, YOU'RE KIDDING, RIGHT!?
JYAKA (CHAK)
DO (BLAM)
GHK ...
DON (BLAM)
YOU VALUE THE LIVES OF THOSE TWO?
HOW DROLL.
NO, NO. I UNDERSTAND EMOTIONS LIKE LOVE AND FRIENDSHIP MYSELF.
I KNOW HUMANS CAN DIE OR SHOW STRENGTH FOR THEIR SAKE.

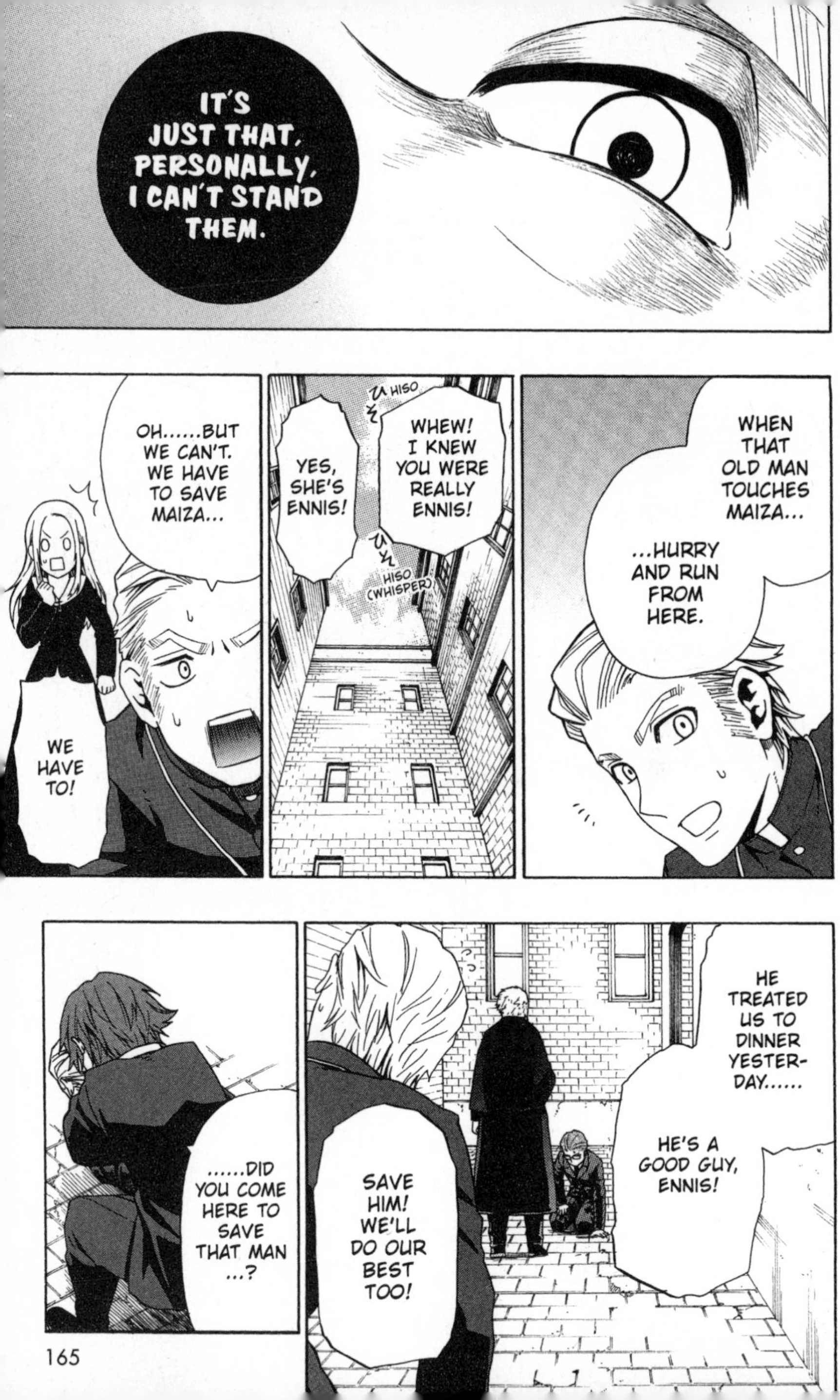
IT'S JUST THAT, PERSONALLY, I CAN'T STAND THEM.
WHEN THAT OLD MAN TOUCHES MAIZA...
...HURRY AND RUN FROM HERE.
HISO
WHEW! I KNEW YOU WERE REALLY ENNIS!
YES, SHE'S ENNIS!
HISO (WHISPER)
OH......BUT WE CAN'T. WE HAVE TO SAVE MAIZA...
WE HAVE TO!
HE TREATED US TO DINNER YESTER-DAY......
HE'S A GOOD GUY, ENNIS!
SAVE HIM! WE'LL DO OUR BEST TOO!
......DID YOU COME HERE TO SAVE THAT MAN ...?

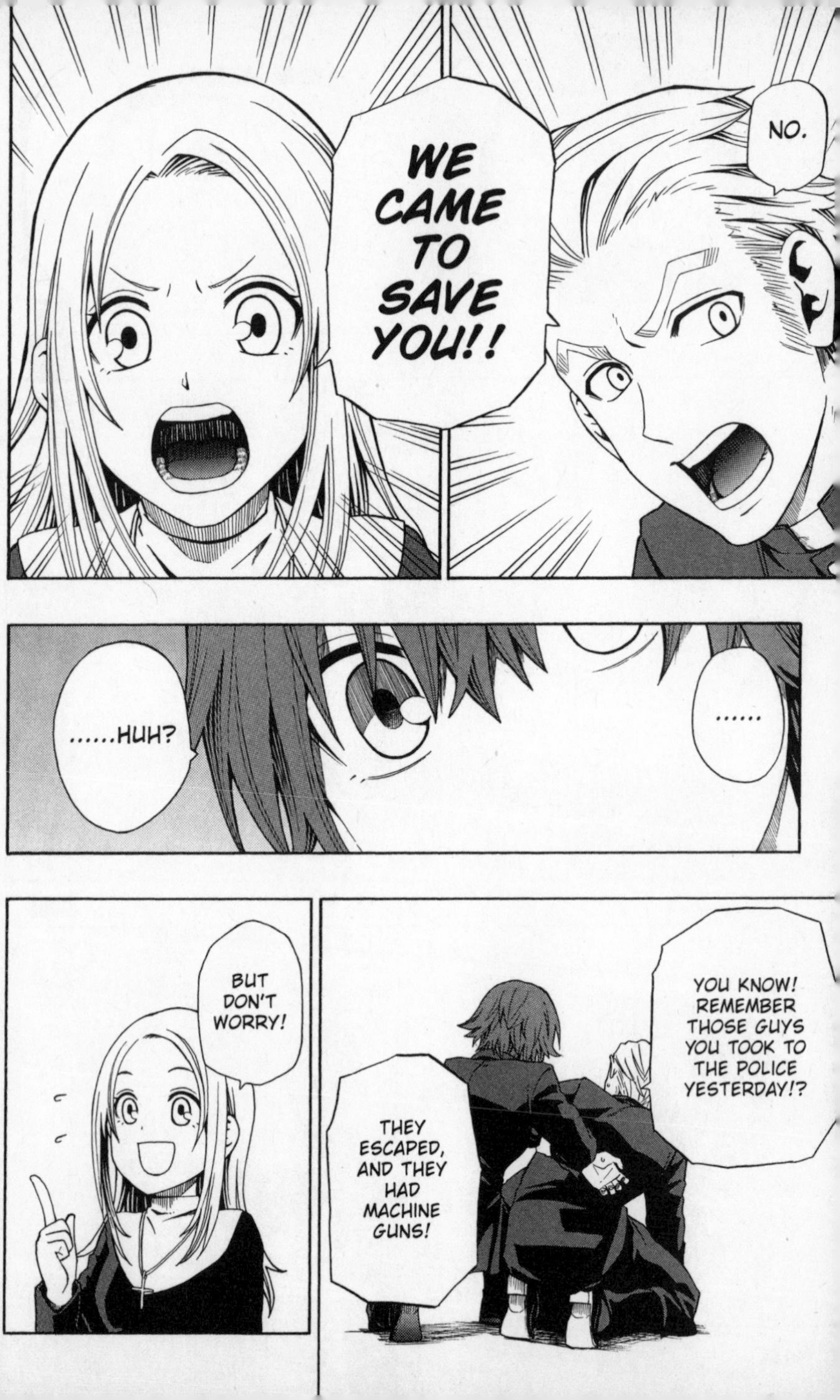
NO.
WE CAME TO SAVE YOU!!
......
......HUH?
YOU KNOW! REMEMBER THOSE GUYS YOU TOOK TO THE POLICE YESTERDAY!?
THEY ESCAPED, AND THEY HAD MACHINE GUNS!
BUT DON'T WORRY!

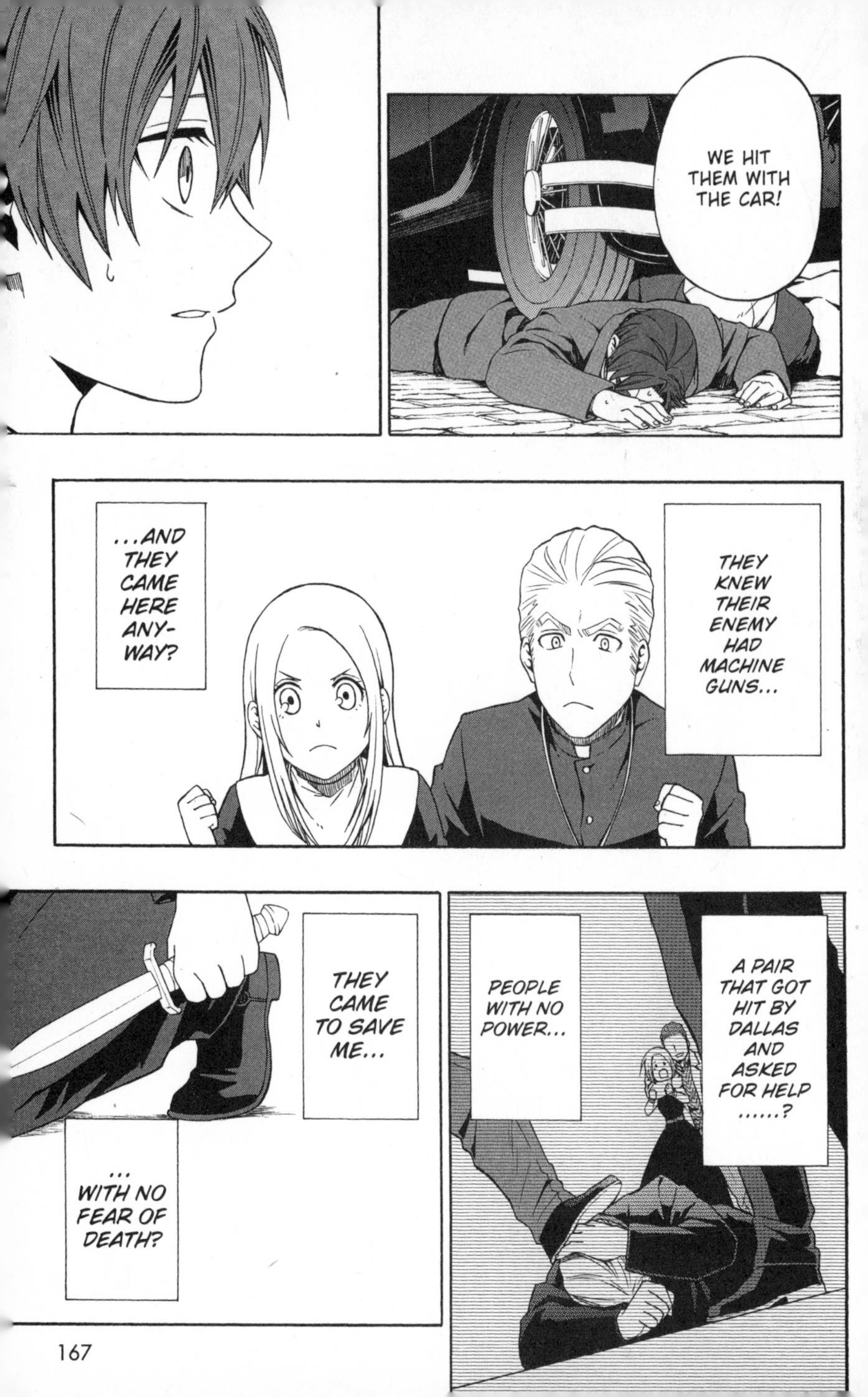
WE HIT THEM WITH THE CAR!
THEY KNEW THEIR ENEMY HAD MACHINE GUNS...
...AND THEY CAME HERE ANY-WAY?
A PAIR THAT GOT HIT BY DALLAS AND ASKED FOR HELP ......?
PEOPLE WITH NO POWER...
THEY CAME TO SAVE ME...
... WITH NO FEAR OF DEATH?

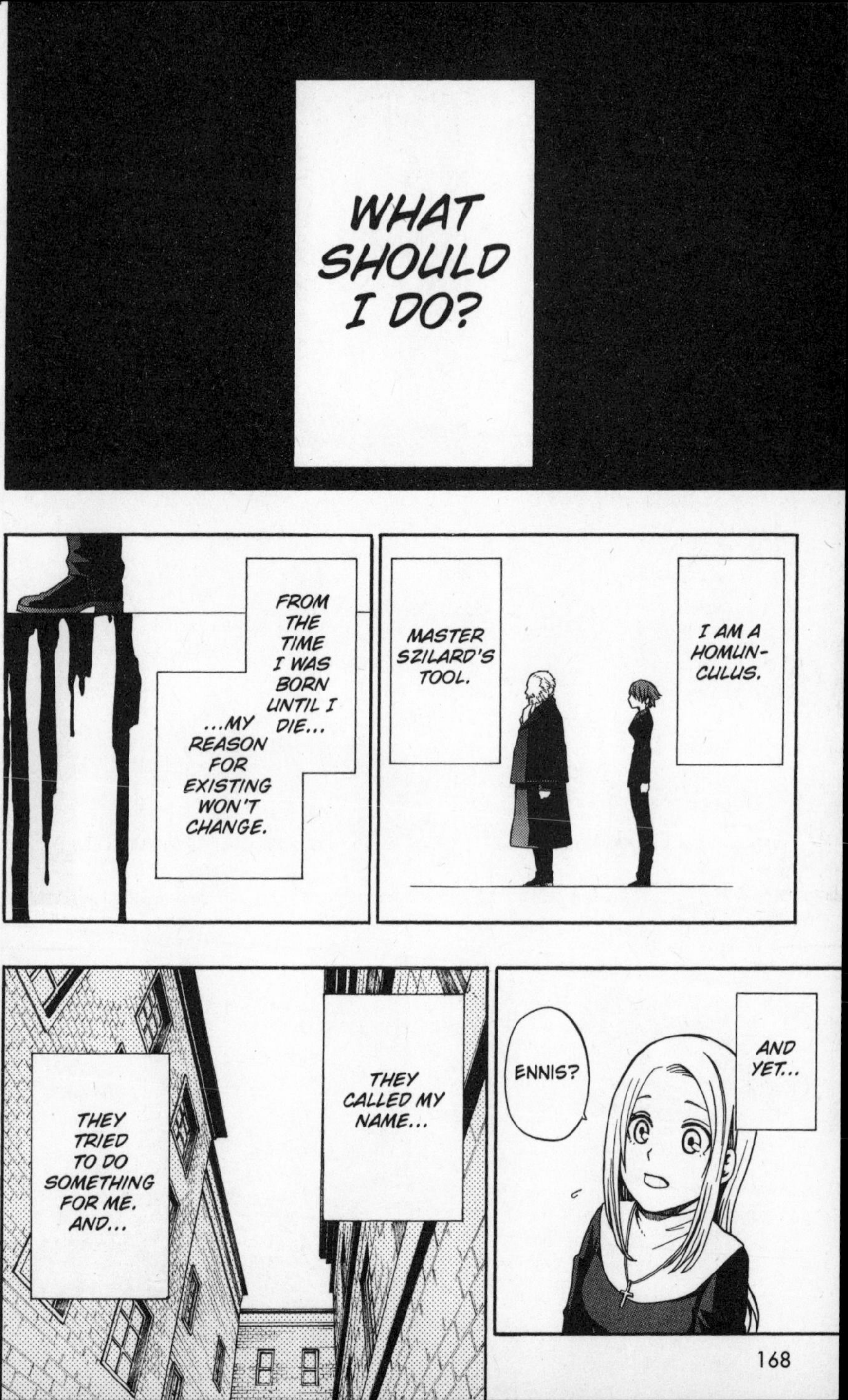
WHAT SHOULD I DO?
I AM A HOMUNCULUS.
MASTER SZILARD'S TOOL.
FROM THE TIME I WAS BORN UNTIL I DIE...
...MY REASON FOR EXISTING WON'T CHANGE.
AND YET...
ENNIS?
THEY CALLED MY NAME...
THEY TRIED TO DO SOMETHING FOR ME. AND...

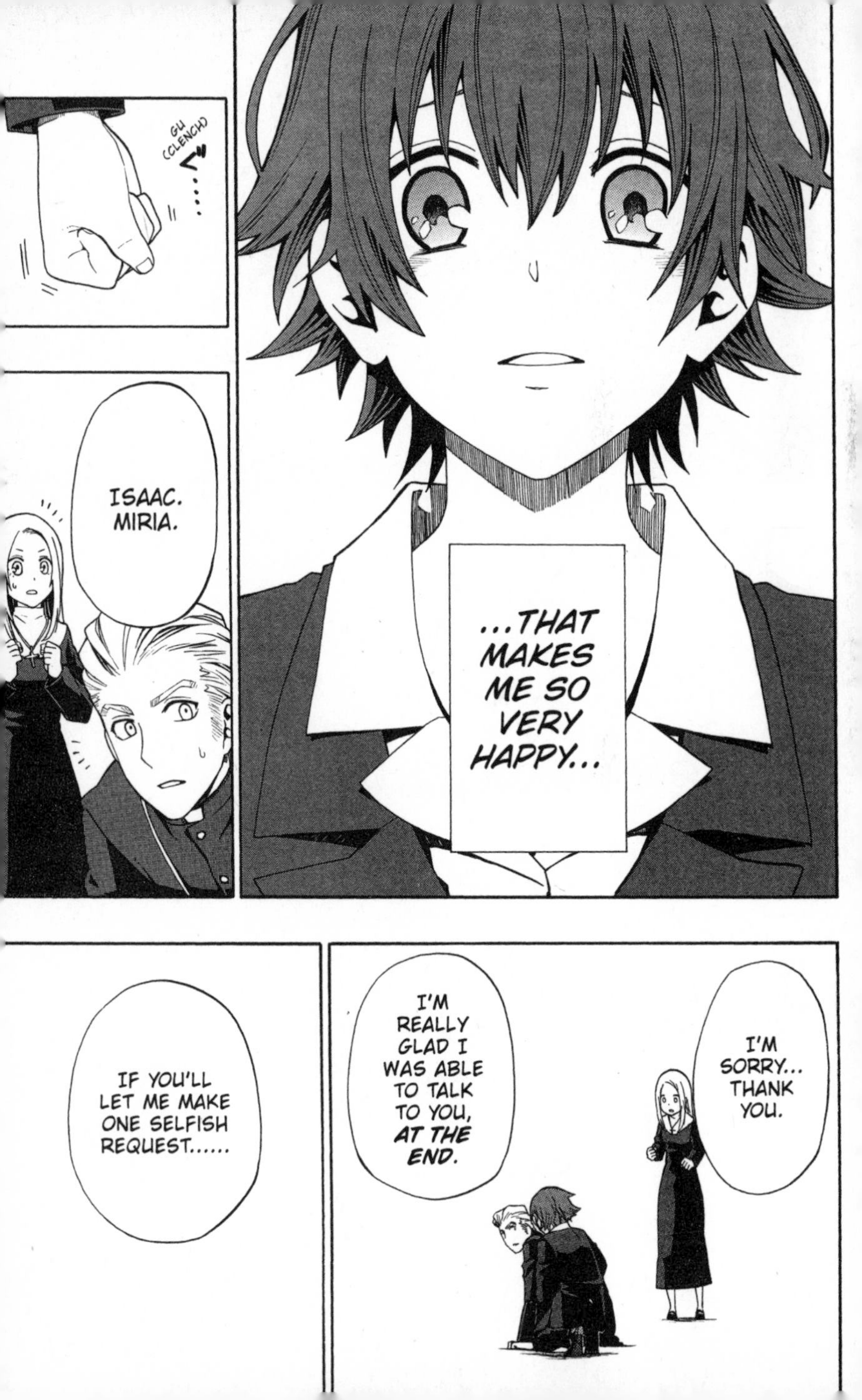
...THAT MAKES ME SO VERY HAPPY...
GU (CLENCH)
ISAAC. MIRIA.
I'M SORRY... THANK YOU.
I'M REALLY GLAD I WAS ABLE TO TALK TO YOU, AT THE END.
IF YOU'LL LET ME MAKE ONE SELFISH REQUEST......

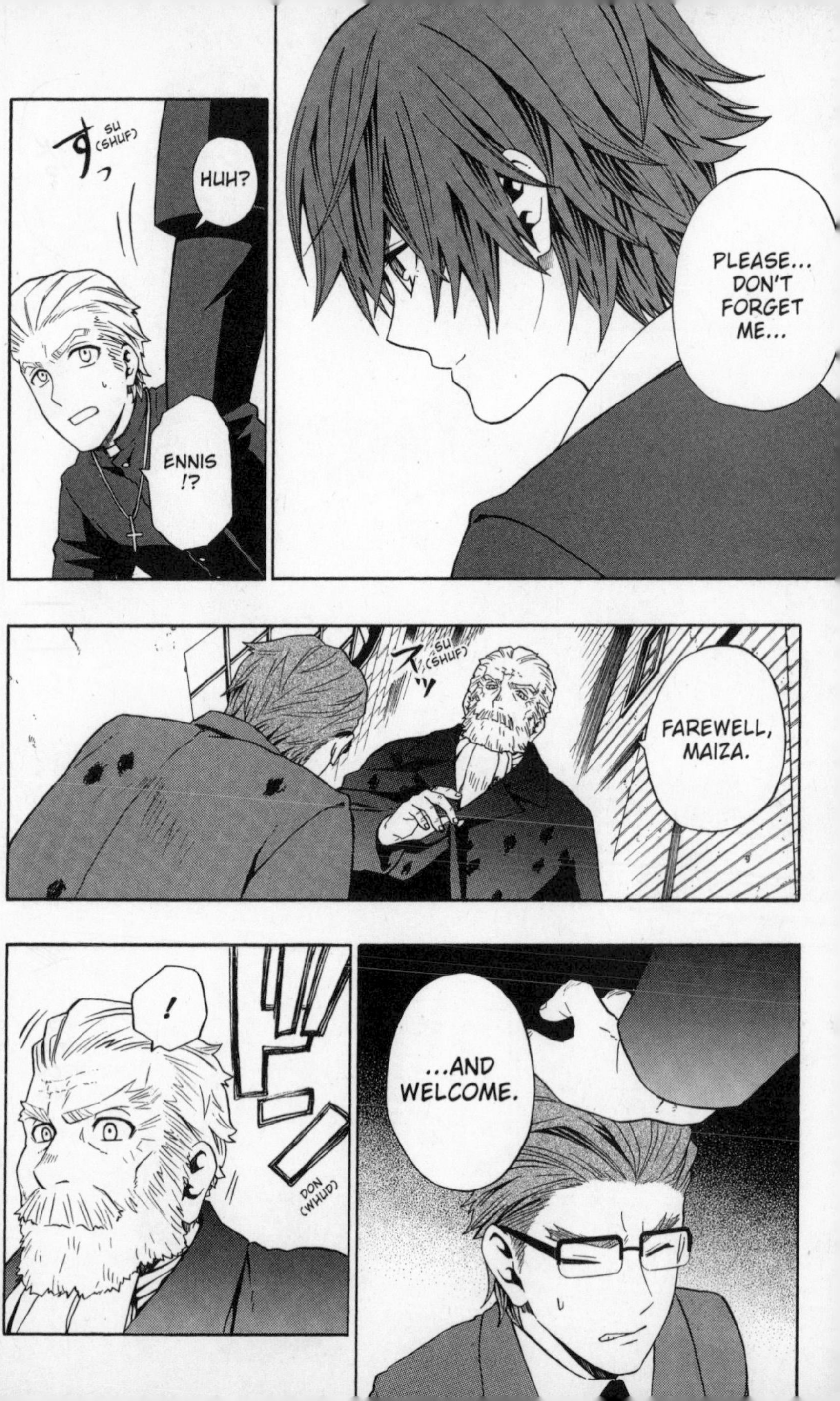
PLEASE... DON'T FORGET ME...
SU (SHUF)
HUH?
ENNIS !?
FAREWELL, MAIZA.
SU (SHUF)
...AND WELCOME.
!
DON (WHUD)

ENNIS... WHAT IS THE MEANING OF THIS?

GIRO (GLARE)

GAHK ...!?

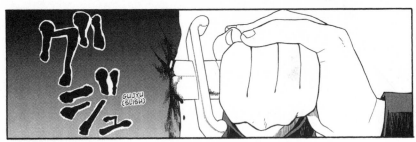

GUJYU (SLISH)

DA (DASH)

BA (BAM)

NO. NEVER MIND. THE TIME FOR EXPLANATIONS IS PAST!

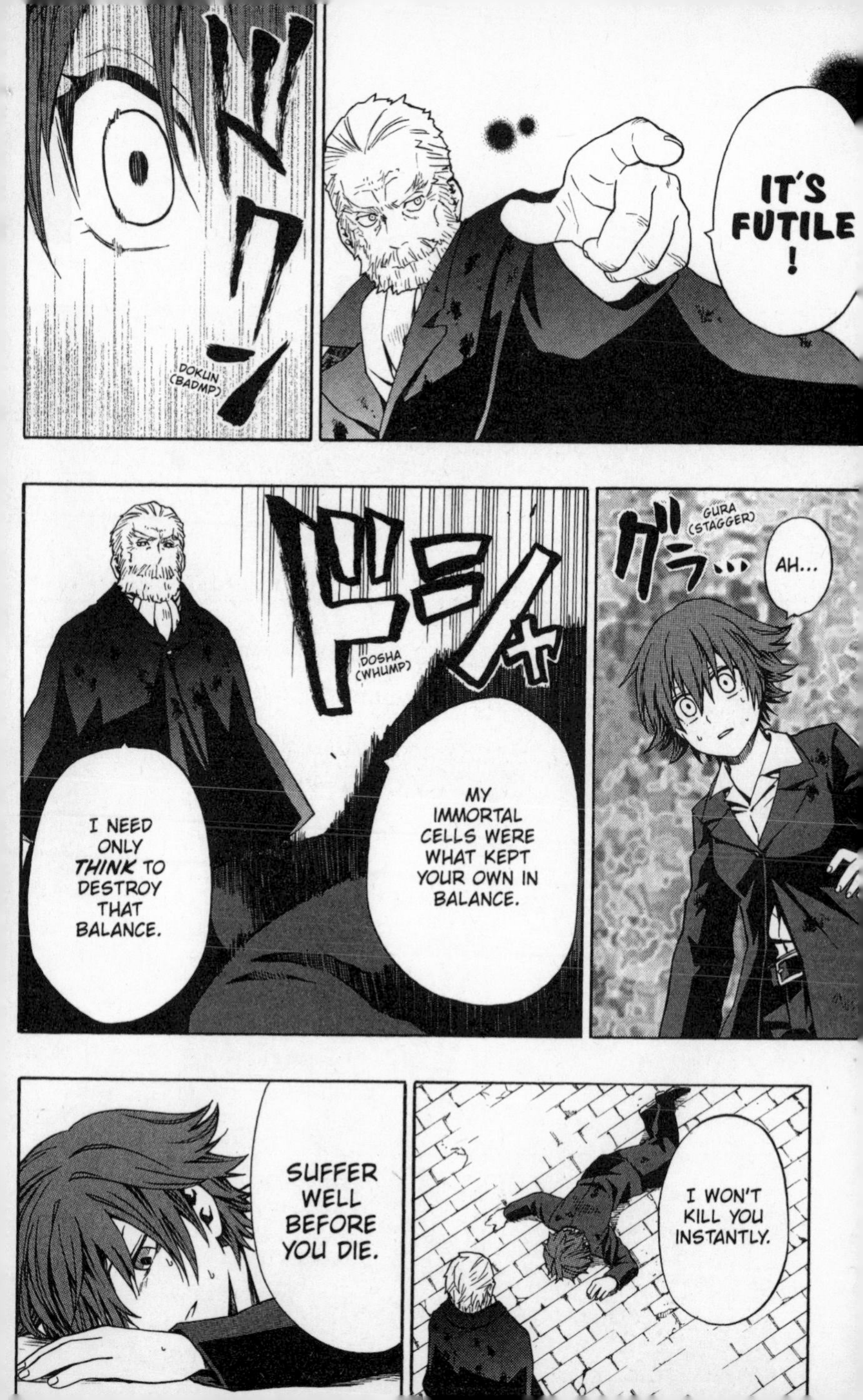
IT'S FUTILE!
DOKUN (BADMP)
GURA (STAGGER)
AH...
DOSHA (WHUMP)
MY IMMORTAL CELLS WERE WHAT KEPT YOUR OWN IN BALANCE.
I NEED ONLY *THINK* TO DESTROY THAT BALANCE.
I WON'T KILL YOU INSTANTLY.
SUFFER WELL BEFORE YOU DIE.

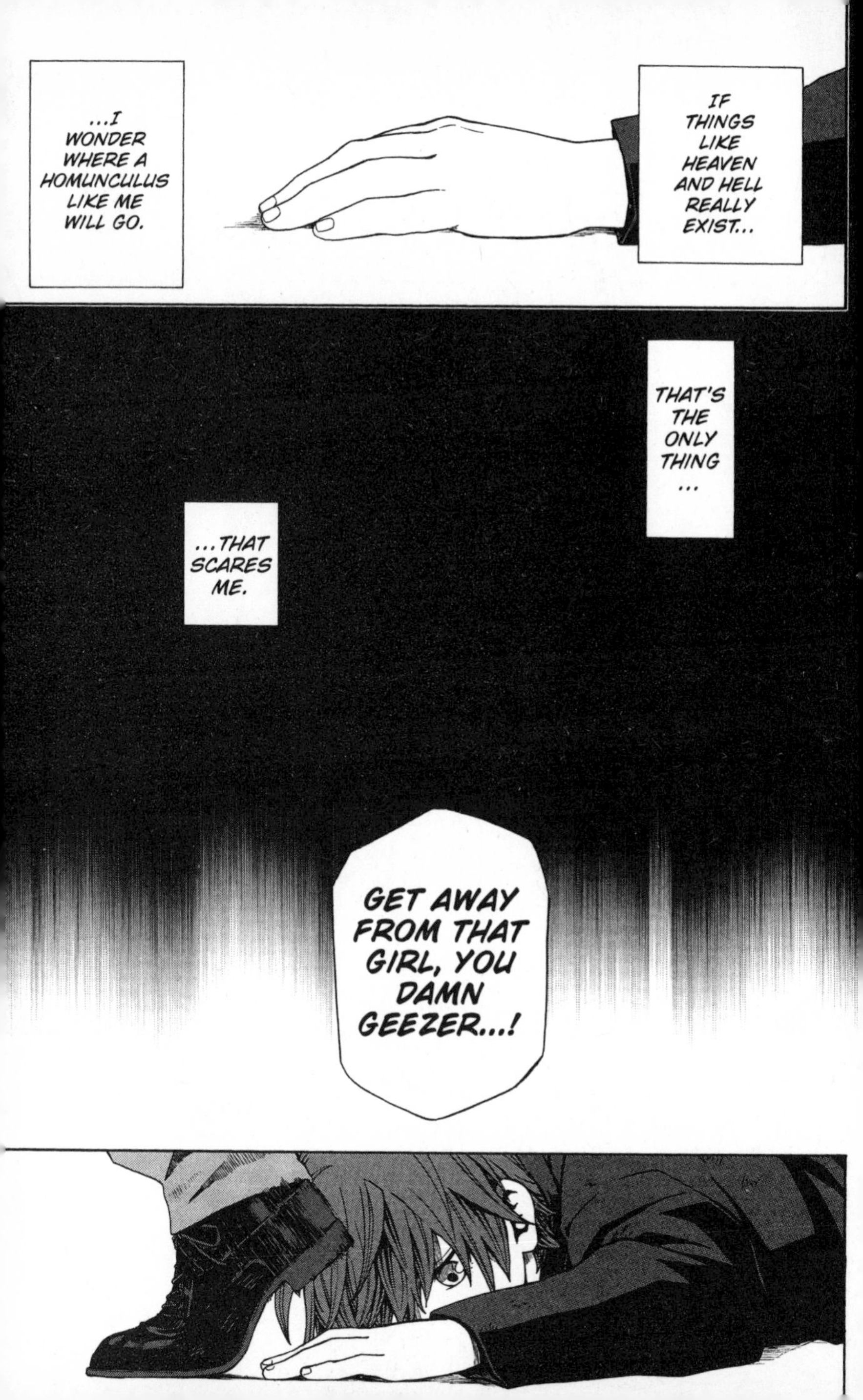
IF THINGS LIKE HEAVEN AND HELL REALLY EXIST...
...I WONDER WHERE A HOMUNCULUS LIKE ME WILL GO.
THAT'S THE ONLY THING ...
...THAT SCARES ME.
GET AWAY FROM THAT GIRL, YOU DAMN GEEZER...!

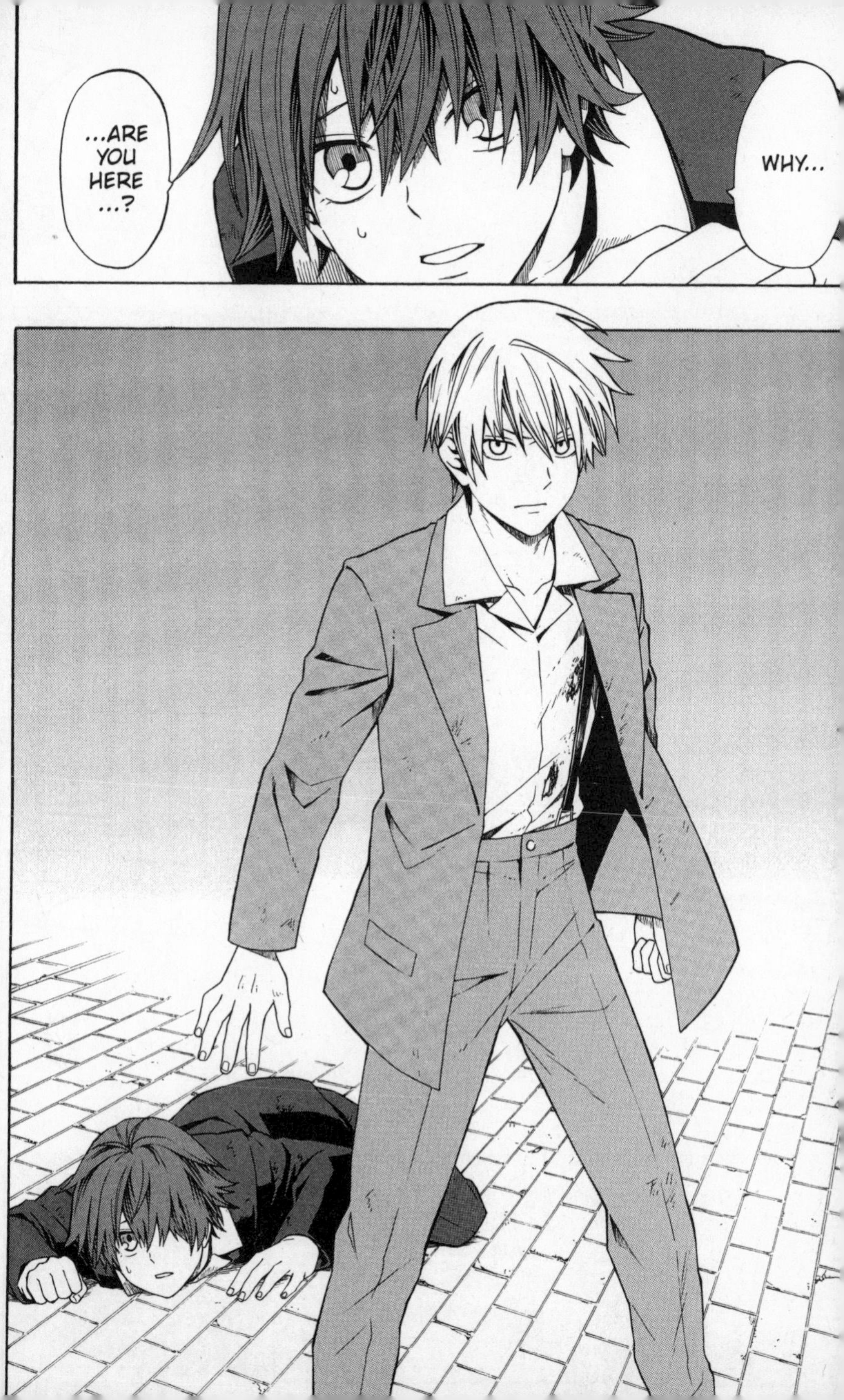
WHY...
...ARE YOU HERE ...?

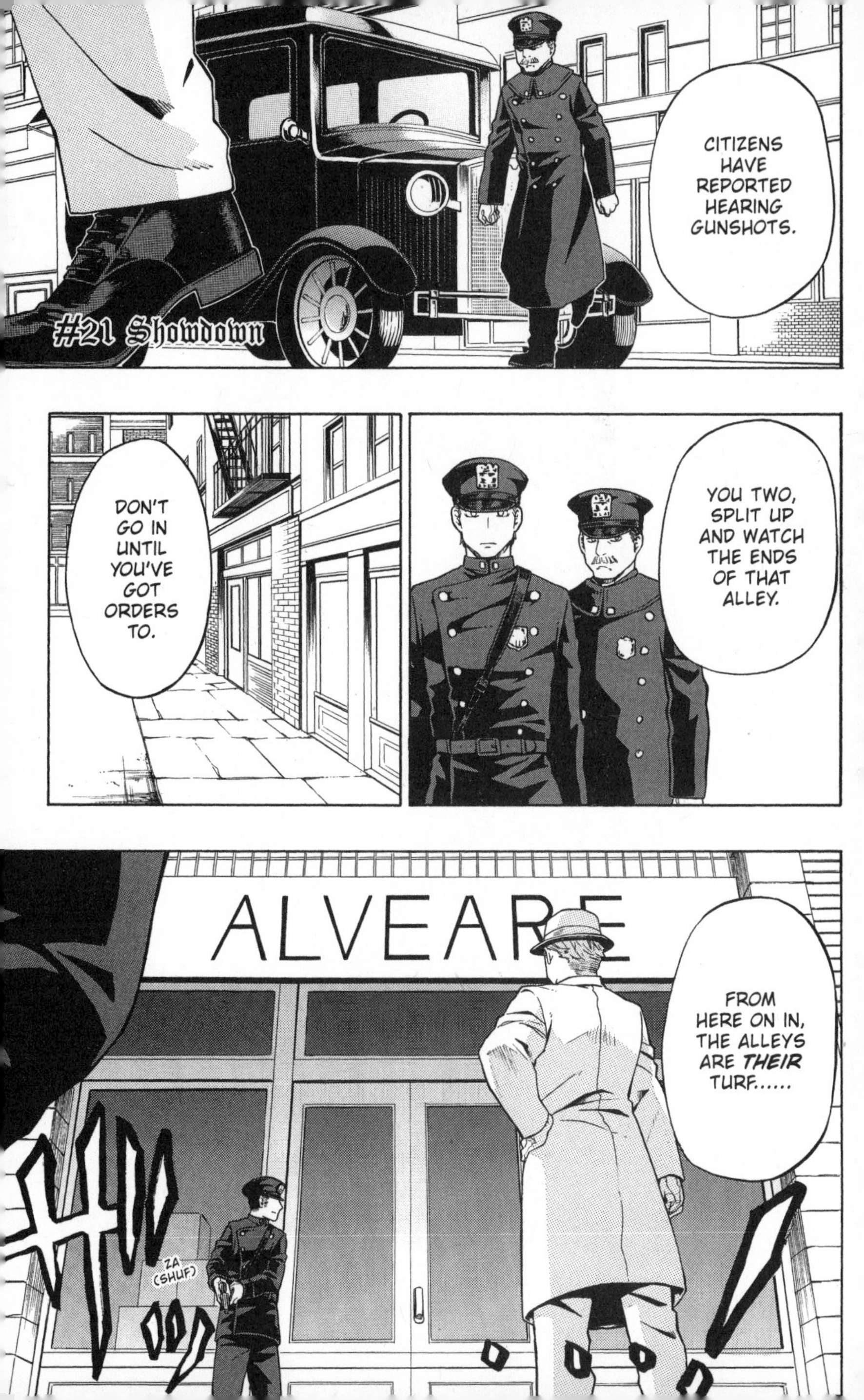
#21 Showdown
CITIZENS HAVE REPORTED HEARING GUNSHOTS.
YOU TWO, SPLIT UP AND WATCH THE ENDS OF THAT ALLEY.
DON'T GO IN UNTIL YOU'VE GOT ORDERS TO.
ALVEARE
FROM HERE ON IN, THE ALLEYS ARE *THEIR* TURF......
ZA (SHUF)

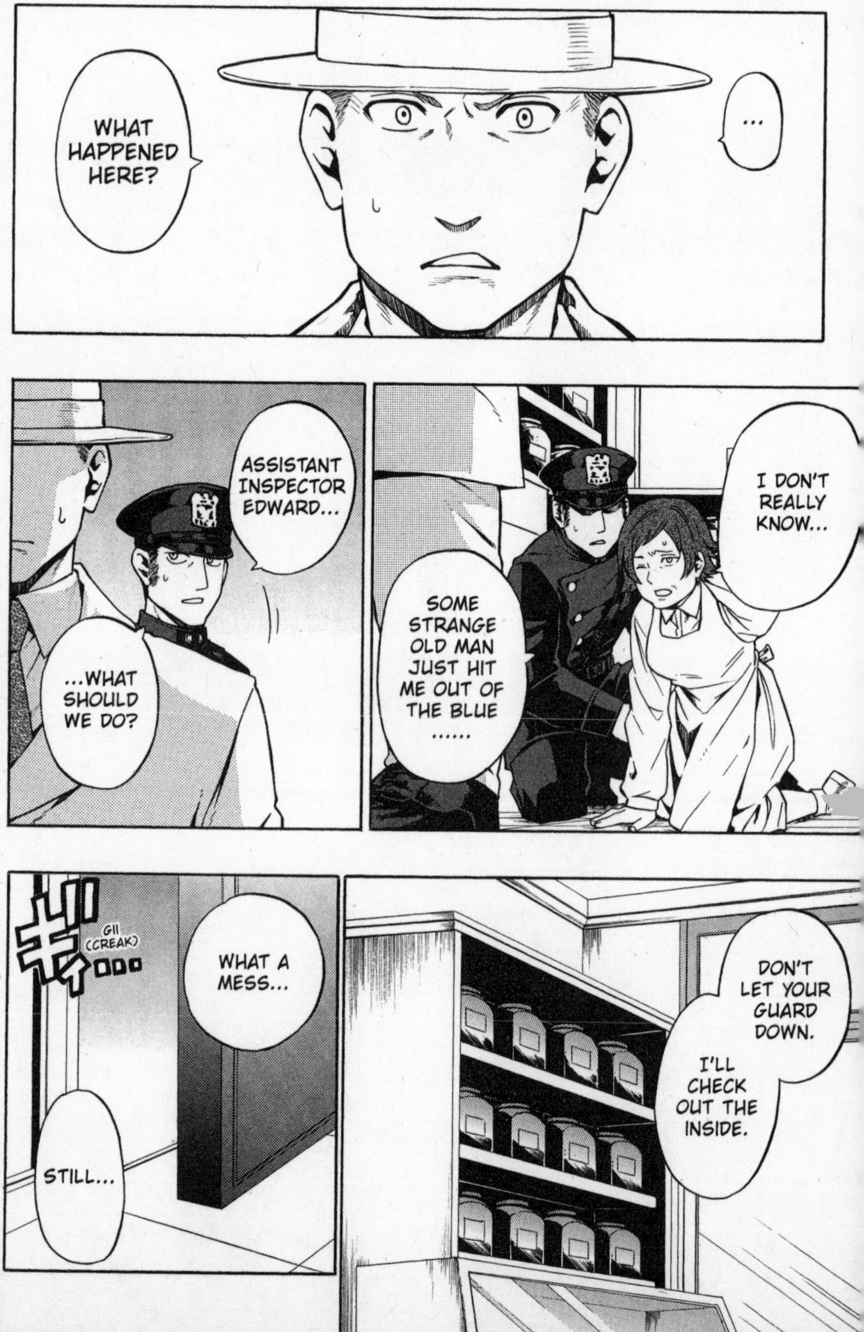
...
WHAT HAPPENED HERE?
I DON'T REALLY KNOW...
SOME STRANGE OLD MAN JUST HIT ME OUT OF THE BLUE ......
ASSISTANT INSPECTOR EDWARD...
...WHAT SHOULD WE DO?
DON'T LET YOUR GUARD DOWN.
I'LL CHECK OUT THE INSIDE.
GII (CREAK)
WHAT A MESS...
STILL...

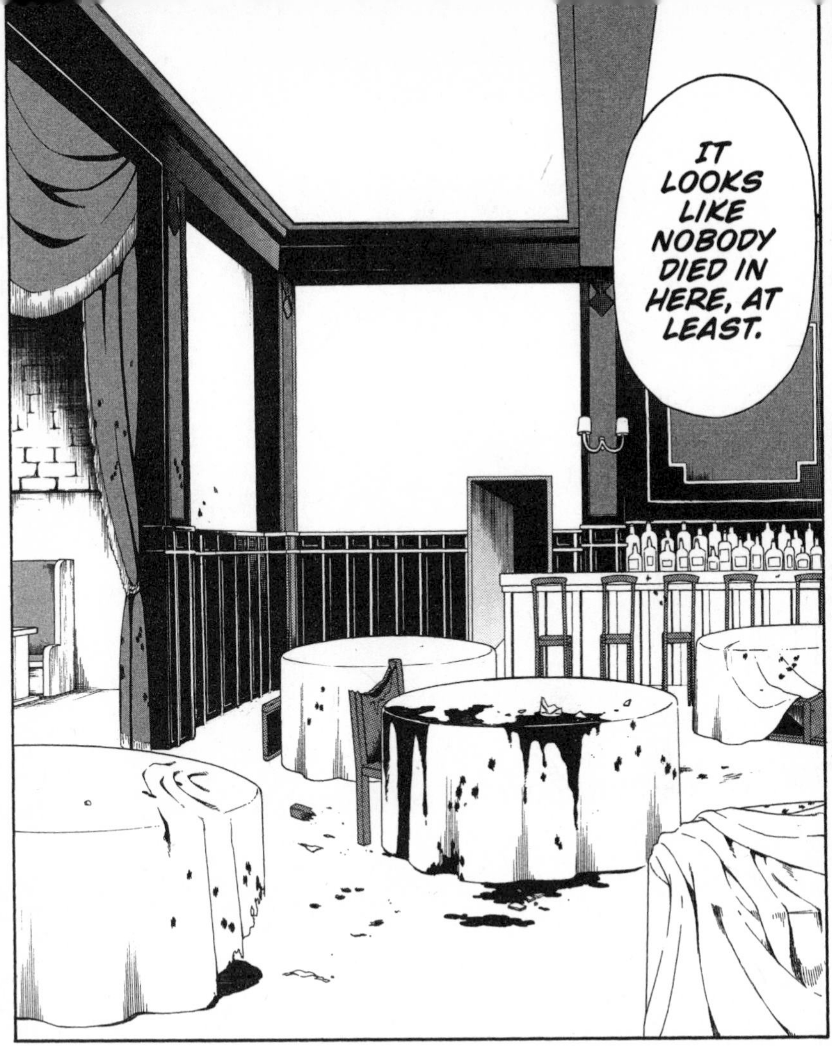
IT LOOKS LIKE NOBODY DIED IN HERE, AT LEAST.

#21 Showdown

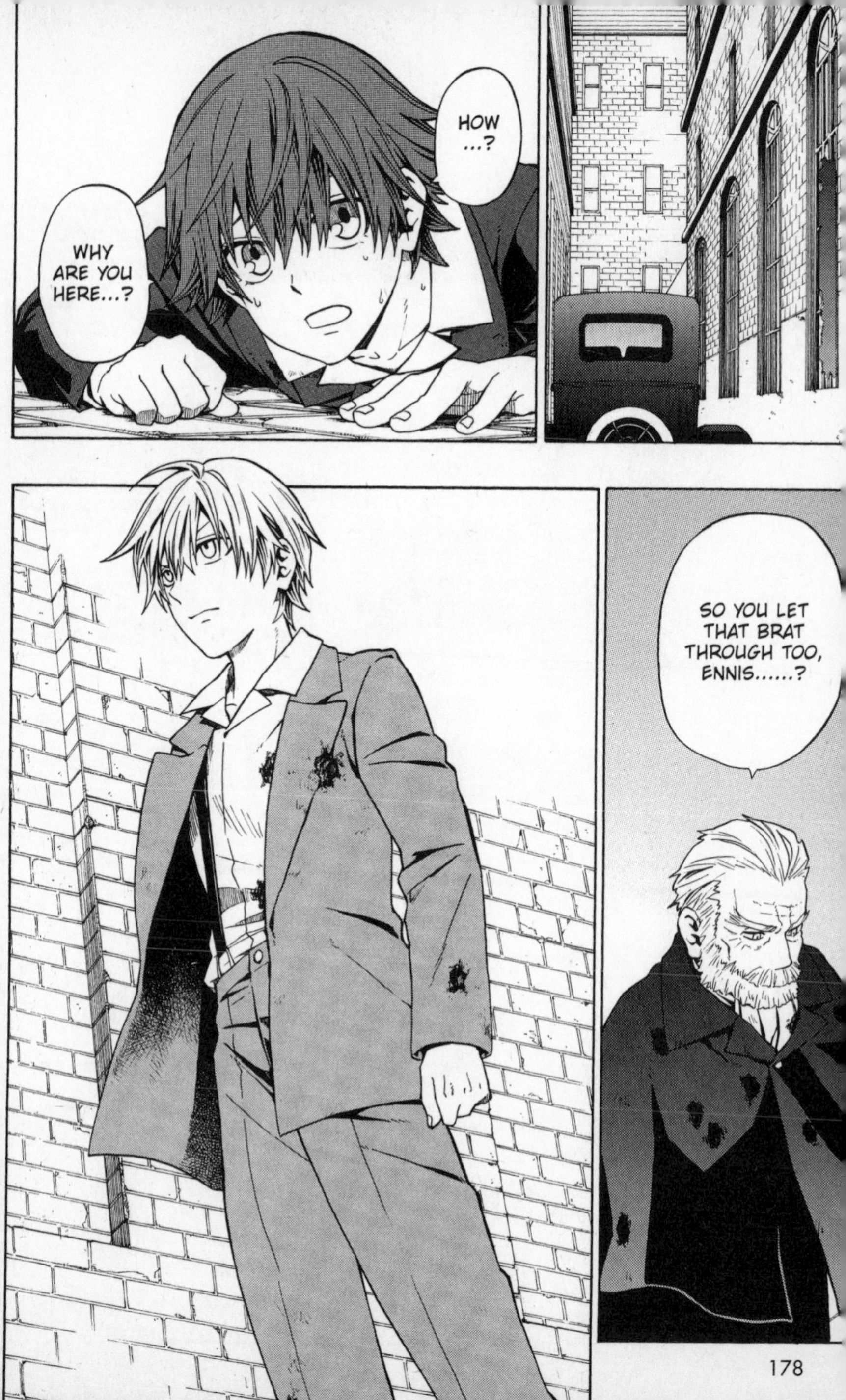
HOW ...?
WHY ARE YOU HERE...?
SO YOU LET THAT BRAT THROUGH TOO, ENNIS......?

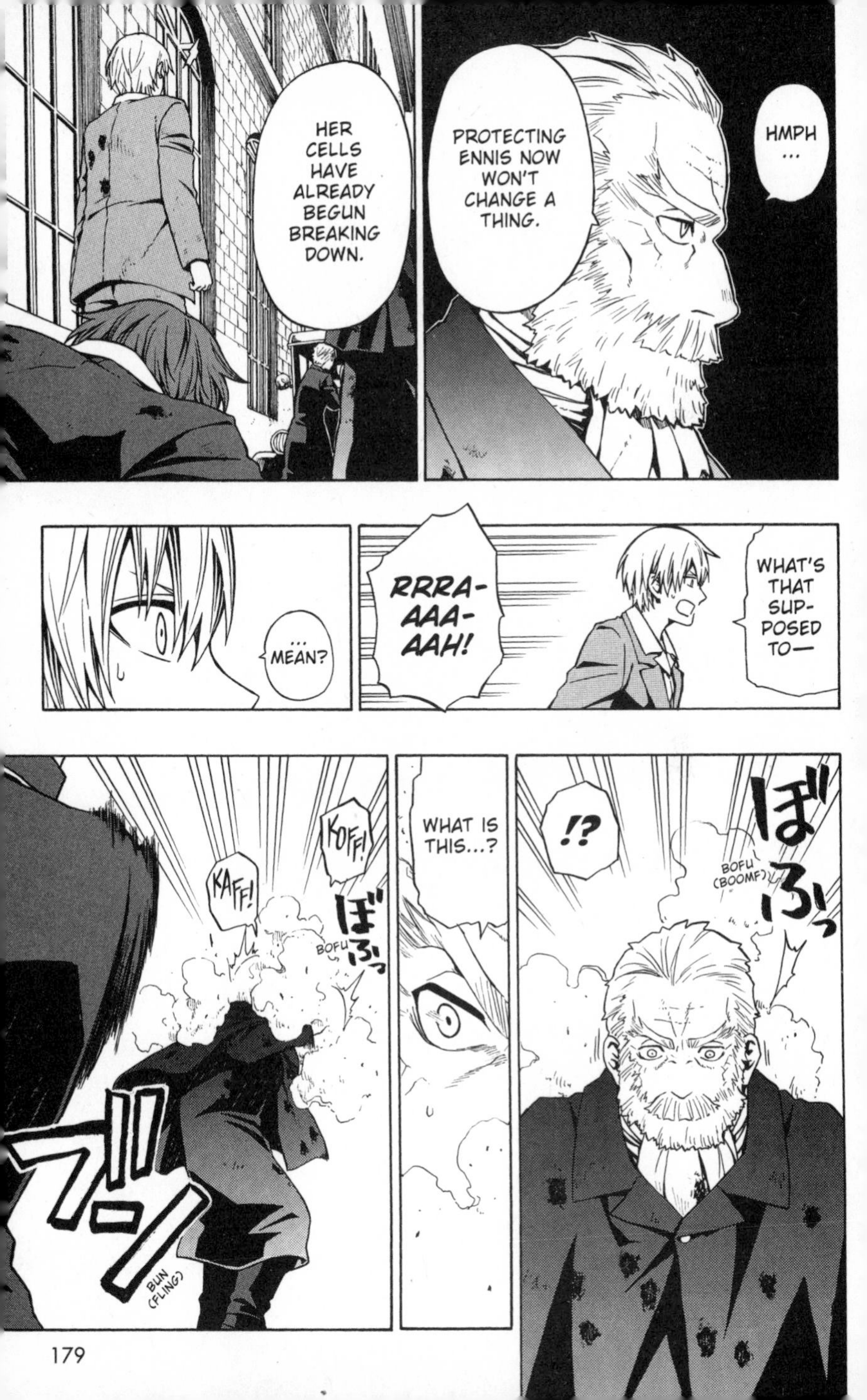

HMPH...
PROTECTING ENNIS NOW WON'T CHANGE A THING.
HER CELLS HAVE ALREADY BEGUN BREAKING DOWN.
WHAT'S THAT SUP-POSED TO—
RRRA-AAA-AAH!
...MEAN?
ぼふっ
BOFU (BOOMF)
!?
WHAT IS THIS...?
KOFF!
KAFF!
ぼふっ
BOFU
ブンッ
BUN (FLING)

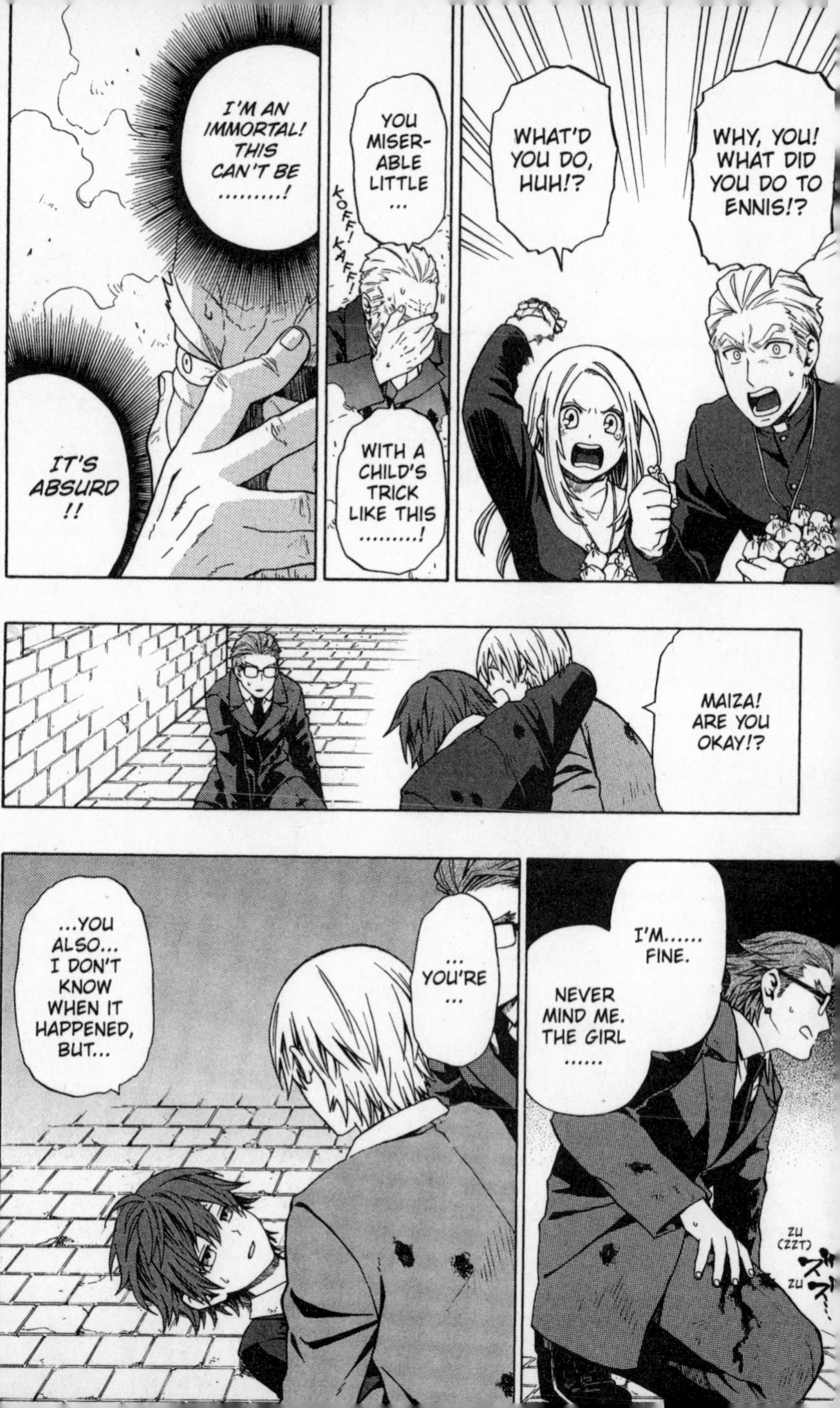
WHY, YOU! WHAT DID YOU DO TO ENNIS!?
WHAT'D YOU DO, HUH!?
YOU MISERABLE LITTLE ...
KOFF! KAFF!
WITH A CHILD'S TRICK LIKE THIS ....!
I'M AN IMMORTAL! THIS CAN'T BE ....!
IT'S ABSURD !!
MAIZA! ARE YOU OKAY!?
I'M...... FINE.
NEVER MIND ME. THE GIRL ......
ZU (ZZT)
ZU
... YOU'RE ...
...YOU ALSO... I DON'T KNOW WHEN IT HAPPENED, BUT...

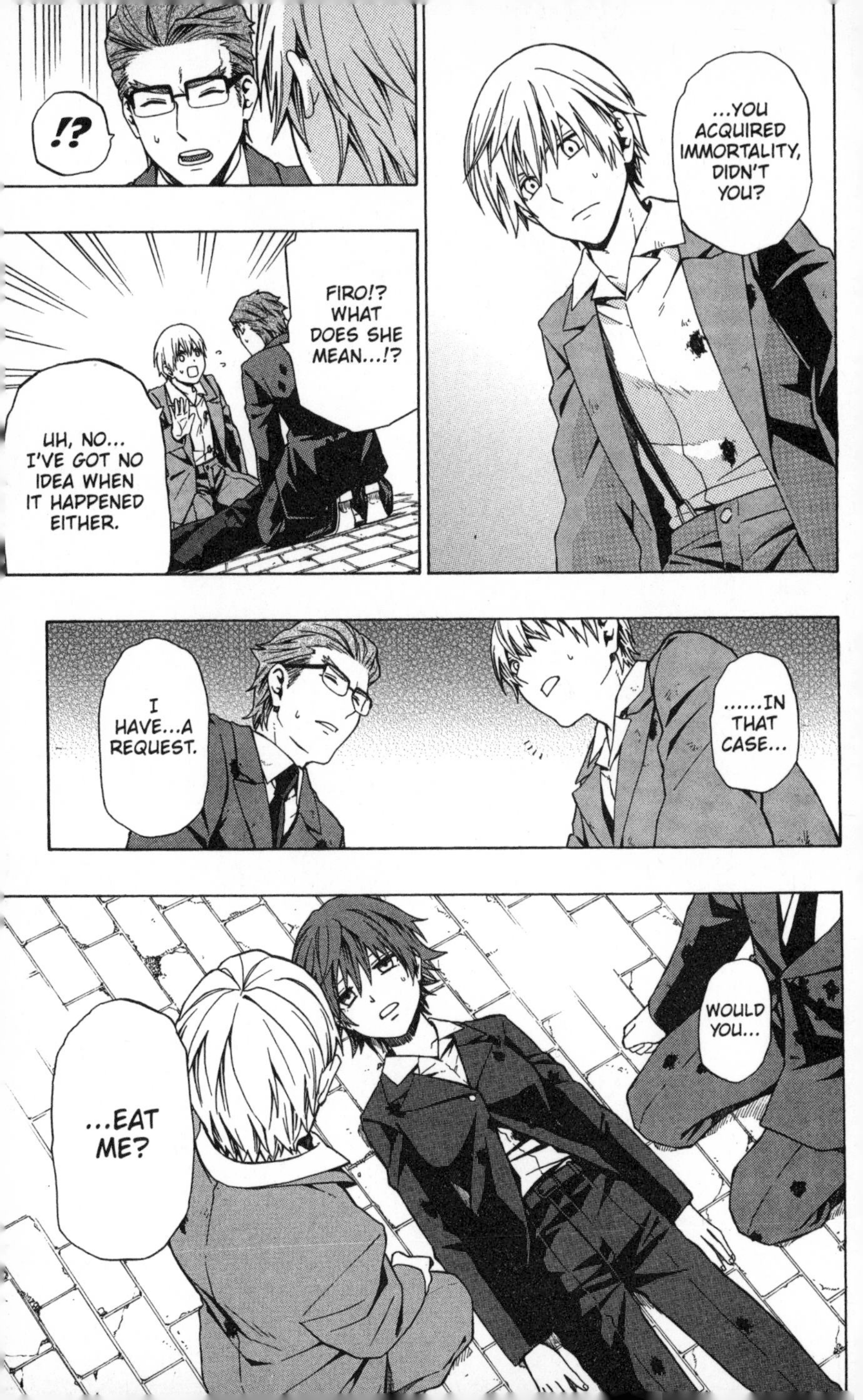
...YOU ACQUIRED IMMORTALITY, DIDN'T YOU?
!?
FIRO!? WHAT DOES SHE MEAN...!?
UH, NO... I'VE GOT NO IDEA WHEN IT HAPPENED EITHER.
......IN THAT CASE...
I HAVE...A REQUEST.
WOULD YOU...
...EAT ME?

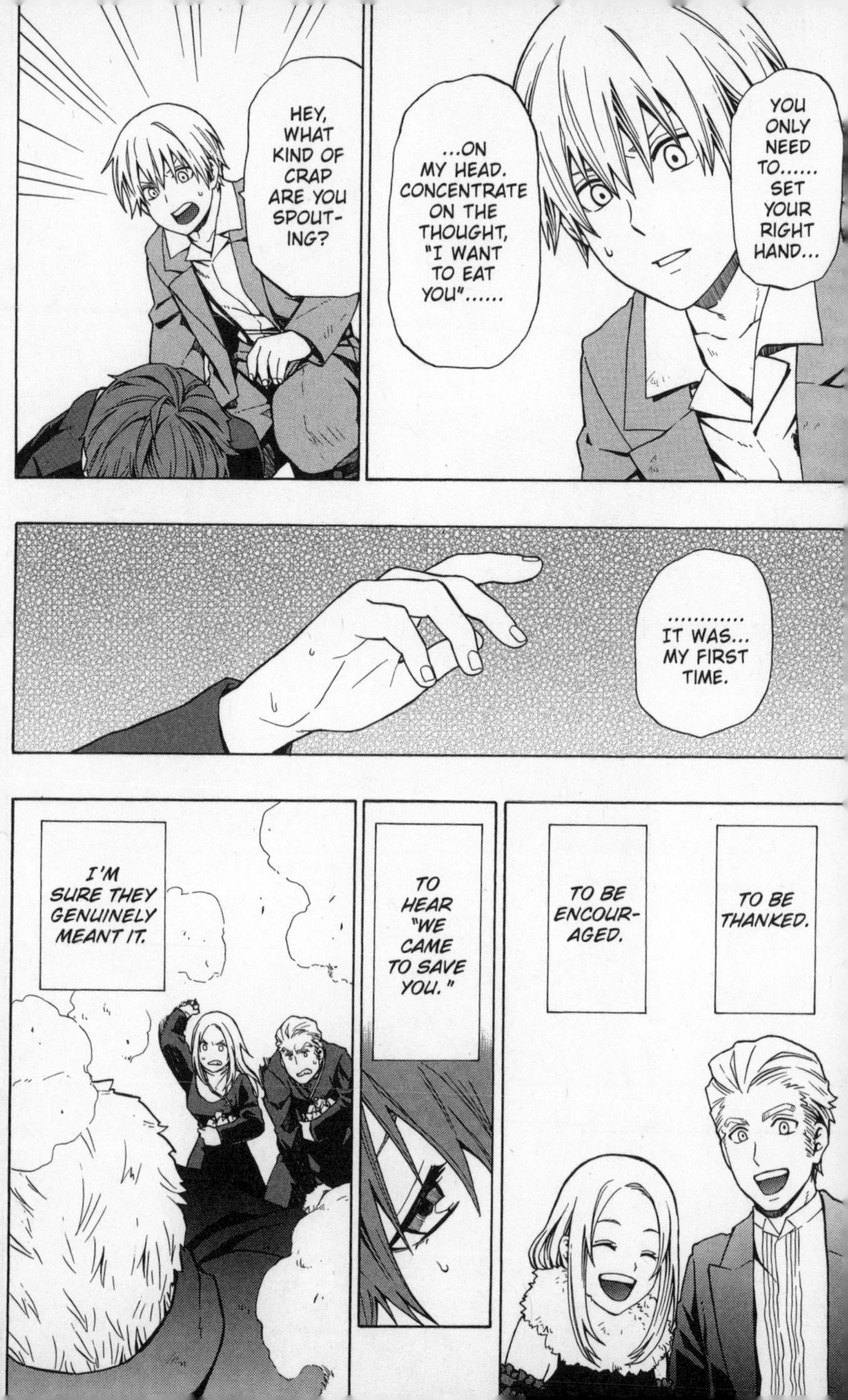
YOU ONLY NEED TO...... SET YOUR RIGHT HAND...
...ON MY HEAD. CONCENTRATE ON THE THOUGHT, "I WANT TO EAT YOU"......
HEY, WHAT KIND OF CRAP ARE YOU SPOUTING?
.... IT WAS... MY FIRST TIME.
TO BE THANKED.
TO BE ENCOURAGED.
TO HEAR "WE CAME TO SAVE YOU."
I'M SURE THEY GENUINELY MEANT IT.

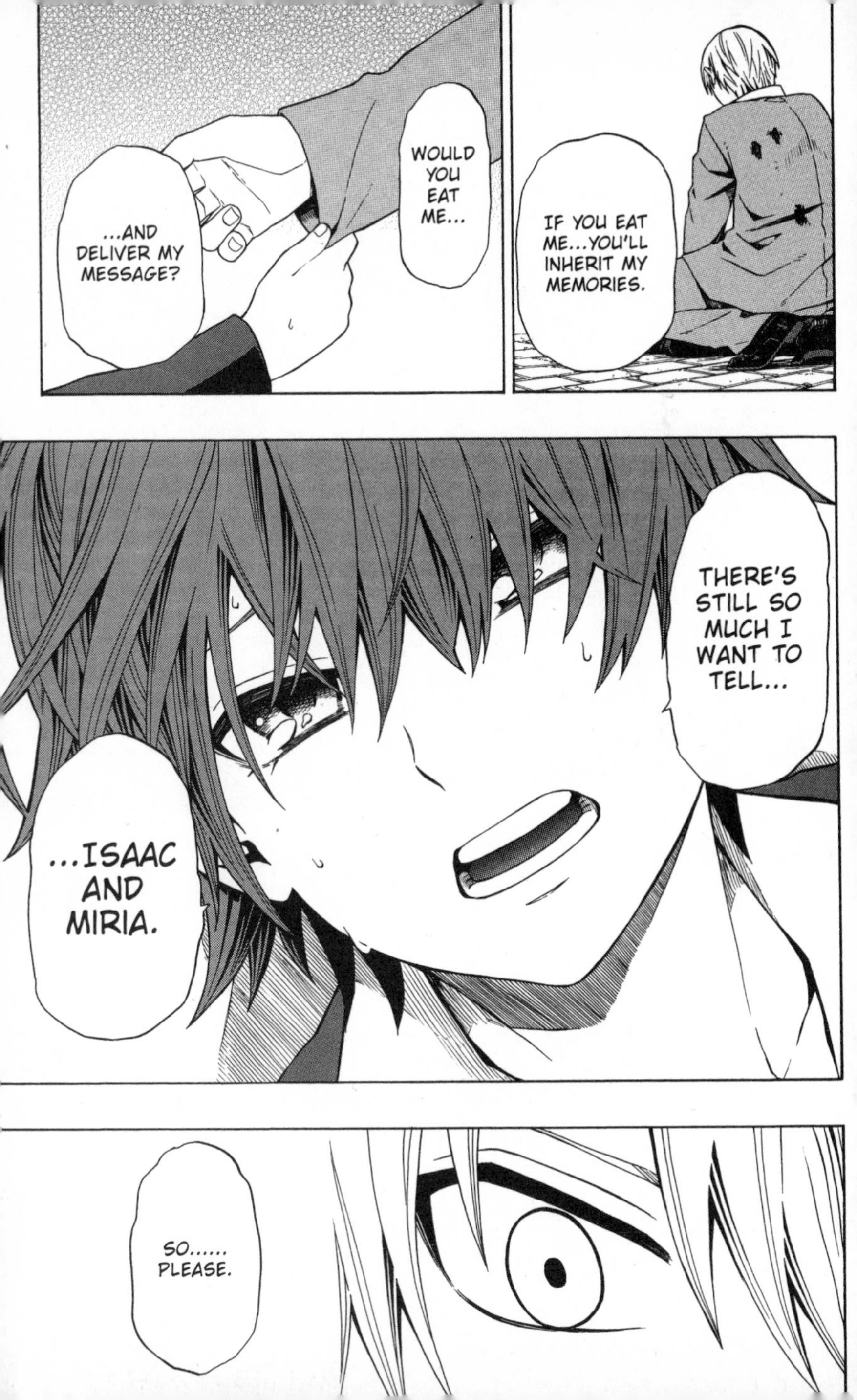
IF YOU EAT ME...YOU'LL INHERIT MY MEMORIES.
WOULD YOU EAT ME...
...AND DELIVER MY MESSAGE?
THERE'S STILL SO MUCH I WANT TO TELL...
...ISAAC AND MIRIA.
SO...... PLEASE.

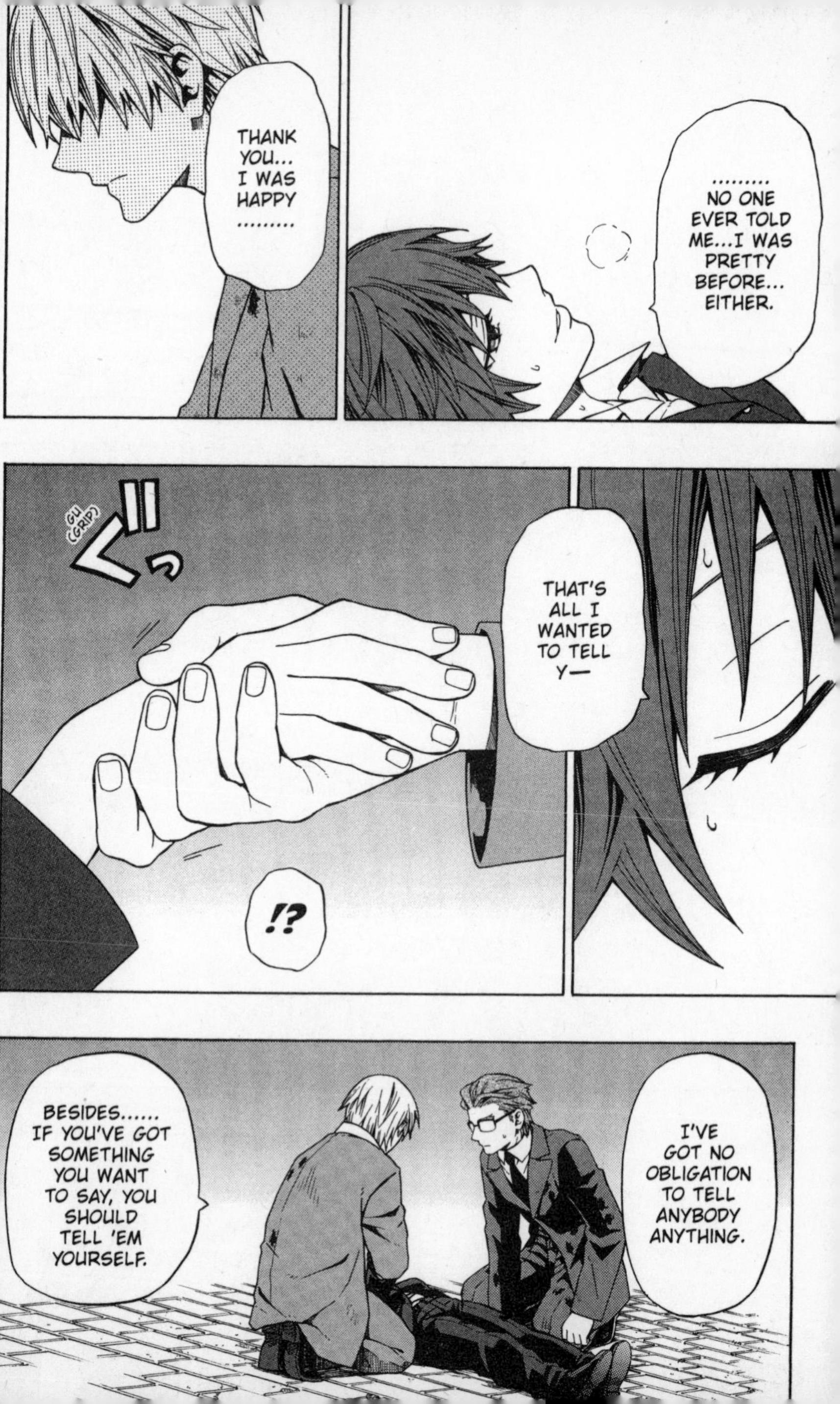
....
NO ONE EVER TOLD ME...I WAS PRETTY BEFORE... EITHER.
THANK YOU... I WAS HAPPY ....
THAT'S ALL I WANTED TO TELL Y—
GU (GRIP)
!?
I'VE GOT NO OBLIGATION TO TELL ANYBODY ANYTHING.
BESIDES...... IF YOU'VE GOT SOMETHING YOU WANT TO SAY, YOU SHOULD TELL 'EM YOURSELF.

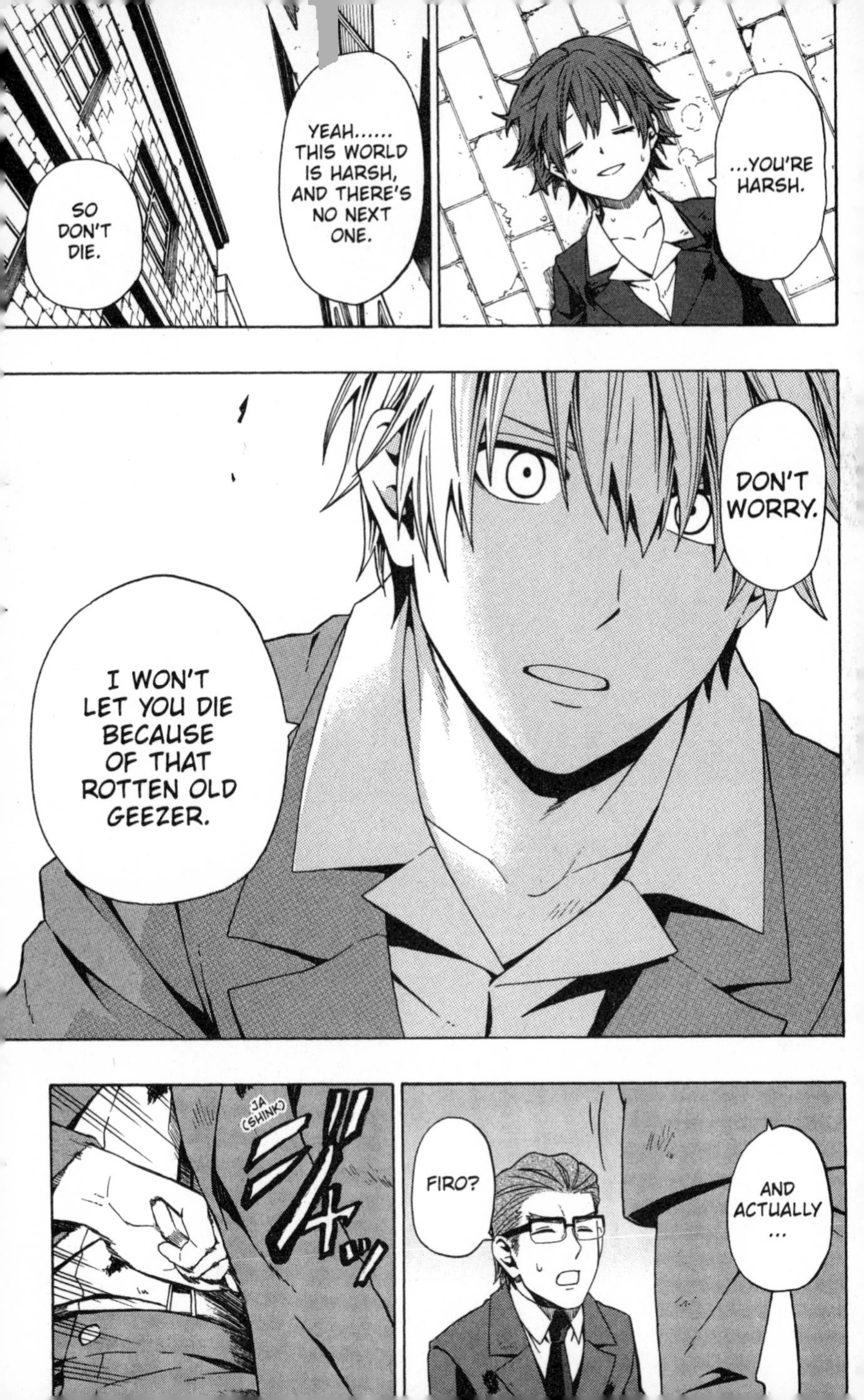
...YOU'RE HARSH.
YEAH...... THIS WORLD IS HARSH, AND THERE'S NO NEXT ONE.
SO DON'T DIE.
DON'T WORRY.
I WON'T LET YOU DIE BECAUSE OF THAT ROTTEN OLD GEEZER.
AND ACTUALLY ...
FIRO?
JA (SHINK)

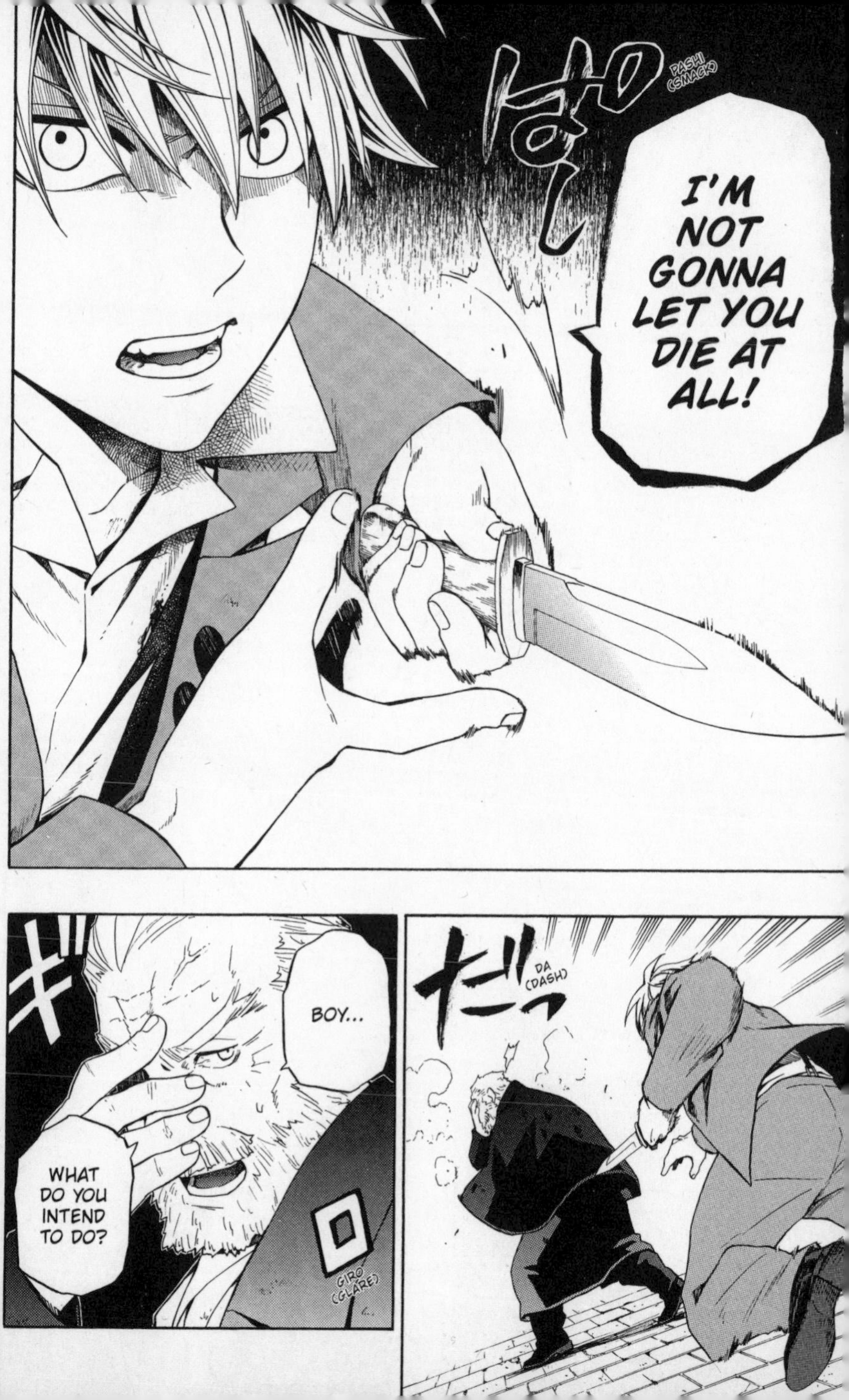
ぱし
PASHI (SMACK)
I'M NOT GONNA LET YOU DIE AT ALL!
DA (DASH)
BOY...
GIRO (GLARE)
WHAT DO YOU INTEND TO DO?

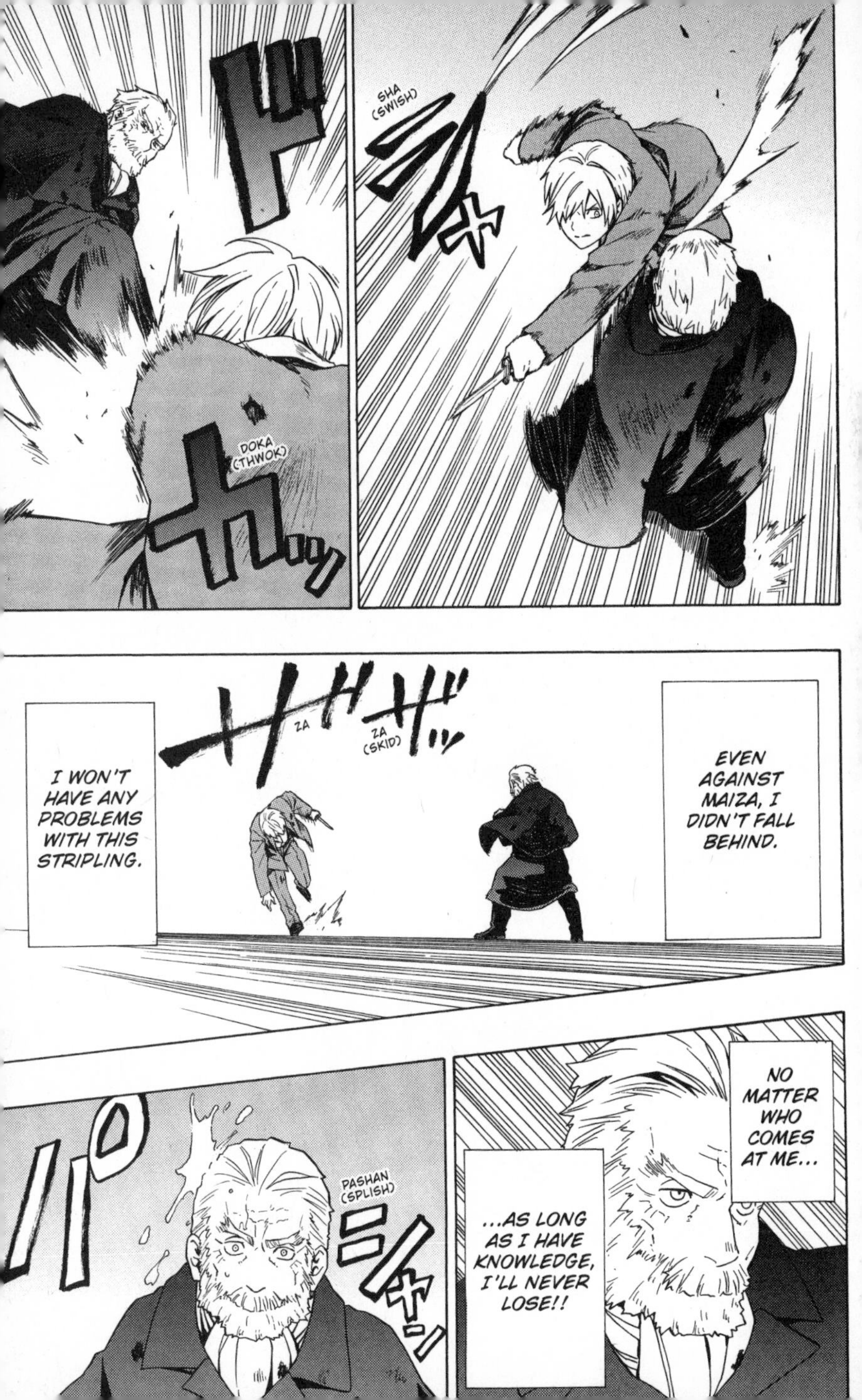
SHA (SWISH)
DOKA (THWOK)
EVEN AGAINST MAIZA, I DIDN'T FALL BEHIND.
ZA (SKID)
ZA
I WON'T HAVE ANY PROBLEMS WITH THIS STRIPLING.
NO MATTER WHO COMES AT ME...
...AS LONG AS I HAVE KNOWLEDGE, I'LL NEVER LOSE!!
PASHAN (SPLISH)

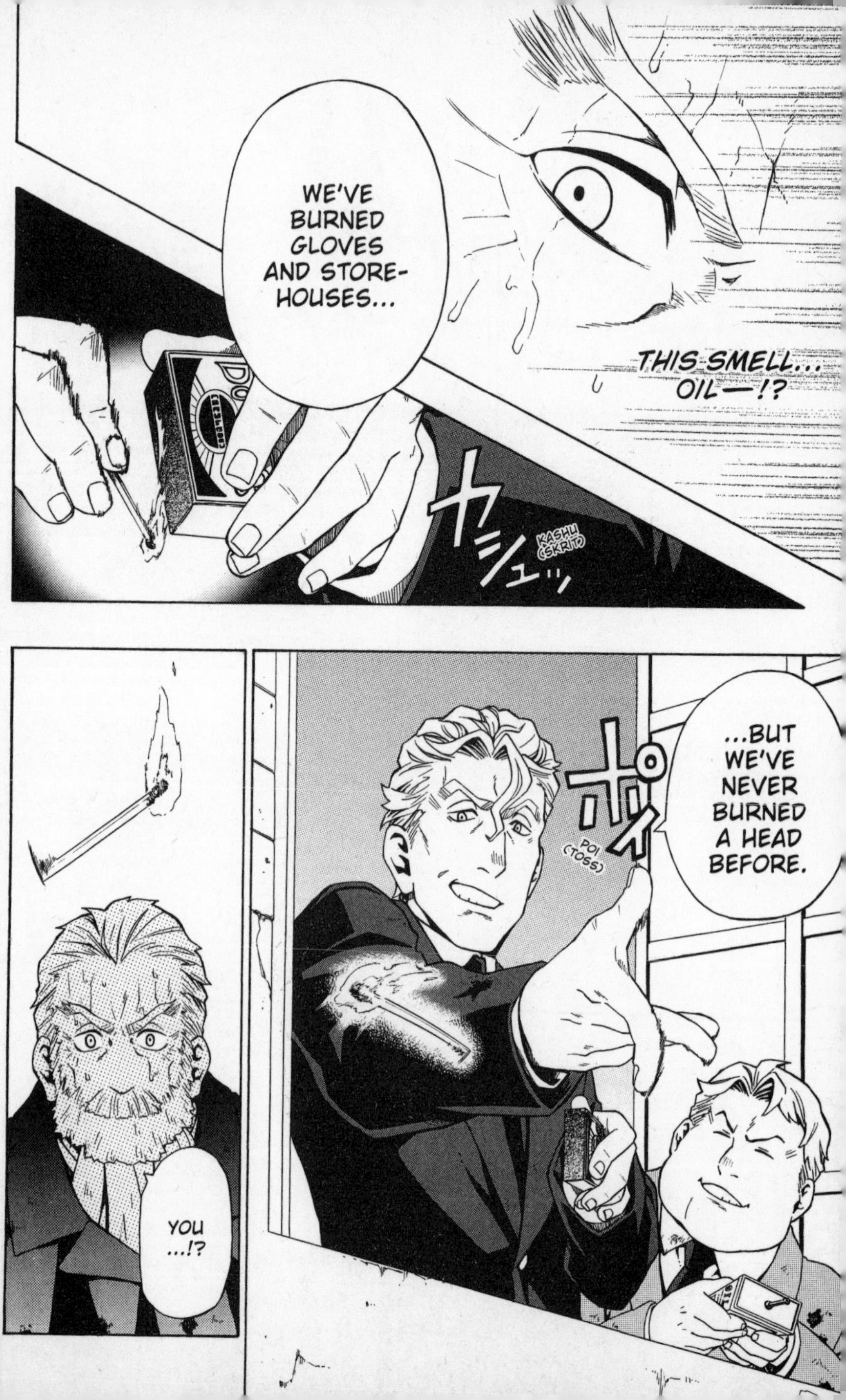
THIS SMELL... OIL—!?
WE'VE BURNED GLOVES AND STORE-HOUSES...
KASHU (SKRIT)
...BUT WE'VE NEVER BURNED A HEAD BEFORE.
POI (TOSS)
YOU ...!?

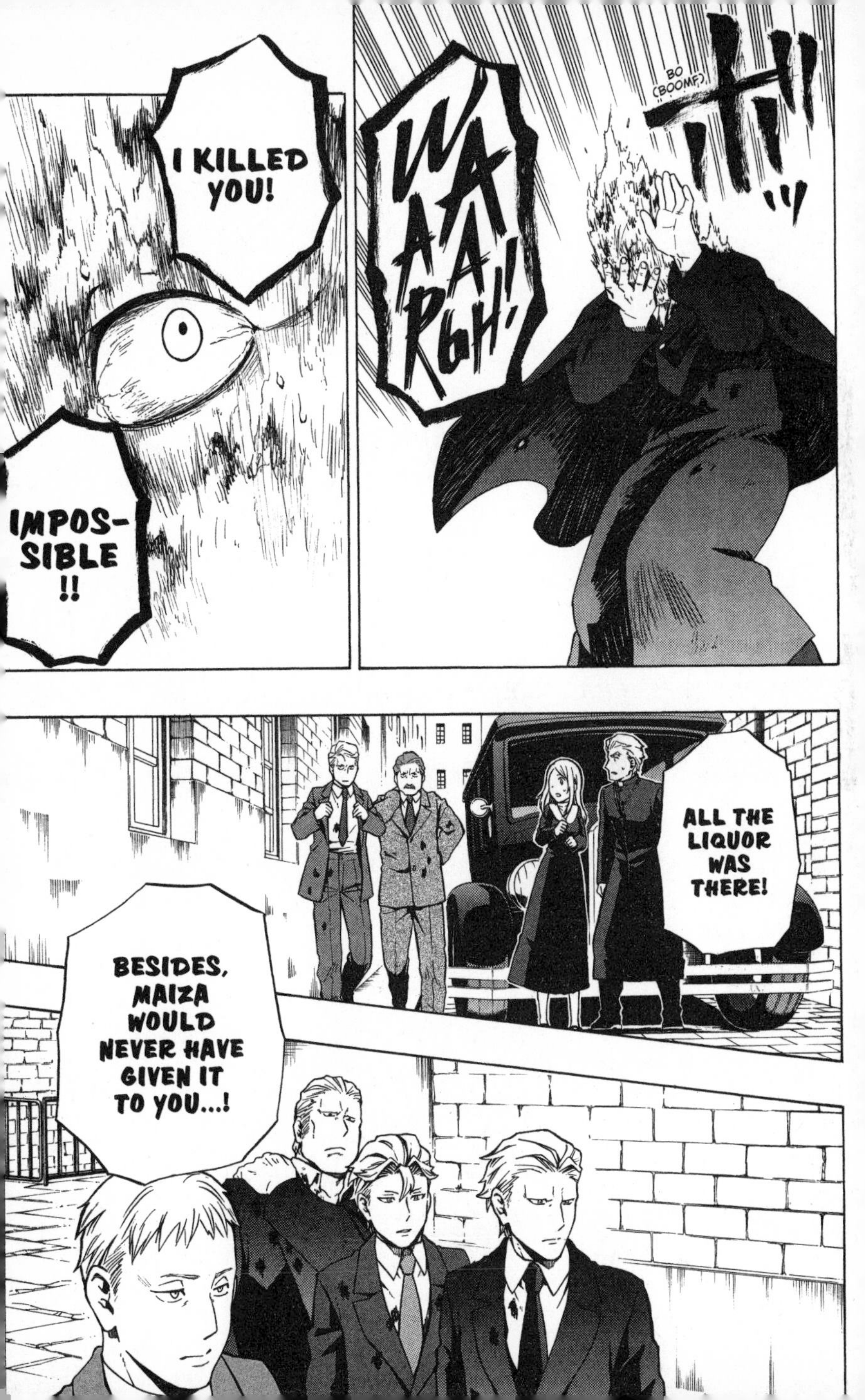
BO (BOOMF)
WAAARGH!
I KILLED YOU!
IMPOSSIBLE!!
ALL THE LIQUOR WAS THERE!
BESIDES, MAIZA WOULD NEVER HAVE GIVEN IT TO YOU...!

DON'T TELL ME...

ARE THEY ALL IMMORTALS?

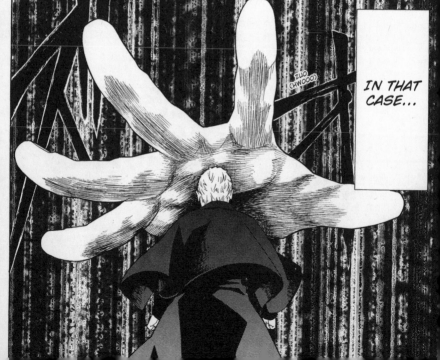

ZUO CHWOOO)

IN THAT CASE...

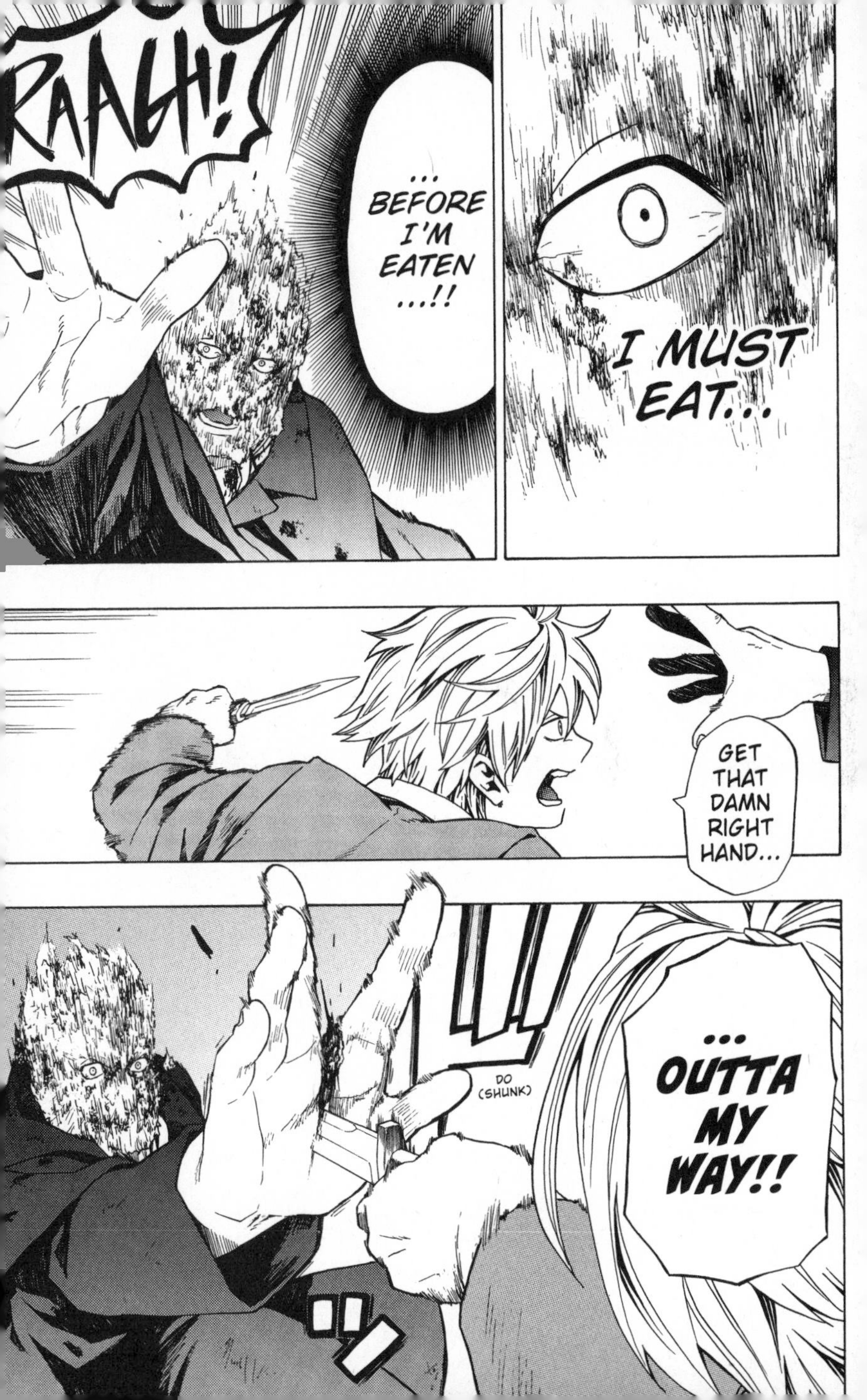
I MUST EAT...
...BEFORE I'M EATEN...!!
RAAGH!
GET THAT DAMN RIGHT HAND...
...OUTTA MY WAY!!
DO (SHUNK)

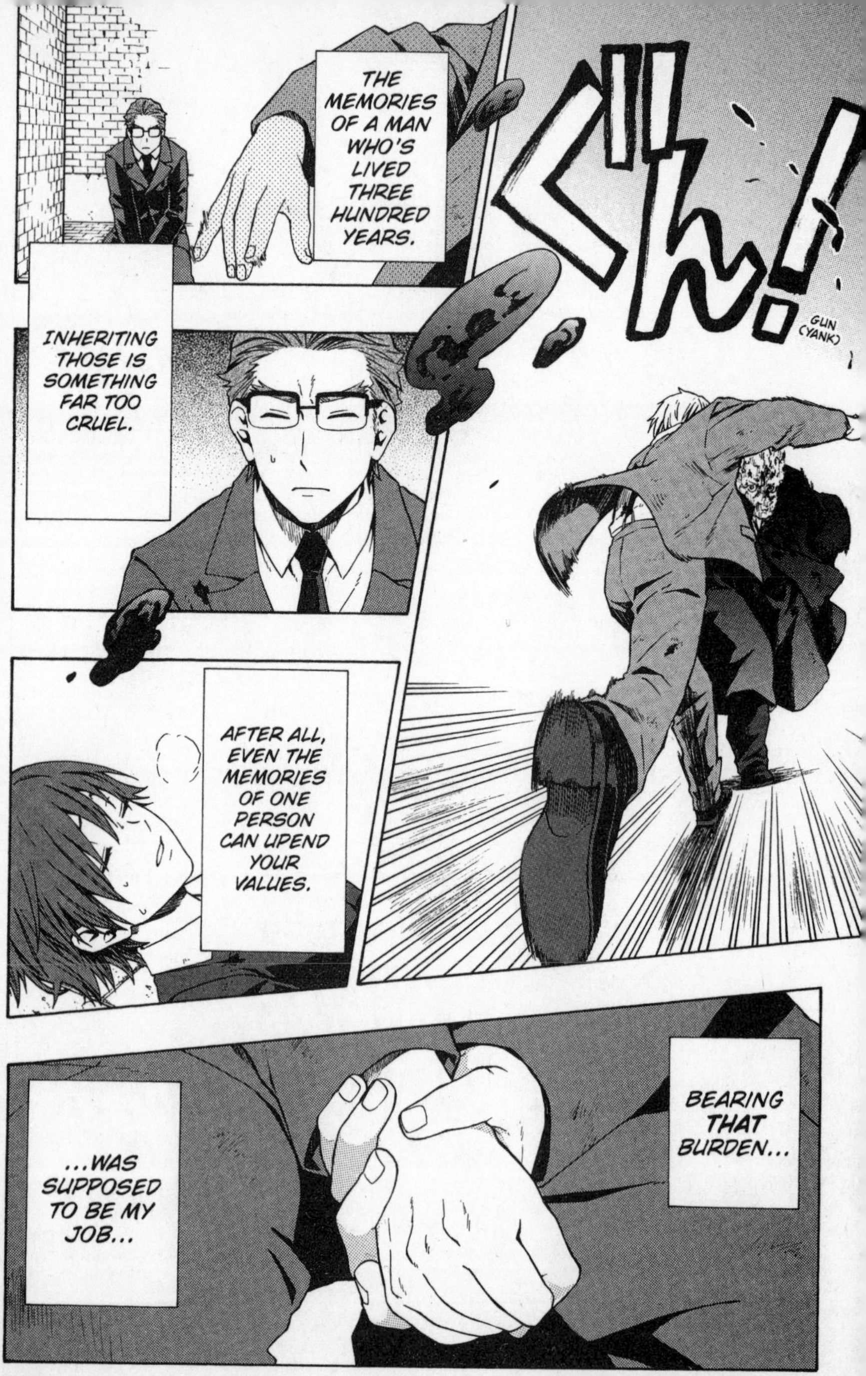
ぐん!
GUN (YANK)
THE MEMORIES OF A MAN WHO'S LIVED THREE HUNDRED YEARS.
INHERITING THOSE IS SOMETHING FAR TOO CRUEL.
AFTER ALL, EVEN THE MEMORIES OF ONE PERSON CAN UPEND YOUR VALUES.
BEARING THAT BURDEN...
...WAS SUPPOSED TO BE MY JOB...

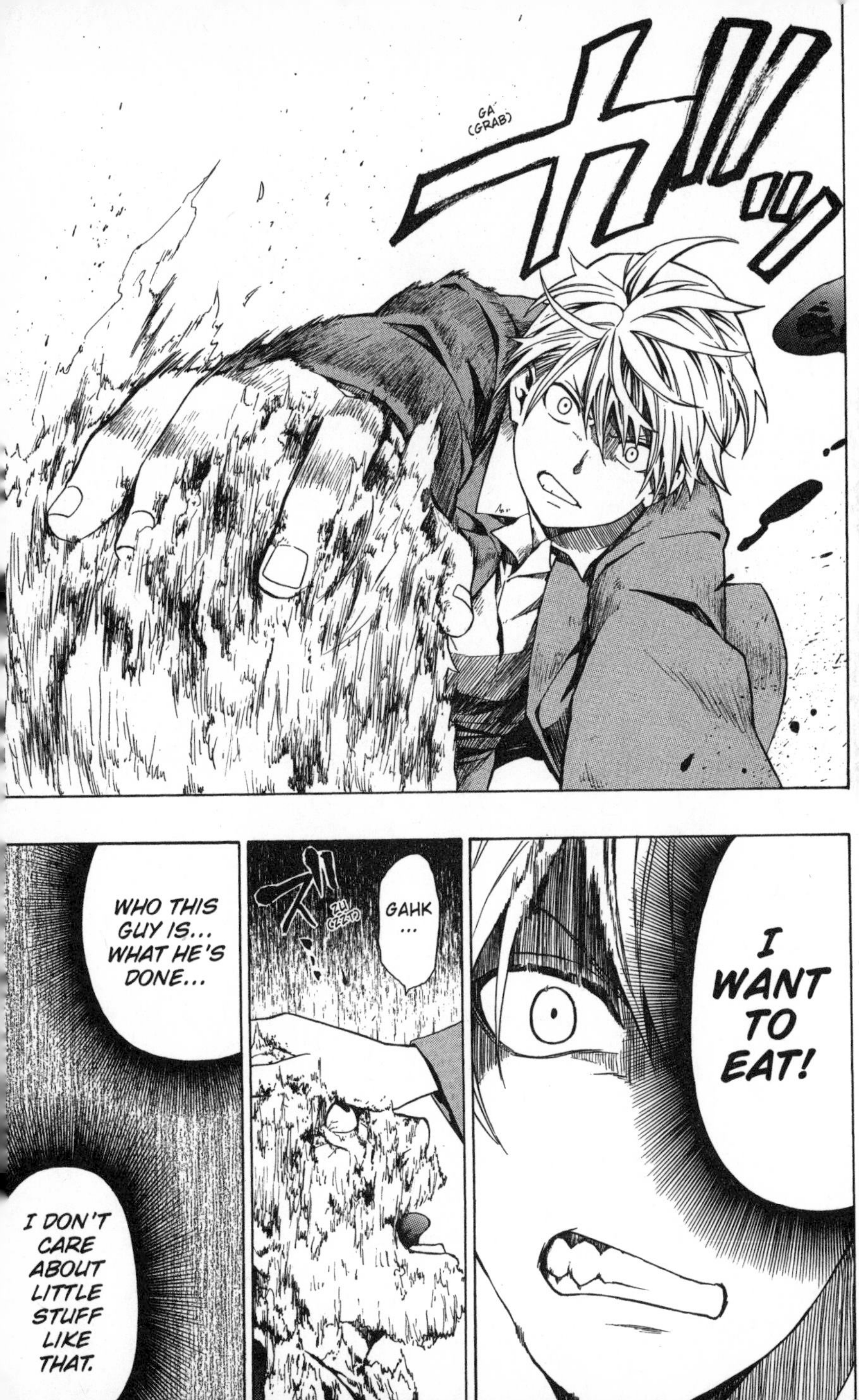
GA (GRAB)
I WANT TO EAT!
ZU (ZZZT)
GAHK ...
WHO THIS GUY IS... WHAT HE'S DONE...
I DON'T CARE ABOUT LITTLE STUFF LIKE THAT.

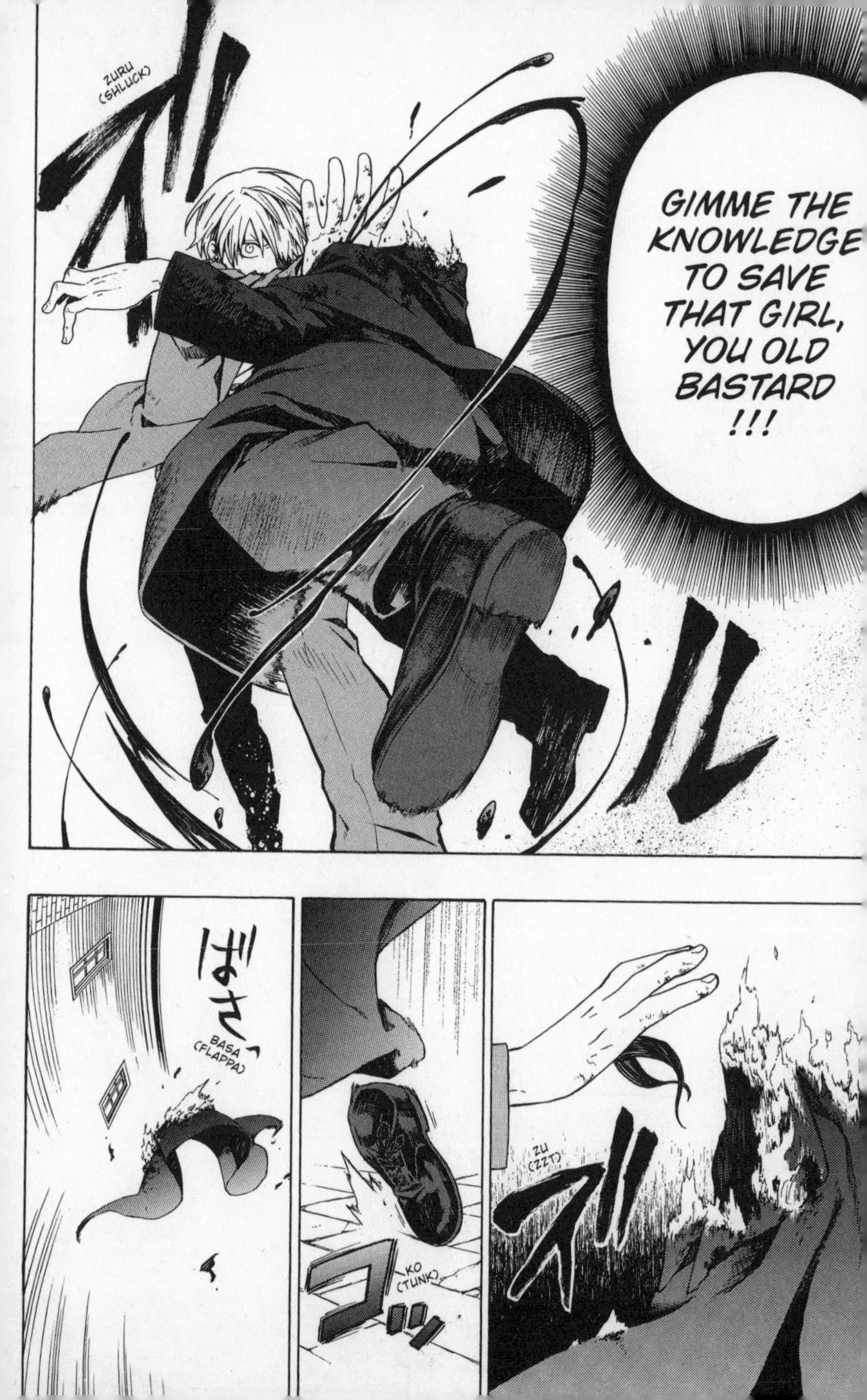
GIMME THE KNOWLEDGE TO SAVE THAT GIRL, YOU OLD BASTARD !!!
ズル
ZURU (SHLUCK)
ズ
ZU (ZZT)
コッ
KO (TUNK)
ばさ
BASA (FLAPPA)

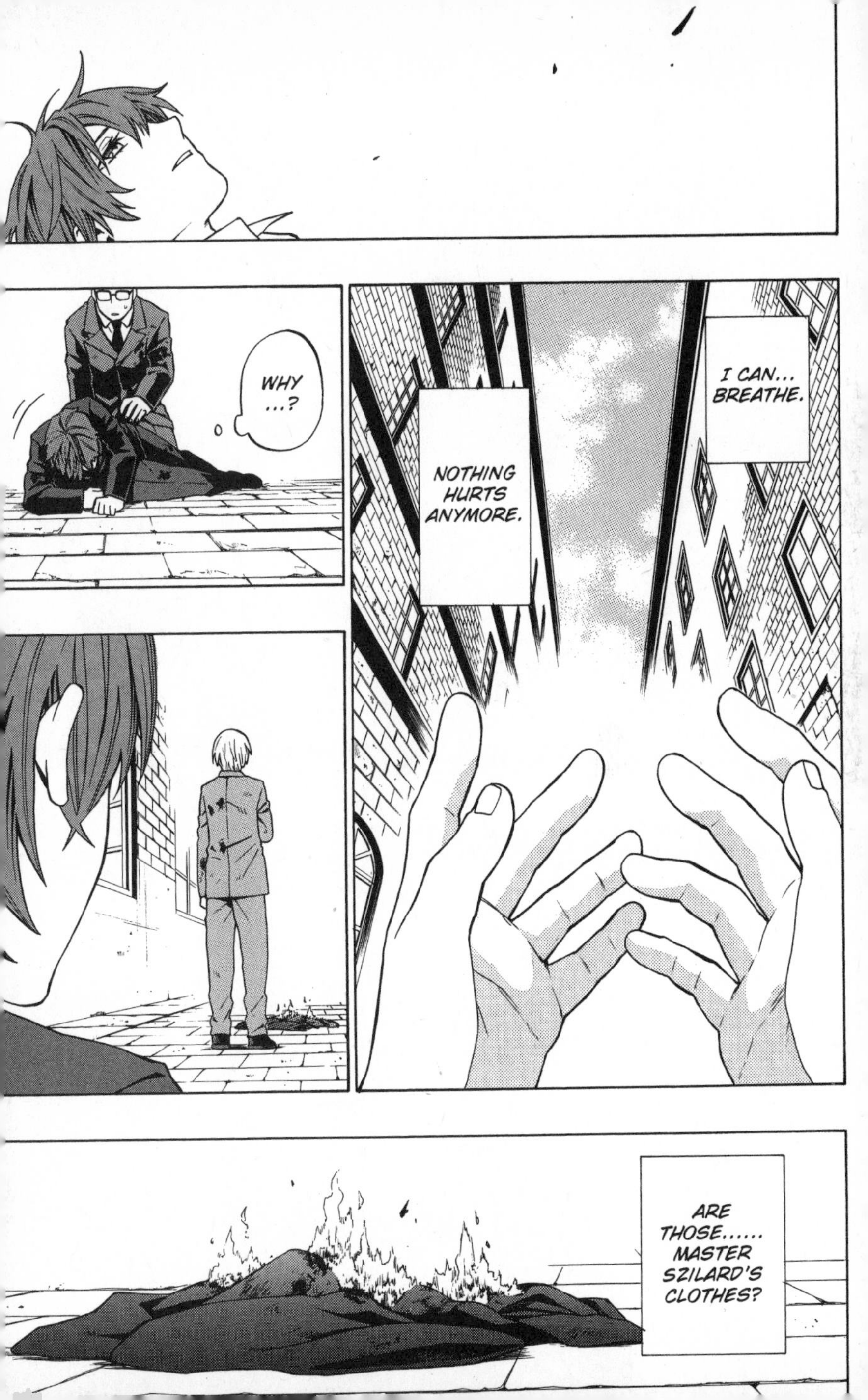
I CAN... BREATHE.
NOTHING HURTS ANYMORE.
WHY ...?
ARE THOSE...... MASTER SZILARD'S CLOTHES?

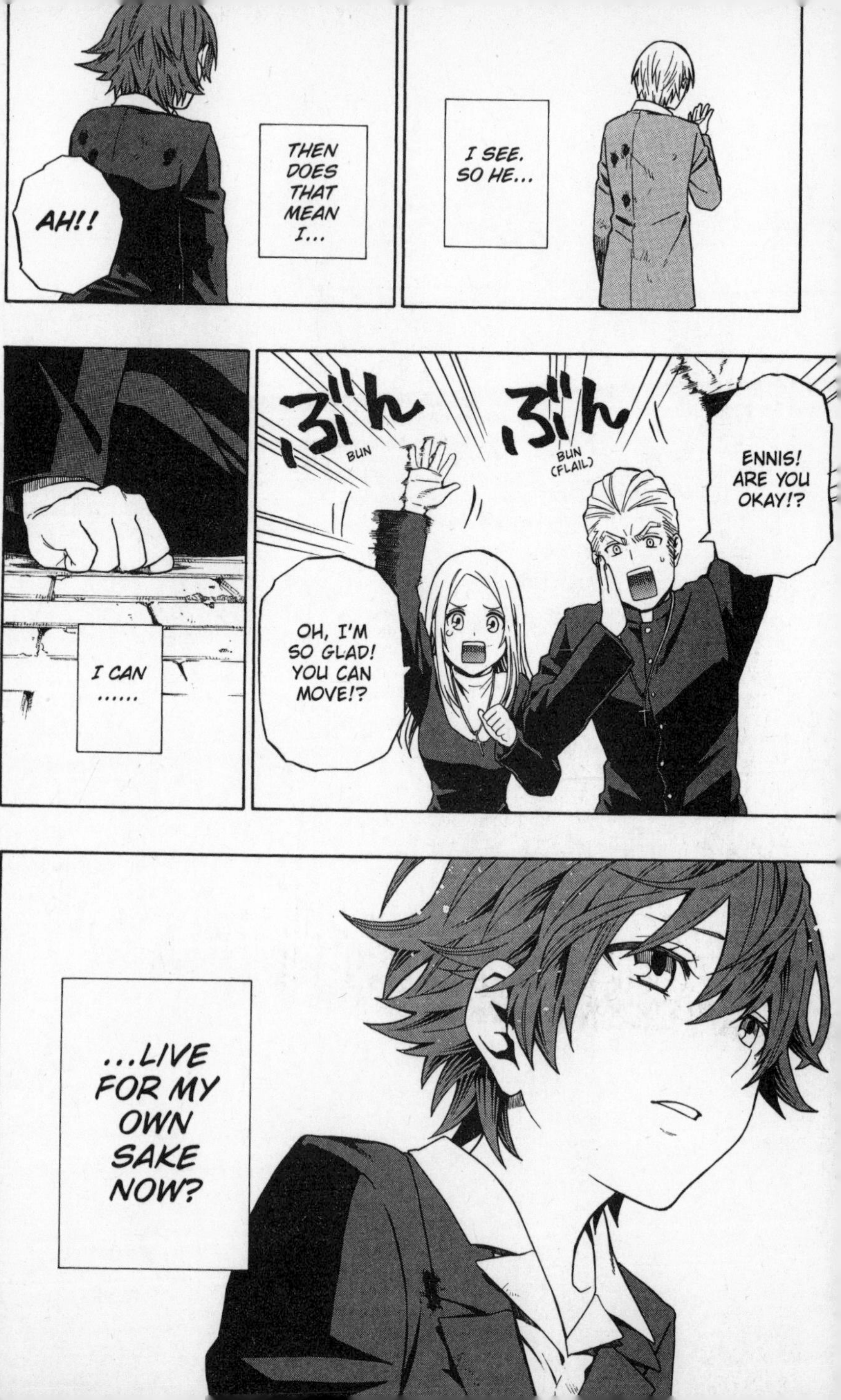
I SEE. SO HE...
THEN DOES THAT MEAN I...
AH!!
ENNIS! ARE YOU OKAY!?
ぶん
BUN (FLAIL)
ぶん
BUN
OH, I'M SO GLAD! YOU CAN MOVE!?
I CAN ......
...LIVE FOR MY OWN SAKE NOW?

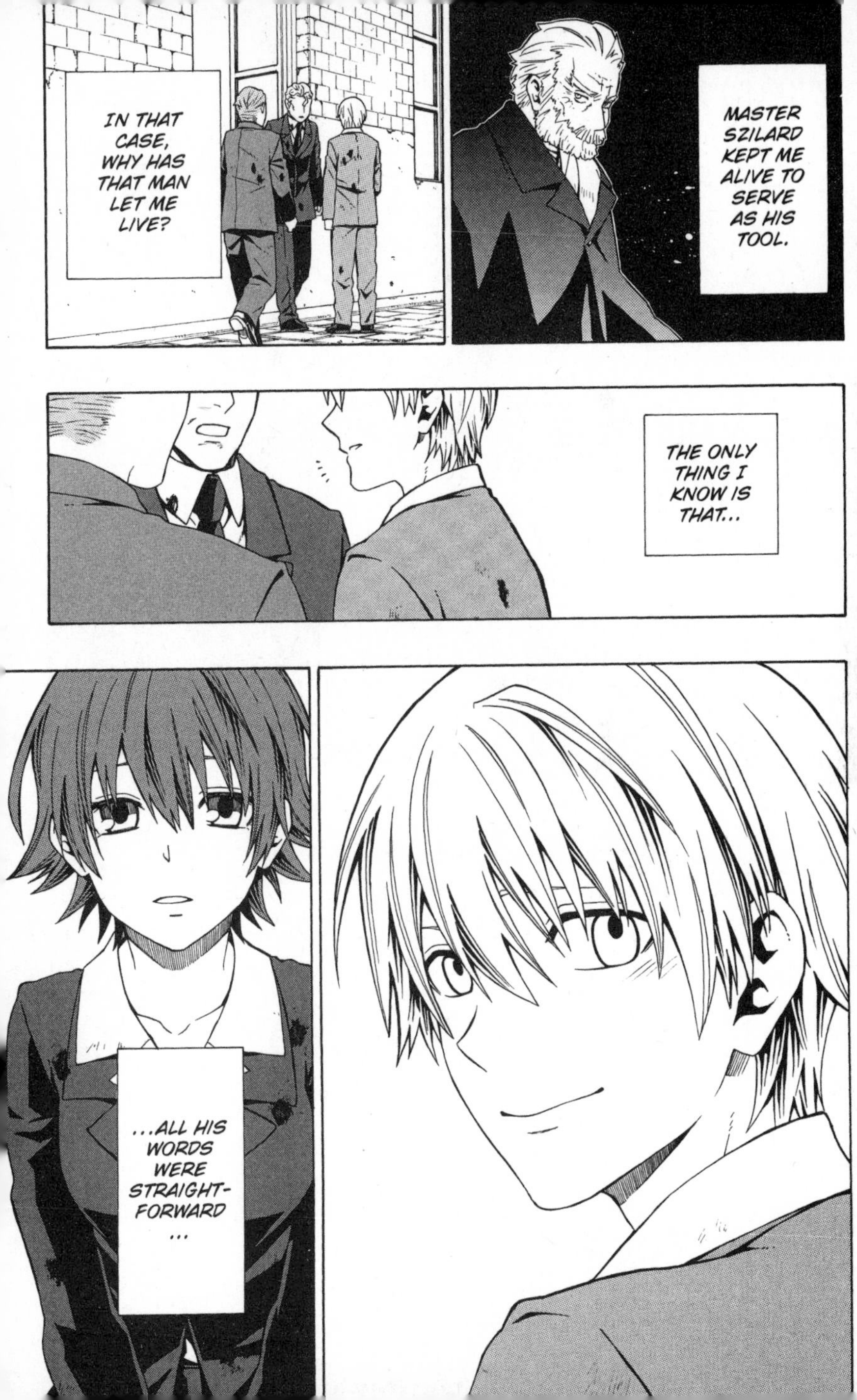
MASTER SZILARD KEPT ME ALIVE TO SERVE AS HIS TOOL.
IN THAT CASE, WHY HAS THAT MAN LET ME LIVE?
THE ONLY THING I KNOW IS THAT...
...ALL HIS WORDS WERE STRAIGHT-FORWARD...

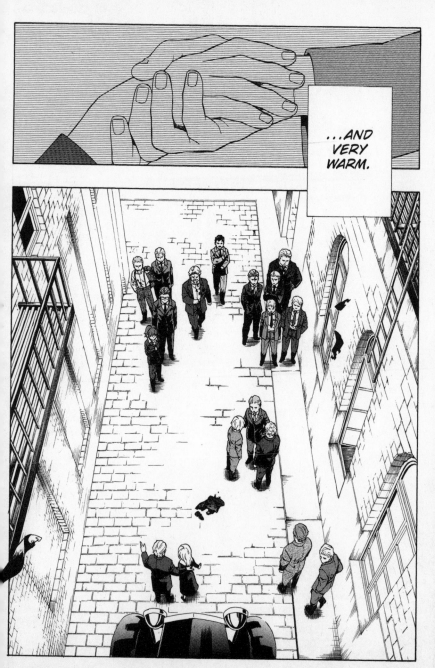

...AND
VERY
WARM.

198

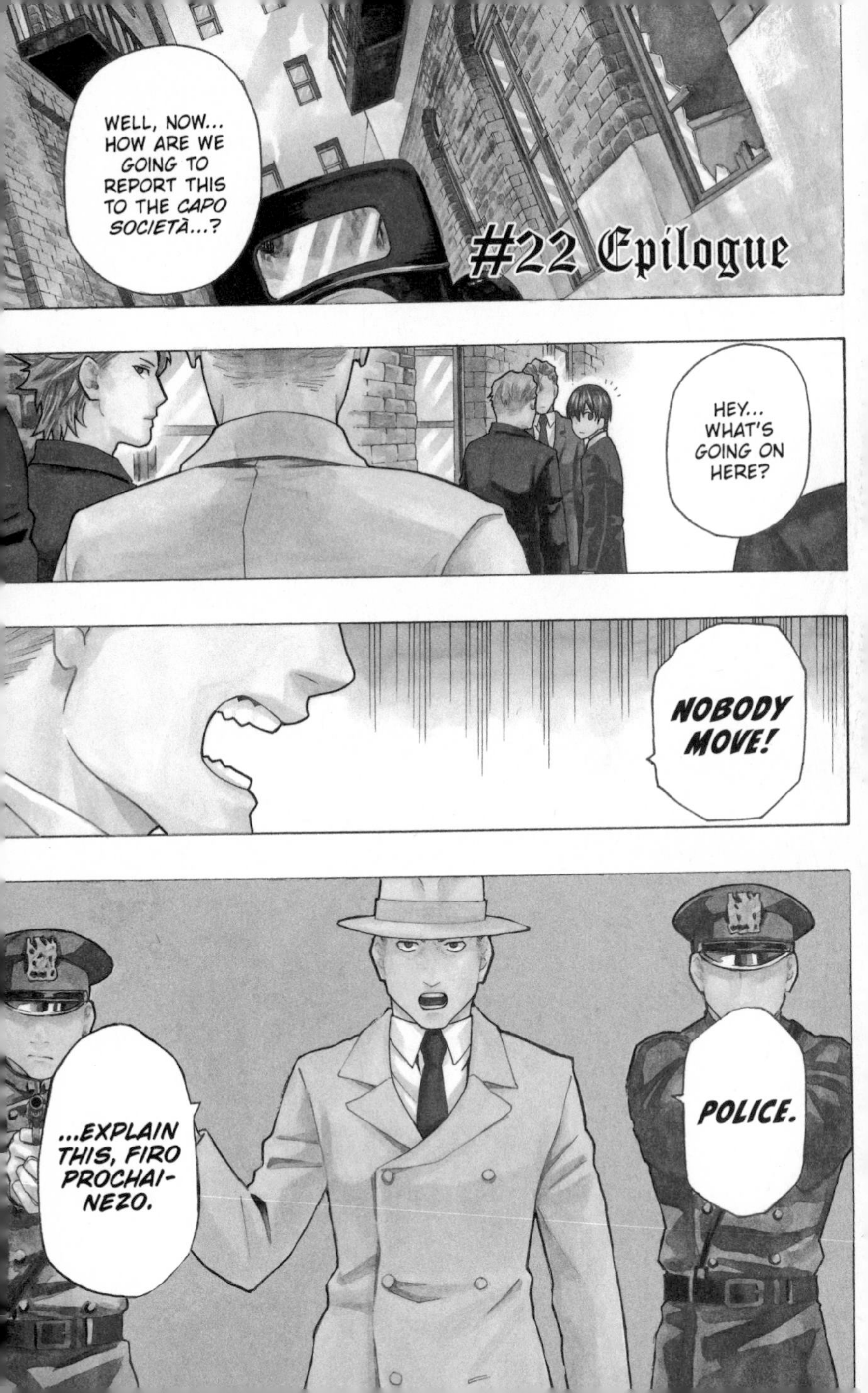
#22 Epilogue
WELL, NOW... HOW ARE WE GOING TO REPORT THIS TO THE CAPO SOCIETÀ...?
HEY... WHAT'S GOING ON HERE?
NOBODY MOVE!
POLICE.
...EXPLAIN THIS, FIRO PROCHAI-NEZO.

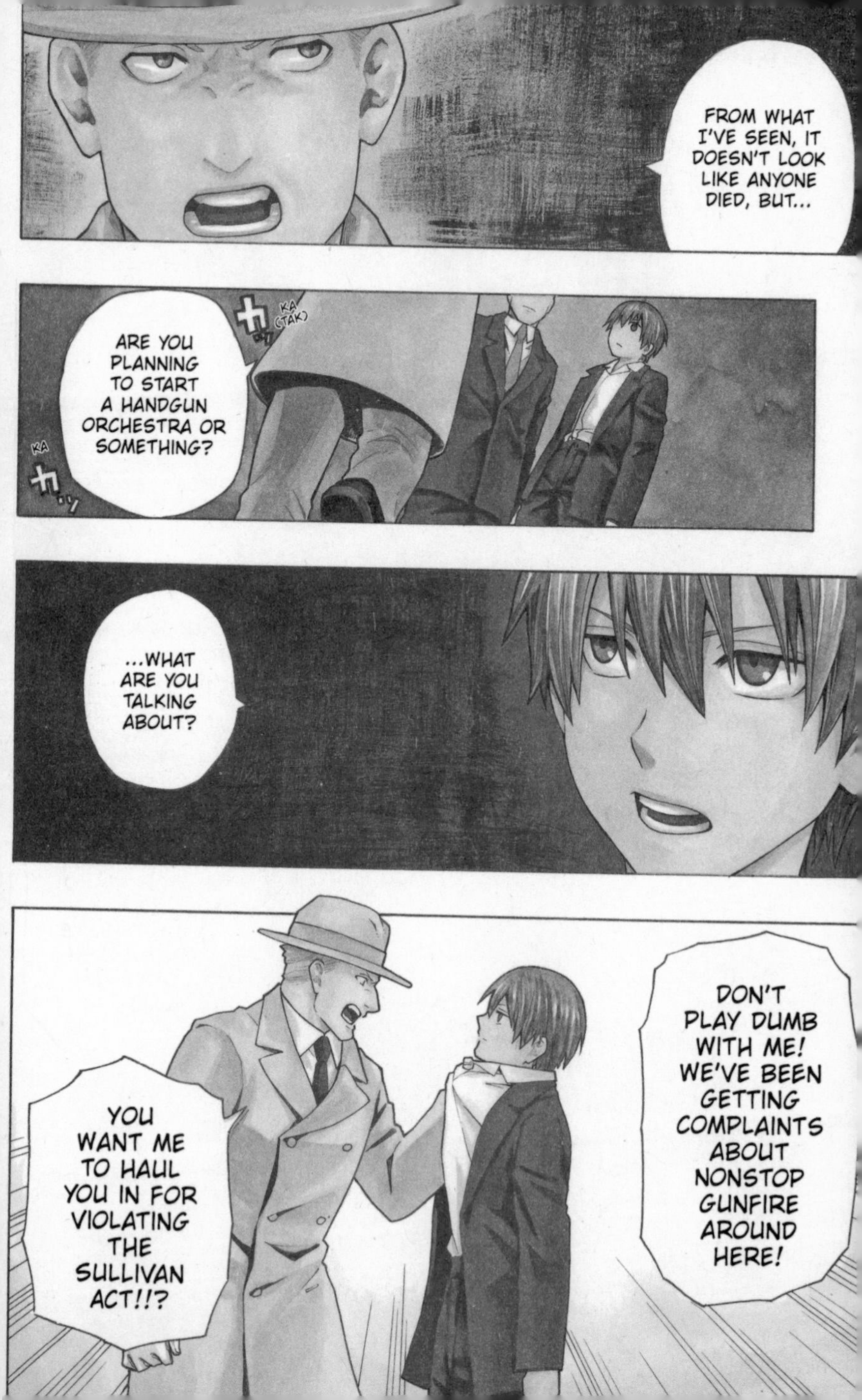
FROM WHAT I'VE SEEN, IT DOESN'T LOOK LIKE ANYONE DIED, BUT...
KA (TAK)
ARE YOU PLANNING TO START A HANDGUN ORCHESTRA OR SOMETHING?
KA
...WHAT ARE YOU TALKING ABOUT?
DON'T PLAY DUMB WITH ME! WE'VE BEEN GETTING COMPLAINTS ABOUT NONSTOP GUNFIRE AROUND HERE!
YOU WANT ME TO HAUL YOU IN FOR VIOLATING THE SULLIVAN ACT!!?

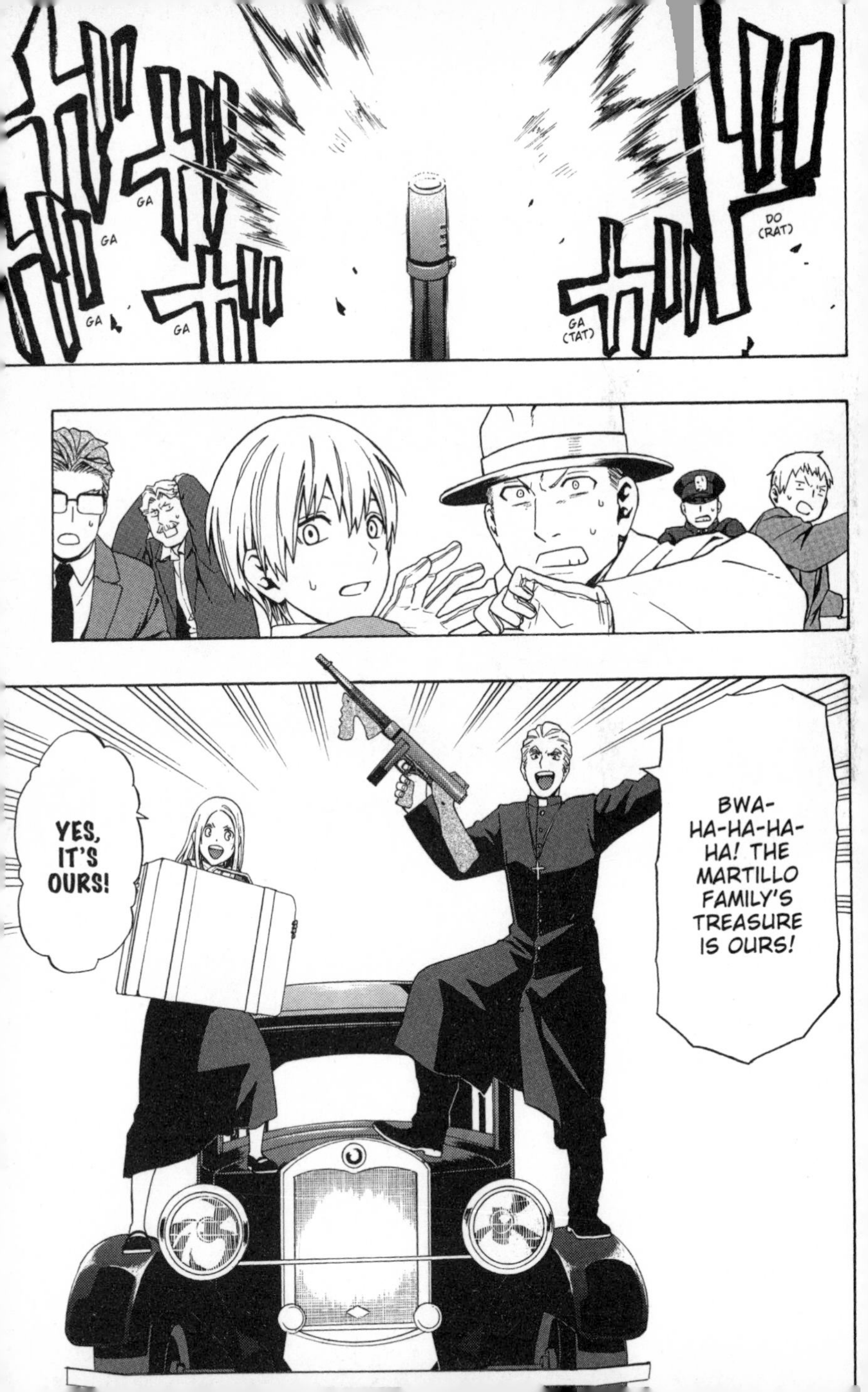
DO (RAT)
GA (TAT)
GA
GA
GA
GA
BWA-HA-HA-HA-HA! THE MARTILLO FAMILY'S TREASURE IS OURS!
YES, IT'S OURS!

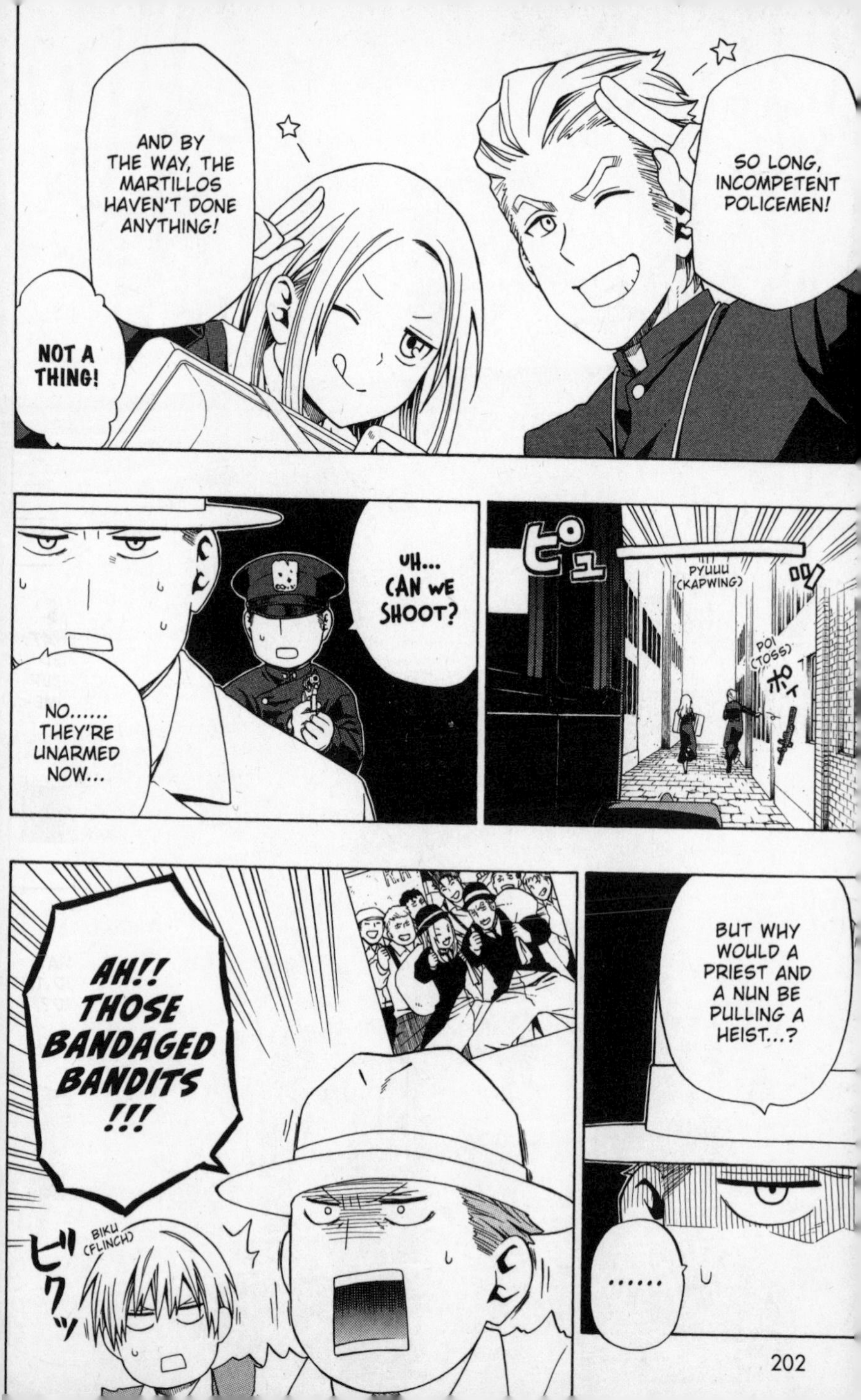

SO LONG, INCOMPETENT POLICEMEN!
AND BY THE WAY, THE MARTILLOS HAVEN'T DONE ANYTHING!
NOT A THING!
ピュ
PYUUU (KAPWING)
ポイ
POI (TOSS)
UH... CAN WE SHOOT?
NO...... THEY'RE UNARMED NOW...
BUT WHY WOULD A PRIEST AND A NUN BE PULLING A HEIST...?
......
AH!! THOSE BANDAGED BANDITS!!!
ビクッ
BIKU (FLINCH)

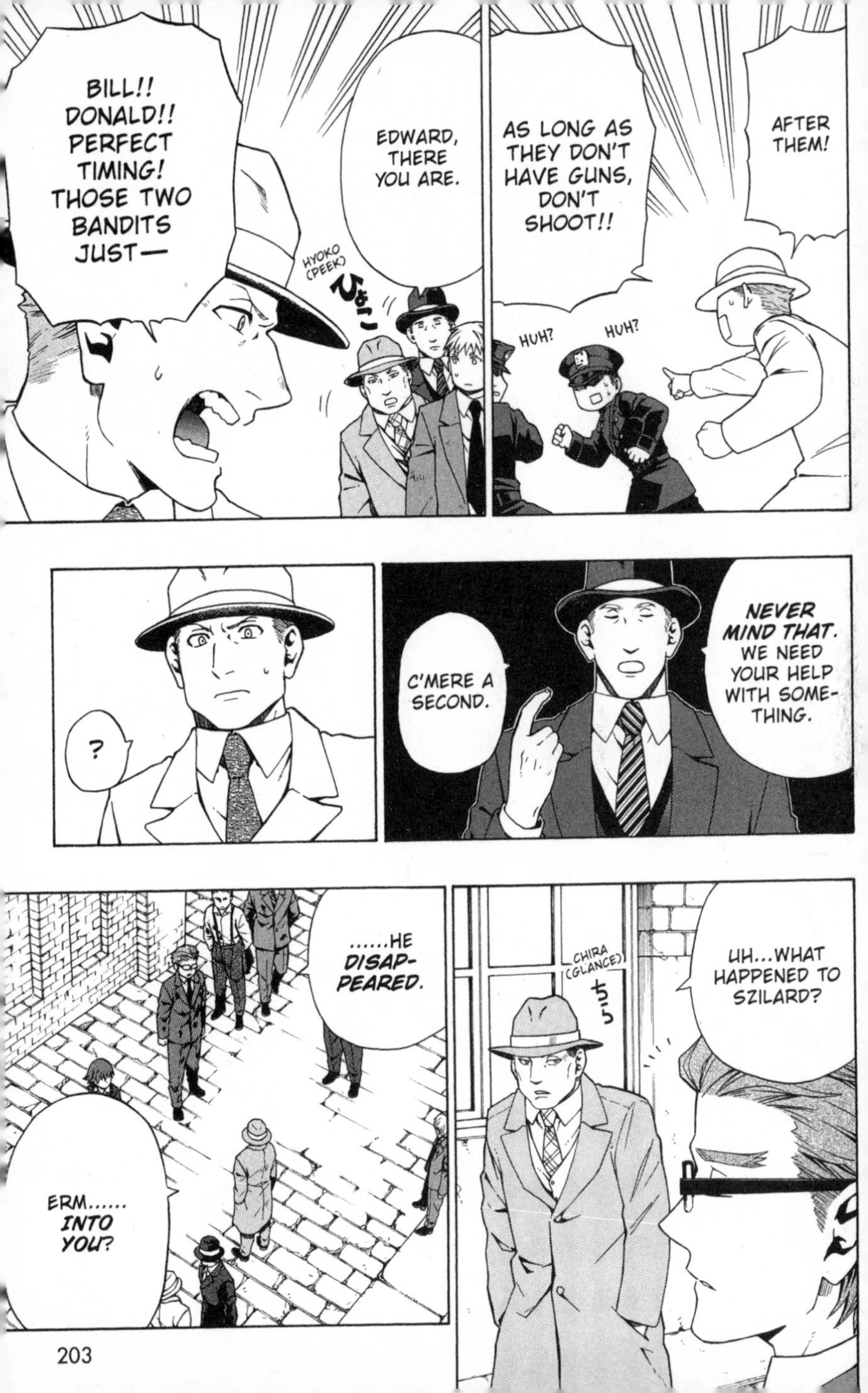
AFTER THEM!
AS LONG AS THEY DON'T HAVE GUNS, DON'T SHOOT!!
HUH?
HUH?
EDWARD, THERE YOU ARE.
HYOKO (PEEK)
BILL!! DONALD!! PERFECT TIMING! THOSE TWO BANDITS JUST—
NEVER MIND THAT. WE NEED YOUR HELP WITH SOMETHING.
C'MERE A SECOND.
?
UH...WHAT HAPPENED TO SZILARD?
CHIRA (GLANCE)
......HE ***DISAPPEARED.***
ERM...... ***INTO YOU?***

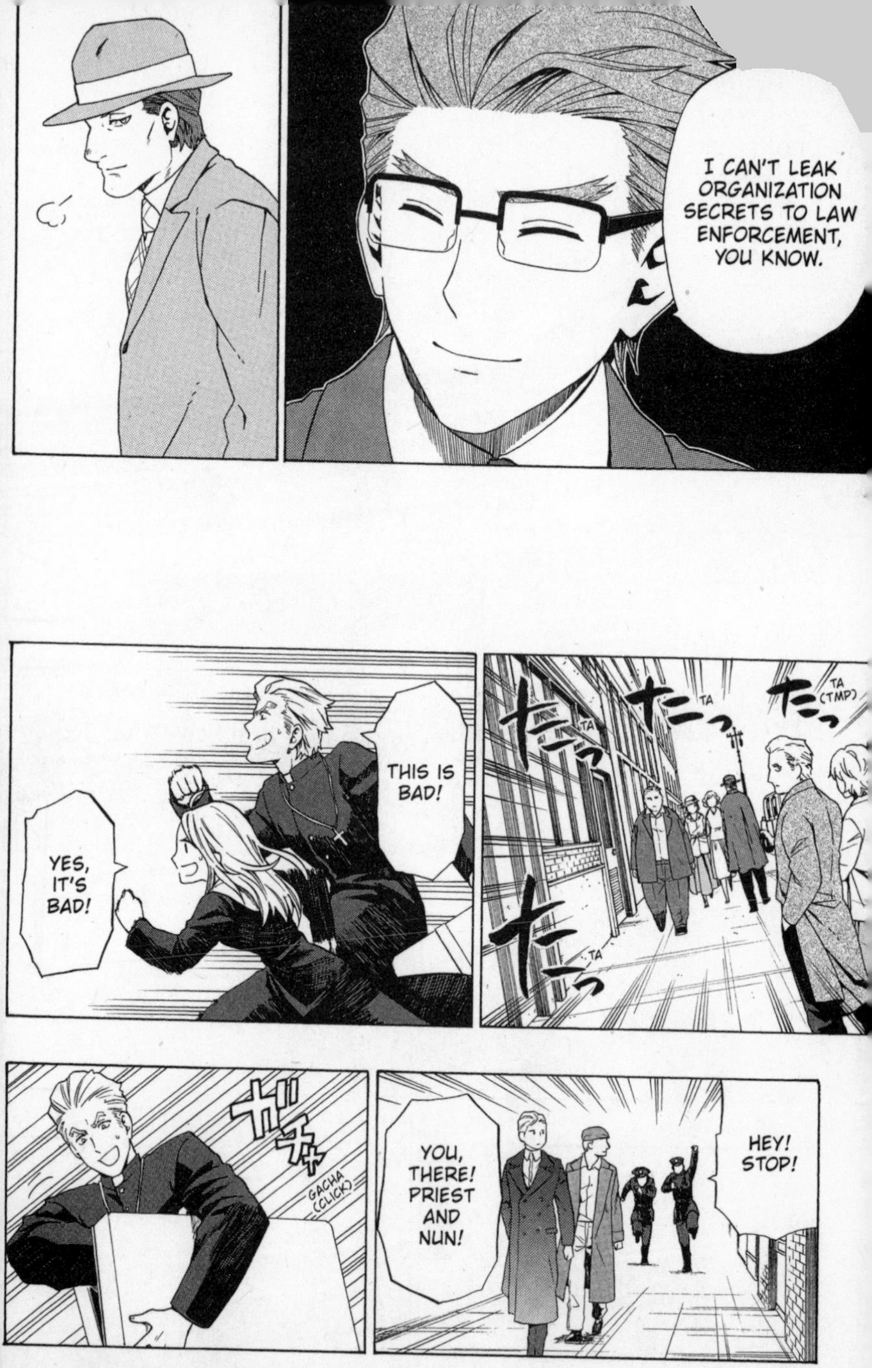
I CAN'T LEAK ORGANIZATION SECRETS TO LAW ENFORCEMENT, YOU KNOW.
たっ
TA (TMP)
たっ
TA
たっ
TA
たっ
TA
THIS IS BAD!
YES, IT'S BAD!
HEY! STOP!
YOU, THERE! PRIEST AND NUN!
ガチャ
GACHA (CLICK)

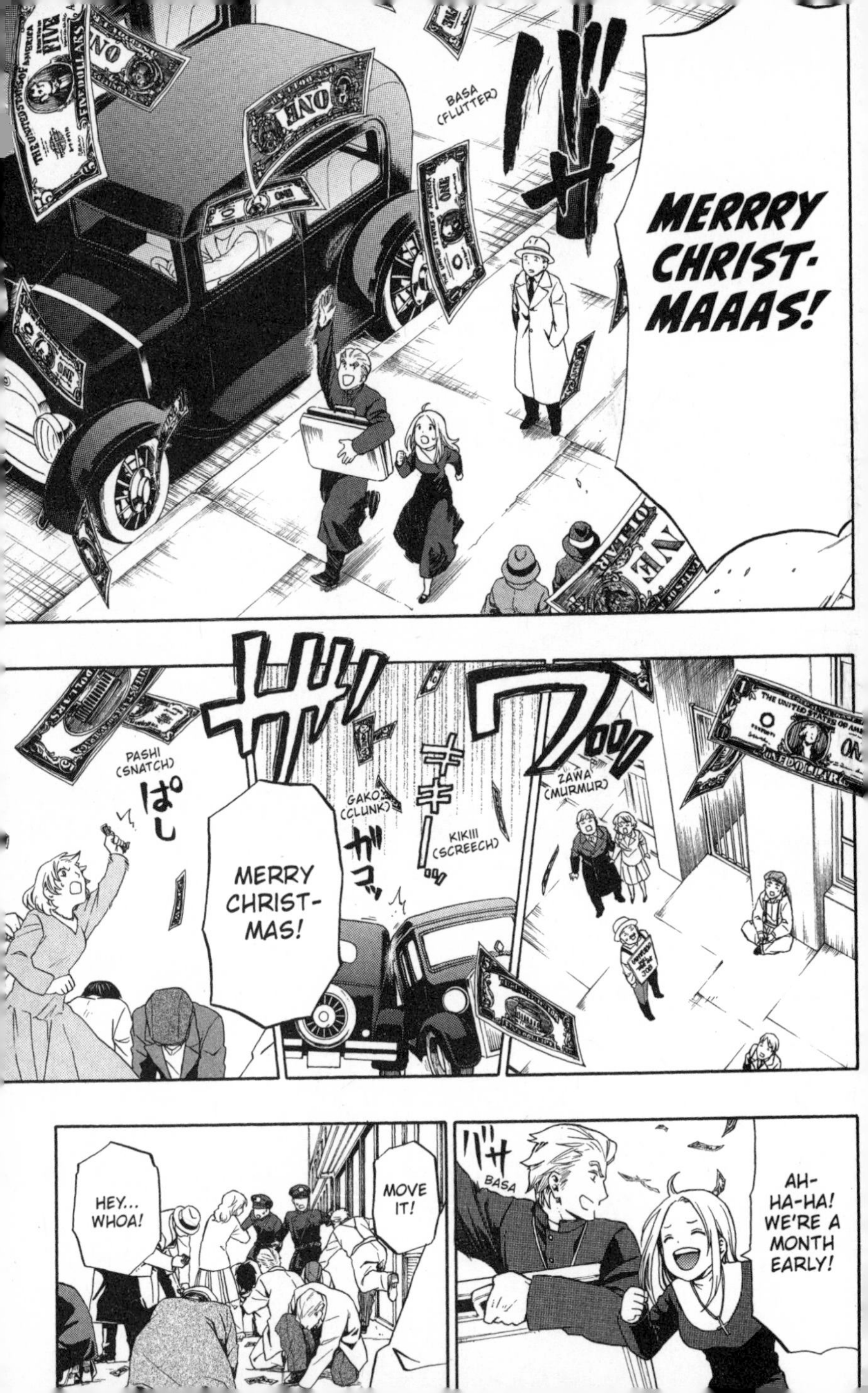
BASA (FLUTTER)
MERRRY CHRIST-MAAAS!
ZAWA (MURMUR)
KIKIII (SCREECH)
GAKO (CLUNK)
MERRY CHRIST-MAS!
PASHI (SNATCH)
ぱし
BASA
AH-HA-HA! WE'RE A MONTH EARLY!
MOVE IT!
HEY... WHOA!

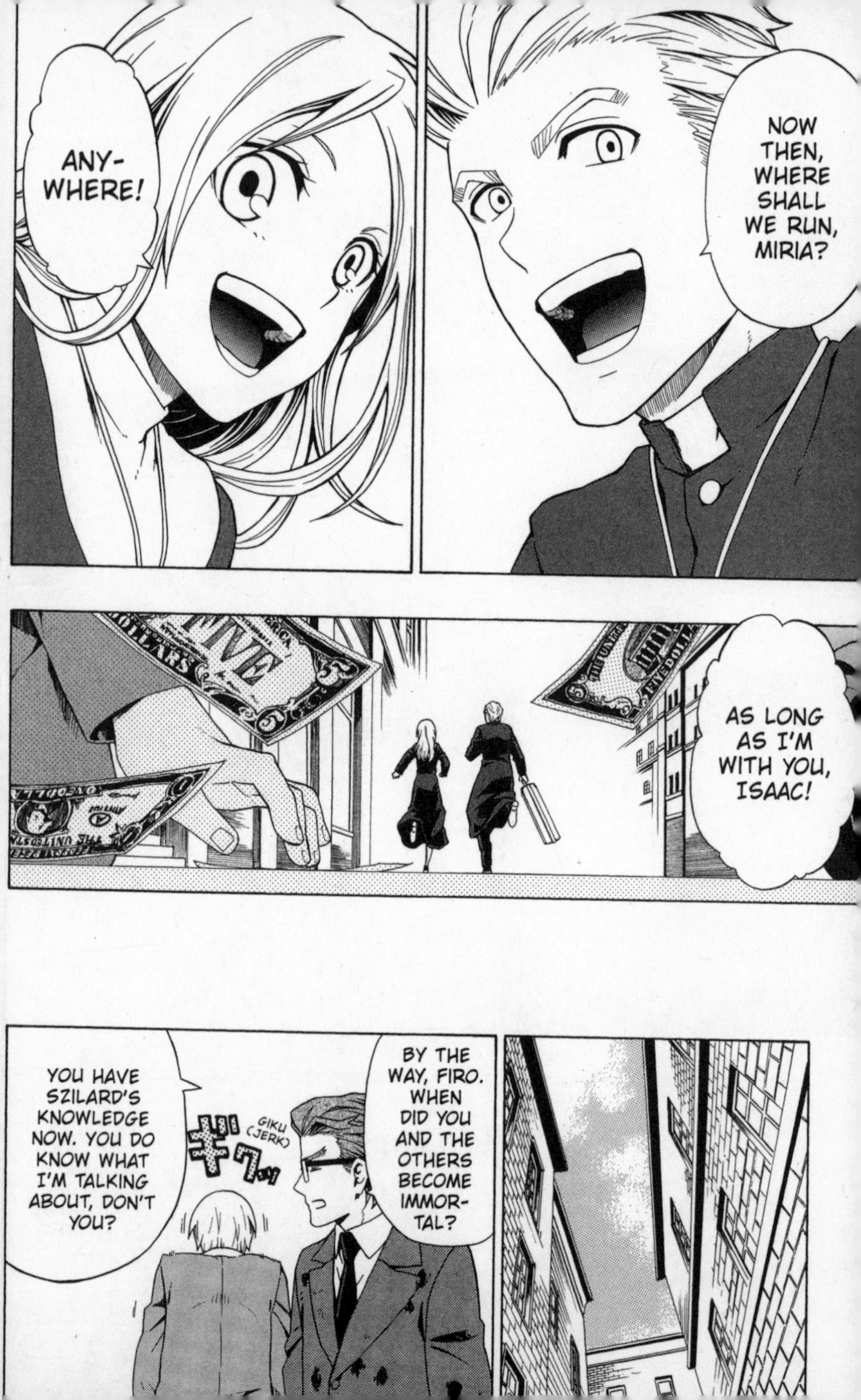
NOW THEN, WHERE SHALL WE RUN, MIRIA?
ANY-WHERE!
AS LONG AS I'M WITH YOU, ISAAC!
BY THE WAY, FIRO. WHEN DID YOU AND THE OTHERS BECOME IMMORTAL?
GIKU (JERK)
YOU HAVE SZILARD'S KNOWLEDGE NOW. YOU DO KNOW WHAT I'M TALKING ABOUT, DON'T YOU?

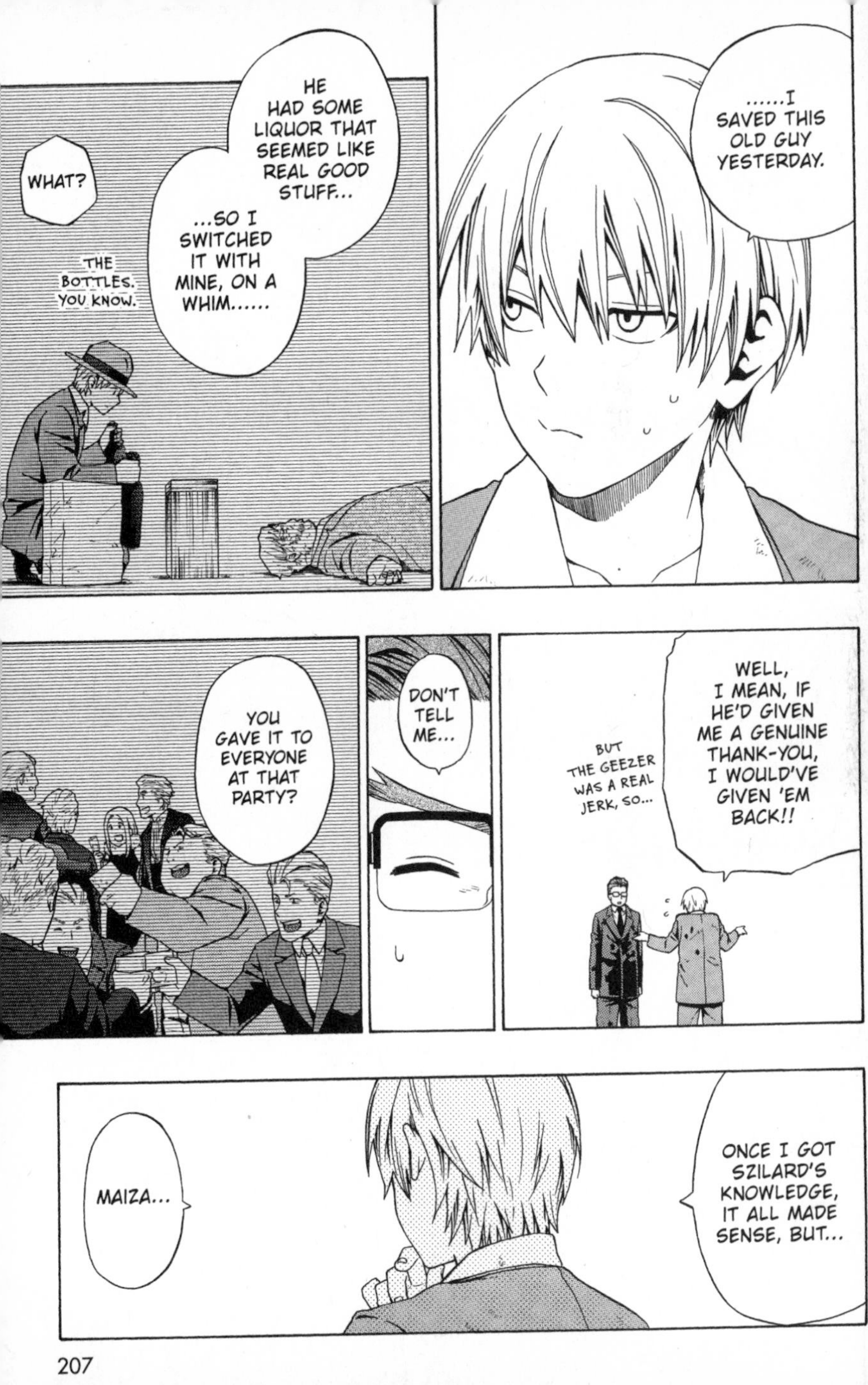
......I SAVED THIS OLD GUY YESTERDAY.
HE HAD SOME LIQUOR THAT SEEMED LIKE REAL GOOD STUFF...
...SO I SWITCHED IT WITH MINE, ON A WHIM......
WHAT?
THE BOTTLES. YOU KNOW.
WELL, I MEAN, IF HE'D GIVEN ME A GENUINE THANK-YOU, I WOULD'VE GIVEN 'EM BACK!!
BUT THE GEEZER WAS A REAL JERK, SO...
DON'T TELL ME...
YOU GAVE IT TO EVERYONE AT THAT PARTY?
ONCE I GOT SZILARD'S KNOWLEDGE, IT ALL MADE SENSE, BUT...
MAIZA...

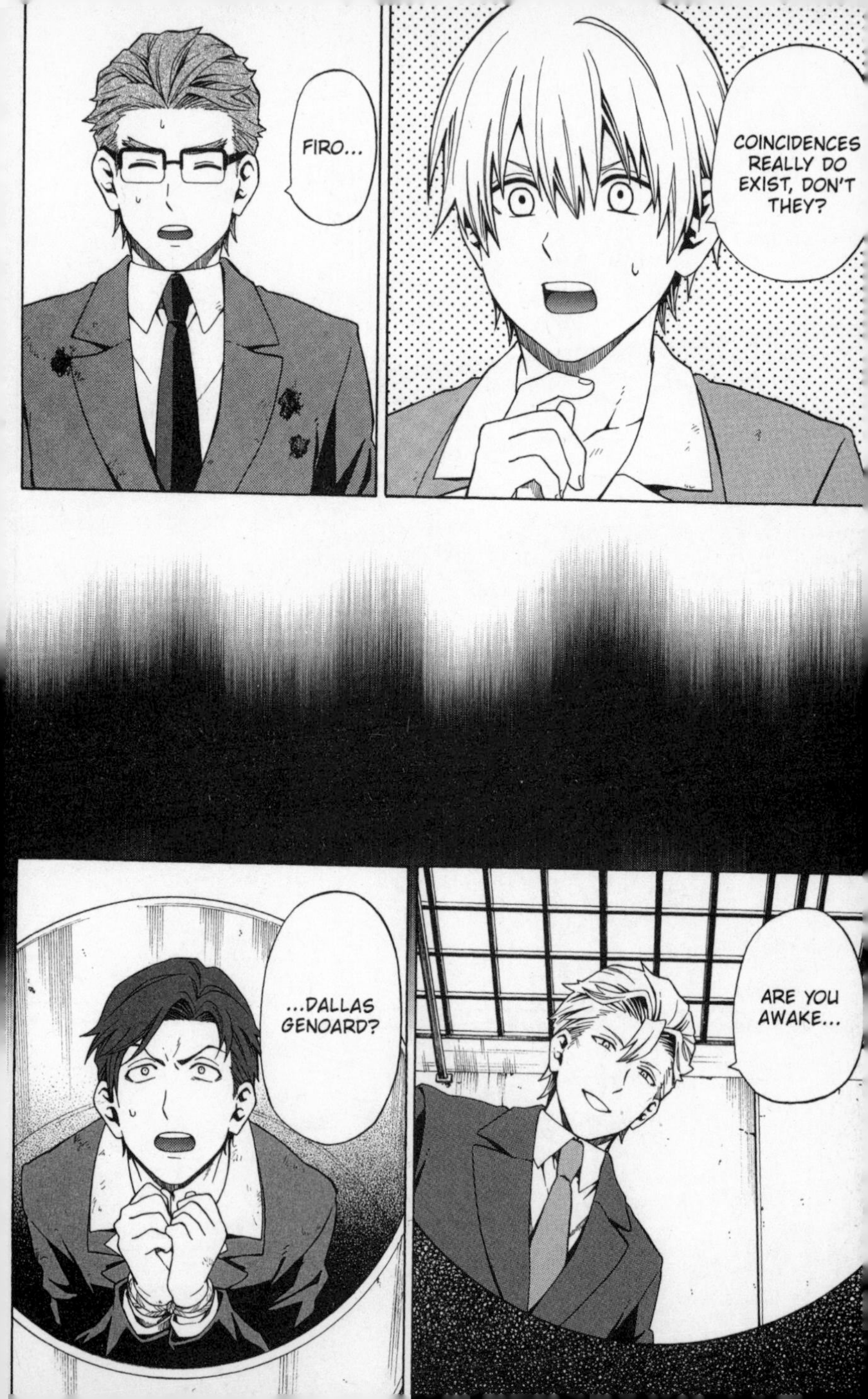
COINCIDENCES REALLY DO EXIST, DON'T THEY?
FIRO...
ARE YOU AWAKE...
...DALLAS GENOARD?

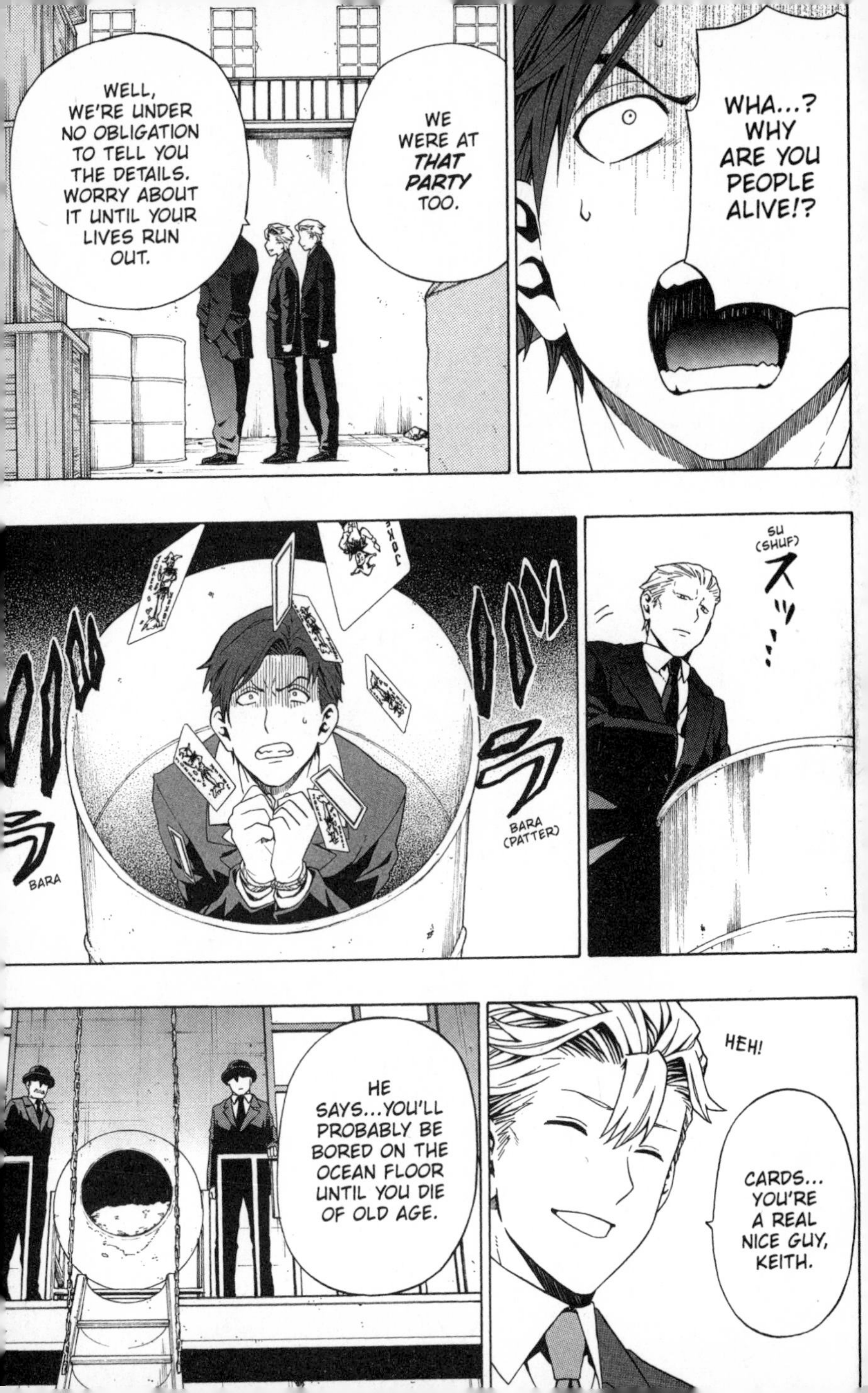
WHA...? WHY ARE YOU PEOPLE ALIVE!?
WE WERE AT *THAT PARTY* TOO.
WELL, WE'RE UNDER NO OBLIGATION TO TELL YOU THE DETAILS. WORRY ABOUT IT UNTIL YOUR LIVES RUN OUT.
SU (SHUF)
BARA (PATTER)
BARA
HEH!
CARDS... YOU'RE A REAL NICE GUY, KEITH.
HE SAYS...YOU'LL PROBABLY BE BORED ON THE OCEAN FLOOR UNTIL YOU DIE OF OLD AGE.

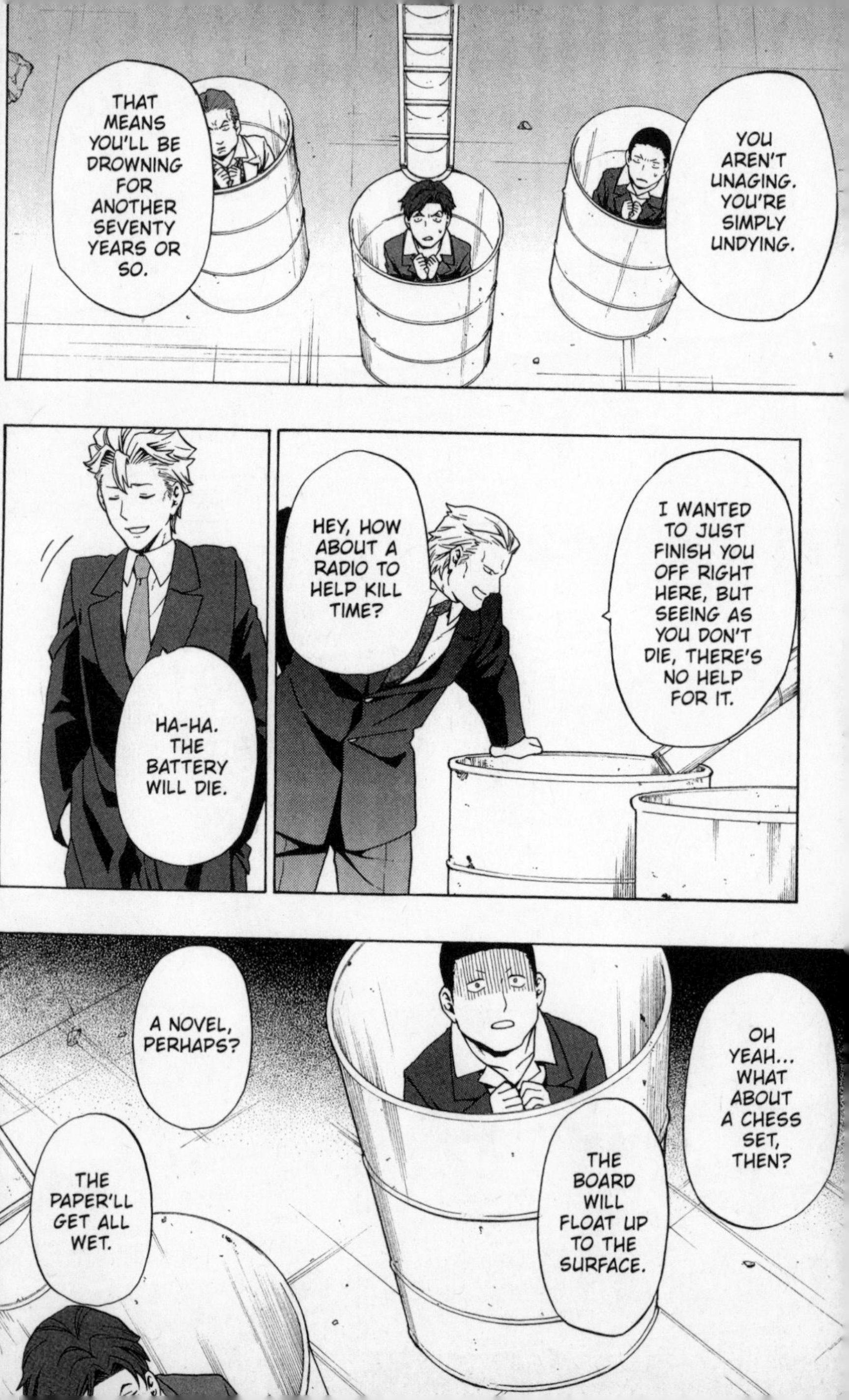
YOU AREN'T UNAGING. YOU'RE SIMPLY UNDYING.
THAT MEANS YOU'LL BE DROWNING FOR ANOTHER SEVENTY YEARS OR SO.
I WANTED TO JUST FINISH YOU OFF RIGHT HERE, BUT SEEING AS YOU DON'T DIE, THERE'S NO HELP FOR IT.
HEY, HOW ABOUT A RADIO TO HELP KILL TIME?
HA-HA. THE BATTERY WILL DIE.
OH YEAH... WHAT ABOUT A CHESS SET, THEN?
THE BOARD WILL FLOAT UP TO THE SURFACE.
A NOVEL, PERHAPS?
THE PAPER'LL GET ALL WET.

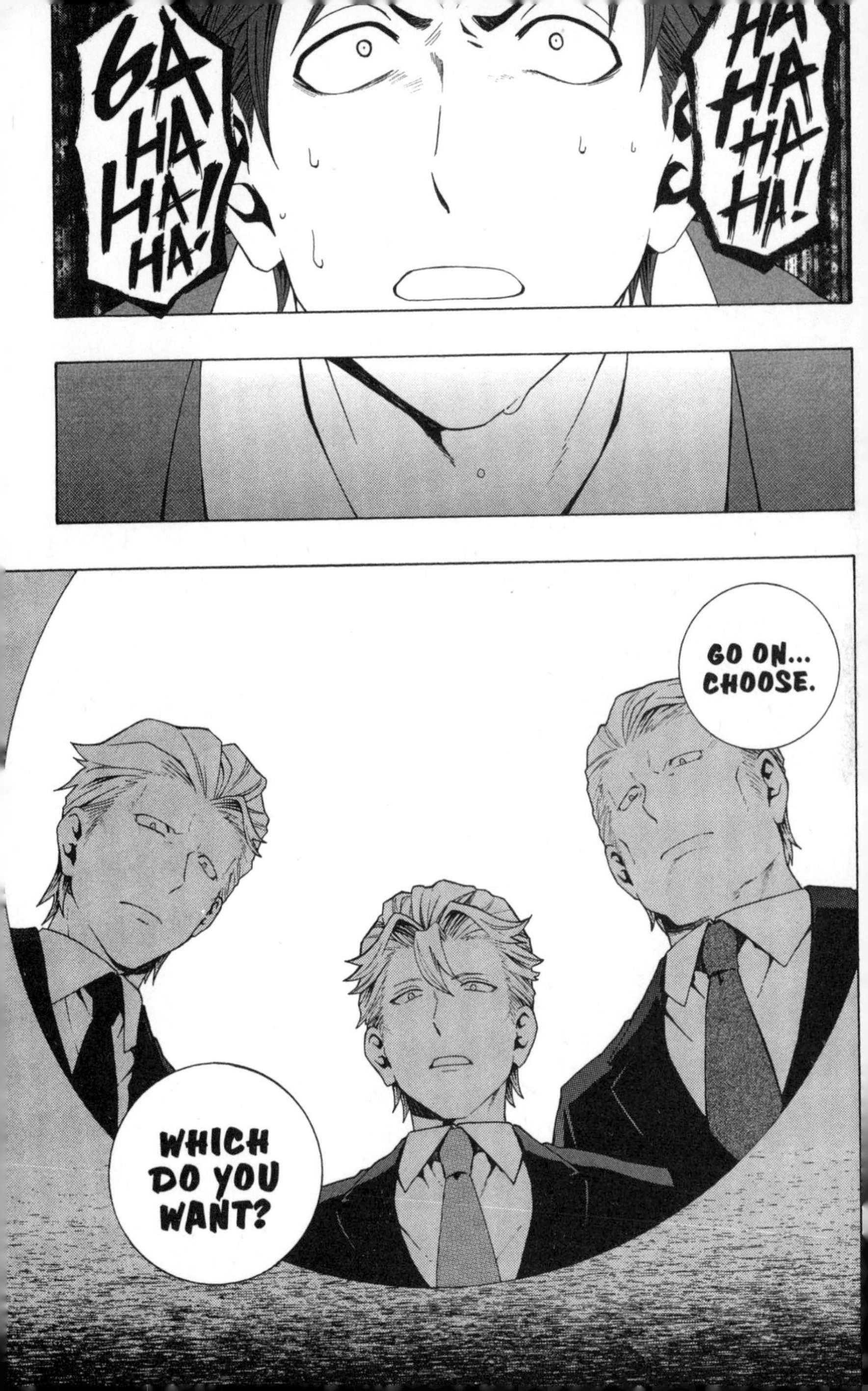
HA HA HA HA HA!
GA HA HA HA! HA-
GO ON... CHOOSE.
WHICH DO YOU WANT?

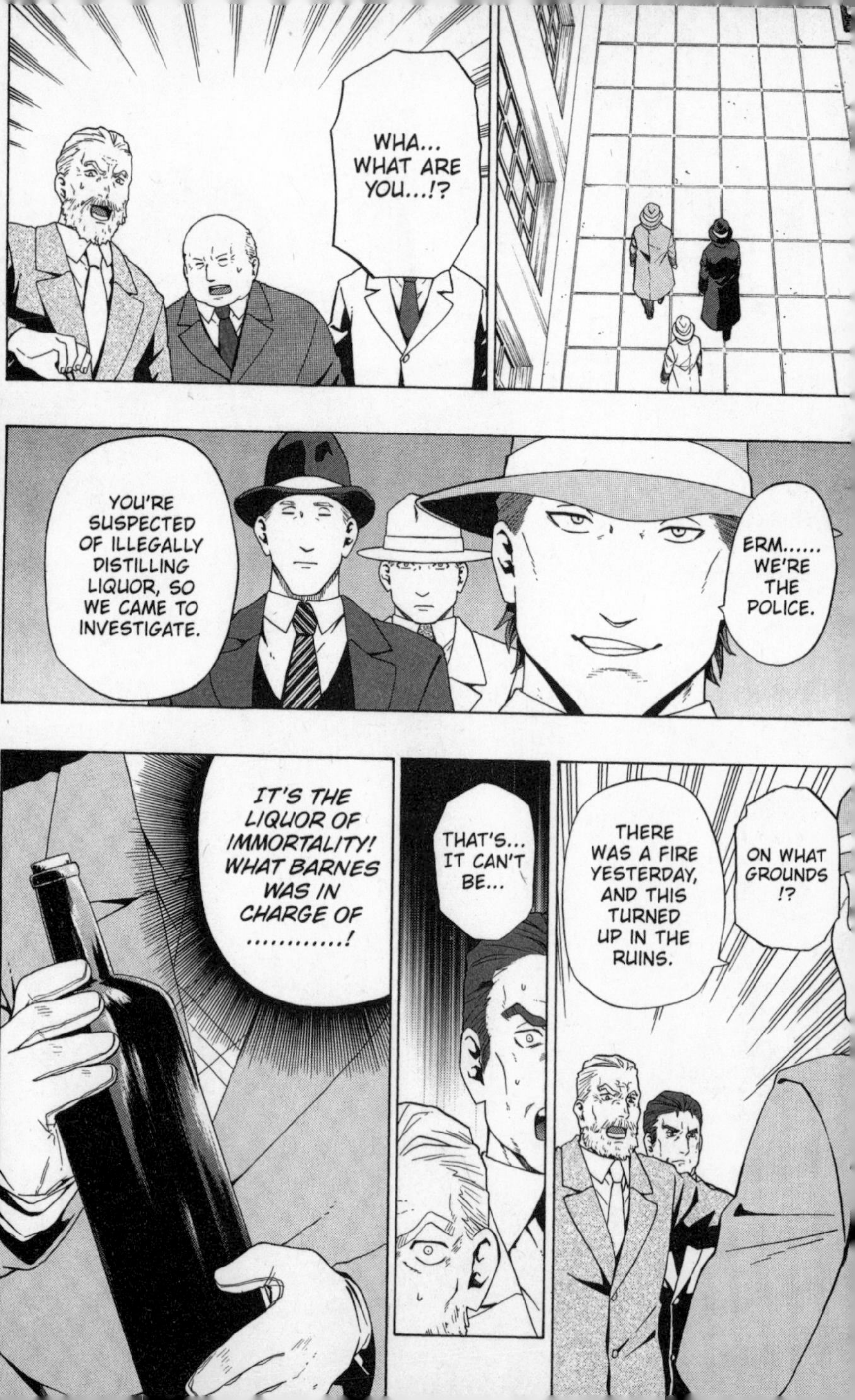
WHA... WHAT ARE YOU...!?
ERM...... WE'RE THE POLICE.
YOU'RE SUSPECTED OF ILLEGALLY DISTILLING LIQUOR, SO WE CAME TO INVESTIGATE.
ON WHAT GROUNDS !?
THERE WAS A FIRE YESTERDAY, AND THIS TURNED UP IN THE RUINS.
THAT'S... IT CAN'T BE...
IT'S THE LIQUOR OF IMMORTALITY! WHAT BARNES WAS IN CHARGE OF ....!

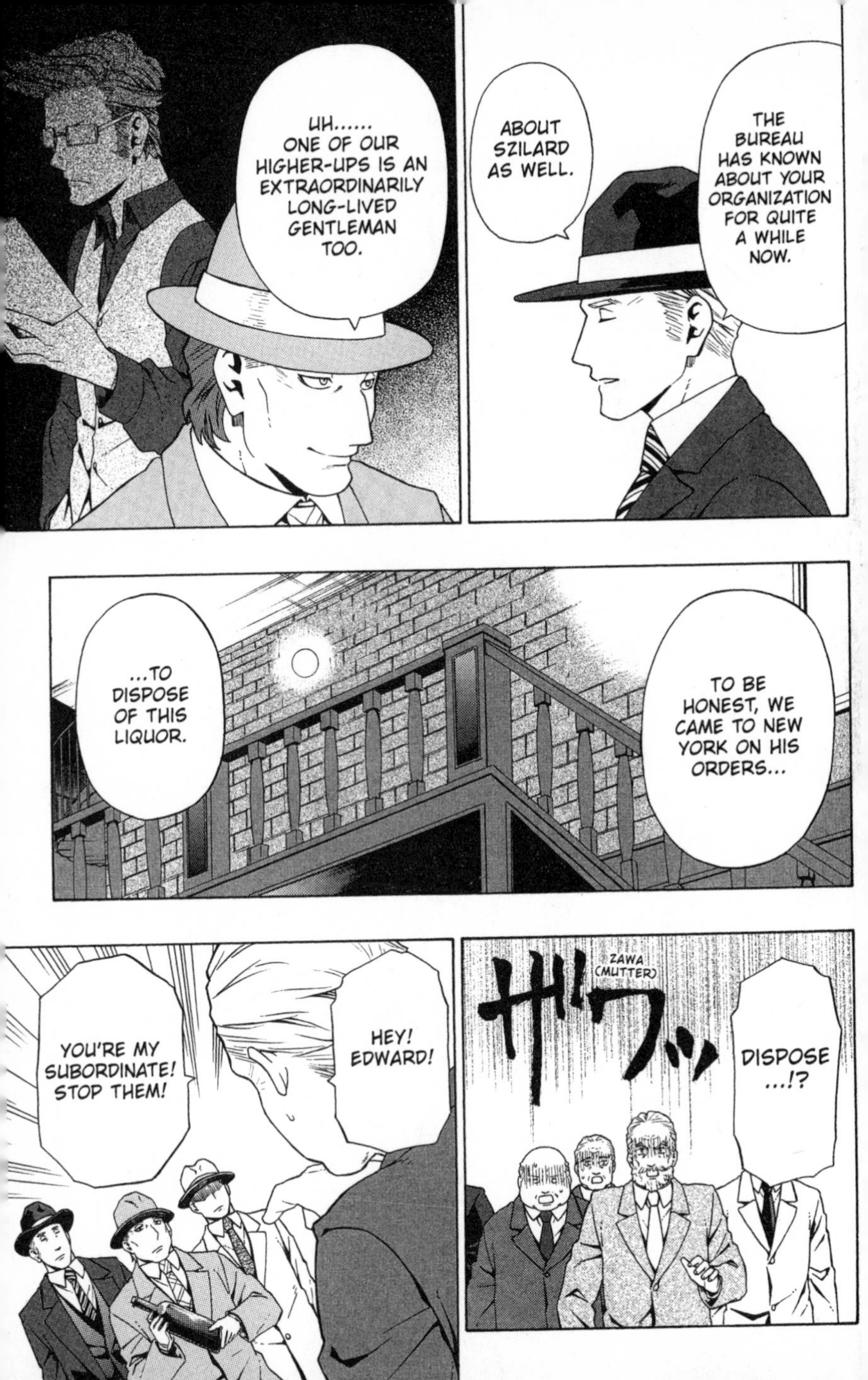
THE BUREAU HAS KNOWN ABOUT YOUR ORGANIZATION FOR QUITE A WHILE NOW.
ABOUT SZILARD AS WELL.
UH...... ONE OF OUR HIGHER-UPS IS AN EXTRAORDINARILY LONG-LIVED GENTLEMAN TOO.
TO BE HONEST, WE CAME TO NEW YORK ON HIS ORDERS...
...TO DISPOSE OF THIS LIQUOR.
ザワッ
ZAWA (MUTTER)
DISPOSE ...!?
HEY! EDWARD!
YOU'RE MY SUBORDINATE! STOP THEM!

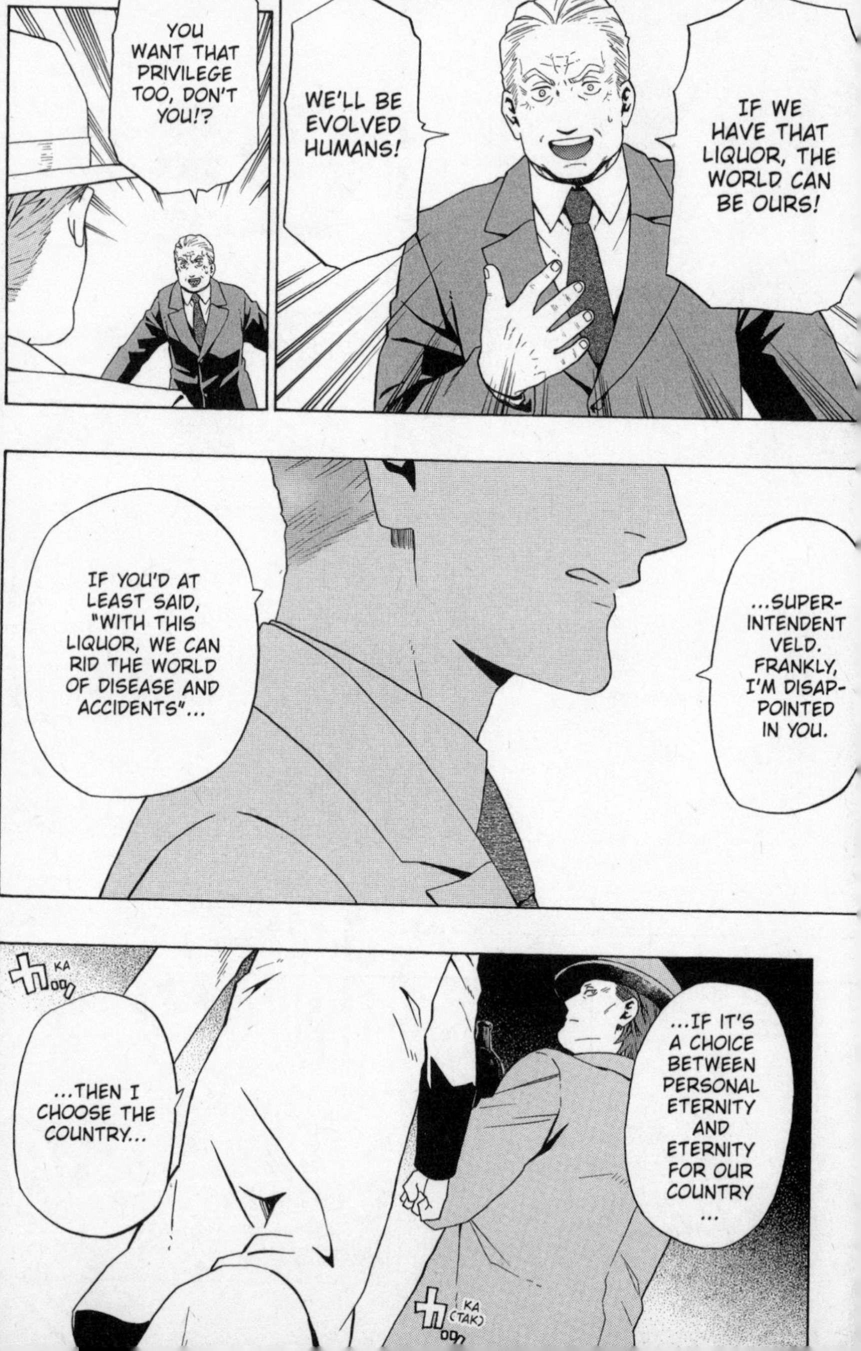
IF WE HAVE THAT LIQUOR, THE WORLD CAN BE OURS!
WE'LL BE EVOLVED HUMANS!
YOU WANT THAT PRIVILEGE TOO, DON'T YOU!?
...SUPER-INTENDENT VELD. FRANKLY, I'M DISAP-POINTED IN YOU.
IF YOU'D AT LEAST SAID, "WITH THIS LIQUOR, WE CAN RID THE WORLD OF DISEASE AND ACCIDENTS"...
...IF IT'S A CHOICE BETWEEN PERSONAL ETERNITY AND ETERNITY FOR OUR COUNTRY ...
KA (TAK)
KA
...THEN I CHOOSE THE COUNTRY...

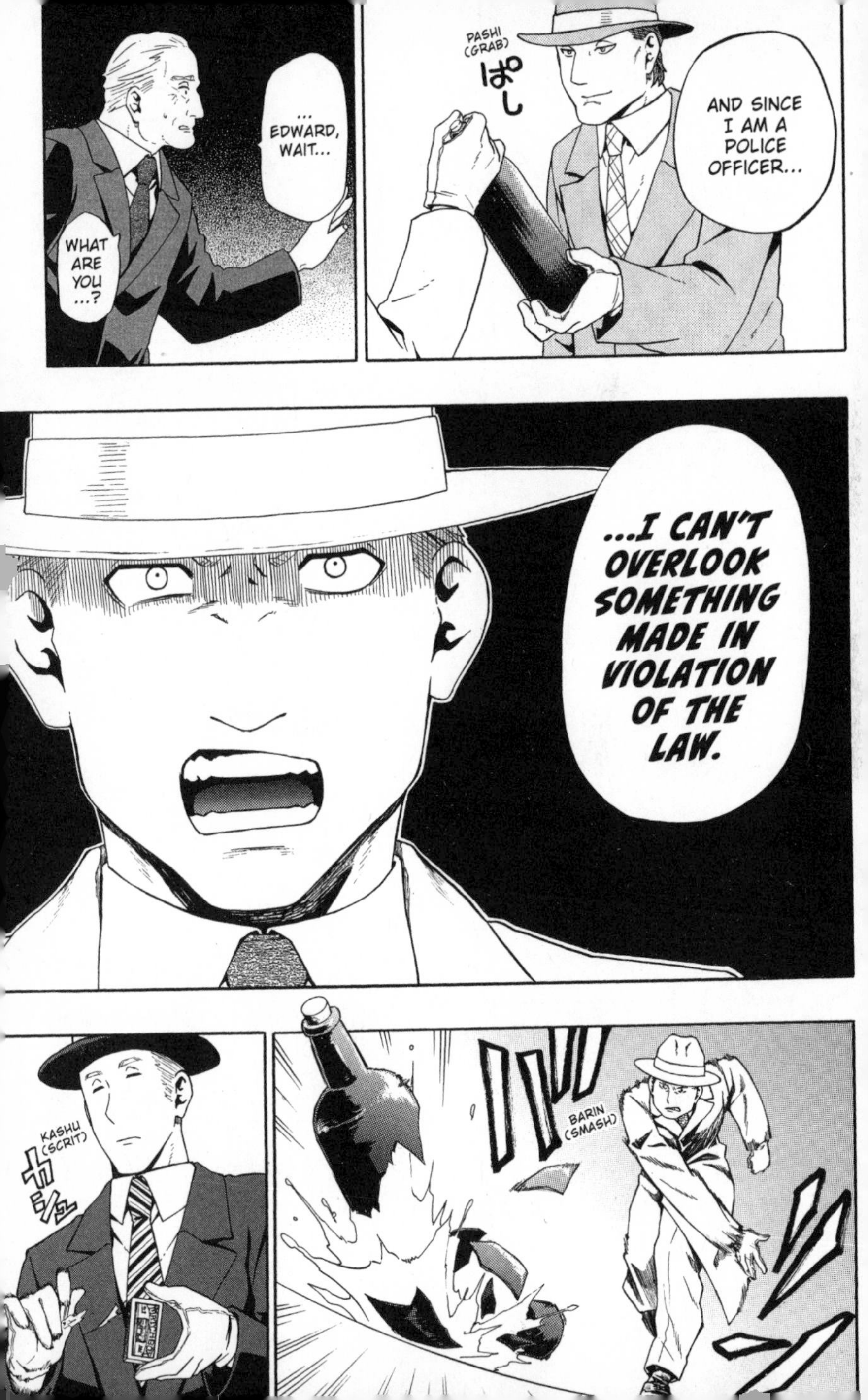
PASHI (GRAB)
ぱし
AND SINCE I AM A POLICE OFFICER...
... EDWARD, WAIT...
WHAT ARE YOU ...?
...I CAN'T OVERLOOK SOMETHING MADE IN VIOLATION OF THE LAW.
BARIN (SMASH)
KASHU (SCRIT)
カシュ

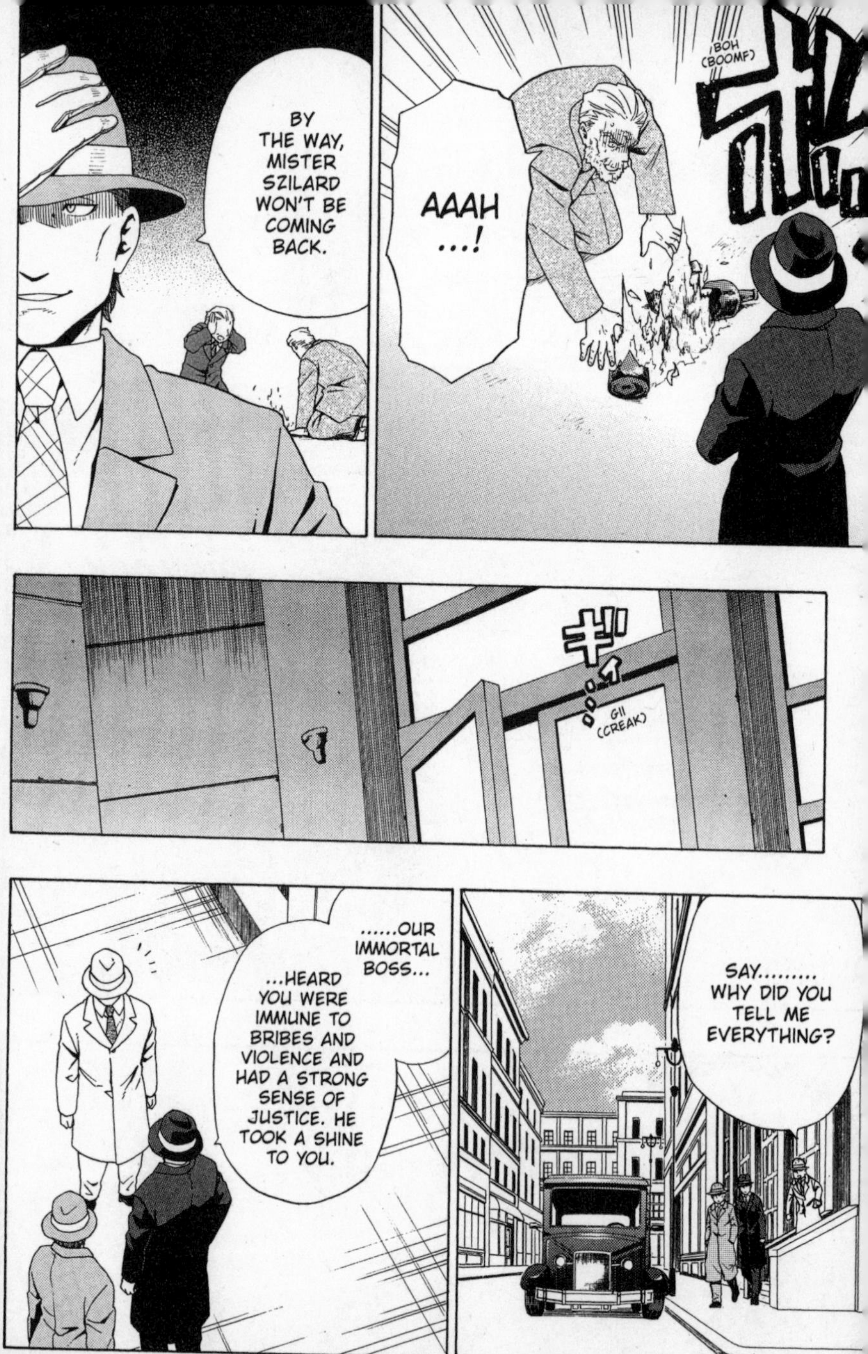
BOH (BOOMF)
AAAH ...!
BY THE WAY, MISTER SZILARD WON'T BE COMING BACK.
GII (CREAK)
SAY......... WHY DID YOU TELL ME EVERYTHING?
......OUR IMMORTAL BOSS...
...HEARD YOU WERE IMMUNE TO BRIBES AND VIOLENCE AND HAD A STRONG SENSE OF JUSTICE. HE TOOK A SHINE TO YOU.

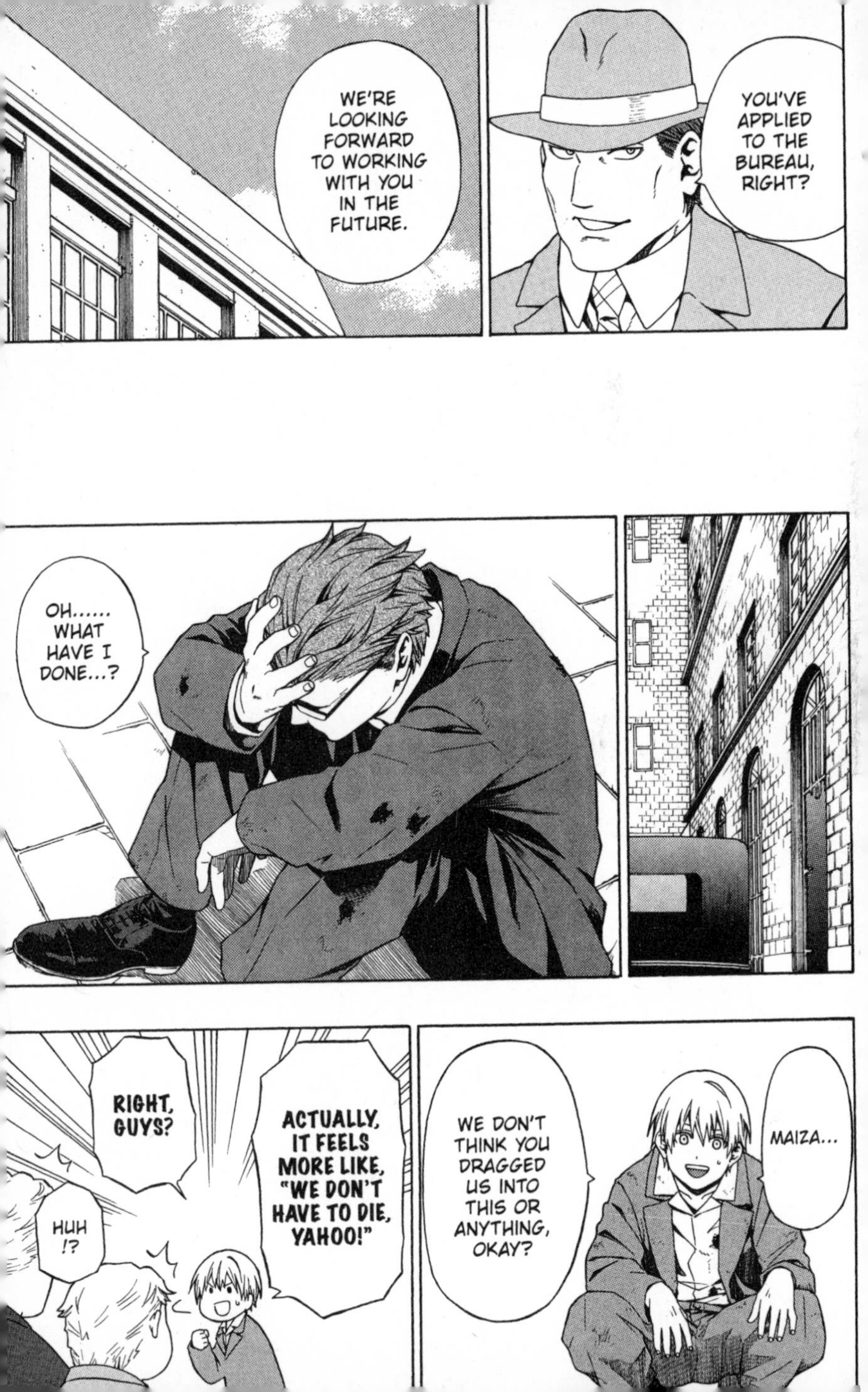
YOU'VE APPLIED TO THE BUREAU, RIGHT?
WE'RE LOOKING FORWARD TO WORKING WITH YOU IN THE FUTURE.
OH...... WHAT HAVE I DONE...?
MAIZA...
WE DON'T THINK YOU DRAGGED US INTO THIS OR ANYTHING, OKAY?
ACTUALLY, IT FEELS MORE LIKE, "WE DON'T HAVE TO DIE, YAHOO!"
RIGHT, GUYS?
HUH!?

YAHOO! CHEER UP, MAIZA!

I DON'T REALLY GET IT, BUT "YAHOO!"

...THE PAIN OF LIVING FOR ETERNITY......

FIRO...... IF YOU HAVE SZILARD'S KNOWLEDGE, THEN YOU KNOW...

I CAN'T DO THAT.

FIRO...... WOULD YOU...?

NOW THAT SZILARD, MY BROTHER'S ENEMY, IS DEAD, THERE'S NO POINT IN LIVING ANY LONGER......

TO BE HONEST... I'M TIRED OF LIVING.

IF YOU'RE GONE...

THE SYNDICATE NEEDS YOU, MAIZA.

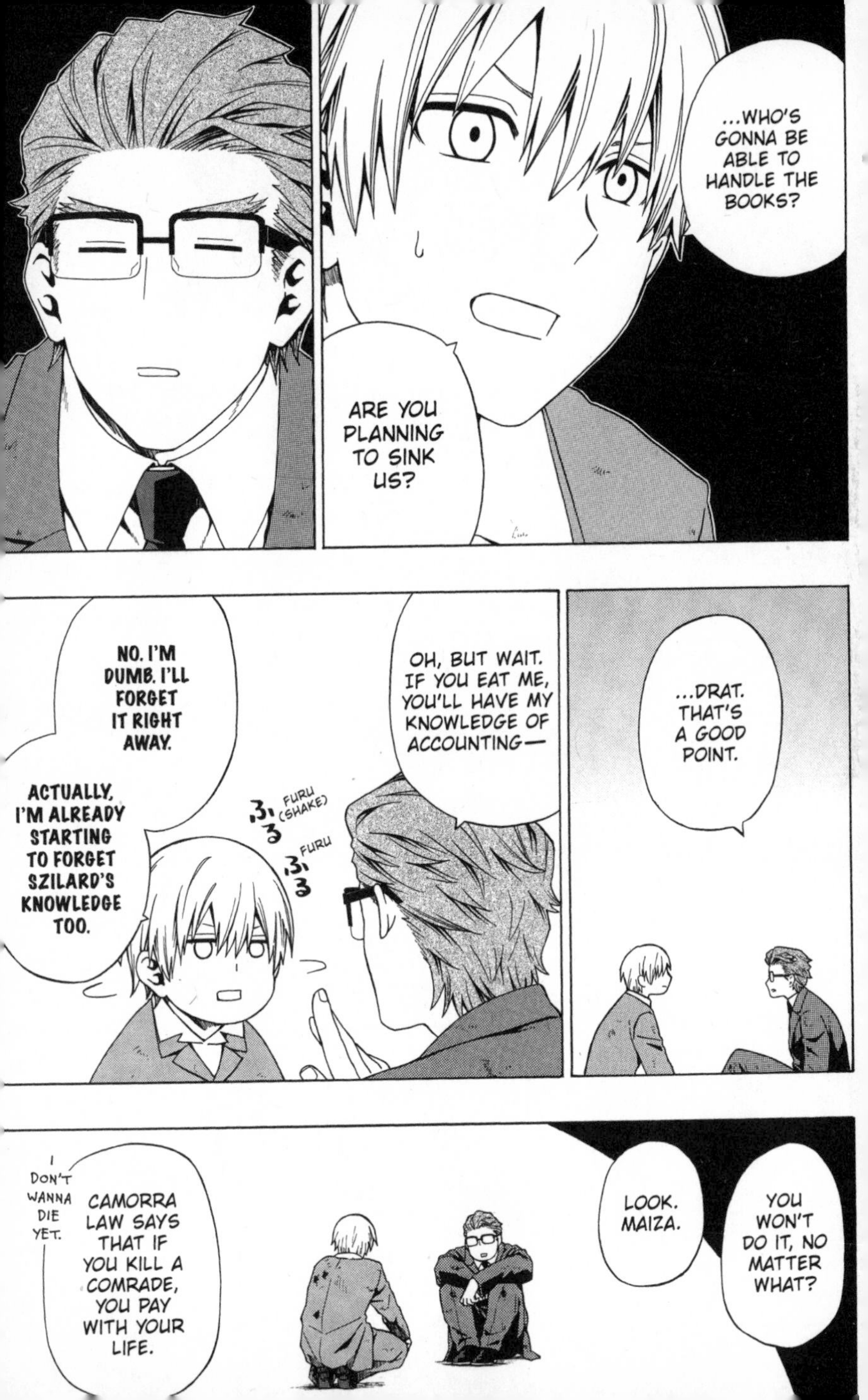
...WHO'S GONNA BE ABLE TO HANDLE THE BOOKS?
ARE YOU PLANNING TO SINK US?
...DRAT. THAT'S A GOOD POINT.
OH, BUT WAIT. IF YOU EAT ME, YOU'LL HAVE MY KNOWLEDGE OF ACCOUNTING—
ふる FURU (SHAKE)
ふる FURU
NO. I'M DUMB. I'LL FORGET IT RIGHT AWAY.
ACTUALLY, I'M ALREADY STARTING TO FORGET SZILARD'S KNOWLEDGE TOO.
YOU WON'T DO IT, NO MATTER WHAT?
LOOK. MAIZA.
CAMORRA LAW SAYS THAT IF YOU KILL A COMRADE, YOU PAY WITH YOUR LIFE.
I DON'T WANNA DIE YET.

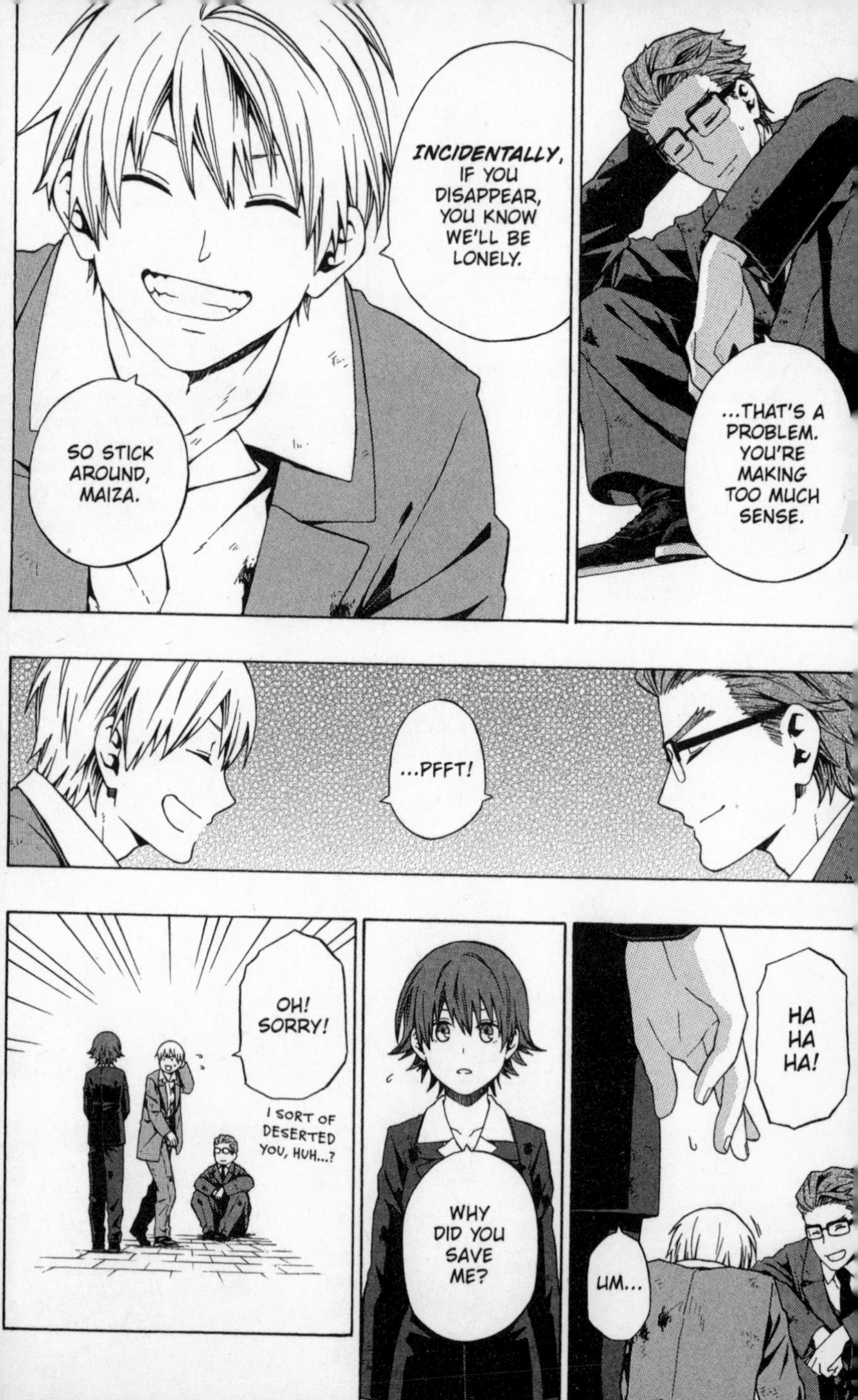
...THAT'S A PROBLEM. YOU'RE MAKING TOO MUCH SENSE.
INCIDENTALLY, IF YOU DISAPPEAR, YOU KNOW WE'LL BE LONELY.
SO STICK AROUND, MAIZA.
...PFFT!
HA HA HA!
UM...
WHY DID YOU SAVE ME?
OH! SORRY!
I SORT OF DESERTED YOU, HUH...?

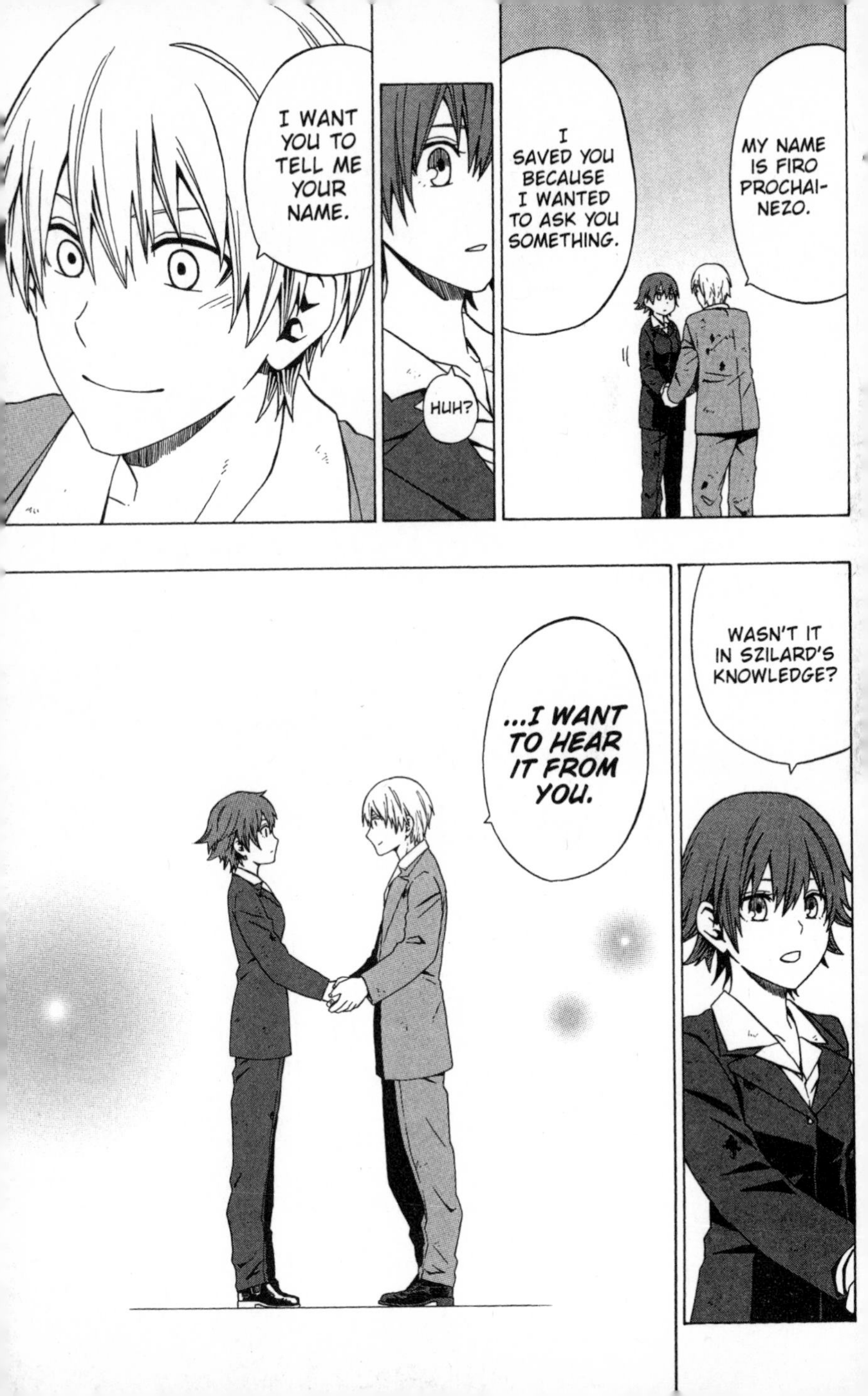
MY NAME IS FIRO PROCHAI-NEZO.
I SAVED YOU BECAUSE I WANTED TO ASK YOU SOMETHING.
HUH?
I WANT YOU TO TELL ME YOUR NAME.
WASN'T IT IN SZILARD'S KNOWLEDGE?
...I WANT TO HEAR IT FROM YOU.

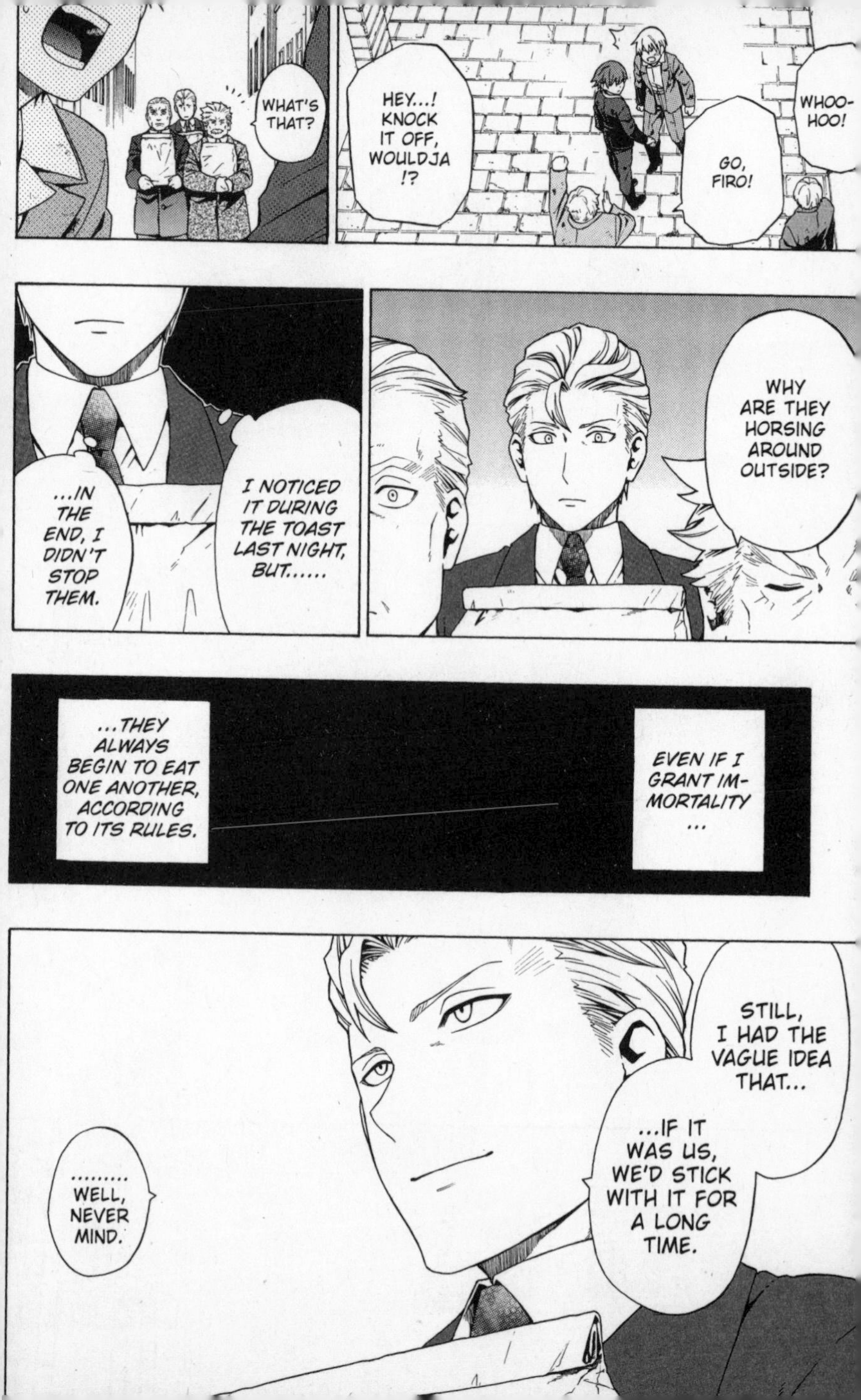
WHOO-HOO!
GO, FIRO!
HEY...! KNOCK IT OFF, WOULDJA!?
WHAT'S THAT?
WHY ARE THEY HORSING AROUND OUTSIDE?
I NOTICED IT DURING THE TOAST LAST NIGHT, BUT......
...IN THE END, I DIDN'T STOP THEM.
EVEN IF I GRANT IMMORTALITY...
...THEY ALWAYS BEGIN TO EAT ONE ANOTHER, ACCORDING TO ITS RULES.
STILL, I HAD THE VAGUE IDEA THAT...
...IF IT WAS US, WE'D STICK WITH IT FOR A LONG TIME.
.... WELL, NEVER MIND.

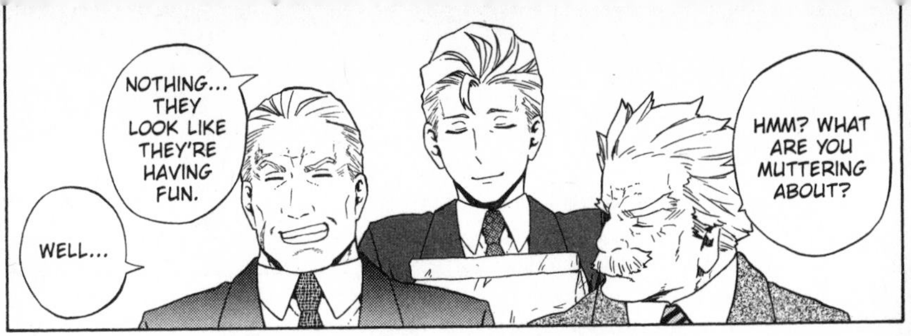
HMM? WHAT ARE YOU MUTTERING ABOUT?
WELL...
NOTHING... THEY LOOK LIKE THEY'RE HAVING FUN.

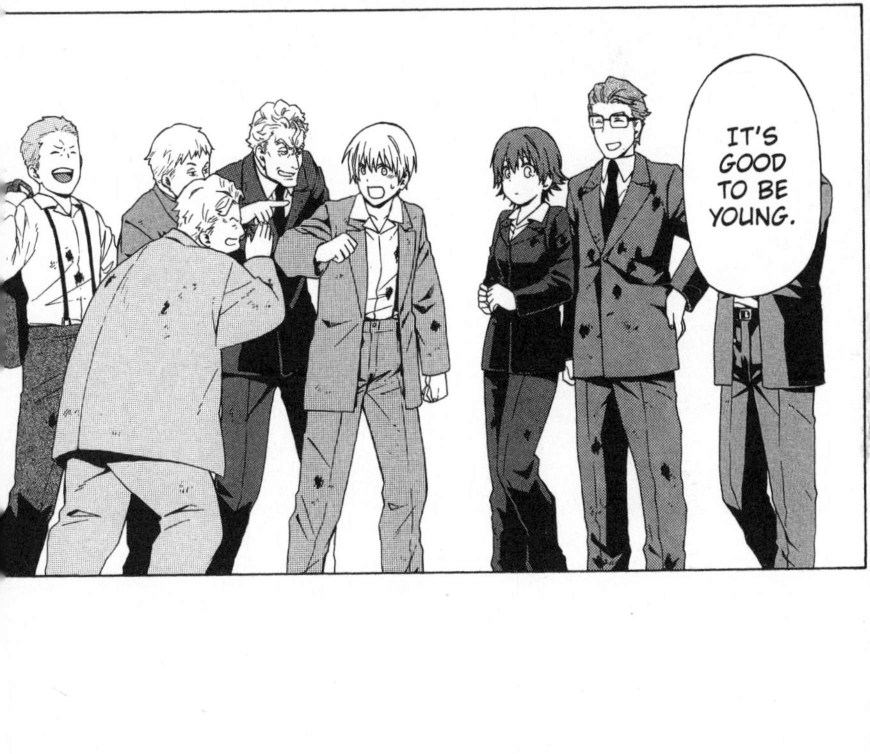
IT'S GOOD TO BE YOUNG.

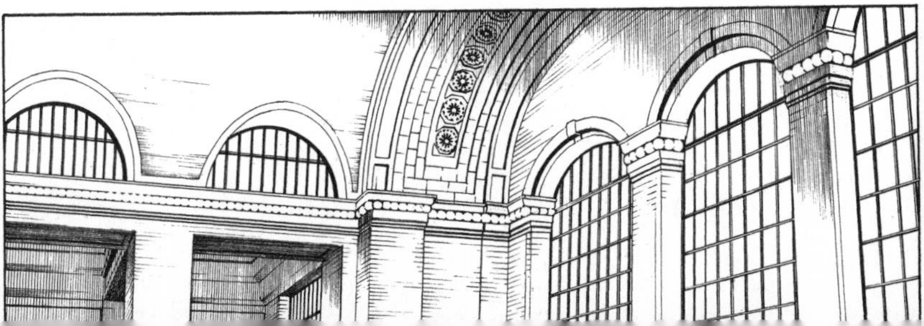

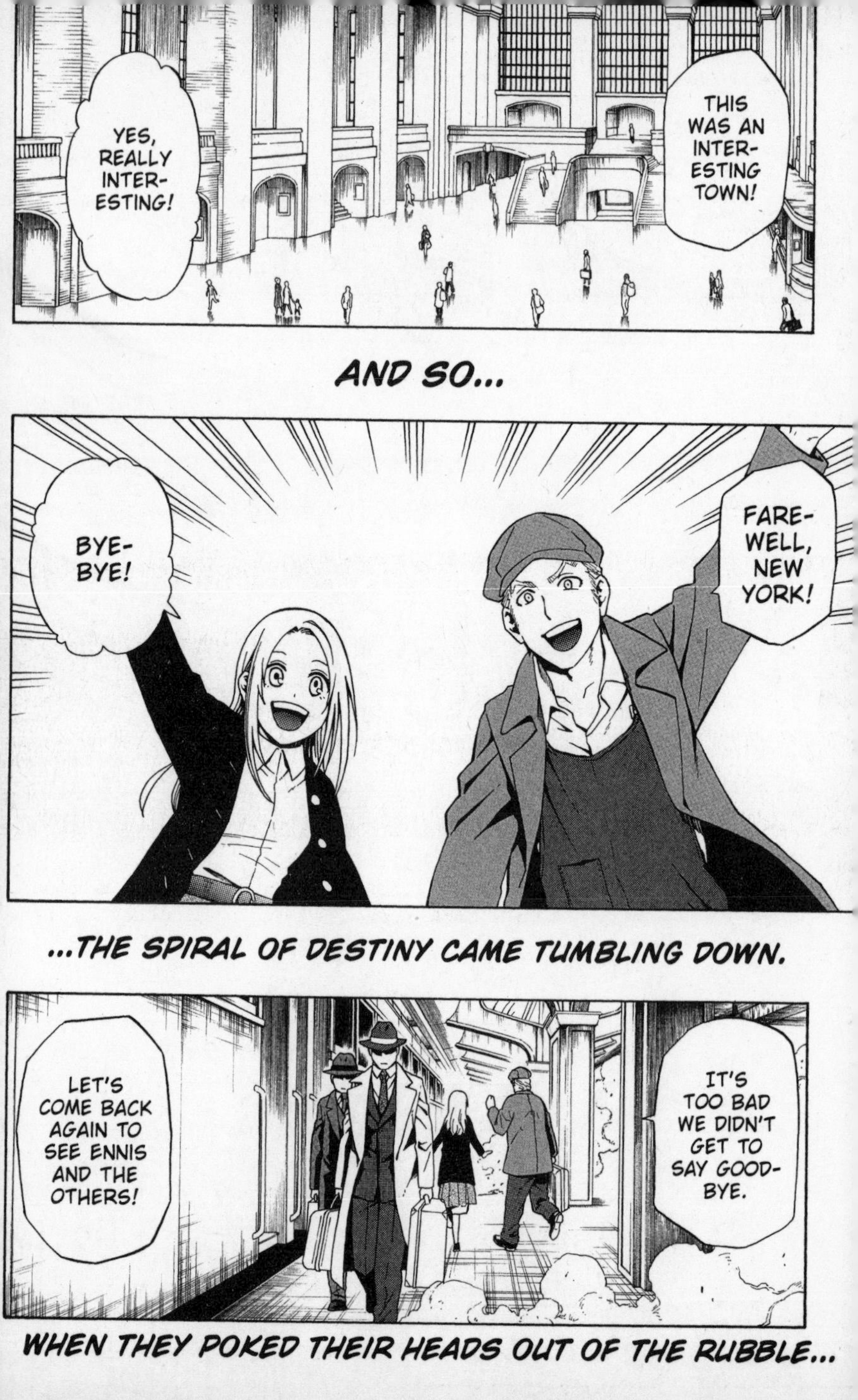
THIS WAS AN INTERESTING TOWN!
YES, REALLY INTERESTING!
AND SO...
FAREWELL, NEW YORK!
BYE-BYE!
...THE SPIRAL OF DESTINY CAME TUMBLING DOWN.
IT'S TOO BAD WE DIDN'T GET TO SAY GOOD-BYE.
LET'S COME BACK AGAIN TO SEE ENNIS AND THE OTHERS!
WHEN THEY POKED THEIR HEADS OUT OF THE RUBBLE...

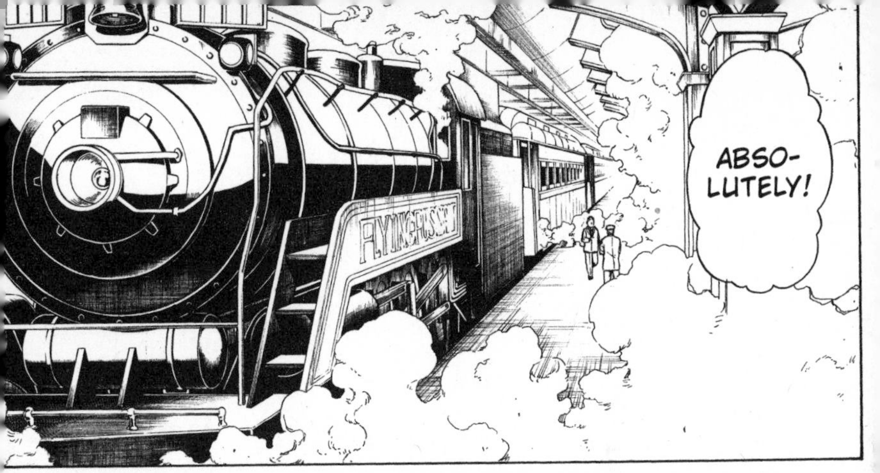
ABSO-
LUTELY!

...THEY FOUND THE BEGINNING OF A NEW SPIRAL.

BACCANO!
1930 The Rolling Bootlegs
THE END

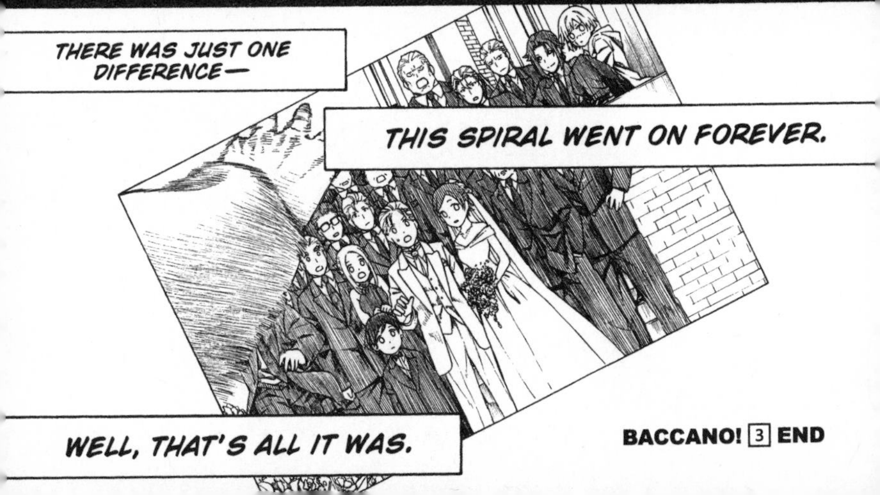
THERE WAS JUST ONE DIFFERENCE—
THIS SPIRAL WENT ON FOREVER.
WELL, THAT'S ALL IT WAS.

BACCANO! 3 END

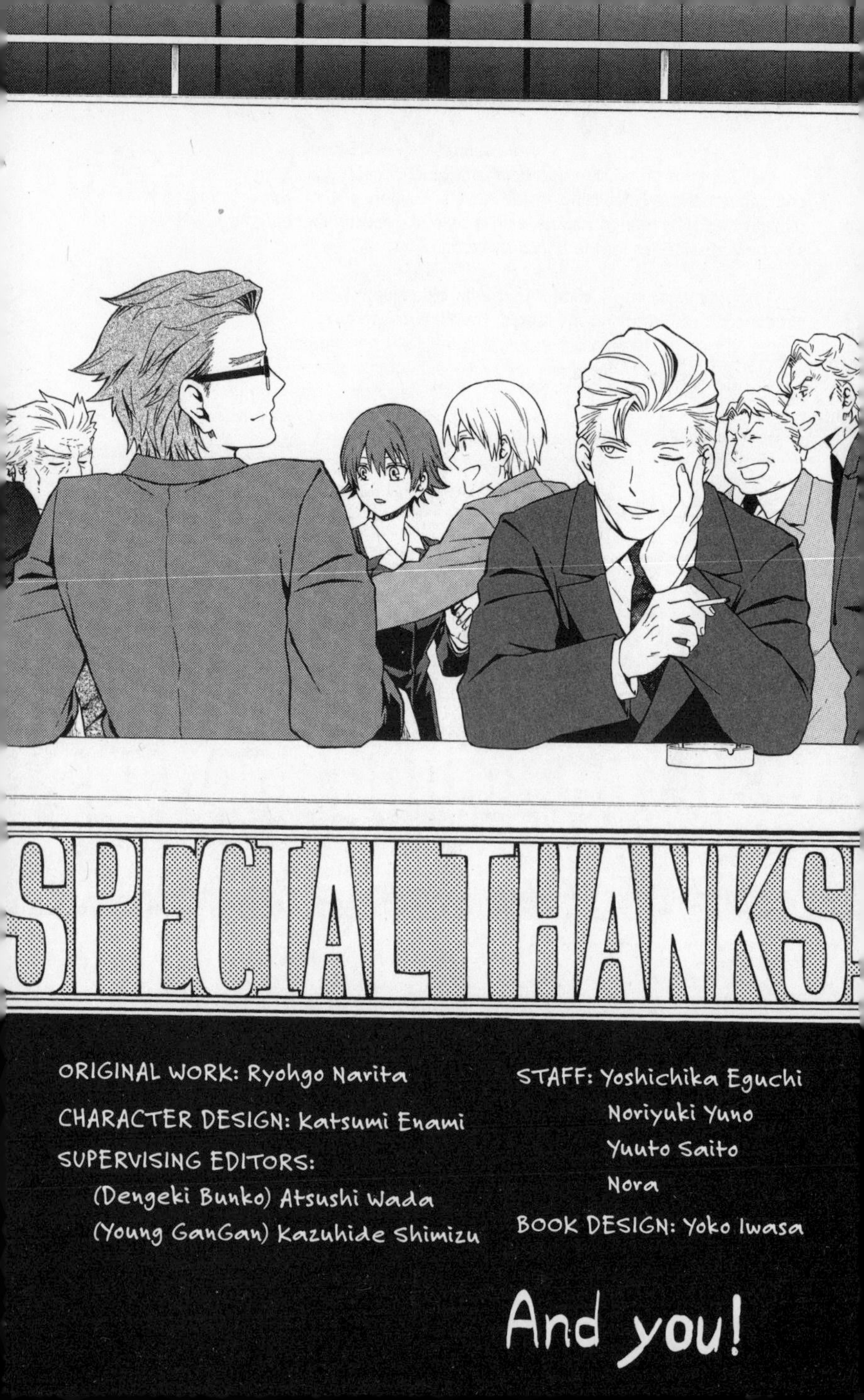

SPECIAL THANKS

ORIGINAL WORK: Ryohgo Narita

CHARACTER DESIGN: Katsumi Enami

SUPERVISING EDITORS:
(Dengeki Bunko) Atsushi Wada
(Young GanGan) Kazuhide Shimizu

STAFF: Yoshichika Eguchi
Noriyuki Yuno
Yuuto Saito
Nora

BOOK DESIGN: Yoko Iwasa

And you!

A COMMENT FROM THE AUTHOR OF THE ORIGINAL WORK, RYOHGO NARITA-SENSEI

Fujimoto-san's *Baccano!* manga was a series of new discoveries for me.

As I supervised the scenario for the original section, I discovered new facets in the characters I'd been depicting in the novels. On top of that, through seeing the story reincarnated with manga visuals, with a style of direction that differed from the anime, I saw new possibilities for the *Baccano!* world.

To begin with, my *Baccano!* text was bland until Katsumi Enami added light and shadow to it with magnificent visuals. Then the anime gave it "sound and heat" through its movement and audio and the cast's enthusiastic performances. In addition, *Baccano!* has gained a variety of other elements through its *Dengeki* comicalization and its drama CDs. However, in Fujimoto-san's manga version, the unique scent (not that this is something I've actually smelled, naturally) of the 1930s, the Prohibition era, is expressed with extraordinary depth in the art, and it made me feel as though the world of *Baccano!* had expanded again.

The anime is over, and as the original work heads toward its completion as well, I'm deeply moved to have been able to see *Baccano!* reborn in a new form this way. I couldn't be more grateful to Fujimoto-san and the members of the *Young GanGan* editorial department.

I hope readers of the original will also discover a new side of *Baccano!* and that those who came into contact with the *Baccano!* world for the first time through Fujimoto-san's manga will enjoy the novels and the anime too so that we'll be able to enjoy the world of *Baccano!* together in the future as well!

And so, to the ones who've kept me company this far: Fujimoto-san, Shimizu-san the editor, the members of the *YG* editorial department, and most of all, the readers—thank you very much!! I hope we'll meet again someday!

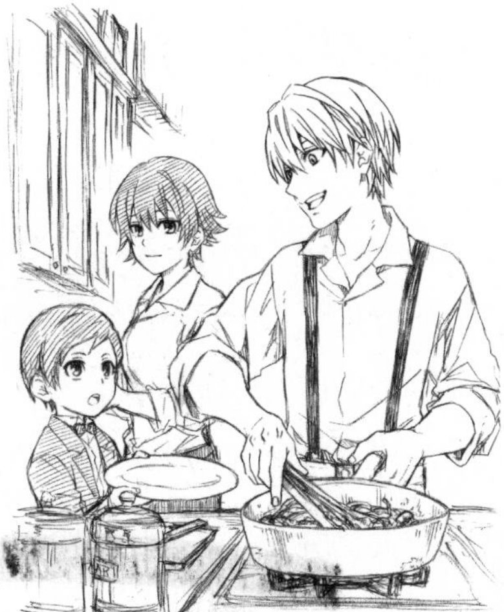

BACCANO! ③

Shinta Fujimoto
Ryohgo Narita
Katsumi Enami

Translation: Taylor Engel • **Lettering: Rochelle Gancio**

This book is a work of fiction. Names, characters, places, and incidents are the product of the author's imagination or are used fictitiously. Any resemblance to actual events, locales, or persons, living or dead, is coincidental.

BACCANO! vol.3
© 2017 Ryohgo Narita
© 2017 Shinta Fujimoto / SQUARE ENIX CO., LTD.
Licensed by KADOKAWA CORPORATION ASCII MEDIA WORKS
First published in Japan in 2017 by SQUARE ENIX CO., LTD. English translation rights arranged with SQUARE ENIX CO., LTD. and Yen Press, LLC through Tuttle-Mori Agency, Inc.

English translation © 2018 by SQUARE ENIX CO., LTD.

Yen Press, LLC supports the right to free expression and the value of copyright. The purpose of copyright is to encourage writers and artists to produce the creative works that enrich our culture.

The scanning, uploading, and distribution of this book without permission is a theft of the author's intellectual property. If you would like permission to use material from the book (other than for review purposes), please contact the publisher. Thank you for your support of the author's rights.

Yen Press
1290 Avenue of the Americas
New York, NY 10104

Visit us at yenpress.com
facebook.com/yenpress
twitter.com/yenpress
yenpress.tumblr.com
instagram.com/yenpress

First Yen Press Edition: May 2018
The chapters in this volume were originally published as ebooks by Yen Press.

Yen Press is an imprint of Yen Press, LLC.
The Yen Press name and logo are trademarks of Yen Press, LLC.

The publisher is not responsible for websites (or their content) that are not owned by the publisher.

Library of Congress Control Number: 2016910571

ISBNs: 978-0-316-44848-2 (paperback)
        978-0-316-44849-9 (ebook)

10 9 8 7 6 5 4 3 2 1

WOR

Printed in the United States of America